Change in International Law

Change in International Law

Paths, Processes, Power

NICO KRISCH
EZGI YILDIZ
PEDRO MARTÍNEZ ESPONDA

OXFORD
UNIVERSITY PRESS

OXFORD
UNIVERSITY PRESS

Great Clarendon Street, Oxford, OX2 6DP,
United Kingdom

Oxford University Press is a department of the University of Oxford.
It furthers the University's objective of excellence in research, scholarship,
and education by publishing worldwide. Oxford is a registered trade mark of
Oxford University Press in the UK and in certain other countries.

Published in the United States of America by Oxford University Press
198 Madison Avenue, New York, NY 10016, United States of America.

British Library Cataloguing in Publication Data
Data available

Library of Congress Control Number: 2025951420

ISBN 9780198918295

DOI: 10.1093/9780198918325.001.0001

Printed and bound by
CPI Group (UK) Ltd., Croydon, CR0 4YY

The manufacturer's authorized representative in the EU for product safety is
Oxford University Press España S.A. of Parque Empresarial San Fernando de Henares,
Avenida de Castilla, 2 – 28830 Madrid (www.oup.es/en or product.safety@oup.com).
OUP España S.A. also acts as importer into Spain of products made by the manufacturer.

MIX
Paper | Supporting
responsible forestry
FSC® C013604

Preface

Plus ça change . . . When we started work on the project behind this book, the world was a rather different place. It was a world before Covid-19, before the Russian attack on Ukraine, before the atrocious conflict in Sudan, and before the horrors of the war in Gaza or the interventions in Venezuela and Iran. International law—the object of our interest—has been increasingly ignored in these conflicts. But already when we began the project, international law was under pressure, and in one way or another, it has been under pressure throughout its existence. International crises are the context in which law operates in international society, and it is often through such crises that change in international law comes about.

Change in international law is what we are trying to understand better with this book. We cannot claim to explain everything about such change, but our combination of theoretical and empirical work helps to paint a broader, more systematic picture than has been available so far. It is also a picture that broadens our gaze beyond the rules themselves to the political and social contexts in which legal change occurs. In this picture, change is remarkably less dependent on state consent and explicit agreement than is usually assumed. Rather, it is often the result of discursive processes with distinct pathways on which institutions and other authorities play a crucial role. Most of this change, we find, does not come about in big leaps and revolutions—it is gradual and incremental, but can nevertheless bring about significant transformations in the rules of international law.

As co-authors, we came to this project with different disciplinary tools and thematic backgrounds, but we were united by a shared interest in understanding how international law changes—not just in moments of rupture but through slower, layered, and sometimes contested processes. For us, this book (and the project from which it emerged) created an interdisciplinary thinking space, where we not only learned from each other but also from a community of scholars grappling with the tensions, transformations, and possibilities within international law today. Writing in the midst of intensifying backlash against liberal norms and institutions, we found it especially meaningful to trace not only how change occurs, but also who drives it, how it is received, and the role of authority and power in shaping its trajectory. We hope this book serves as a resource for scholars, practitioners, and students navigating the future of international law and global governance with curiosity, scepticism, and perhaps also hope.

Arriving at this picture was an exciting, if not always easy, journey. It required a team ready to explore many instances of change across the different fields of international law, from international human rights law to trade, investment, and environmental law, and to take an active part in building the theoretical frame of the project step by step. We are especially grateful to Dorothea Endres, whose untiring engagement has advanced both the framework and many of the case studies tremendously, and she has contributed very directly to Chapter 3, in which we compare change processes across issue areas. Without her, this book would look very different. Nina Teresa Kiderlin also provided research assistance in the early years of the project. Matthew Daminato and Adhira Menon were of great editorial help in the finishing stages of the book. We also thank Peter Stevens and Umut Yüksel for their thoughtful conversations and feedback, which helped sharpen the quantitative analyses and conceptual design of several of the figures in the book.

Yet the book is the product of many more hands (and brains) beyond our team. We have been lucky to be able to bring together an amazing group of colleagues from the disciplines of international law and international relations interested in similar questions—colleagues willing to share their thoughts and ideas through written texts and recurring discussions. We were especially fortunate to host a number of visiting scholars in Geneva who actively engaged with our work, including Wayne Sandholtz, Nina Reiners, Mark Pollack, and Umut Yüksel. They and many others have taken part in the workshops and conferences that were part of our project, in Geneva, in cyberspace (yes, Covid-19), and then in the wonderful Chateau de Bossey. Many have also contributed to our edited volume, *The Many Paths of Change in International Law*, which appeared a couple of years ago. We cannot name them all here, but we deeply appreciate their engagement throughout.

The project could not have come to fruition without much work behind the scenes, and we have been fortunate to enjoy the constant support of the Geneva Graduate Institute's Global Governance Centre. Clarissa Brack Burdeu, Camila Moraes Silva, and especially Sylvia Nissim have been a great support for all things administrative, including the organization of our events, workshops, and the final conference. We are immensely grateful to them. Last but not least, their and our work would not have been possible without the generous financial support we received through an Advanced Grant from the European Research Council.

Books are like mountains—as you get closer, you realize how much effort they require. We therefore also thank our partners and families for bearing with us during the many hours we spent writing and revising the different chapters—and meeting to discuss these. As we dispersed across continents once the project had formally ended, these meetings typically took place virtually and at strange hours—early in the morning in Mexico and California, in the evening in Geneva. For us, this work was stimulating all along. Now we hope that you, the readers, will likewise find the outcome helpful, interesting, and perhaps even exciting. And we hope that the world remains a place in which thinking and writing about international law continue to be meaningful.

Geneva, Brunswick ME, Mexico City
March 2026

Acknowledgements

This book is part of 'The Paths of International Law: Stability and Change in the International Legal Order', a project that has received funding from the European Union's Horizon 2020 research and innovation programme under grant agreement No. 740634.

Although funded by the European Union, the views and opinions expressed are those of the author(s) only and do not necessarily reflect those of the European Union or the European Research Council Executive Agency. Neither the European Union nor the granting authority can be held responsible for them.

European Research Council

Established by the European Commission

Contents

Detailed Contents

Figures and Tables

Figures

Tables

Abbreviations

AB	World Trade Organization Appellate Body
AD Agreement	Anti-Dumping Agreement
APs	Additional Protocols to the Geneva Conventions
ASEAN	Association of Southeast Asian Nations
BITs	Bilateral Investment Treaties
CEDAW	Committee on the Elimination of All Forms of Discrimination Against Women
CESCR	UN Committee on Economic, Social and Cultural Rights
CITES	Convention on International Trade in Endangered Species of Wild Fauna and Flora
COPs	Conferences of the Parties
CRCs	Cobalt-Rich Crusts
CSW	Committee on the Status of Women
ECOSOC	United Nations Economic and Social Council
ECtHR	European Court of Human Rights
EU	European Union
FAO	Food and Agriculture Organization
FET	Fair and Equitable Treatment
FTAs	Free Trade Agreements
G-77	Group of 77
GA	United Nations General Assembly
GATS	General Agreement on Trade in Services
GATT	General Agreement on Tariffs and Trade
GIL	General International Law
IACtHR	Inter-American Court of Human Rights
ICC	International Criminal Court
ICJ	International Court of Justice
ICL	International Criminal Law
ICRC	International Committee of the Red Cross
ICS	European Union's Investment Court System
ICSID	International Centre for the Settlement of International Disputes
ICTR	International Criminal Tribunal for Rwanda
ICTY	International Criminal Tribunal for the former Yugoslavia
IEL	International Environmental Law
IHL	International Humanitarian Law
IHRL	International Human Rights Law
IIL	International Investment Law
ILC	International Law Commission
ISA	International Seabed Authority

ITL	International Trade Law
ITLOS	International Tribunal of the Law of the Sea
IUU	Illegal, Unreported, and Unregulated Fishing
LoS	Law of the Sea
MC12	World Trade Organization 12th Ministerial Conference
MOPs	Meetings of the Parties
NAFTA	North American Free Trade Agreement
NATO	North Atlantic Treaty Organization
NGO	Non-Governmental Organization
NIEO	New International Economic Order
OECD	Organisation for Economic Co-operation and Development
Paris Agreement	Paris Agreement on Climate Change
PMNs	Polymetallic Nodules
PMSs	Polymetallic Sulphides
RCEP	Regional Comprehensive Economic Partnership
SADC	Southern African Development Community
SCM	Agreement on Subsidies and Countervailing Measures
SD-NSA	Self-Defence against Non-State Actors
SPS Agreement	Agreement on the Application of Sanitary and Phytosanitary Measures
TRIPs	Trade Related Aspects of Intellectual Property Rights Agreement
TWAIL	Third World Approaches to International Law
UDHR	Universal Declaration of Human Rights
UK	United Kingdom of Great Britain and Northern Ireland
UN	United Nations
UNCITRAL	United Nations Commission on International Trade Law
UNCLOS	United Nations Convention on the Law of the Sea
UNCTAD	United Nations Conference on Trade and Development
UNEP	UN Environmental Programme
UNESCO	United Nations Educational, Scientific and Cultural Organization
UNGA	United Nations General Assembly
UNGPs	UN Guiding Principles on Business and Human Rights
UNHCR	United Nations High Commissioner for Refugees
UNHRC	UN Human Rights Council
UNSC	United Nations Security Council
US	United States
USCC	Use—Select—Change—Create model
VCLT	Vienna Convention on the Law of Treaties
WHO	World Health Organization
WTO	World Trade Organization

1
Transformations of International Law

'[I]nternational law is more static than any other law', Hersch Lauterpacht wrote ninety years ago, and he meant it in a descriptive rather than critical way.[1] At the time, he argued, international law largely regulated the external relations of states and was not much affected by the changes in social and economic circumstances that typically triggered changes in domestic law. The absence of a legislature to effect change in international law—a topic much discussed at the time—was thus not a significant cause of concern for him up until the point 'when the political organization of the international community has undergone a fundamental change, so as to regulate in detail the life of its individual members in its internal aspects'.[2]

That change has come, but legislative mechanisms for adapting international law are still largely absent. International law today does indeed regulate 'in detail the life of its individual members', through rules on trade and investment, environmental protection, or human rights (and many more), and it reaches deep into the domestic affairs of states and touches on many sensitive issues of national politics, society, and economic relations. International law is no longer just 'adjective', a mere delimitation of competencies of states vis-à-vis one another.[3] It is, instead, today 'substantive' through and through. But the modes of change in international law have, at least on the surface, largely remained the same as they were a century ago. Formal change still occurs primarily through treaties that require the consent of the parties and through customary law, which, at least notionally, requires a widespread and uniform practice of states. In a world of almost two hundred states, this leads to tensions and frustration: in many contexts, international law is seen as insufficiently responsive to new circumstances and demands. Major shocks may bring about transformations at a larger scale, as at the end of World War II with the adoption of the UN Charter. But such shocks are rare, and in the normal course of international law, change is more difficult to bring about. Nowhere is this more evident than in the case of climate change, where progress is excruciatingly slow and burdensome, and international legal rules lag far behind what the world would require to contain global warming.

[1] Hersch Lauterpacht, *The Function of Law in the International Community*, 2nd ed. (Oxford University Press, 2011), p. 257.
[2] ibid.
[3] ibid.

Change in International Law. Nico Krisch, Ezgi Yildiz, and Pedro Martínez Esponda, Oxford University Press.
 DOI: 10.1093/9780198918325.003.0001

Yet smoother mechanisms to effect change have not been established, in any case not formally. This is primarily because states do not want to lose control. The existing high hurdles for change, especially those linked with state consent, protect them from the imposition of obligations they do not support. States are loath to lower those hurdles. Even when they have done so—for example, for adjustments to international environmental agreements—the scope often remains limited to technical matters with states retaining opt-out possibilities to ensure they are not simply outvoted.[4] In the eyes of many, then, international law is simply not fit for purpose in an accelerated world.[5]

Yet, in reality, international law is hardly as static as this picture suggests. It may not have proper formal legislative processes, but it is nevertheless constantly in motion. Over the past few decades, new human rights have been created, trade rules have been adjusted to new economic circumstances, more stringent standards of treatment under investment law have taken hold, and atrocities in internal conflicts have been criminalized. Remarkably, all of these largely occurred, at least initially, without formal agreements and in many cases over the objections of some, even powerful states. When the United Kingdom and the United States opposed a new right to water, for example, they soon found that the right became established regardless, through processes in different UN bodies, and they eventually jumped onto the bandwagon.[6] Likewise, the United States fervently resisted looser rules on subsidies in international trade law, but that loosening nevertheless occurred through successive interpretations by the World Trade Organization's Appellate Body, such that the changes were eventually acknowledged by most members of the organization.[7]

It is this dynamism that we explore in the present book. We want to understand better how international law develops gradually, in the absence of formal change through treaties—and despite the high hurdles which, according to traditional legal doctrine, stand in the way of new rules or interpretations. We are interested in the paths on which such change travels, the actors that propel it, and the conditions under which change occurs. Rather surprisingly, such change processes are not well understood so far. While scholars of international law often focus on

[4] See, e.g., Jutta Brunnée, 'COPing with Consent: Law-Making under Multilateral Environmental Agreements', *Leiden Journal of International Law* 15, (2002): p. 1.

[5] See, e.g., William D Nordhaus, 'Paul Samuelson and Global Public Goods', in *Samuelsonian Economics*, edited by Michael Szenberg and others (Oxford University Press, 2006), p. 88: 'To the extent that global public goods may become more important in the decades ahead, one of our major challenges is to devise mechanisms that overcome the bias toward the status quo and the voluntary nature of current international law in life-threatening issues. To someone who is an outsider to international law, the Westphalian system seems an increasingly dangerous vestige of a different world.'

[6] See Nina Reiners, 'Despite or Because of Contestation? How Water Became a Human Right', *Human Rights Quarterly* 43, (2021): p. 329.

[7] Nina Kiderlin, 'World Trade Law and the Rise of China: Struggles over Subsidy Rules', in *The Many Paths of Change in International Law*, edited by Nico Krisch and Ezgi Yildiz (Oxford University Press, 2023).

formal, doctrinal criteria rather than actual change processes, international relations scholars have paid much more attention to treaty-making than to the less formal mechanisms in view here.[8] Yet we can build on a growing body of literature tracing those processes in particular areas as well as a broader scholarly shift towards understanding international law as a social practice well beyond formalistic representations or official rules and institutions. In this book, we substantiate our inquiry into the paths of international law through a thorough analysis of twenty-five cases of change over the past decades.[9]

The international law that emerges from our inquiry—the one we lay out in this and the following chapters—is not as dynamic as some would hope, but it is significantly more dynamic than many would expect. It is also not uniform; in fact, change happens very differently across the different issue areas of international law. Which institutions and actors matter, both to drive change and to block it, heavily depends on the authority constellations formed in particular institutional contexts. This also means that the politics of change differ significantly—material power matters more in some areas than in others. International law travels on many 'paths', and not always does it do the bidding of the most powerful actors around. Powerful states get their way more easily through (bilateral) treaties, and they can also decide to ignore international law and bear the corresponding costs. But they are less able to bring about (and often even to block) change on many of the paths we take into view. At the same time, change processes also rarely simply reflect the views of the weak or translate demands of justice into legal obligations. International legal change is typically born from struggle, but from a particular, bounded, and often institutionalized kind of struggle.

In this introduction, we outline our core argument about gradual change and explore the competing pressures between which change processes in international law are caught. We begin, in section 1, by contrasting the traditional understanding of a relatively static international law—characterized by high hurdles and punctuated equilibria—with a more dynamic picture that attends to the myriad informal processes through which established norms are reinterpreted and new ones emerge. In section 2, we analyse in more detail the competing forces that have historically made it difficult to establish smoother, more structured mechanisms of formal change, and we show how these forces continue to shape the politics of legal change today. Against this background, section 3 outlines the structure of the book and its different chapters. In section 4, we conclude by explaining why understanding change in international law requires attention not only to major

[8] See, e.g., James Crawford, *Chance, Order, Change: The Course of International Law: General Course on Public International Law* (Hague Academy of International Law, 2014); Barbara Koremenos, *The Continent of International Law: Explaining Agreement Design* (Cambridge University Press, 2016).

[9] Pedro Martinez Esponda and others (eds.) *The Paths of Change in International Law: Case Studies* (SSRN, 2023).

transformations but also—and especially—to the gradual adjustments that are the focus of this book.

1. International Law between Stasis and Change

The conventional picture of a relatively static international law is closely connected with the formal categories in international legal doctrine that define how change is recognized and validated. These categories are built around high hurdles, most notably the requirement of state consent (or at least acquiescence) to new rules. When change is defined in these terms, international legal development is expected to take the form of long periods of stability interspersed with short periods of movement. This image, however, obscures the actual processes of gradual change through which most transformations of international law come about.

Punctuated Equilibria: The Traditional Picture

The restrictiveness of the traditional framework of international legal change finds its doctrinal expression in the requirements for the emergence of new rules through treaty-making and change in customary law. Both of these require widespread agreement: in the case of treaties, agreement between all parties; in the case of customary law, a widespread and consistent practice and *opinio juris*.[10] The latter is not normally understood to require full universality, but a degree of support (or at least acquiescence) close to universal. When it comes to treaties, certain changes can also come about through 'subsequent practice'—whereby states express their understanding of a treaty's meaning. This is often thought to be limited to 'interpretive' change rather than a change in the rules, although it is not clear that a line between the two can be drawn consistently. In any event, to be consequential, such practice too is understood to require a convergence of all parties to a treaty.[11] And while there is today an increasing recognition that other actors—individuals, NGOs, companies, etc.—are 'participants' in law-making processes, the authority to effect change is still widely seen to lie with states.[12] The UN International Law

[10] See, e.g., James Crawford, *Brownlie's Principles of Public International Law*, 9th ed. (Oxford University Press, 2019), ch. 2.

[11] Georg Nolte, ed., *Treaties and Subsequent Practice* (Oxford University Press, 2013).

[12] See Rosalyn Higgins, *Problems and Process: International Law and How We Use It* (Clarendon Press, 1995), ch. 3; Jean d'Aspremont, ed., *Participants in the International Legal System: Multiple Perspectives on Non-State Actors in International Law* (Taylor & Francis, 2011). On challenges of the traditional sources doctrine, see also Chapter 2 below, and Samantha Besson and Jean d'Aspremont, eds., *The Oxford Handbook on the Sources of International Law* (Oxford University Press, 2017).

Commission (ILC) has just recently reaffirmed this general approach in two projects on customary international law and the subsequent practice to treaties.[13]

Because of these high thresholds, episodes of change appear as few and far between, at least when it comes to rules with global reach. Agreement among a large number of countries is notoriously hard to obtain—the decade-long negotiations on the UN Convention on the Law of the Sea are an emblematic (but by no means singular) case in point. Sufficiently converging practice to create new custom is likewise usually elusive and typically takes a long time to form. Major change in customary international law, in the eyes of some observers, then comes about primarily through rare 'Grotian moments'.[14]

This imagery—of long periods of stasis interspersed by relatively brief moments of movement leading to new settlement and stability—is one typically associated with models of punctuated equilibria. Such models, originating in evolutionary biology, have come to be widely used in the social sciences.[15] They also underpin the most prominent recent account of change in international law from an international relations perspective, Paul Diehl and Charlotte Ku's *Dynamics of International Law*. Diehl and Ku argue that most international legal change happens relatively quickly and in response to significant shocks to the system—shocks that undermine an existing *status quo* and allow actors to overcome path dependence and its contributing factors, such as bureaucratic inertia, standardized procedures, and the transaction costs inherent in negotiations.[16] This model is, in part, a reflection of the central place of treaties in Diehl and Ku's account, while their treatment of customary international law is less clear-cut. Other observers have, however, applied similar models to custom. Pierre-Hugues Verdier and Erik Voeten, for example, have suggested that the development of customary international law follows a tipping point model, in which longer phases of stability alternate with short periods of activity. Using the example of state immunity, they demonstrate that, once a critical mass of states accepts a new rule, other states are likely to follow, generating a cascade effect that leads to consolidated change in a short period.[17]

[13] ILC, 'Draft Conclusions on Identification of Customary International Law' (2018); ILC, 'Draft Conclusions on Subsequent Agreements and Subsequent Practice in Relation to the Interpretation of Treaties' (2018). On the former, see Wouter Werner, 'The Making of Lawmaking: The ILC Draft Conclusions on the Identification of Customary Law', in *The Many Paths of Change in International Law*, edited by Nico Krisch and Ezgi Yildiz (Oxford University Press, 2023).

[14] Michael P Scharf, *Customary International Law in Times of Fundamental Change: Recognizing Grotian Moments* (Cambridge University Press, 2013).

[15] See, e.g., B Guy Peters, Jon Pierre and Desmond S King, 'The Politics of Path Dependency: Political Conflict in Historical Institutionalism', *The Journal of Politics* 67, (2005): p. 1275, 1288–90.

[16] Paul F Diehl and Charlotte Ku, *The Dynamics of International Law* (Cambridge University Press, 2010), pp. 64–71.

[17] Pierre-Hugues Verdier and Erik Voeten, 'Precedent, Compliance, and Change in Customary International Law: An Explanatory Theory', *American Journal of International Law* 108, (2014): p. 389.

Such a tipping-point model fits the high thresholds erected by doctrine; it has become common in the literature on international norm change;[18] and it also reflects a common theme in the broader literature on institutional change in (domestic) politics. Historical institutionalism—the political science tradition that focuses on how institutions evolve over time and how this evolution shapes political outcomes[19]—has long emphasized punctuated equilibria as structuring institutional change processes. When institutions are 'sticky' because of path dependence driven by internalization or increasing returns, change requires a major shock. As a result, change will occur infrequently and, when it does occur, tends to take the form of significant, sudden change.[20] Critical junctures are often cited as paradigmatic moments of systemic ruptures,[21] although not all shocks need to rise to that level to unsettle an existing equilibrium.

In such a framework, we will expect international law to evince limited adaptability outside exceptional moments of disruption.[22] Some events or challenges are likely to lead to change, but more often than not, international law will lack a convincing answer to new problems or transformations in its political context. Diehl and Ku drily note that 'this means that some problems will not be addressed'.[23] International law's dynamism is bound to be low according to this model, and its limited responsiveness might mean that actors pushing for change will either seek to overturn international law's strictures or find ways around it—especially in today's accelerating environment in which new challenges appear at an ever more rapid pace.

Change in Small Steps

The traditional picture of change in international law then is overall rather static. As demands for greater dynamism are met by political divergence, the traditional avenues for change in the rules of international law—treaties, as well as custom—are easily blocked.

[18] See Martha Finnemore and Kathryn Sikkink, 'International Norm Dynamics and Political Change', *International Organization* 52(4) (1998): p. 887; Gary Goertz, *International Norms and Decision Making: A Punctuated Equilibrium Model* (Rowman & Littlefield, 2003); Wayne Sandholtz and Kendall W Stiles, *International Norms and Cycles of Change* (Oxford University Press, 2009).

[19] See Orfeo Fioretos, Tulia G Falleti and Adam Sheingate, eds., *The Oxford Handbook of Historical Institutionalism* (Oxford University Press, 2016).

[20] See Stephen D Krasner, 'Sovereignty: An Institutional Perspective', *Comparative Political Studies* 21, (1988): p. 66.

[21] See Giovanni Capoccia and R Daniel Kelemen, 'The Study of Critical Junctures: Theory, Narrative, and Counterfactuals in Historical Institutionalism', *World Politics* 59, (2007): p. 341.

[22] See also the emphasis on critical junctures in the design of international courts by Karen J Alter, 'The Evolution of International Law and Courts', in *International Politics and Institutions in Time*, edited by Orfeo Fioretos (Oxford University Press, 2017).

[23] Diehl and Ku (n 16), p. 63.

This does not mean that change through treaties or convergent state practice is not taking place at all; after all, there have been major breakthroughs on the conventional path in recent decades. This was especially visible in the 1990s, with the environmental agreements coming out of the Rio Conference, the agreements establishing the World Trade Organization, or the Rome Statute creating the International Criminal Court. In the interim, we have seen successes in treaty-making in certain areas, such as the Paris Agreement on Climate Change (for all its flaws), the Convention on the Rights of Persons with Disabilities, or the Agreement on Marine Biodiversity of Areas Beyond National Jurisdiction. But multilateral negotiations—always lengthy and complicated—have by all accounts become almost impossible to conclude, and this trend is reflected in the decline in the number of treaties concluded since the turn of the millennium.[24] In the punctuated equilibria image of international legal development, the periods of movement appear increasingly rare, while phases of stability grow longer, making stasis the most frequent outcome.

But is this an accurate reflection of reality? It certainly contrasts with the picture observers and practitioners paint of developments in many subfields of international law. They report a considerable amount of movement across the board, from international criminal law to human rights, and from investment law to the law of international organizations. New crimes have been established, new rights created, new protections for investors instituted, and new powers for international organizations have been recognized as well.[25] We trace such developments across different issue areas in greater detail in Chapter 3. This movement is typically not related to treaty-making, at least not directly. Even if it is sometimes portrayed as a change in customary law, it tends to have little to do with a consistent practice of states—it instead usually proceeds through institutions and interpretive acts. It is an 'informal' change in the sense that it does not fit into the traditional forms of change in international law and nevertheless is registered as such by participants in international legal practice.

This movement suggests a dynamism that is distinct from—and greater than—what we would expect on the basis of the traditional sources and the punctuated-equilibria model outlined above, and it suggests that change in international law takes place in a rather different way than is typically imagined. It is

[24] Joost Pauwelyn, Ramses A Wessel and Jan Wouters, 'When Structures Become Shackles: Stagnation and Dynamics in International Lawmaking', *European Journal of International Law* 25, (2014): p. 733; Amitav Acharya, Antoni Estevadeordal and Louis W Goodman, 'Multipolar or Multiplex? Interaction Capacity, Global Cooperation and World Order', *International Affairs* 99, (2023): p. 2339, 2349–52.

[25] See, e.g., Nolte (n 11); Guy Fiti Sinclair, *To Reform the World: International Organizations and the Making of Modern States* (Oxford University Press, 2017); Federico Ortino, *The Origin and Evolution of Investment Treaty Standards: Stability, Value, and Reasonableness* (Oxford University Press, 2019); Andreas von Arnauld, Kerstin von der Decken and Mart Susi, *The Cambridge Handbook of New Human Rights: Recognition, Novelty, Rhetoric* (Cambridge University Press, 2020); Nora Stappert, 'Practice Theory and Change in International Law: Theorizing the Development of Legal Meaning through the Interpretive Practices of International Criminal Courts', *International Theory* 12, (2020): p. 33.

this dynamism—a dynamism of small steps, of gradual change—that we seek to understand better in this book. We seek to understand not only its importance but also its shape—the actors and institutions involved, the conditions that enable or hinder it, and the political economy underlying such informal change. In order to get a better sense of the kind of processes we focus on, we begin this inquiry with two illustrative vignettes.

Change in Practice: Two Vignettes

The first such vignette concerns climate change, probably the most pressing challenge the world currently faces. The 2015 Paris Agreement, the one major negotiation success in recent years, is not necessarily a breakthrough: although negotiations were drawn out over two decades, they resulted in commitments and mechanisms so limited that the Agreement's effective contribution to tackling climate change has long been in doubt. Gridlock has thus become a common diagnosis in this field. However, if we look below the surface of major treaty conferences and inter-governmental agreements, we can observe significantly greater dynamism in meaningful norm-making. This is evident in myriad non-state initiatives—from sustainable forestry standards to accounting rules—that populate today's transnational climate governance regime complex.[26] It is also evident in domestic regulation, where numerous initiatives have emerged to counter global warming, many of which have a transnational component.[27] Yet, movement is also visible in the rules of international law as such. This concerns the reception of climate-related concerns in other areas (such as human rights, trade, investment, and energy law), both formally, through treaty amendments and new agreements, and informally, through judicial and arbitral practice.[28] At a more general level, movement has also reached international courts, with two recent advisory opinions—in 2024 by the International Tribunal of the Law of the Sea and in 2025 by the International Court of Justice (ICJ)—marking significant steps in the development of international law on climate change.[29]

[26] See Kenneth W Abbott, 'The Transnational Regime Complex for Climate Change', *Environment and Planning C: Government and Policy* 30, (2012): p. 571; Harriet Bulkeley and others, *Transnational Climate Change Governance* (Cambridge University Press, 2014).

[27] Joanne Scott, 'Unilateralism, Extraterritoriality and Climate Change', in *Climate Change Law*, edited by Daniel A Farber and Marjan Peeters (Edward Elgar Publishing, 2016).

[28] See Daniel Bodansky, Jutta Brunnée and Lavanya Rajamani, *International Climate Change Law* (Oxford University Press, 2017), ch. 9.

[29] See ITLOS, *Request for an Advisory Opinion submitted by the Commission of Small Island States on Climate Change and International Law* (Advisory Opinion of 21 May 2024); ICJ, *Obligations of States in respect of Climate Change* (Advisory Opinion) [2025] ICJ Rep 2025. For assessments, see Jiangtao Qian, Kangjie Sun and Yen-Chiang Chang, 'The Impact of the ITLOS Climate Change Advisory Opinion on the Development of International Law', *Marine Policy* 170, (2024): p. 106406; John H. Knox, 'Obligations of States in Respect of Climate Change (Advisory Opinion)', *American Journal of International Law* 120, (2026): forthcoming.

More broadly, while climate regime negotiations bore limited results, related developments in the human rights sphere continued and intensified on a variety of other paths.[30] After much action in regional human rights systems, especially in the Americas and Africa, momentum at the universal level towards a human right to a healthy environment picked up in the 2010s. The UN Human Rights Council appointed a special rapporteur, and a powerful statement from the Inter-American Court of Human Rights generated further impetus, eventually culminating in recognition of the right by the Human Rights Council in 2021 and the UN General Assembly in 2022.[31] Meanwhile, courts and quasi-judicial bodies have increasingly used international human rights law to articulate obligations to prevent, mitigate, and remedy climate change related harm.[32] This is evident, for example, in the practice of the UN Human Rights Committee as regards climate refugees and indigenous groups affected by climate change.[33] It is also reflected in the jurisprudence of the European Court of Human Rights, most notably in its *KlimaSeniorinnen* judgment, which addresses measures to tackle climate change more broadly.[34] In 2025, the Inter-American Court of Human Rights has rendered an important advisory opinion on the climate emergency and human rights, triggered by a request from Chile and Colombia.[35] Likewise, domestic courts are increasingly active in specifying international legal standards in this area. For example, the Supreme Court of the Netherlands has used (European) human rights law in combination with developments in the UN climate regime to derive obligations of the Dutch government to enact stricter measures to limit emissions.[36] These developments can, of course, hardly compensate for the limitations of the Paris Agreement, but they reflect a different kind of dynamism than can be gleaned from looking at major inter-governmental conferences and treaty-making alone.

A similar story emerges in other areas, such as international humanitarian law (IHL). Pressures to adapt and develop IHL were traditionally absorbed primarily through treaty-making processes, up until the adoption of the Additional Protocols in 1977. But already the negotiations of the Protocols were fraught with friction, and Western states—especially the US—soon decided that the conventional

[30] Dorothea Endres, 'Case Study 17: The Human Right to a "Good" Environment', in *The Paths of International Law: Case Studies*, edited by Pedro Martínez Esponda and others (SSRN, 2023). See also John H Knox and Ramin Pejan, *The Human Right to a Healthy Environment* (Cambridge University Press, 2018).

[31] UNHRC Res 48/13 (8 October 2021) UN Doc A/HRC/RES/48/13; UNGA Res 76/L.75 (28 July 2022) UN Doc A/76/L.75.

[32] See César Rodríguez-Garavito, ed., *Litigating the Climate Emergency: How Human Rights, Courts, and Legal Mobilization Can Bolster Climate Action* (Cambridge University Press, 2022).

[33] UN Human Rights Committee, *Teitiota v New Zealand* (2019) No. 2728/2016; *Daniel Billy and Others v Australia* (2023) UN Human Rights Committee No. 3624/2019.

[34] ECtHR, *Verein KlimaSeniorinnen Schweiz and Others v Switzerland* [2024] App. no. 53600/20.

[35] IACtHR, *Climate Emergency and Human Rights* (Advisory Opinion AO-32/25 of 29 May 2025), https://www.corteidh.or.cr/docs/opiniones/seriea_32_en.pdf

[36] Supreme Court of the Netherlands, *Urgenda Foundation v States of Netherlands* [2019] ECLI:NL:HR:2019:2007; Hague District Court, *Milieudefensie and Others v Royal Dutch Shell plc* [2021] ECLI:NL:RBDHA:2021:5339.

route had become too resistant to their own aims. With treaty-making blocked, IHL faced stagnation, but movement began to shift to other contexts.[37] These included the international criminal tribunals set up by the UN Security Council in the 1990s, which, through the identification and expansion of international criminal law, also clarified and developed the laws of war.[38] Movement also occurred through other non-state actors, most notably the International Committee of the Red Cross (ICRC). The ICRC had long been a major institution in the field, with a particularly strong role in the preparation and organization of treaty conferences. In the absence of such conferences, another function of the ICRC moved to the forefront—the clarification and restatement of IHL.[39] The ICRC had been active in publishing commentaries to the Geneva Conventions from early on, and from the 1990s onwards, this aspect of its work became more central and elaborate. The shift became most visible in its study on customary IHL, originally presented in 2005. The study, based on a broad analysis of international practice, provided a restatement which, at least from the standpoint of some observers, went beyond existing rules to include a fair share of progressive development as well. Despite criticism from some countries—most prominently the United States—the customary law study soon became a core reference point for arguments about IHL today.[40] Not all efforts of the ICRC have borne similar fruit—the guidance on direct participation in hostilities, for example, has met with more widespread contestation, and its role in international legal discourse has remained less weighty.[41]

In IHL, as in climate change, informal and gradual change was present throughout, often alongside more traditional forms. But in both areas, it became more relevant—and more pronounced—as traditional law-making (especially treaty-making) faced greater obstacles. This informal change may have been less effective than many would have hoped; after all, it did not present revolutions or big leaps, but instead incremental developments. Over time, these may still amount to significant transformations; in any event, in a context otherwise characterized by stagnation, they have become particularly consequential.

[37] See Giovanni Mantilla, 'From Treaty to Custom: Shifting Paths in the Recent Development of International Humanitarian Law', *Leiden Journal of International Law* 37, (2024): p. 1; see also Sandesh Sivakumaran, 'Making and Shaping the Law of Armed Conflict', *Current Legal Problems* 71, (2018): p. 119.

[38] See, e.g., Christopher Greenwood, 'The Development of International Humanitarian Law by the International Criminal Tribunal for the Former Yugoslavia', *Max Planck Yearbook of United Nations Law Online* 2, (1998): p. 97.

[39] See Mantilla (n 37); Linus Mührel, *The Authority of the International Committee of the Red Cross* (DeGruyter Brill, 2024).

[40] Marko Milanovic and Sandesh Sivakumaran, 'Assessing the Authority of the ICRC Customary IHL Study: How Does IHL Develop?', *International Review of the Red Cross* 104, (2022): p. 1856.

[41] See Ka Lok Yip, 'The ICRC's Interpretive Guidance on the Notion of Direct Participation in Hostilities: Sociological and Democratic Legitimacy in Domestic Legal Orders', *Transnational Legal Theory* 8, (2017): p. 224; Dorothea Endres, 'Case Study 8: Direct Participation in Hostilities', in *The Paths of International Law: Case Studies*, edited by Pedro Martínez Esponda and others (SSRN, 2023).

Gradual Change

The picture of incremental, informal change that emerges from the two vignettes stands in contrast with the punctuated-equilibria model typically employed to capture processes of international legal change. That model helps us understand certain forms of change, but it leaves out a host of other instances—some of these perhaps of smaller scale, but others amounting to broader transformations of the respective fields.

Shifting our attention towards more incremental, gradual change also reflects broader developments in how political and institutional change is understood among historical institutionalists. The classical model of institutional development—centred on sudden ruptures induced by external shocks as introduced above—has given way to broader accounts that encompass forms of gradual change driven by endogenous processes. In these, change occurs 'in the "gaps" or "soft spots" between the rule and its interpretation or the rule and its enforcement'.[42] Depending on the flexibility in existing rules and the veto possibilities in the institutional context, change proceeds either through a reinterpretation or through the enactment of new rules which replace or 'layer' onto existing ones.[43] Such incremental processes of change have also attracted greater attention in international relations in recent years.[44]

A rise in the importance of gradual processes of change is fuelled by the institutionalization of international politics throughout the twentieth century. The increasing density of institutions has led to a corresponding rise of authority in the international order, often described as a 'system change' away from a more strongly anarchical conception of international relations.[45] Institutions can play a central role in the gradual processes we take into view here, as they allow for an accretion of authority in favour of a new position over time—sometimes in ways that do not fully depend on states.[46] This is especially true of a particular form

[42] James Mahoney and Kathleen Thelen, 'A Theory of Gradual Institutional Change', in *Explaining Institutional Change: Ambiguity, Agency, and Power*, edited by James Mahoney and Kathleen Thelen (Cambridge University Press, 2010), p. 14.

[43] See, e.g., Wolfgang Streeck and Kathleen Thelen, 'Introduction: Institutional Change in Advanced Political Economies', in *Beyond Continuity: Institutional Change in Advanced Political Economies*, edited by Wolfgang Streeck and Kathleen Thelen (Oxford University Press, 2005); Mahoney and Thelen (n 42).

[44] See, e.g., Orfeo Fioretos, 'Historical Institutionalism in International Relations', *International Organization* 65, (2011): p. 367; Thomas Rixen and Lora Anne Viola, 'Historical Institutionalism and International Relations: Towards Explaining Change and Stability in International Institutions', in *Historical Institutionalism & International Relations*, edited by T Rixen, L A Viola and M Zürn (Oxford University Press, 2016); Michael Zürn, 'Historical Institutional and International Relations: Strange Bedfellows?', in *Historical Institutionalism & International Relations*, edited by T Rixen, L A Viola and M Zürn (Oxford University Press, 2016).

[45] Michael Zürn, *A Theory of Global Governance: Authority, Legitimacy, and Contestation* (Oxford University Press, 2018).

[46] On the importance of authority in international legal change, see Ingo Venzke, *How Interpretation Makes International Law: On Semantic Change and Normative Twists* (Oxford University Press, 2012);

of institutionalization, the 'judicialization' of international relations, marked by a growing number of international courts and tribunals competent to interpret international legal rules.[47] In both our vignettes, change ultimately came to be recognized through a cumulative build-up of authority across different institutions and courts.

Such gradual change is, of course, not alien to students of international law. Reinterpretation has been a core element in the toolbox of lawyers, and judges and other experts keep finding new meaning in old rules, both in treaties and in customary international law. The remaking of the law of state responsibility by the ILC and the ICJ, with only limited involvement of states, offers a telling example.[48] However, as a matter of international legal doctrine, such moves are often treated as inconsequential. The ILC itself, in its work on the identification of custom and on the subsequent practice to treaties, limits the formal effects of such instances of reinterpretation to that of subsidiary instruments (at best)—always secondary (and subject) to the law-making action of states.[49]

Yet an important part of contemporary changes in international law takes place through such informal, gradual steps of reinterpretation and remaking, often eschewing the classical, doctrinal frames (and sometimes leaving states on the sidelines). Scholars have recognized this in particular for customary international law and have pointed to the emergence of concepts such as 'modern custom', 'custom on a sliding scale', or have recast custom in a common-law light.[50] Much of the scholarly attention to gradual change has come from the process school of international law. Most prominently, the proponents of the New Haven School—Myres McDougal, Harold Lasswell, and Michael Reisman—regarded international law less as a structure of norms than as a process of authoritative

Fuad Zarbiyev, 'Saying Credibly What the Law Is: On Marks of Authority in International Law', *Journal of International Dispute Settlement* 9, (2018): p. 291.

[47] See Karen J Alter, Emilie M Hafner-Burton and Laurence R Helfer, 'Theorizing the Judicialization of International Relations', *International Studies Quarterly* 63, (2019): p. 449.

[48] See, e.g., Pedro Martínez Esponda, 'The Concept of Internationally Wrongful Act', in *The Paths of Change in International Law: Case Studies*, edited by Pedro Martínez Esponda and others (SSRN, 2023); Fernando Lusa Bordin, 'Reflections of Customary International Law: The Authority of Codification Conventions and ILC Draft Articles in International Law' *International & Comparative Law Quarterly* 63, (2014): p. 535. For examples related to treaty law, see Danae Azaria, '"Codification by Interpretation": The International Law Commission as an Interpreter of International Law', *European Journal of International Law* 31, (2020): p. 171.

[49] But see also Fuad Zarbiyev, 'A Quiet Revolution in the Making? The Changing State Authority in Treaty Interpretation', in *The Many Paths of Change in International Law*, edited by Nico Krisch and Ezgi Yildiz (Oxford University Press, 2023).

[50] See more generally Anthea Roberts, 'Traditional and Modern Approaches to Customary International Law: A Reconciliation', *American Journal of International Law* 95, (2001): p. 757; Frederic L Kirgis, 'Custom on a Sliding Scale', *American Journal of International Law* 81, (1987): p. 146; Curtis A Bradley, 'Customary International Law Adjudication as Common Law Adjudication', in *Custom's Future: International Law in a Changing World*, edited by Curtis A Bradley (Cambridge University Press, 2016).

decision-making: a continuous flow of authoritative and controlling decisions.[51] Rosalyn Higgins, later a judge at the ICJ, built on this approach to reconceive many core elements of classical international legal sources and doctrine.[52] Other process scholars, such as Abram Chayes, Thomas Ehrlich, and Andreas Lowenfeld, later in particular Harold Koh, likewise moved away from traditional, rule-focused approaches. In so doing, they further broadened the range of actors and sites relevant in the continuous making and remaking of international legal norms.[53]

While these approaches primarily stemmed from, and responded to, the American legal realism that had become influential since the early twentieth century, process thinking—and with it, greater attention to the steps of gradual change—has also entered international law from other directions. One of them is critical legal scholarship, with an emphasis on the indeterminacy of texts, which led scholars such as David Kennedy or Martti Koskenniemi—and many other scholars since the 1990s—to shift attention from texts towards the discourses that produce meaning.[54] More recently, scholars drawing on socio-legal approaches have come to emphasize the social practices that constitute law and legality in the international realm, thereby also foregrounding the fluidity of meaning and the plurality of actors involved in the formation of normative understandings.[55]

All of these approaches provide important building blocks for our enterprise, and we will come back to them—especially the social-practice tradition—in Chapter 2 and at later points in the book. But they all come with important limitations, too. Adherents of the New Haven School often blur their positive analysis with a particular normative project (and a very contestable one at that).[56] The international legal process tradition of Chayes and colleagues places greater emphasis on the relevance of law in the political process than on the process of law-making and interpretation itself; Harold Koh's focus on questions of compliance is a case in point.[57] For critical scholars, the discourse itself—once liberated from the strictures of text—often seems so malleable as to accommodate virtually any meaning. Likewise, much of the social-practice scholarship emphasizes the

[51] See, e.g., Myres S McDougal, Harold D Lasswell and W Michael Reisman, 'The World Constitutive Process of Authoritative Decision', *Journal of Legal Education* 19, (1966): p. 253; see also Higgins (n 12).

[52] Higgins (n 12).

[53] Abram Chayes, Thomas Ehrlich and Andreas F Lowenfeld, *International Legal Process: Materials for an Introductory Course; in Two Volumes* (Little, Brown, 1968); Harold Hongju Koh, 'Transnational Legal Process', *Nebraska Law Review* 75, (1996): p. 181.

[54] David Kennedy, *International Legal Structures* (Nomos, 1987); Martti Koskenniemi, *From Apology to Utopia: The Structure of International Legal Argument* (Cambridge University Press, 2005).

[55] See, e.g., Jutta Brunnée and Stephen J Toope, *Legitimacy and Legality in International Law: An Interactional Account* (Cambridge University Press, 2010); Venzke (n 46); Tanja Aalberts and Thomas Gammeltoft-Hansen, *The Changing Practices of International Law* (Cambridge University Press, 2018).

[56] See Andrea Bianchi, *International Law Theories: An Inquiry into Different Ways of Thinking* (Oxford University Press, 2016), pp. 108–109. See also Rían Derrig, *The New Haven School: American International Law* (Oxford University Press, 2025), chs. 4, 5.

[57] Harold Hongju Koh, 'Why Do Nations Obey International Law?', *The Yale Law Journal* 106, (1997): p. 2599.

importance of practice (over words, text, etc.) but often without specifying further the constraining and conditioning features that give such practices their structure and force.[58]

International law thus appears more dynamic in many of these accounts, but they tend to be relatively unspecific about the foundations of this dynamism. We are often left with an impression of unbounded complexity and a multitude of actors and fora, as well as a sense of fluidity without an anchor. This is well visible in Monica Hakimi's recent attempt to provide a real-world conception of customary international law—a 'practice' account indebted to the New Haven School, in which the process of customary international law appears as 'enigmatic', 'highly unstructured', and 'messy'.[59] This might capture an important aspect of the development of customary international law—or of any international law apart from treaty-making—but it also seems to surrender too early in the search for patterns and regularities in the process.

With this book, we build on the insights from these approaches and advance towards a more specific understanding of the process and practice of international law. Using empirical material, we seek to detect patterns, convergences, and variation in the way change actually occurs in international law. This allows us to present—in Chapters 3 to 7—a more structured account of the way in which actors, authorities, and ideational contexts shape the trajectory of international norms.

2. Competing Forces: The Politics of Change

The gap between formal structures and actual practices we have begun to explore in the previous section may be surprising at first, but it can be understood as the result of an unresolved tension between competing political forces. Change processes in international law are caught between the need to solve common global problems and the interest of states in retaining control over the obligations they are subject to. The tension between both forces has long shaped debates about change in international law, and it has prevented—at least on a formal level—the recognition of more fluid forms of change. In the following, we outline the contours of this tension, trace (unsuccessful) historical attempts at resolving it in more satisfactory ways, and on that basis seek to better understand the politics (and distributional issues) that have contributed to states' reluctance to accept more dynamic forms of international legal change.

[58] See the critique in Wim Zimmermann, 'Self-Presentation in International Law: On Reputation and Interpretation', *German Law Journal*, forthcoming.

[59] Monica Hakimi, 'Making Sense of Customary International Law', *Michigan Law Review* 118, (2020): p. 1487, 1491–92, 1504.

Common Problems versus National Control

Pressures towards more flexible change in international law have grown considerably over the past century. When Lauterpacht wrote in the 1930s about change and stability—as in the quote with which we opened this chapter—international law was still largely understood in terms of coexistence. States were seen as masters of their own territories and populations, and the main function of international law was the delimitation and protection of boundaries between them.

Today's international law is one not merely of coexistence, but also of cooperation, community, and governance. As a corollary, it features much higher levels of interaction in dealing with common issues—be they environmental challenges, the regulation of a globalized economy, or human rights concerns across borders.[60] With this greater level of interdependence, the expectations for international legal responses have risen sharply, and the need for change is exacerbated further by the acceleration of social life. Most obviously, such acceleration is caused by the pace of technological change, which by most accounts has increased significantly over the past centuries and decades. Acceleration is also characteristic of economic relations, which in late capitalism rely ever more on constant innovation, disruption, and reordering. And acceleration—partly because of the factors already mentioned, partly because of a greater fluidity of social relations and expectations—now defines how individuals experience their lives and the changes in them.[61]

These factors push for a greater dynamism in international regulation to tackle issues ranging from cybersecurity to supply chains, from marine biodiversity to financial stability, from cryptocurrencies to climate change. This push is also carried forward by many more actors than was previously the case—civil society actors, just as business organizations, are now regularly making claims for change. But the demand for common rules is not easily met by an international law that, as intimated at the outset, usually requires widespread agreement for rules of universal or quasi-universal reach.[62]

But at the same time, requirements for state consent and widespread agreement are not simply a technicality or a relic from earlier times when sovereignty reigned supreme. They respond to the widely felt desire of countries to be able to determine for themselves what obligations they accept and what rules they live

[60] See Wolfgang Friedmann, *The Changing Structure of International Law* (Columbia University Press, 1964); Joseph H H Weiler, 'The Geology of International Law: Governance, Democracy and Legitimacy', *Zeitschrift für ausländisches öffentliches Recht und Völkerrecht* 64, (2004): p. 547.

[61] See Hartmut Rosa, *Beschleunigung: Die Veränderung der Zeitstrukturen in der Moderne* (Suhrkamp Verlag, 2005).

[62] Daniel Bodansky, 'What's in a Concept? Global Public Goods, International Law, and Legitimacy', *European Journal of International Law* 23, (2012): p. 651; Nico Krisch, 'The Decay of Consent: International Law in an Age of Global Public Goods' *American Journal of International Law* 108, (2014): pp. 1, 2–7.

by—a desire closely connected to principles of (democratic) self-determination. The importance of such self-determination is obvious for moral nationalists, but it is highly relevant also for cosmopolitans concerned about issues of domination.[63] Such requirements protect national decision-making space, at least to some extent, against formal-legal domination by others. They thus figure high on the agenda, especially of countries in the Global South with a long experience of external interference and colonial or quasi-colonial subjection.[64] Yet they are also defended (and perhaps even more vigorously) by powerful states seeking to avoid the imposition of rules on them.[65]

The emphasis on such protections has only increased in recent years with the rise of anti-internationalist sentiments that seek to 'take back control' from international processes. Such sentiments in part reflect a loss of influence in the face of a globalized economy. They are also fuelled by a stronger sense of difference and diversity. The 1990s' supposed end of history had led to a widespread belief that core political and ideological divisions were a thing of the past, replaced by convergence around one basic model of liberal democracy and free markets.[66] Yet today we see a more self-confident assertion of alternatives, often merely through an emphasis on a country's own traditions and history, at other times with a clearer anti-liberal approach.[67] Faced with such differences, political integration at an international level or the loosening of consent-based protections in law-making remains even more elusive.

The effects of greater diversity and stronger anti-internationalism are further amplified by the shift in power that has taken place in international society over the past few decades and continues to take place today. The Western dominance of the twentieth century—contested during the Cold War, then consolidated in the 1990s—has abated, but the transition to a multipolar order remains unfinished. Amid growing political and ideological divergence, commentators have diagnosed a fractured world—one riven with disagreement and great power rivalry, where concerns about relative gains often outweigh the perceived benefits of cooperation.[68]

[63] See, e.g., David Miller, *National Responsibility and Global Justice* (Oxford University Press, 2007); and with a view to Europe see Richard Bellamy, *A Republican Europe of States: Cosmopolitanism, Intergovernmentalism and Democracy in the EU* (Cambridge University Press, 2019).

[64] On the emphasis on sovereignty protections among newly independent states, see, e.g., Antony Anghie, 'Bandung and the Origins of Third World Sovereignty', in *Bandung, Global History, and International Law: Critical Pasts and Pending Futures*, edited by Luis Eslava, Michael Fakhri and Vasuki Nesiah (Cambridge University Press, 2017).

[65] See Nico Krisch, 'International Law in Times of Hegemony: Unequal Power and the Shaping of the International Legal Order', *European Journal of International Law* 16, (2005): p. 369.

[66] See the classical account in Francis Fukuyama, *The End of History and the Last Man* (Penguin UK, 1993) with more nuance than is usually acknowledged.

[67] On some of the broader transformations, see G John Ikenberry, 'Three Worlds: The West, East and South and the Competition to Shape Global Order', *International Affairs* 100, (2024): p. 121.

[68] We adopt the expression 'fractured world' from Andrew Hurrell. See also Paul Tucker, *Global Discord: Values and Power in a Fractured World Order* (Princeton University Press, 2022).

The confluence of such countervailing factors—an increased need for dynamic responses to a rapidly changing world with ever more pronounced political divisions—has led to gridlock in many areas. Initiatives for new rules or policies are often halted as a result of disagreement among key players.[69] Scholars have highlighted stagnation in new law-making efforts, especially in the conclusion of multilateral treaties, and they have observed shifts to other, more informal instruments.[70] What movement there is seems to occur primarily through informal means, bilateral or regional arrangements, or even unilateral action—working around a formal international law that often appears as too inflexible.[71] But amid growing political divisions, states are ever less willing to accept more dynamic law-making processes, given concerns that such processes could be leveraged by rival actors to advance their own agendas.

Contested Modes of Change

The conflicting forces around change have come to the fore—in different constellations—at various points during the past century, and they have led to a number of (ultimately unsuccessful) attempts at softening the rigid formal modes of international legal change. Two instances stand out: the debate on peaceful change in the 1930s, and the adjustment to a decolonized world in the 1960s and 1970s, both of which allow us to better appreciate the political obstacles on the way to a formal rearticulation of the tension between common problems and national control. Debates around the dynamism of international law—or the lack thereof—were particularly vehement in discussions of 'peaceful change' in the inter-war period. This debate was triggered by growing discontent with the post-First World War settlement, especially on the part of Germany with the Versailles Treaty, and by a broader sense that the order created in 1919 had become outdated and was no longer in keeping with the 'realities' of international politics.[72] The issue became pressing when revisionist states used increasingly violent means to achieve their goals, and many observers and political actors sought forms of 'peaceful change' that could adapt treaties to new political and factual circumstances.[73] As

[69] Thomas Hale, David Held and Kevin Young, *Gridlock: Why Global Cooperation Is Failing When We Need It Most* (Polity, 2013).

[70] Robert A Denemark and Matthew J Hoffmann, 'Just Scraps of Paper? The Dynamics of Multilateral Treaty-Making', *Cooperation and Conflict* 43, (2008): p. 185; See Pauwelyn, Wessel and Wouters (n 24).

[71] See Krisch (n 62).

[72] Another attempt at treaty revision around the same time—concerning the 'unequal treaties' imposed on China, Siam, and other countries in the nineteenth century—attracted comparatively less attention. See Gerrit W Gong, *The Standard of 'Civilization' in International Society* (Clarendon Press, 1984).

[73] See Peter Marcus Kristensen, '"Peaceful Change" in International Relations: A Conceptual Archaeology', *International Theory* 13, (2021): p. 36; Torbjørn L Knutsen, 'Peaceful Change: The Interwar Era and the Disciplinary Context', in *The Oxford Handbook of Peaceful Change in International Relations*, edited by T V Paul and others (Oxford University Press, 2022).

one commentator put it, '[p]erhaps no other problem of international law play[ed] . . . such an important rôle as the problem of revision'.[74]

The starting point of this debate was the unsatisfactory nature of an international order geared excessively towards the *status quo*—the result of tying treaty revision to the unanimous consent of all parties. But views diverged heavily as to ways out of this situation.[75] Some commentators thought that international law contained the resources for solving much of the problem itself, especially by way of judicial adaptation.[76] For others, these tools did not go far enough or relied too much on judges to resolve essentially political questions.[77] Yet the political mechanisms that existed were also not promising. Article 19 of the Covenant of the League of Nations addressed the issue, but gave the Assembly of the League only advisory powers.[78]

Attention thus shifted to the creation of new mechanisms. Proposals ranged from gradual amendments to the Covenant to the creation of a supranational legislature or of an 'international equity court' which could decide disputes on the basis of equity and thus remedy perceived injustices in existing law.[79] Such ideas obviously faced significant obstacles, not only in terms of feasibility, but also regarding the conditions that would need to be in place for them to function. A legislative mechanism with (qualified) majority decision-making was for some a goal to strive towards, but it was also seen to clash with the structure of international society—it ran 'the risk of being unreal unless it form[ed] part and parcel of a comprehensive political organization of mankind'.[80] Some thus hoped that smaller improvements to the operation of the organs of the League, and to the weight of their pronouncements, may generate political dynamics that would allow for fair revisions to existing treaties.[81] But even such smaller improvements were practically out of reach—given the prevailing diversity and distrust among countries, countries' interest in keeping control trumped the desire for smoother mechanisms for legal change.

74 Josef L Kunz, 'The Problem of Revision in International Law', *American Journal of International Law* 33, (1939): p. 33, 33.

75 See, e.g., the debate in *International Affairs* 14, (1935): pp. 818–36; C A W Manning, ed., *Peaceful Change: An International Problem* (Macmillan, 1937).

76 Lauterpacht (n 1), ch. XI.

77 See, e.g., Kunz (n 74), p. 41; Sir John Fischer Williams, *International Change and International Peace* (Oxford University Press, H Milford, 1932), pp. 7–14; E H Carr, *The Twenty Years' Crisis, 1919-1939* (Springer, 2016), pp. 185–89.

78 G M Gathorne-Hardy, 'Territorial Revision and Article 19 of the League Covenant', *International Affairs* 14, (1935): pp. 818, 820–24; David Mitrany, 'Territorial Revision and Article 19 of the League Covenant', *International Affairs* 14, (1935): pp. 827, 830.

79 See, e.g., Fischer Williams (n 77); Karl Strupp, *Legal Machinery for Peaceful Change* (Constable & Company Limited, 1937); for a survey see Kunz (n 74), pp. 48–55.

80 Hersch Lauterpacht, 'The Legal Aspect', in *Peaceful Change: An International Problem*, edited by C A W Manning (Macmillan, 1937), p. 164.

81 Fischer Williams (n 77), pp. 59–76.

When it came to designing the new world organization—the United Nations—in 1945, one might have imagined a greater readiness among countries to establish a legislative mechanism to tackle common problems early enough, and thus to prevent the recurrence of war. However, they did so only in a tightly circumscribed fashion, by allowing the UN Security Council to enact binding resolutions to address concrete threats to international peace. This was an important but limited act of delegation (for most member states, but not for the permanent members which, because of their veto power, retained control).[82] Yet there was little openness to go further: a proposal by the Philippines to grant the General Assembly legislative powers was rejected almost unanimously in the respective committee at the San Francisco Conference, and the Assembly was therefore left with a largely recommendatory function.[83]

A few decades later, questions of change and adaptability came to the centre of attention again from a different perspective, namely as a result of the decolonization process. While many newly independent states initially aimed for integration into existing international law, they soon began to call for stronger protections against intervention and for steps towards a more solidaristic international order—and for more effective mechanisms to realize such change.[84]

Some of the goals pursued by developing countries were taken up in treaties, such as the 1969 Vienna Convention on the Law of Treaties, with the inclusion of provisions on *jus cogens* and the invalidity of treaties concluded under the threat of force. But on the most central issues—especially those relating to greater solidarity and a fairer new international economic order (NIEO)—treaty-making was elusive as Western countries remained reluctant to accept Southern demands.[85] The core battleground was the United Nations and, in particular, the General Assembly in which the developing world had a distinct numerical advantage. General Assembly resolutions thus became the preferred vehicle for generating change, and in some cases, this path proved successful. The 1970 Friendly Relations Declaration, for example, was soon regarded as having clarified and developed key principles of the international legal order, especially with a view to a stronger prohibition of intervention.[86] Agreement was more difficult to find on

[82] On those powers and their later expansion, see Nico Krisch, 'Chapter VII Powers: The General Framework and Articles 39 to 43', in *The United Nations Charter: A Commentary*, edited by Bruno Simma and others (Oxford University Press, 2012).

[83] *Documents of the United Nations Conference on International Organization* (United Nations, 1945), vol. IX, 70.

[84] Georges M Abi-Saab, 'The Newly Independent States and the Rules of International Law', *Howard Law Journal* 8, (1962): p. 95. See also Jorge Castañeda, 'The Underdeveloped Nations and the Development of International Law', *International Organization* 15, (1961): p. 38.

[85] See Antony Anghie, *Imperialism, Sovereignty and the Making of International Law* (Cambridge University Press, 2007), ch. 4.

[86] See Georges M Abi-Saab, *International Change and the International Legal Order* (The Ecumenical Institute Bossey World Council of Churches, 1970); Jorge E Viñuales, ed., *The UN*

further-reaching demands—the 1974 Charter on Economic Rights and Duties of States, which contained core elements of the NIEO project, was adopted with a vote of 115:6:10, reflecting broader North–South divisions.[87]

The question of change in international law here became, once again, eminently practical. Could a General Assembly resolution, passed with an overwhelming majority but not unanimously, be regarded as creating new law? Developing countries pushed in this direction, but met with the resistance of Western states which knew that they could be easily outvoted.[88] The doctrinal debates on these developments persisted, but a 'legislative' power of the General Assembly increasingly became a minority proposition in the following decades.

A stronger role of the Assembly was only accepted in the context of customary international law, and only when the Assembly acted by consensus. Following discussions around (unanimous) GA resolutions on the law of outer space in the 1960s,[89] convergence grew around the notion that new custom could be 'crystallized' in a GA resolution[90]—a point also underscored by the ICJ and the ILC.[91] But even as this flexibilizes legal change, it merely reproduces the problem that change is hampered as long as there is disagreement among countries. The ILC recently captured this explicitly: '[r]esolutions which attract negative votes or abstentions are unlikely to be regarded as reflecting customary international law.'[92]

In these instances of contestation over the modes of change, the conflicting forces introduced above are clearly on display: the need for effectuating change more flexibly contrasts with the interest of states in controlling what kind of change and which obligations are brought about. Amid a diverse and divided international society, in which different sides fear being sidelined, the tension between both forces remains unresolved, and the traditional, restrictive frame of change remains intact, at least on a formal level.

Friendly Relations Declaration at 50: An Assessment of the Fundamental Principles of International Law (Cambridge University Press, 2020).

87 UNGA Res 3281 (XXIX) (12 December 1974).

88 See, e.g., Jorge G Castañeda, *Legal Effects of United Nations Resolutions* (Columbia University Press, 1969); Mark E Ellis, 'The New International Economic Order and General Assembly Resolutions: The Debate over the Legal Effects of General Assembly Resolutions Revisited', *California Western International Law Journal* 15, (1985): p. 647.

89 See Bin Cheng, 'United Nations Resolutions on Outer Space: "Instant" International Customary Law?', *Indian Journal of International Law* 5, (1965): p. 23.

90 See, e.g., the contributions by Luigi Condorelli and Gaetano Arangio-Ruiz in *Change and Stability in International Law-Making*, edited by Antonio Cassese and Joseph H H Weiler (Walter de Gruyter, 1988). See Roberts (n 50).

91 ICJ, *Military and Paramilitary Activities in and against Nicaragua (Nicaragua v United States of America)* [1986] ICJ Rep 392, pp. 99–100, para. 188; ILC, 'Draft Conclusions on the Identification of Customary International Law' (2018) UN Doc A/73/10.

92 ILC, 'Draft Conclusions on the Identification of Customary International Law' (n 13), p. 148. See also *Legality of the Threat or Use of Nuclear Weapons* (Advisory Opinion) [1996] ICJ Rep 226, paras. 70–73.

The Politics of Change

The historical struggles over the modes of change, rooted in the tension between national control and effective common rules, provides us with a helpful background to better understand the politics of change. This question—especially regarding the political economy of change processes—is inscribed in the broader debate on the politics of international law, which is marked by two core approaches opposing each other. The first of these—a more 'idealist' one—presents a rather egalitarian image of international law. Consent-based law is seen here as protecting weaker states from the dominance of the materially powerful. Even if sovereign equality is primarily a formal notion,[93] it is seen to contribute to the protection of diversity and self-government.[94] On this view, the rule of law remains a counterpoint to power politics.[95]

This juxtaposition of law and politics stands in stark contrast with realist or critical approaches, which see international law primarily as a political tool, and a tool of the powerful at that. For realists, state consent and its supposedly protective function are largely fictions, as powerful states are often able to coerce or induce consent.[96] Classical and constructivist-minded realists also highlight the ideational processes through which dominant ideas influence the preferences of weaker states, thereby facilitating their consent to rules that reflect those ideas—developing countries' widespread acceptance of bilateral investment treaties is a case in point.[97] As a result, international law tends to reflect the vision of the great powers of the day to a significant extent.[98] This vision parallels Marxist accounts for whom law appears primarily as a superstructure of material forces; for them, '[t]he international rule of law is not counterposed to force and imperialism: it is an expression of it'.[99] Many postcolonial approaches echo this view, frustrated not only with the colonial origins of international law but also with the limited success of efforts to change its unequal structure following the formal independence of former colonies.[100]

[93] See Nico Krisch, 'More Equal than the Rest? Hierarchy, Equality and US Predominance in International Law', in *United States Hegemony and the Foundations of International Law*, edited by M Byers and G Nolte (Cambridge University Press, 2003).

[94] Benedict Kingsbury, 'Sovereignty and Inequality', *European Journal of International Law* 9, (1998): p. 599.

[95] See, e.g., Terry Nardin, 'Theorising the International Rule of Law', *Review of International Studies* 34, (2008): p. 385.

[96] Richard H Steinberg, 'Wanted—Dead or Alive: Realism in International Law', in *Interdisciplinary Perspectives on International Law and International Relations: The State of the Art*, edited by J L Dunoff and M A Pollack (Cambridge University Press, 2012), p. 161.

[97] On the ideational background, see Quinn Slobodian, *Globalists: The End of Empire and the Birth of Neoliberalism* (Harvard University Press, 2018), ch. 4. But see also the competing explanations in Zachary Elkins, Andrew T Guzman and Beth A Simmons, 'Competing for Capital: The Diffusion of Bilateral Investment Treaties, 1960-2000', *International Organization* 60, (2006): p. 811.

[98] Wilhelm G Grewe, *The Epochs of International Law* (Walter de Gruyter, 2000).

[99] China Miéville, *Between Equal Rights: A Marxist Theory of International Law* (Brill, 2005), p. 8.

[100] See, e.g., Anghie (n 85).

Apart from conflicting theoretical commitments, these two approaches diverge on two main points. The first concerns the assessment of the *status quo*—a relatively static system tends to protect the *status quo*, and those who are seen to benefit from the existing situation will also benefit from strict requirements for change. While the first camp highlights the benefits existing rules offer the weak—such as the impartiality and generality of rules over the whims of power politics—the second camp underscores how these rules benefit the powerful—especially by consolidating and legitimizing an international order largely created by European states and insulated by high barriers to change. The second core difference relates, as already intimated, to the political economy of consent. While the first approach sees consent as a valuable tool of protection for the weak, the second approach highlights consent's utility for the powerful: while it prevents the imposition of rules on *them* and helps to legitimize rules crafted in their favour, it is actually of little use for weaker states because their consent can be bought, forced, or induced through discursive frames construed by the powerful in the first place.

The contrast between both approaches may not be resolvable in principle, but they constitute a helpful starting point for a comparative institutional analysis. From such an angle, the requirements of consent and widespread agreement in classical change processes in international law may well be open to exploitation, but they also impose heavier constraints on powerful actors than other forms of international politics. International law may then be simultaneously instrumental *and* resistant to the pursuit of power—and more resistant than other tools such as diplomacy, unilateral pressures, or coercion. This might help to explain the ambivalent relationship of many powerful states with international legal rules and institutions.[101] Such a comparative analysis might also be helpful for a comparison of the politics of different avenues of international law-making and change. Bilateral treaty negotiations are typically more open to the influence of material power than processes leading to multilateral agreements; and law-making through the Security Council offers (some) powerful actors far more control than conventional or customary processes.[102]

How do the gradual, informal change processes we take into view here fare in such a comparative analysis? How do they compare to traditional processes of change through treaties or customary law? The answer is not necessarily straightforward, and the debate on customary international law may serve as a guide. Many observers highlight the resistance of powerful states to a more flexible approach to custom—one that, for example, downplays consistent state practice in favour of *opinio juris*—because they fear a loss of control.[103] We have encountered

[101] See Krisch (n 65).

[102] ibid pp. 387–88, 398–99; see also Detlev F Vagts, 'Hegemonic International Law', *American Journal of International Law* 95, (2001): p. 843.

[103] Steinberg (n 96), p. 162.

such resistance already in the debate over the status of UN General Assembly resolutions in the context of the NIEO campaign. But critical scholars also stress the challenges that a lower threshold for new customary rules poses for weaker states. These challenges arise partly because of the outsized attention typically paid to the practice of Western, powerful states in the construction of custom and partly because developing countries often view consent as a vital tool of protection.[104]

These contrasting observations on custom apply to other avenues of informal change as well: flexibilizing legal change brings with it possibilities but also risks for powerful and weak actors alike. The balance may not be the same across the board—change through courts is subject to different politics than that through expert bodies, multilateral fora, or private authority. The politics of change then throw us back onto the politics of the institutions or actor constellations relevant in a particular setting. We will return to these in greater detail later in the book.

Despite such nuances, it is probably fair to assume that, overall, powerful states are particularly ill at ease with more flexible change mechanisms. They benefit more directly from the *status quo*, have the means to influence the consent of other states, and they can often achieve desired change through other, unilateral avenues. They will thus feel less of a need to accept the risks that come with shifts away from consent-based law-making, especially when it involves independent experts. Their reluctance to accept international dispute settlement or the authority of quasi-judicial bodies is symptomatic of their approach.[105]

Less powerful states—often less content with the existing rules in the first place—typically do not have easy alternatives and often need to rely on broad norm-making processes to achieve their aims on a global scale. They may still be wary of abandoning the protections that come with consent.[106] But on some of the paths of gradual change—especially the more discursive, interpretive ones—material power may matter less, and weaker states may be able to draw on interpretive power through discourse mobilization (a theme we will return to in Chapter 5). Overall, then, more fluid change processes can be expected to benefit weaker states more than powerful states.

Nevertheless, most countries are unlikely to give up the formal protections of consent, except in very circumscribed circumstances for more technical issues or in contexts of tighter, regional integration with like-minded states.[107] They may support flexibility if it suits their interests in a given case.[108] If it is coupled with

[104] See B S Chimni, 'Customary International Law: A Third World Perspective', *American Journal of International Law* 112, (2018): p. 1; Nils Gilman, 'The New International Economic Order: A Reintroduction', *Humanity* 6, (2015): p. 1.

[105] See Krisch (n 65), and also 'The (Contested) Paths of the Present' in Chapter 7.

[106] On the tension in the NIEO context see Gilman (n 104), p. 5.

[107] See, on delegation to international organizations, Liesbet Hooghe, Tobias Lenz and Gary Marks, *A Theory of International Organization* (Oxford University Press, 2019).

[108] Krisch (n 65), pp. 392–94; Michael Byers, 'Preemptive Self-Defense: Hegemony, Equality and Strategies of Legal Change', *Journal of Political Philosophy* 11, (2003): p. 171.

sufficient protections for them, they may also accept that more flexible paths generate legally binding outcomes more generally. Powerful countries do so for the UN Security Council, and they also show support for General Assembly resolutions as long as they are unanimous. As the United States asserted in 1963, in the context of rules for outer space, '[w]hen a General Assembly resolution proclaimed principles of international law . . . and was adopted unanimously, it represented the law as generally accepted in the international community'.[109] Likewise, as we have seen in the NIEO debate, developing countries supported General Assembly law-making with qualified majorities—knowing that their strength in numbers would protect them from overly adverse law-making.

Short of such protections, countries—weak and powerful alike—are thus likely to reject more flexible processes of international legal change, at least formally. But they may be ready to tolerate them if they retain a certain 'safety valve' by keeping the results of such processes contestable. This may be the case as long as these results can be portrayed as non-binding—as merely 'emerging', 'soft', 'informal', or generally below the threshold of creating formal obligations. Countries may still go along with the outcome if they do not harbour strong objections. But if they strongly disagree, such contestability affords them space to reject the outcome and thus provides a measure of control—a point we take up in greater depth in Chapter 7. More flexible forms of international legal change may then lack full formal recognition, and the consolidation of norms will often be the result of *ex post* processes of acceptance over time.

3. Change in International Law: An Outline

In this book, we ask: how does change in international law come about beyond treaty-making—through what mechanisms, with what actors, and under what conditions? And: who wins and who loses—whose efforts and which ideas prevail when change attempts are successful or unsuccessful? As we have seen, both questions have elicited widely diverging answers—between those who understand change in punctuated equilibria and those who see it happen more gradually; and between those who see change processes dominated and controlled by the powerful versus those who see such change processes as potential entry points for weaker actors.

In the following chapters, we seek to scrutinize these competing visions and get closer to the actual ways in which international law changes. We do so in the first place through a focus on empirics—many of the questions about the structure and speed of change can only be answered by paying close attention to instances of change (and non-change) as they occur in reality. To this end, we look at change

[109] UN Doc A/AC.105/C.2/SR.20 (22 April 1963), p. 11.

processes described in the existing literature, but also carry out a detailed analysis of twenty-five original case studies of change processes over the past decades. Likewise, our questions can be answered only if we take into view both micro- and macro-perspectives—if we zoom in *and* out again so as to be able to perceive the fine-grained interactions of actors around change attempts as well as the bigger picture and conditions of change obscured when seen from up close. And, connected to that, answering those questions requires us to adopt a methodological stance that does not pre-empt one or the other ontology but instead remains open to different constructions of what international law is and how it changes.

Our cases cover general international law as well as different issue areas, ranging from international trade and investment law to international environmental law, the law of the sea, international criminal law, human rights and humanitarian law. As mentioned above, we do not include cases that centred on change through treaty-making—treaties are much better understood than the other paths we take into view. Our cases span roughly five decades, from around 1970 to 2020, allowing us to capture variation over time. We explain our case selection and design in more detail in Chapter 3.

In our analysis, we are interested in how change comes about (or fails to come about), and we conceptualize change as a discursive shift in the understanding of international legal norms. Such change may proceed in different directions, including the expansion or contraction of existing understandings, as well as the establishment or reconfigurations of norms and rules. By contrast, questions of compliance are of secondary importance to our analysis. Non-compliance becomes analytically relevant only where it is accompanied by an active discursive challenge to the rule in question, or where it triggers broader discursive shifts among other actors.

This also means that we do not examine, at least not directly, recent actions by great powers that deliberately violate, erode, or hollow out established legal obligations. In Chapter 7, we address such developments in the context of the 'changing modes of change' in a new geopolitical environment. Our primary concern here, however, lies with the general conditions under which change efforts succeed in producing discursive settlement over longer periods of time. Violations—even of central rules, such as those governing the use of force, as in Russia's invasion of Ukraine or the United States' intervention in Venezuela—do not in themselves amount to legal change so long as other states continue to reaffirm existing rules. They may lead to change over time if they generate a broader shift in international understandings of what counts as the relevant law, but whether and to what extent this will occur remains an open question.

In Chapter 2, we lay out our theoretical framework and the building blocks of our analysis of change in greater detail. We build on a conception of international law as a social practice which endogenously generates understandings of applicable norms, relevant actors, and recognized authorities, and we seek to make this account more concrete than is typical in the existing literature. We do so by developing a typology of the different paths on which we expect change to occur. Each path is characterized by its own actors, dynamics, and authority structures, and we expect significant variation in the relevant path(s) across different issue areas, depending on the recognition by the actors in a given field. These paths form a core structuring element of our comparative analysis of change processes across international law. They allow us to ask more systematically on which paths international law travels, which actors play a role around them, and which factors matter more or less when a particular path is pursued.

Chapter 3 uses our theoretical framework and the findings from our cases—triangulated with material from existing scholarship—to present a comparative picture of international legal change across different issue areas. Change processes, we find, travel on strongly varying paths, with some areas dominated by classical, decentralized interactions of states and others focused on international institutions, courts, or quasi-judicial bodies. In several areas, it is the interaction of different paths that favours successful change outcomes. The available paths also condition access: in some areas, private actors (whether from business or civil society) find receptive institutions, while in others, their change attempts are frustrated unless they can find governments to advance them. International law here appears as not so much one field, but instead as a multiplicity of connected fields, each with its own ways of making and changing law.

In Chapter 4, we explore the conditions and factors behind successful change in international law and present the results of our empirical analysis, on the basis of both descriptive statistics and a regression analysis. We evaluate competing accounts of norm change—ranging from statist explanations to those focusing on norm characteristics—and find the strongest support for an authority-based institutionalist account. Perhaps most importantly, we find that state positions matter less for change attempts than is typically assumed. In many of our cases, states seem to be more effective in blocking change attempts than in driving them. Another finding relates to the role of authority: change attempts that are processed by a focal authority in a given field—a court or institution—are significantly more likely to be successful than those that take place in the context of more peripheral, diffuse authority settings. The effect of authority configurations becomes yet more pronounced in cases where state opposition is present. Even in the face of significant state opposition, we find, change attempts are more likely to succeed when they receive support from focal authority. Authority, more than state positions, thus appears as a major explanatory factor for change.

While Chapters 3 and 4 provide broader, cross-cutting accounts of change across our cases and fields, Chapters 5 to 7 focus in greater depth on particular aspects of our findings. Chapter 5 does so by zooming in on the role of power in international legal change. By most accounts, material power is of central importance to legal change in the international context, but this expectation did not hold in our cases. In fact, both major power support and major power opposition had very limited effects on the success of change attempts—powerful states were neither able to make change happen nor were they able decisively to block it outright. While material power may play a more pronounced role in treaty-making, it has limited explanatory force for the more gradual, informal change processes we analyse here. Instead, our cases point to the importance of non-material forms of power. In particular, we focus on ideational power which, in a discursive social practice such as law, plays a particularly important role. The chapter explores how actors engage in discourse mobilization to advance change and examines factors that tamper, undercut, or propel different forms of power in international legal change processes. The prominence of ideational power along many interpretive paths of change—paths that often privilege actors other than states—helps explain the ambivalence of materially powerful states towards international law in general—and towards non-state paths of change in particular.

Chapter 6 seeks to understand the paths of change in international law amid the institutional complexity of global politics. Among the multiplicity of paths potentially available to change agents, which paths does international law travel on, and why? We draw on a historical institutionalist frame to show how, in many of our cases, change takes a 'path of least resistance', on which change agents avoid institutions with greater resistance and build their case by accumulating authority in more receptive but potentially peripheral sites before accessing more central (but initially less sympathetic) institutions. This often includes moving across issue areas, thus using a fragmented landscape in the hope of generating change across the board. Complexity and multiplicity thus facilitate greater dynamism in international law, but this dynamism remains limited, and many change attempts face obstacles as a result. Change agents frequently react by turning to other forms and fora—informal, domestic, informational—to pursue their goals. 'Paths of least resistance' often lead outside international law.

Chapter 7 explores the role of contestation in international legal change. Contestation is a key driver of change, but it also leads to the destabilization of rules and meanings. The likelihood of unsettled understandings increases in contexts of diffuse authority. As these are the norm rather than the exception in international law, we often find international law 'in degrees' rather than in binary form. Contestation also operates on another level—that of the paths themselves. Even as they follow non-state authorities in practice, states typically challenge suggestions of a formal interpretive or law-making authority of non-state paths. Some states have engaged in further-reaching backlash, especially against international courts, leading in certain cases to the effective disabling of judicial institutions. This highlights the changeability of the paths of international law themselves—their timebound nature and the way in which, through different periods in the development of international law, the paths of change have undergone significant transformation. The constellation of paths we focus on throughout the book—in part a product of the post-Cold War international order—is then also likely to undergo change as its political context shifts towards greater division and multipolarity, potentially leaving international law itself 'fractured'.

Chapter 8 synthesizes the findings of the book and outlines further directions these findings point us towards. It presents eight core lessons—around the role of states, power, authority, and the paths of international legal change—and then focuses on implications for the study of international law and international relations. These implications provide challenges in different respects: for international legal sources doctrine, for the literature on norm change in international politics, and for rationalist accounts of international law. In a third step, the conclusion sketches elements of a normative assessment of the mechanisms of change in international law, emphasizing the tension between the need for dynamic responses to global challenges and the importance of checks on the risk of domination that comes with non-consensual processes. We end by pointing to some of the (potentially gloomy) paths ahead.

Apart from the discussion in the conclusion, we do not, in this book, engage in a broader normative inquiry into the legitimacy and justification of different forms of change processes. Such a normative assessment would raise questions central to political philosophy, including the appropriate fora for law-making, the character of international society, the meaning and implications of self-determination, or the relevance and content of democratic standards for global political processes. These are big and important questions, and ones to which political theorists have not always given direct or comprehensive answers.[110] Tackling them would have required a different, and much broader, project than we can undertake here. Certain normative considerations will, of course, appear throughout the book, and we will return to them in the conclusion. But we also hope that others will take up the task of a more sustained normative engagement with the international legal change processes we describe and analyse here.

4. Between Adjustment and Transformation

The picture we paint in this book is one of gradual shifts in many sites, propelled by a great variety of actors and institutions and resulting in a great number of adjustments. It is a picture of movement beneath the more visible—and far more studied—surface of treaty-making and state practice leading to customary norms, and beneath the surface of the formal sources and accepted modes of legal change. It is also a more dynamic picture than is usual in accounts of international legal

[110] Some attempts can be found in Samantha Besson and John Tasioulas, eds., *The Philosophy of International Law* (Oxford University Press, 2010); Chris Brown and Robyn Eckersley, eds., *The Oxford Handbook of International Political Theory* (Oxford University Press, 2018).

change, quite in contrast with the imagery of punctuated equilibria and high hurdles associated with traditional forms.

This dynamism is, we believe, central to understanding international law today. But this claim raises important questions. Some may ask: how relevant is it really—is it perhaps all about small, insignificant changes? They might think that it would be more meaningful to study major transformations—such as those that affect the structure of the international legal order—to be able to draw conclusion on the degree of dynamism (and the politics) of international law as such.[111]

Studying major transformations is obviously of great importance, and some of these have brought about structural change directly. The adoption of the United Nations Charter may have been such a moment; for the area of trade law, the establishment of the World Trade Organization. But most examples of major change were not so sudden, and their effects were often more indirect. This is true for most cases further back in time—the freedom of the seas emerged gradually out of a long-standing struggle, with shifting coalitions on both sides, from the seventeenth century onwards;[112] the transformation of subjecthood through the inclusion of entities outside Europe and North America in the structure of international law proceeded from the early nineteenth century up until the mid-twentieth century.[113] Many momentous shifts after 1945, too, did not come about instantly. The UN Convention on the Law of the Sea is a good reflection of this—it brought with it new rules, but in many respects, it was a continuation, culmination, or codification of prior change processes; in others, it was the starting point of a development of norms left vague in the negotiations.[114] Likewise, current transformations in international law—as a result of power shifts, the demise of the 'liberal international order' or the United States under Donald Trump—are likely to be reflected in international law not through one major instrument or design, but instead through many processes of adaptation in different fields.

In this book, we thus shift the focus away from big, sudden moments of change in international law, which are anyway few and far between. We instead pay attention to the many smaller processes that shift international rules on a daily basis—and may contribute to broader transformations over time. If we think of the

[111] We thank Umut Özsu for emphasizing this point. See also B S Chimni, 'Epilogue: Fragmentary Thoughts on Informal Change', in *The Many Paths of Change in International Law*, edited by Nico Krisch and Ezgi Yildiz (Oxford University Press, 2023).

[112] See Andrea Weindl, 'Grotius's Mare Liberum in the Political Practice of Early-Modern Europe', *Grotiana* 30, (2009): p. 131.

[113] See Hedley Bull and Adam Watson, eds., *The Expansion of International Society* (Oxford University Press, 1984).

[114] See Rozemarijn J Roland Holst, *Change in the Law of the Sea: Context, Mechanisms and Practice* (Brill, 2022); see also Ezgi Yildiz, 'Case Study 14: Evolving Rules of Continental Shelf Delimitation: The Fate of the Equidistance Principle', in *The Paths of International Law: Case Studies*, edited by Pedro Martínez Esponda and others (SSRN, 2023); Ezgi Yildiz and Umut Yuksel, 'The Delocalizing Effect of International Courts: Evidence from Maritime Delimitation Practices', *The Review of International Organizations* 20, (2025): p. 825.

'greening of international law', we do not only look at the treaties concluded in and around Rio, but also at the many paths on which environmental concerns—such as the precautionary principle—came to pervade other areas of international law, from trade to human rights.[115] If we think of the ways in which capitalism has constituted and transformed international law, we might think of the changing rules on maritime use and territorial acquisition at the heart of European empires, but also changes in the protection of foreign property (later 'investments'), brought about through an amalgamation of customary law, bilateral treaties, and their interpretative expansion.[116]

As these examples show, such transformations through small steps are not limited to the past few decades, and they will continue to characterize international law even in the face of current challenges. Many will think that, with the rise of great-power competition, and a more fractured international society more radical shifts are likely and that such shifts will occur in other ways than we describe here. This is a possibility, but as we discuss further in Chapter 7, it is not the most likely one. International law may indeed be disregarded more than in the past, and thus its norms may, to some extent, erode. It may also face greater resistance to change by certain countries, and therefore, change processes might be limited to smaller groups of states. But it is not obvious that any of the actors—including the major powers, given their divergences—would be able to bring about large-scale change in the norms and understandings of international law in a short time-frame. As in previous phases of upheaval, international law is instead likely to avoid sudden collapse or transformation, with much of its change coming through the gradual processes we focus on in this book.

International law has had few 'revolutions'. For the most part, change has come retail, not wholesale—through an accumulation of more circumscribed moves and shifts in meaning. International legal change is a 'strong and slow boring of hard boards'—perhaps even more so than the politics Max Weber talked about,[117] given the deep-seated resistance to change that characterizes law, and especially international law. But this does not mean that international law stands still; it only forces us to shift focus. If we want to understand the transformations of international law, we need to understand the many paths (and small steps) through which it changes. This is what we set out to do in the following chapters.

[115] See, e.g., Philippe Sands, ed., *Greening International Law* (Routledge, 1993). See also Ezgi Yildiz, 'Case Study 19: The Precautionary Principle', in *The Paths of International Law: Case Studies*, edited by Pedro Martínez Esponda and others (SSRN, 2023).

[116] See, e.g., the inquiries in Miéville (n 99); Ntina Tzouvala, *Capitalism As Civilisation: A History of International Law* (Cambridge University Press, 2020); Karen J Alter, 'From Colonial to Multilateral International Law: A Global Capitalism and Law Investigation', *International Journal of Constitutional Law* 19, (2021): p. 798.

[117] Max Weber, *Politik als Beruf*, 2nd ed. (Duncker & Humblot, 1926), p. 67.

2
The Process of Change

If we want to understand international law's gradual change, the dynamism of its actual operation, we cannot stop at texts or formal expressions; we have to take into view the social processes through which the law is made and remade. As legal anthropologist Sally Falk Moore put it in the introduction to her *Law as Process*, 'in the long term all legal "systems" are built by accretion'; 'all legal systems are piecemeal aggregates'.[1] Understanding the processes and politics of change in international law requires discerning the ways in which this accretion happens.

To say that international law is a process in this sense helps to contrast our approach with alternatives which focus either on reified texts, held together in coherent legal systems, or on rules created by unencumbered actors—actors who choose and use the law according to their preferences at a given moment.[2] The process vision sits between these, highlighting on the one hand that texts only gain meaning and relevance in and through social processes, and on the other hand that actors are always embedded in processes and structures that help shape the way they act. Yet, in and of itself, a reference to process poses more questions than it answers. It does not tell us which kind of process we are talking about; nor does it indicate who and what matters in these processes. In this chapter, we seek to get closer to these questions by construing the building blocks of our theory and the conceptual tools that guide our empirical exploration.

The frame we construct here revolves around the notion that international law, as a social practice, generates itself the actors, authorities, and criteria for its reproduction and change. 'Sources' of international law do not lie outside that practice, as doctrinal accounts imply, but are instead constituted by it. We reconstruct the ways in which change occurs on the basis of a typology of five 'paths', all of which come with particular actors, authorities, and dynamics; the state-action path has very different politics than, say, the judicial or private-authority path. Not all of these paths are available everywhere, however—some are strictly reserved for states; others are open to individuals, companies, or other non-state actors. What is more, each area of international law comes with its own practice of assigning weight and authority to some paths and not to others. As the constellation

[1] Sally Falk Moore, *Law as Process: An Anthropological Approach* (Routledge & Kegan Paul, 1978), pp. 9, 12.

[2] See, e.g., Campbell McLachlan, *The Principle of Systemic Integration in International Law* (Oxford University Press, 2024); Eric A Posner and A O Sykes, *Economic Foundations of International Law* (Harvard University Press, 2013).

Change in International Law. Nico Krisch, Ezgi Yildiz, and Pedro Martínez Esponda, Oxford University Press.
 DOI: 10.1093/9780198918325.003.0002

of paths in different issue areas and institutional or geographical contexts varies, international law fragments, resulting in multiple international laws rather than a single unified one.

This chapter explores the process of international legal change, dissecting its key components to provide a rigorous understanding of its dynamics. It begins by interrogating the concept of 'change' in international law, advocating for an inductive approach that transcends formal criteria to encompass shifts in interpretation, discourse, and practice (section 1). The chapter then examines the pivotal roles of actors, practices, and sources of authority, emphasizing how the social practices of international law construct and reconfigure the parameters of change (section 2). Building on this foundation, the chapter introduces a typology of five ideal-typical paths of change, analysing their distinct logics, accessibility, and implications for the pace and scope of legal transformation (section 3). Finally, it compares the defining features of different pathways of change and presents a three-stage framework to understand how change unfolds—from initial selection, through construction, to broader reception (section 4). Together, these sections construct a comprehensive framework, providing a sophisticated lens to study the social, institutional, and strategic dimensions of international legal change and laying the ground for a deeper inquiry in the following chapters.

1. Identifying 'Change'

Before we go further, we should clarify a fundamental notion for our inquiry—that of 'change'. We will often know change in international law when we see it, but in many contexts, actors might disagree—not only on whether change has occurred but also on what constitutes change itself. So, when can we actually speak of 'change' in international law?

An Inductive Approach

Lawyers typically employ a deductive approach to this question. They start from doctrinal criteria and ask whether these have been met—for example, whether state practice and states' *opinio juris* have been sufficiently widespread and uniform to constitute a new rule of customary international law, or whether we can identify a convergence among treaty parties that amounts to subsequent practice under paragraph 3 of Article 31 of the Vienna Convention on the Law of Treaties. While this is a worthwhile endeavour for many purposes—not the least for any argument in court—it limits the positive inquiry in a significant way. Most importantly, it obscures processes that, while not meeting these criteria, may still have resulted in widely recognized change within the field. For example, it might fail to recognize the emergence of a right to a healthy environment as an episode of change simply because it has transpired through channels that are traditionally seen as incapable of producing binding obligations.[3] Doctrinally, one can, no doubt, argue this point, but for the purposes of understanding change, we cannot ignore processes such as these, which have led to a significant shift in the way actors practise (and argue about) international law.

We thus take an inductive approach and try to tackle the question from the other end. We first ask whether, in the view of participants, the law at t_1 differs from the law at t_0. In doing so, we centre the understandings and perceptions of those who engage with the law—its practitioners, interpreters, and enforcers—as the primary yardstick for assessing its state and evolution. Only then do we inquire into the ways in which this change has come about, including the doctrinal criteria used by participants and observers, but also the actors, institutions, and mechanisms relevant to the change. Methodologically, this allows us to scrutinize the discursive prevalence of formal criteria, but most importantly, it allows us to gain a more comprehensive picture of change, including those processes that take place outside traditional forms. We acknowledge that an inductive approach, too, will always make prior choices about its object.[4] By treating the question 'what is law' as endogenous to the practice itself, we aim to foster greater inclusiveness and to take seriously the idea that international law constitutes its own normative and epistemic boundaries.

We follow the same, inclusive line by taking into view any modification of the burden of argument for a particular position on the content of the law,[5] thus going well beyond the idea that change requires the full replacement of one norm with another. Rather than portraying such a black-and-white picture, we acknowledge the many shades of grey in legal practice—recognizing that change can occur in varying degrees and that, in practice, no clear line separates a mere shift in interpretation from the emergence of a new rule. At any given point in time, we will find ourselves confronted with various interpretations of a given norm, with some being more widely accepted, others occupying more marginal positions. Change occurs when the scope of possible interpretations or the weight of particular views in legal discourse has shifted over time. This standard of change is admittedly broad

[3] On this case, see 'Change in Practice: Two Vignettes' in Chapter 1.

[4] Stefan Talmon, 'Determining Customary International Law: The ICJ's Methodology between Induction, Deduction and Assertion', *European Journal of International Law* 26, (2015): p. 417; Donald J Puchala and Raymond F Hopkins, 'International Regimes: Lessons from Inductive Analysis', *International Organization* 36, (1982): p. 245; Wouter Werner, 'The Making of Lawmaking: The ILC Draft Conclusions on the Identification of Customary Law', in *The Many Paths of Change in International Law*, edited by Nico Krisch and Ezgi Yildiz (Oxford University Press, 2023).

[5] This account of legal change goes back to a suggestion by Ingo Venzke: Ingo Venzke, *How Interpretation Makes International Law: On Semantic Change and Normative Twists* (Oxford University Press, 2012); Ingo Venzke, 'What Makes for a Valid Legal Argument?', *Leiden Journal of International Law* 27, (2014): p. 811. See also, Nico Krisch and Ezgi Yildiz (eds), *The Many Paths of Change in International Law* (Oxford University Press, 2023).

in the first place, but it enables further inquiries into the nature of the change, such as its degree of consolidation or the extent of its acceptance. And it provides us with a framework through which we can understand not only the stable states of the law—those rare moments of consensus—but also the more common instances marked by varying degrees of instability. Destabilizing international law is, after all, often a more viable and less demanding route of change than reconsolidating a new meaning.[6]

In this endeavour, we do not a priori differentiate between different types of international law. Discursive statements are often not clearly associated with treaties, custom, or general principles, but instead contain assertions about the state of international law as such—relatively unspecific examples like 'targeted killing is unlawful' or 'including extra-European flights in European emissions trading violates principles of international law' abound. When statements are more specific, we may be able to draw conclusions about potential differences in the thresholds for change applied in various contexts—for instance, whether change within the treaty context genuinely requires greater unanimity than in the customary law context, as implied by the subsequent practice standard. But this is a potential outcome of our inquiry, not its starting point.

Our approach takes a different tack than a more traditional, sources-based inquiry into change in international law—it proceeds inductively, and it is not primarily interested in whether rules have changed as a matter of doctrine. But our findings are likely to be relevant, even if indirectly, for an understanding of the doctrinal side as well. For even though typical international legal argument is deductive—it applies secondary rules on law-making to particular circumstances—the secondary rules themselves need a basis. That basis is typically gained inductively by analysing the ways in which actors understand the law. This is the case in theory—take, for example, H.L.A. Hart's account of the social basis of the rule of recognition, or the applications of it in international law by Jean d'Aspremont.[7] But it is also the case in practice. When we look at the approach of the UN International Law Commission in its recent work clarifying the sources of international law, we find the same methodology, at least as a matter of rhetoric.[8] On the identification of customary law, for example, the Commission writes: 'The draft conclusions reflect the approach adopted by States, as well as by international courts and

[6] Pedro Martínez Esponda, 'Norm-Instability as a Strategy in International Law-Making: The Case of Self-Defence against Non-State Actors', in *The Many Paths of Change in International Law*, edited by Nico Krisch and Ezgi Yildiz (Oxford University Press, 2023).

[7] See H L A Hart, *The Concept of Law*, 2nd ed. (Clarendon Press, 1994); Jean d'Aspremont, *Formalism and the Sources of International Law: A Theory of the Ascertainment of Legal Rules* (Oxford University Press, 2011).

[8] See also Werner (n 4). For an account of sources that attempts to take this approach seriously, see Anthea Roberts and Sandesh Sivakumaran, 'The Theory and Reality of the Sources of International Law', in *International Law*, 5th ed., edited by Malcolm D Evans (Oxford University Press, 2018).

organizations and most authors.'[9] In the preparatory report, the Commission's rapporteur goes to some length to show that the 'two-element approach' employed to identify custom is indeed a reflection of the practice of states and courts.[10] If that is the case, then our inductively gained findings on when change occurs should also be relevant for an analysis of the sources of international law—in one way or another. We will return to this question in our concluding chapter.

Limitations

Our inquiry, although broad, nevertheless knows a number of limitations. First, its focus lies on 'informal' change and not on change through treaty-making as such. Treaties are rather well understood, not just in international law, but also in international relations scholarship. As mentioned in Chapter 1, the study by Paul Diehl and Charlotte Ku on the *Dynamics of International Law* focuses on treaties, and so does, for example, Barbara Koremenos's *Continent of International Law.*[11] Likewise, the legalization literature that burgeoned after 2000 placed particular emphasis on formal agreements and international courts;[12] other ways of doing international law were largely outside the picture.[13] This focus on treaty-making may be partly responsible for the emphasis on punctuated equilibria that is widespread in accounts of international legal change, as we showed in Chapter 1. We do not downplay the important role of treaties, but we are primarily interested in other, less typical forms of law and legal change. Our interest lies in understanding how the meaning of norms changes over time, even in the absence of formal treaty amendments, and how treaties interact with and shape other norms, especially customary international law. In so doing, we focus—in the first place—on individual norm change rather than on systemic shifts or transformations of the legal order, setting our approach apart from much of the classic literature on change.[14]

[9] ILC, 'Draft Conclusions on Identification of Customary International Law' (2018) UNDOC A/73/10, p. 123.

[10] ILC, 'Second Report on Identification of Customary International Law, by Sir Michael Wood, Special Rapporteur' (22 May 2014) UN Doc A/CN.4/672, pp. 171–73.

[11] Paul F Diehl and Charlotte Ku, *The Dynamics of International Law* (Cambridge University Press, 2010); Barbara Koremenos, *The Continent of International Law: Explaining Agreement Design* (Cambridge University Press, 2016).

[12] Judith L Goldstein and others, eds., *Legalization and World Politics* (MIT Press, 2001). See also, more recently, Karen J Alter, 'The Evolution of International Law and Courts', in *International Politics and Institutions in Time*, edited by Orfeo Fioretos (Oxford University Press, 2017).

[13] See Martha Finnemore and Stephen J Toope, 'Alternatives to "Legalization": Richer Views of Law and Politics', *International Organization* 55, (2001): p. 743; Christian Brütsch and Dirk Lehmkuhl, eds., *Law and Legalization in Transnational Relations* (Routledge, 2007).

[14] For example, James Crawford, *The International Law Commission's Articles on State Responsibility: Introduction, Text and Commentaries* (Cambridge University Press, 2002); Jan Klabbers, Anne Peters and Geir Ulfstein, *The Constitutionalization of International Law* (Oxford University Press, 2009); Campbell McLachlan, *The Principle of Systemic Integration in International Law* (Oxford University Press, 2024).

Secondly, we limit our exploration to discourses about international law as such, in the sense of norms understood to contain binding obligations for states in their international relations. The study of soft international law, transnational law, or other legalities is of great interest for many purposes,[15] but it would overburden the present inquiry. It would also lead into a somewhat different direction because, outside formal international law, expectations for the emergence of new norms or the transformation of existing ones are less defined. It is probably fair to say that this leads to a greater potential for dynamism in such alternative contexts, attracting actors who seek more substantial and far-reaching changes than what might be achievable within the constraints of formal law.[16] We will return to this theme when we discuss moves outside of international law in Chapter 6.

Finally, we are here concerned primarily with *discursive* changes—with changes in the ways in which norms are understood by actors in the different fields of international law. Relevant change can, of course, also take place in other ways, most notably in the application of those norms. Whether norms are upheld or disregarded can reveal the degree to which they are respected or ignored, offering insights into their practical influence. In some contexts, such as the authoritarian challenge to international human rights law, much interesting movement may take place in this factual realm. These include processes of norm erosion, where adherence diminishes over time, rather than explicit changes in discourse or formal legal structures.[17] But studying these systematically would require a different approach, and far larger resources, than we could employ. We thus focus here on the discursive side, which allows us to take into view processes of contestation both with regard to the meaning and the validity of existing norms,[18] and we leave questions of compliance and implementation to others.

2. Actors, Practices, Authority: The Social Frame of Change

Law is a social practice. Lawyers may often think about texts and their interpretation, but texts acquire meaning only through and in use, and change in meaning

[15] See, e.g., Joost Pauwelyn, Ramses Wessel and Jan Wouters, eds., *Informal International Lawmaking* (Oxford University Press, 2012); Peer Zumbansen, ed., *The Oxford Handbook of Transnational Law* (Oxford University Press, 2021); Nico Krisch, ed., *Entangled Legalities beyond the State* (Cambridge University Press, 2021).

[16] See Joost Pauwelyn, Ramses A Wessel and Jan Wouters, 'When Structures Become Shackles: Stagnation and Dynamics in International Lawmaking', *European Journal of International Law* 25, (2014): p. 733; Nico Krisch, 'The Decay of Consent: International Law in an Age of Global Public Goods', *American Journal of International Law* 108, (2014): p. 1.

[17] Wayne Sandholtz, 'Resurgent Authoritarianism, Rights, and Legal Change', in *The Many Paths of Change in International Law*, edited by Nico Krisch and Ezgi Yildiz (Oxford University Press, 2023).

[18] On the distinction between both, see Nicole Deitelhoff and Lisbeth Zimmermann, 'Things We Lost in the Fire: How Different Types of Contestation Affect the Robustness of International Norms', *International Studies Review* 22, (2020): p. 51.

is normally driven by actors.[19] As in other discursive practices, change does not simply happen but is pursued and constructed—new ideas are proposed, find reception by some, then by others, until they become so widespread as to be normalized again.[20] The moves in this process may be strategic, but they are not necessarily always so; pushes for new understandings can also stem from a changed sense of what is appropriate or normal.[21] They can be induced by changing external circumstances—environmental or technological—but they become new, intersubjectively shared normative understandings only through social action.

Actors in Processes and Practices

Our account of change in international law also starts—like most accounts of norm change in international relations[22]—from actors. Actors, whom we call *change agents*, initiate change processes; others take them forward or oppose them, engage with them in their roles as government officials, judges, or experts, and position themselves vis-à-vis their results. This is not limited to states or their agents but instead can include all kinds of other actors. Especially at the beginning of change processes, 'norm entrepreneurs' are often civil society groups urging new understandings—for recognizing rape as a war crime, for accommodating environmental measures among trade exceptions, etc. Business associations, just as academics or other experts, may also take a significant role in the process alongside public actors from the executive, legislative, or judicial branches of the state and officials of international organizations.[23] Likewise, private actors as well as states might also become active on the other side of the change process—as norm 'antipreneurs'.[24]

[19] Antje Wiener, 'Enacting Meaning-in-Use: Qualitative Research on Norms and International Relations', *Review of International Studies* 35, (2009): p. 175.

[20] With a view to norms more generally, see Wayne Sandholtz and Kendall W Stiles, *International Norms and Cycles of Change* (Oxford University Press, 2009); Antje Wiener, *Contestation and Constitution of Norms in Global International Relations* (Cambridge University Press, 2018); Wayne Sandholtz, *Prohibiting Plunder: How Norms Change* (Oxford University Press, 2007); Sassan Gholiagha, Phil Orchard and Antje Wiener (eds), *The Oxford Handbook of Norms Research in International Relations* (Oxford University Press, 2025).

[21] See, e.g., Steven Bernstein and Marion Laurence, 'Practices and Norms: Relationships, Disjunctures and Change', in *Conceptualizing International Practices: Directions for the Practice Turn in International Relations*, edited by Alena Drieschova, Christian Bueger and Ted Hopf (Cambridge University Press, 2022).

[22] See only the overview in Wayne Sandholtz, 'International Norm Change', Oxford Research Encyclopedia of Politics, 2017, https://oxfordre.com/view/10.1093/acrefore/9780190228637.001.0001/acrefore-9780190228637-e-588.

[23] See, e.g., Martha Finnemore and Kathryn Sikkink, 'International Norm Dynamics and Political Change', *International Organization* 52, (1998): pp. 887, 896–99; Math Noortmann, August Reinisch and Cedric Ryngaert, eds., *Non-State Actors in International Law* (Bloomsbury Publishing, 2015).

[24] Alan Bloomfield and Shirley V Scott, eds., *Norm Antipreneurs and the Politics of Resistance to Global Normative Change* (Taylor & Francis, 2016).

Branding all these as 'participants' in change processes—as many scholars writing in the tradition of the New Haven School do[25]—is useful to broaden our gaze, but it lacks specificity regarding their actual roles and positions. After all, not everybody is equal in international law or international relations. A formalist (or rationalist) perspective would draw a clear line between states (and their agents) and other actors, the latter being relegated to secondary or subsidiary roles. But this line may result from normative and doctrinal preconceptions and not reflect the actual distribution of roles, at least not across the entirety of international law. Even in formalist contexts, variations are recognized in certain areas, such as the law of international organizations, where the organizations themselves often have a particular role to play.[26]

This suggests that the distribution of roles in the international legal process is context-dependent, and that different contexts over time generate different understandings of who occupies which position. This insight connects with sociological accounts and especially with the more practice-based conceptions of international law we briefly mentioned in the previous chapter. Practices, according to this understanding, are 'patterned actions that are embedded in particular organized contexts and, as such, are articulated into specific types of action and are socially developed through learning and training'.[27] They are constituted by competent performances that rest on a certain background knowledge of participants about what is at stake and what marks a competent performance, thus tying together the material world of action with the discursive one of ideas.[28] 'A practice is a routinized type of behavior which consists of several elements, interconnected to one another: forms of bodily activities, forms of mental activities, 'things' and their use, a background knowledge in the form of understanding, know-how, states of emotion and motivational knowledge.'[29]

Focusing on practices helps to connect agency and structure by linking both to enacted knowledge stored in everyday patterns of action. It is easy to see how this connects with the world of law, which is made up of a myriad of everyday performances, and in which competence is clearly marked out on the basis of professional standards recognized by actors as distinctive.[30] This dynamic extends to international law, which is practised in a great many sites by actors with specialized legal expertise. International legal practice, however, is not always closely tied to specific

[25] See Rosalyn Higgins, *Problems and Process: International Law and How We Use It* (Clarendon Press, 1995), ch. 3.

[26] See ILC, 'Draft Conclusions on Subsequent Agreements and Subsequent Practice in Relation to the Interpretation of Treaties' (2018), pp. 93–106.

[27] Emanuel Adler and Vincent Pouliot, 'International Practices', *International Theory* 3, (2011): pp. 1, 5.

[28] ibid pp. 6–7.

[29] Andreas Reckwitz, 'Toward a Theory of Social Practices: A Development in Culturalist Theorizing', *European Journal of Social Theory* 5, (2002): pp. 243, 249.

[30] Tommaso Soave, *The Everyday Makers of International Law: From Great Halls to Back Rooms* (Cambridge University Press, 2022).

institutions, such as courts, as is the case with domestic law.[31] Strategic action is not absent from its terrain; rather, it is embedded within and derives its meaning from a shared understanding of what law and legal interactions represent, and how they differ from other forms of interactions in international politics. Law, in this view, is not merely a collection of texts but a set of evolving understandings that emerge through users' engagement with norms in their practices. What kind of arguments are acceptable in legal discourse is endogenously defined through the practices of law within each social field. These practices typically align with, yet also introduce variations to, the rules regarding sources and interpretations found in other domains and in 'general' international law.[32]

Approaching these as 'practices' in a narrower sense[33] appears fruitful also because they are not simply external to actors and thus at their disposal to accept, reject, or modify. They instead provide the structure in which actors operate. Moreover, these practices are not just discourses in an ideational realm. They are embodied by actors: proper participants in legal interactions are only those who understand 'how to' make legal arguments, how to work within the field. Being an international lawyer (or an international human rights lawyer, international criminal lawyer, etc.) is largely defined by the practical mastery of key techniques and an understanding of the social positions and authority of different actors within the field.[34] Interventions that seek to shift legal understandings need to be recognizable for such mastery—less so in treaty negotiations, but significantly more in debates about codification or courtroom arguments.[35]

The practice focus also helps to make sense of the relative stickiness of law, which is difficult to capture through other approaches—especially those centred on rational action or on individual interpretive choices, as seen in much of critical theory.[36] Practices are relatively stable in the first place, also because they provide structures for action. However, they are not immutable; rather, they are open to reflection, contestation, and reinterpretation, as long as they remain recognized

[31] Tanja Aalberts and Ingo Venzke, 'Moving beyond Interdisciplinary Turf Wars: Towards an Understanding of International Law as Practice', in *International Law as a Profession*, edited by Jean D'Aspremont and others (Cambridge University Press, 2017); see also Jutta Brunnée and Stephen J Toope, *Legitimacy and Legality in International Law: An Interactional Account* (Cambridge University Press, 2010); Jens Meierhenrich, 'The Practice of International Law: A Theoretical Analysis', *Law and Contemporary Problems* 76, (2013): p. 1.

[32] Nikolas M Rajkovic, Tanja E Aalberts and Thomas Gammeltoft-Hansen, 'Introduction: Legality, Interdisciplinarity and the Study of Practices', in *The Power of Legality: Practices of International Law and their Politics*, edited by Nikolas M Rajkovic, Tanja E Aalberts and Thomas Gammeltoft-Hansen (Cambridge University Press, 2016), pp. 9–21; Aalberts and Venzke (n 31), pp. 305–309.

[33] Christian Bueger and Frank Gadinger, *International Practice Theory*, 2nd ed. (Springer, 2018).

[34] See Adler and Pouliot (n 27), pp. 4–13.

[35] See Nora Stappert, 'Practice Theory and Change in International Law: Theorizing the Development of Legal Meaning through the Interpretive Practices of International Criminal Courts', *International Theory* 12, (2020): p. 33.

[36] See also Wim Zimmermann, 'Self-Presentation in International Law: On Reputation and Interpretation', *German Law Journal* (2025): 1–36.

as the framework shaping the identity of actors within the field.[37] Change in the 'ground rules' of practice within the fields of international law is thus likely to be gradual and slow. At the same time, these ground rules define the conditions under which ordinary legal change is recognized, specifying what acts or statements are sufficient to modify existing norms. These conditions may be strict or permissive; they may erect high hurdles or allow for rapid change. As an example, the ground rules of international law may themselves be resistant to change, but they allow for (relatively quick) legal change through the adoption of treaties. In some fields, they may recognize particular authorities, such as the courts, as central to processes of norm change. In others, they may channel the traditional approach and assign a greater weight to domestic courts, diplomatic pronouncements, or state consent. Ultimately, who and what matter in processes of international legal change is determined by the practice of international law itself.

Constellations, Communities, and Fields

When we think about actors in international legal processes, we thus first look to the practices they are engaged in and the roles these practices assign to them. Different practices hold different roles for them: for example, civil society actors are typically excluded from inter-state diplomacy on security issues, whereas they play a constitutive role in global environmental conferences.[38] Similarly, actors' specific roles in international law are likely to depend on the practices that define the various subfields within international law—practices that, even to a casual observer, differ significantly between areas such as human rights law and the law on the use of force.

The definition of actors' positions is then endogenous to the practices themselves, and it is also through those practices that certain types of resources—material or ideational—gain relevance, as we explore more deeply in Chapter 5. To take an obvious contrast, material power has a different importance in bilateral negotiations than in multilateral fora or judicial settings. Actors' capital, in Bourdieusian terms, may rest on a variety of sources, but it is constituted through the social interactions in a given field.[39]

Seen from the perspective of practices, actors never come alone. They are typically part of a group of actors clustered around a particular practice, some more closely connected to it, others in a looser fashion. Many scholars who use

[37] Ted Hopf, 'Change in International Practices', *European Journal of International Relations* 24, (2018): p. 687. See also the problematization in Bueger and Gadinger (n 33), pp. 100–06.

[38] On different forms of multilateral practices, see Vincent Pouliot, *International Pecking Orders: The Politics and Practice of Multilateral Diplomacy* (Cambridge University Press, 2016).

[39] See Pierre Bourdieu and Loïc J D Wacquant, *An Invitation to Reflexive Sociology* (University of Chicago Press, 1992).

practice theory to understand international law have come to portray the participants in these interactions as members of distinct communities—'interpretive communities', 'epistemic communities', or, indeed, 'communities of practice'.[40] Such communities are typically regarded as relatively cohesive groups that share core commitments about the ways in which texts and norms—and the world more broadly—are interpreted.[41]

Realistically, however, the actors participating in the practice of international law often have relatively little in common. Between a French environmental non-governmental organization (NGO) and a Russian foreign office lawyer, we will hardly detect significant overlaps in worldviews, values, or even interpretative principles. Each is more likely to share commonalities with actors of the same kind—other NGOs, for example—or with those sharing their national background, than with one another. Often, they will belong to multiple social fields, differentiated by functional, national, or social lines.[42] If we thus speak of 'communities of practice', we need to recognize the existence of not one, but multiple interpretive communities even within particular subfields.[43] Practices can be engaged in by actors independently of belonging to any such community—they may merely share a set of thin common understandings, for example, about core issues in a given context or about frames of argument or relevant institutions. Rather than starting from a presumption of relative cohesion, it is thus better to think of participants in the practices of international law as forming part of a constellation such as a 'social field' in which connections are primarily defined by a common understanding of what is at stake.[44]

The degree of commonality and cohesion around international legal practices is then bound to vary. This will also affect the position of actors within their fields—in some contexts, social positions will be clearly defined, with certain actors recognized as occupying such a central position that they can also determine the terms on which other actors compete for influence.[45] In others, actors may not agree on who is central, with different allegiances or understandings existing alongside one

[40] See, e.g., Ian Johnstone, 'The Power of Interpretive Communities', in *Power in Global Governance*, edited by M Barnett and R Duvall (Cambridge University Press, 2005), p. 185; Brunnée and Toope (n 31); Michael Waibel, 'Interpretive Communities in International Law', in *Interpretation in International Law*, edited by Andrea Bianchi, Daniel Peat and Matthew Windsor (Oxford University Press, 2014); Andrea Bianchi, 'Epistemic Communities', in *Concepts for International Law*, edited by Jean d'Aspremont and Sahib Singh (Edward Elgar Publishing, 2019).

[41] Johnstone (n 40), pp. 190–91. See generally Etienne Wenger, *Communities of Practice: Learning, Meaning, and Identity* (Cambridge University Press, 1999), ch. 2.

[42] See Nico Krisch, 'The Many Fields of (German) International Law', in *Comparative International Law*, edited by Anthea Roberts and others (Oxford University Press, 2018).

[43] Waibel (n 40).

[44] See Bourdieu and Wacquant (n 39); Neil Fligstein and Doug McAdam, *A Theory of Fields* (Oxford University Press, 2012).

[45] See Ole Jacob Sending, *The Politics of Expertise: Competing for Authority in Global Governance* (Michigan University Press, 2015); Ole Jacob Sending, 'Recognition and Liquid Authority', *International Theory* 9, (2017): p. 311.

another. In European human rights law, with a relatively tight community engaged in a common practice, the European Court of Human Rights faces little challenge as the core interpreter of the law, even as actors diverge on the interpretation of certain rights.[46] In international humanitarian law, in contrast, different actors attach different weights to the pronouncements of UN expert bodies, the International Committee of the Red Cross (ICRC), or military manuals of powerful states, leading to divergent communities with significant contestation about social positions as well as substantive questions—even as actors converge on the fact that their action has a common focus, namely the discourse of the law regulating armed conflict.[47]

Authority in and through Practice

If positions within a field are endogenously constructed by social practice, the same applies to positions of 'authority', a central element of processes of norm change. 'Authority', understood as the recognized ability to induce deference, has come to occupy an increasingly central place in accounts of international politics in recent years.[48] This shift reflects a move away from the presumption of anarchy towards a thicker, more socially grounded understanding of interactions beyond the state.[49] Some observers have associated the rise of authority relations with a 'system change' in the structure of the global order.[50]

In the context of law, authority acquires particular prominence in its connection with the meaning of texts and norms. This concerns, in the first place, the authority to *make* law—political authority grounded in the recognition by actors that the power to establish new legal norms rests with a single actor or group, and that the norms they create are, in principle, to be followed. Yet in international law, this kind of authority is in short supply and largely limited to the collective of states

[46] See Mikael Madsen, 'The Challenging Authority of the European Court of Human Rights: From Cold War Legal Diplomacy to the Brighton Declaration and Backlash', *Law and Contemporary Problems* 79, (2016): p. 141.

[47] Dorothea Endres, 'Whose International Law Is Changing? The Practice of Fragmented Communities Constructing Legal Change', in *The Many Paths of Change in International Law*, edited by Nico Krisch and Ezgi Yildiz (Oxford University Press, 2023).

[48] Richard Friedman, 'On the Concept of Authority in Political Philosophy', in *Authority*, edited by Joseph Raz (New York University Press, 1990), pp. 63–71.

[49] See, e.g., David A Lake, 'Rightful Rules: Authority, Order, and the Foundations of Global Governance', *International Studies Quarterly* 54, (2010): p. 587; Deborah D Avant, Martha Finnemore and Susan K Sell, 'Who Governs the Globe?', in *Who Governs the Globe?*, edited by Deborah Avant, Martha Finnemore and Susan K Sell (Cambridge University Press, 2010); Jorg Kustermans and Rikkert Horemans, 'Four Conceptions of Authority in International Relations', *International Organization* 76, (2022): p. 204.

[50] Michael Zürn, 'On the Role of Contestations, the Power of Reflexive Authority, and Legitimation Problems in the Global Political System', *International Theory* 13, (2021): pp. 192, 195; see also Michael Zürn, *A Theory of Global Governance: Authority, Legitimacy, and Contestation* (Oxford University Press, 2018).

and certain bodies of international organizations, often for narrowly defined purposes.[51] A much more widespread, but also more circumscribed form of authority in international law is interpretive or semantic—the authority to *ascertain* what the law is and what a particular norm means.[52] This is a form of epistemic authority, connected with expertise about what is already binding, rather than a power to bind anew. While such authority is often exercised by institutions, it may also be held by individual experts or professional communities whose interpretations are treated as credible or persuasive—thus positioning them as authorities in their own right. Finally, while authority often describes a relation between actors, it can also point to relations with texts or symbols. Codifications, for example, often enjoy an authority that is independent from, or exceeds, the authority of their makers.[53]

Authority—especially in the international context—is not limited to 'solid' analogues of national governments, legislatures, or courts, but includes a wider range of forms.[54] Deference then does not have to be absolute—it need not force an actor to entirely 'suspend their judgment', as some have considered essential to authority. Instead, it can be *relative* and exist in varying degrees. It also need not apply universally; authority is *relational* in that it is inscribed in and produced by a relationship between actors in which the authority holder plays as much a role as those actors recognizing her or his authority.[55] This entails that authority may be limited to a particular community or social field, and that its strength may likewise vary across the relations it extends to. The pope's authority is mostly limited to believers in the Catholic faith—beyond this group, he may have a weaker moral authority or none at all. Likewise, a body such as the UN Human Rights Committee may appear authoritative to some participants in international human rights practice and not to others.[56]

Authority is often presented as the result of a formal ascription or delegation, as in the constitutionally conferred authority of parliaments or courts. In the international realm, an analogous imagery has been used to measure the authority of international organizations.[57] This includes *authority by mandate*, where the legitimacy and influence of bodies like the UN Security Council or the Human Rights

[51] See, e.g., José E Alvarez, *International Organizations as Law-Makers* (Oxford University Press, 2005), ch. 4.

[52] Venzke, *How Interpretation Makes International Law* (n 5).

[53] See also Fuad Zarbiyev, 'A Quiet Revolution in the Making? The Changing State Authority in Treaty Interpretation' in Nico Krisch and Ezgi Yildiz (eds), *The Many Paths of Change in International Law* (Oxford University Press, 2023).

[54] Avant, Finnemore and Sell (n 49) pp. 9–14; Nico Krisch, 'Liquid Authority in Global Governance' *International Theory* 9, (2017): p. 237.

[55] Krisch (n 54) pp. 240–42.

[56] See also Fuad Zarbiyev, 'Saying Credibly What the Law Is: On Marks of Authority in International Law', *Journal of International Dispute Settlement* 9, (2018): pp. 291, 309–10.

[57] Liesbet Hooghe, Tobias Lenz and Gary Marks, *A Theory of International Organization* (Oxford University Press, 2019). See also David A Lake, 'Relational Authority and Legitimacy in International Relations', *American Behavioral Scientist* 53, (2009): p. 331.

Council derive from the specific responsibilities entrusted to them, even though their decisions ultimately depend on the votes and actions of member states. But as becomes clear from the outline of our practice account above, this is neither the sole mode of generating authority nor the most common one. Whether political or epistemic, authority is often grounded in, or enhanced by, processes of recognition embedded in social practices.[58] In the global realm, the social construction of authority, outside of delegatory frames, is most clearly visible with respect to private authorities, such as the ICRC or independent expert groups. It also applies to courts whose formal jurisdiction extends only to the parties to a dispute, but whose interpretations generate deference among a much wider range of actors.[59] The material sources of authority—the reasons for which an authority is recognized—may lie in law and delegation, but also in expertise, procedures, or (moral) principle.[60] Authority thus produced also tends to come in different forms, not only as complete deference to commands, but can instead be 'reflexive' and graduated.[61]

A consequence of socially produced, rather than formally delegated, authority is that it often exists not only in varying degrees but also in plurality, with multiple authorities coexisting within a given field.[62] Authority may sometimes be *focal*, with one actor or institution a central reference point. More often, authority beyond the state is *diffuse*—most areas are characterized by a multiplicity of actors and institutions recognized as having a certain authority. Cumulatively, such authority may still be strong, but its dynamics differ from the more consolidated, focal constellation. Importantly, different authorities vary in their relational reach and thus elicit deference from different sets of actors. Their interventions are typically spread out over time and may also diverge considerably in content. Much authority in the international realm has thus been described as 'liquid', subject to competition, or in constant flux, spread out over a process in which the locus of authority is hard to identify.[63]

Such diffuse authority will often leave norms somewhat unsettled and contribute to the perception that norms, in the international sphere, always remain a

[58] See Friedman (n 48); Joelle Dumouchel, 'For a Practice Approach to Authority: The Emergence of Central Bankers' International Authority', in *Conceptualizing International Practices: Directions for the Practice Turn in International Relations*, edited by Alena Drieschova, Christian Bueger and Ted Hopf (Cambridge University Press, 2022).

[59] See Karen J Alter, Laurence R Helfer and Mikael Rask Madsen, eds., *International Court Authority* (Oxford University Press, 2018).

[60] See Michael Barnett and Martha Finnemore, *Rules for the World: International Organizations in Global Politics* (Cornell University Press, 2004); Zarbiyev (n 56).

[61] Michael Zürn, *A Theory of Global Governance: Authority, Legitimacy, and Contestation* (Oxford University Press, 2018), ch. 2; Krisch (n 54), p. 237, https://www.cambridge.org/core/journals/international-theory/article/liquid-authority-in-global-governance/DF9A703FC187A120D4F827698548AF6B.

[62] Ole Jacob Sending, *The Politics of Expertise: Competing for Authority in Global Governance*, reprint ed. (University of Michigan Press, 2015).

[63] Krisch (n 54); Sending (n 62); Martha Finnemore, 'Dynamics of Global Governance: Building on What We Know', *International Studies Quarterly* 58, (2014): p. 221.

work-in-progress;[64] this is a point we will return to in Chapter 7. How diffuse authority is, however, depends largely on the social and institutional constellation in a given context. Some contexts have their own focal institution—such as the World Trade Organization (WTO) Appellate Body in its day—while others have a multiplicity of bodies with greater or lesser weight, as in the case of international human rights law.[65]

How change travels in international law, we surmise, will depend to a large extent on elements produced by the social practice that underlies it—the relevant actors and communities, the types of arguments that count, and the authorities relevant in a given field. These may or may not correspond with international lawyers' doctrinal categories; likewise, they may or may not be the same across the different issue areas, as we will explore further in Chapter 3. What we have seen so far suggests a rather unruly picture, one shaped by markedly different practices of international law across issues and institutional contexts.

3. Paths of Change

The theoretical framework laid out above helps us to sharpen our lenses for tracing change processes in international law. It directs attention away from formal criteria and institutional rules towards the greater variety of social practices through which international law is continuously transformed, and it urges us to pay attention to the manifold actors, communities, and authorities engaged in such transformation. If this pushes us towards analyses at the micro-level, we also need a framework to compare these at a meso- or macro-level so as to be able to get closer to a broader picture of how change in international law unfolds.[66]

We begin here to develop such a framework, drawn from existing accounts of individual change processes, with a view to structuring our inquiry. We propose a set of ideal-typical categories to better understand the specific constellations and dynamics at play in different contexts—not only regarding actors and authorities but also in a temporal sense, focusing on the stages through which change processes typically unfold.

We build this framework around five main, ideal-typical pathways of change. Some of them are more traditionally recognized as law-making channels; others

[64] Anette Stimmer and Lea Wisken, 'The Dynamics of Dissent: When Actions Are Louder than Words', *International Affairs* 95, (2019): p. 515.

[65] See, e.g., the broader accounts in Avant, Finnemore and Sell (n 49); Alter, Helfer and Madsen (n 59).

[66] But see also Kratochwil's scepticism towards attempts at generalizing from practices; Friedrich Kratochwil, 'Practices and a "Theory" of Action? Some Conceptual Issues Concerning Ends, Reasons and Happiness', in *Conceptualizing International Practices: Directions for the Practice Turn in International Relations*, edited by Alena Drieschova, Christian Bueger and Ted Hopf (Cambridge University Press, 2022).

less so. Our aim is to explore the extent to which change processes can be observed following these paths. We are also interested in the particular dynamics associated with them. Each path comes with its own operating logic and is linked with different sets of actors and sources of authority. Distinguishing them should help us not only to gain a clearer view, but also to generate conjectures about the potential and limitations of the different paths—for instance, the extent to which they enable major change versus incremental steps, or the degree to which powerful actors are likely to exert influence through them.

The State Action Path

The state action path is central to most lawyers' image of how international law changes, as change in this modality comes about when states modify their behaviour and make corresponding statements. This mechanism, therefore, effectively reflects the typical notion of customary international law and the subsequent practice to treaties. Let us illustrate this with an example from the law on the use of force.[67] After the adoption of the UN Charter and up until the 1990s, it was widely accepted that states could use self-defence when attacked by other states, but not against attacks emanating from non-state actors. With the rise of transnational terrorism in the 1990s, however, this agreement crumbled and self-defence against non-state actors found greater recognition. This was in large part a result of state action, most decisively after the attacks of 11 September 2001, when the US notified the UN Security Council that it was exercising its right to self-defence against the Taliban and Al-Qaeda. This was met with support from some states and acquiescence from others, and it initiated a wider use of self-defence against non-state actors also in other circumstances. These were partly criticized, but typically not with the argument that there was no right to target non-state actors, but on other grounds, such as a lack of proportionality. It was primarily after the Western attacks on ISIS in Syria in 2014 that more principled challenges were raised against the argument, for example, by Brazil and Mexico.[68]

We will come back to some of the complexities of the case later, but it is worth highlighting here how much of this change process travelled on the classical state-action path. This path derives its legitimacy from the collective authority of states and their continued recognition as the 'masters' of international law. Change attempts are typically initiated by a few states acting as change agents. Compared to

[67] On this case, see Martínez Esponda (n 6); Pedro Martínez Esponda, 'Self-Defense Against Non-State Actors', in *The Paths of International Law: Case Studies*, edited by Pedro Martínez Esponda and others (SSRN, 2023).

[68] Martínez Esponda (n 6). But see also the discussion in Jutta Brunnée and Stephen J Toope, 'Self-Defence against Non-State Actors: Are Powerful States Willing but Unable to Change International Law?', *International & Comparative Law Quarterly* 67, (2018): p. 263.

the other paths described below, this path is characterized by more unilateral action, although its success ultimately depends on generating broader support for the proposal. The mechanism of change typically consists of two steps: proposing a new norm or establishing a new practice—which destabilizes existing understandings, pushes existing boundaries, or goes beyond set standards—and then shoring up international backing.

Apart from treaty-making, the state-action path is widely seen to be the main path of open law *creation*, rather than mere interpretation, and it allows, in principle, for radical shifts in the content of the law. Activating it, however, faces significant problems of collective action in a world of many states. How much of a problem this poses depends on the thresholds required for change to be recognized. Traditionally, change on this path is thought to require a form of consensus understood as virtually universal acceptance or acquiescence, either among all states (for customary international law) or the parties to a treaty (in the case of subsequent practice to treaties).[69] However, there has been a long-standing debate about whether the practices of certain 'specially affected' countries carry greater weight. More broadly, there are indications that, in practice, the threshold for change may be lower than universal agreement or uniform practice, allowing change to occur even in the face of objections from some states.[70]

The politics of this path also depend in part on the threshold question—and thus on the degree (and kind) of opposition necessary to derail a change attempt. In any event, the state-action path has long been seen to favour powerful states—it is they who can generate sufficient visibility and engineer support for a proposal, while smaller states' efforts in this respect often go unnoticed or remain inconsequential.[71] It is telling that, in the the self-defense against non-state actors example above, a potential shift in the law was recognized only after the US took action and brought the issue to the fore, while the earlier practice of other states was either not registered or treated as exceptional.[72] The same may be said of perhaps the most classical case for change on this path, the extension of coastal state authority over resources in the adjacent continental shelf after the 1945 proclamation by US President Harry S. Truman. This shift quickly attracted favourable practice of other states, thus bringing about a relatively smooth transformation of the customary international law of the sea. But the similar moves by other countries

[69] ILC, 'Articles on Responsibility of States for Internationally Wrongful Acts' (2001), art. 8; ICJ, *North Sea Continental Shelf Cases (Federal Republic of Germany v Denmark; Federal Republic of Germany v Netherlands)* [1969] ICJ Rep 3, para. 74, *Military and Paramilitary Activities in and against Nicaragua (Nicaragua v United States of America)* [1986] ICJ Rep 392, pp. 99–100, para. 186.

[70] See, e.g., Anthea Roberts, 'Traditional and Modern Approaches to Customary International Law: A Reconciliation', *American Journal of International Law* 95, (2001): p. 757.

[71] See, e.g., the critique in B S Chimni, 'Customary International Law: A Third World Perspective', *American Journal of International Law* 112, (2018): p. 1.

[72] See Esponda (n 6).

in the previous decades—especially smaller ones such as Ceylon, Venezuela, and Panama—failed to trigger similar attention and were regarded as circumscribed exceptions rather than the beginning of a new rule.[73] For most actors, most of the time, change on the state-action path might thus be out of reach.

The Multilateral Path

On the second path, the multilateral path, change is generated through statements issued by many states within a multilateral framework, typically an international organization, global conferences, or conferences of the parties (COPs) to a treaty. It relies on the collective authority of states, but also the institutional authority of the organization that serves as a forum. A resolution adopted by the UN Human Rights Council, for example, will appear as more authoritative than a collective statement by the same states outside the organizational framework. Recall the example of the emergence of a right to a healthy environment, briefly discussed in Chapter 1, in which a resolution by the Human Rights Council was central to the consolidation of the right.[74]

Multilateral bodies are usually seen as more accessible and egalitarian than the state action path. Consequently, as we also saw in Chapter 1, the 1960s and 1970s saw an intense debate about law-making through the UN General Assembly, driven by developing countries in the context of their attempt to establish a new international economic order.[75] Although they had some isolated successes, this was ultimately unsuccessful, but the multilateral path has remained a core focus of change attempts, typically realized by means of the introduction of new proposals via declarations and resolutions, or through the adoption of formal treaties that might shift opinion on customary rules.[76] Multilateral fora are, in some contexts, a tool for less powerful states to create common fronts against more powerful states, offering a pathway to circumvent big powers.[77] Perhaps the most prominent example of law-making in this fashion is the UN General Assembly's 1970 Friendly Relations Declaration, addressing the issues of the use of force, intervention, and

[73] See Michael P Scharf, *Customary International Law in Times of Fundamental Change: Recognizing Grotian Moments* (Cambridge University Press, 2013), ch. 5.

[74] See 'Change in Practice: Two Vignettes' in Chapter 1.

[75] International Committee on Legal Aspects of a New International Economic Order, 'Third Report of the International Committee on Legal Aspects of a New International Economic Order' in International Law Association Report of the Sixty-first Conference (International Law Association, 1965); Declaration on the Establishment of a New International Economic Order, UNGA Res 3201 (1974) UN Doc A/RES/3201(S-VI)).

[76] For example, they successfully contributed to designing new rules to govern global commons. For more, see Stephanie J Rickard, 'International Negotiations over the Global Commons', *The Review of International Organizations* 20, (2024): p. 999.

[77] See Amrita Narlikar, *International Trade and Developing Countries: Bargaining Coalitions in GATT and WTO* (Routledge, 2004).

sovereignty. It quickly came to be seen by many observers as reflecting and crystallizing customary law, even in areas where it extended beyond prior understandings.[78] Another potent but different example is the UN Security Council's expansion of its powers in the 1990s and early 2000s—shedding constraints on the types of situations the Council could act on as well as on the tools it has at its disposal.[79]

The threshold for the recognition of change on this path will depend on the institutional status of the forum in which statements are made. Certain law-making powers of inter-governmental bodies are formally recognized—as in the Security Council or the COPs under multilateral environmental agreements.[80] Beyond this, the weight of the multilateral path will depend on the areas concerned. In general, international lawyers have long debated whether statements alone, without corresponding practice, can shift understandings; proponents of 'modern custom' have seen actual practice moving in that direction.[81] It is likely, however, that this question finds different answers in the social practices of human rights law than in those pertaining to, say, the law on the use of force or the law of the sea.[82]

The Bureaucratic Path

Change on the bureaucratic path is the result of decisions or statements produced by international organizations in contexts that do not involve the direct participation of states in the decision-making process. This includes officials in international organizations' secretariats—at times the heads of these secretariats themselves—as well as experts or expert bodies operating within international organizations, such as the UN Special Rapporteurs.

This path draws on a variety of sources of authority, often simultaneously. Delegated authority plays a role alongside bureaucratic authority derived from expertise, capacity, and procedures, while principled moral authority frequently contributes as well.[83] The UN's International Law Commission (ILC), for example, derives its weight from both its mandate and the recognized expertise of its

[78] See Jorge E Viñuales, ed., *The UN Friendly Relations Declaration at 50: An Assessment of the Fundamental Principles of International Law* (Cambridge University Press, 2020).

[79] See, e.g., Nico Krisch, 'Chapter VII Powers: The General Framework and Articles 39 to 43', in *The United Nations Charter: A Commentary*, 3rd ed., edited by Bruno Simma and others (Oxford University Press, 2012).

[80] See José E Alvarez, *International Organizations as Law-Makers* (Oxford University Press, 2005), pp. 109–22; Jutta Brunnée, 'COPing with Consent: Law-Making under Multilateral Environmental Agreements', *Leiden Journal of International Law* 15, (2022): p. 1.

[81] Roberts (n 70), p. 757.

[82] See also the various chapters on sources in different areas of international law in Samantha Besson and Jean d'Aspremont, eds., *The Oxford Handbook on the Sources of International Law* (Oxford University Press, 2017).

[83] On the authority of international organizations, see Barnett and Finnemore (n 60), ch. 2.

members. Special Rapporteurs appointed by the Human Rights Council can base their work similarly on mandates and expertise, but often also on a broader moral basis. Likewise, the UN Secretary-General, as a norm entrepreneur, often draws on moral authority, speaking on behalf of the international community.[84] A defining characteristic of the bureaucratic path is its claim to impartiality and independence. Actors on this path often present their work as technical or expert-driven rather than political, even when addressing questions that are inherently political in nature—a framing that enhances the perceived legitimacy of their contributions.

More than the two previous paths, this one typically operates through clarification and interpretation, often through texts and restatements, and thus in a more legal-technical vein. Although such attempts may sometimes involve new norms and organizational mission creep, they usually avoid open pretensions to legal change. Codifications are a typical instrument here—they can develop the law significantly but have to do so primarily within the framework of restating existing law rather than creating new obligations.[85] The ILC's Articles on State Responsibility are a case in point and, although some of its elements can be seen as novel, the ILC has insisted on its function as identifying existing law, and the Articles have also been widely recognized as reflecting the law in the area.[86] To take another prominent example, the United Nations High Commissioner for Refugees (UNHCR) has been centrally involved in developing international refugee law and the 1951 Convention.[87] Its *Handbook* is regularly used as persuasive authority, including in domestic court proceedings, and the effects of UNHCR's normative activism are visible throughout the field, for example, in the expansion of the category of protected persons through the recognition of gender-based persecution as a ground for refugee status.[88] The scope for creating new norms and understandings on this path is likely to vary—with the authority basis, but also with the opportunity space created by the social environment. Crises in particular are likely to enhance the possibility of moving forward on this path, especially for actors who can invoke moral authority on a given issue. Kofi Annan's push, as the UN Secretary-General,

[84] See Ian Johnstone, 'The Secretary-General as Norm Entrepreneur' in Simon Chesterman, ed., *Secretary or General? The UN Secretary-General in World Politics* (Cambridge University Press, 2007).

[85] See Werner (n 4); also Wouter Werner, *Repetition and International Law* (Cambridge University Press, 2022).

[86] See Fernando Lusa Bordin, 'Reflections of Customary International Law: The Authority of Codification Conventions and ILC Draft Articles in International Law', *International & Comparative Law Quarterly* 63, (2014): p. 535.

[87] Venzke (n 5), ch. III; Corinne Lewis, *UNHCR and International Refugee Law: From Treaties to Innovation* (Routledge, 2012).

[88] Nicole laViolette, '"UNHCR Guidance Note on Refugee Claims Relating to Sexual Orientation and Gender Identity": A Critical Commentary', *International Journal of Refugee Law* 22, (2010): p. 173. See, e.g., the reception in the UK House of Lords (UKHL), *Secretary of State for the Home Department v Fornah* [2006] UKHL 46.

towards a 'responsibility to protect' in response to Kosovo and other atrocities of the 1990s, used such greater space effectively.[89]

The Judicial Path

The judicial path is perhaps the most recognizably 'legal' of the various paths—change here is the result of decisions and findings of courts and quasi-judicial bodies. It relies on judicial expert authority and often also on the delegation from states, although this delegation may not cover all of the law-creating function that courts sometimes assume. At least in the international sphere, the jurisdiction of courts and tribunals is typically limited to the resolution of disputes and the interpretation of the law *inter partes*. Advisory opinions on broader legal questions—available in a variety of settings, from the International Court of Justice to the International Tribunal for the Law of the Sea or the Inter-American Court of Human Rights—are usually 'advisory' and thus non-binding.

The broader normative ripple effects of the findings of judicial bodies, their de facto authority over the development of international law, will often be more 'extensive', serving as a guiding influence on a wider audience within the relevant legal field.[90] In some areas, such as European human rights law, courts have emerged as focal reference points when it comes to identifying and shaping legal rules and their content.[91] Even when they are not in such a central position, the findings of judicial or quasi-judicial bodies are often nevertheless consequential in broader change processes. Just take the two examples we mentioned at the beginning of Chapter 1—in the case of a right to a healthy environment, the Inter-American Court of Human Rights played an important role;[92] in the transformation of international humanitarian law since the end of the Cold War, the international criminal tribunals created in the 1990s were important drivers.[93]

Our exploration of this path includes a broad range of bodies whose authority is based on judicial expertise, ranging from formal international courts to quasi-judicial bodies such as the WTO panels and Appellate Body to less well-known and more informal institutions such as the Organisation for Economic Co-operation and Development (OECD) National Contact Points.[94] We also include domestic

[89] See Charles Cater and David M Malone, 'The Origins and Evolution of Responsibility to Protect at the UN', *International Relations* 30, (2016): p. 278.

[90] Karen Alter, Laurence Helfer and Mikael Madsen, 'How Context Shapes the Authority of International Court', *Law and Contemporary Problems* 79, (2016): p. 1.

[91] See Madsen (n 46); Ezgi Yildiz, *Between Forbearance and Audacity: The European Court of Human Rights and the Norm against Torture* (Cambridge University Press, 2023).

[92] See 'Change in Practice: Two Vignettes' in Chapter 1; Endres (n 47).

[93] See 'Change in Practice: Two Vignettes' in Chapter 1; also Giovanni Mantilla, 'From Treaty to Custom: Shifting Paths in the Recent Development of International Humanitarian Law', *Leiden Journal of International Law* 37, (2024): p. 359.

[94] See also the range of institutions covered in Ruth Mackenzie and others, *Manual on International Courts and Tribunals* (Oxford University Press, 2010).

courts when they interpret international (rather than national) law—in many areas of international law, for example on immunity issues, these courts form part of transnational judicial discourses and are recognized by other actors not because they represent the position of their state, but because they have weighty views on how best to interpret a particular norm.

Legal change on this path is usually framed, even more exclusively than on the bureaucratic path, as mere interpretation of treaties or the ascertainment of customary international law, which judges are deemed 'competent' to undertake. Such change might channel views expressed in other legal instruments (both soft and hard), but typically does not openly claim to effect change and is framed as being limited to a mere clarification of law produced elsewhere and by other actors. The ICJ's efforts to establish new guidelines for the delimitation of the continental shelf, for instance, were framed as reflecting state practice, even though this practice did not necessarily provide a conclusive picture.[95] Only in a few instances do we find more open acknowledgements of a broader role, most notably in the European Court of Human Rights' dynamic, evolutive approach to interpretation—but here, too, the Court tends to base itself, at least rhetorically, on a European consensus.[96]

Judicial proceedings are often presented as a contrast to political negotiations. Yet courts and tribunals are politicized in their own ways and typically have particular commitments (to rights, free trade, investment, etc.) as well as institutional rules (on access, composition, appointments, etc.) that shape their operation.[97] Moreover, they are also responsive to their political and social environment—the WTO Appellate Body, for example, has been found to reorient its jurisprudence significantly when its decisions are met with non-compliance.[98] More generally, international courts are likely to be responsive in the face of attacks on their authority, which should never be assumed as absolute or unassailable.[99] While not

[95] Ezgi Yildiz, 'Evolving Rules of Continental Shelf Delimitation: The Fate of the Equidistance Principle', in *The Paths of International Law: Case Studies*, edited by Pedro Martínez Esponda and others (SSRN, 2023); Ezgi Yildiz and Umut Yüksel, 'The Defocalizing Effect of International Courts: Evidence from Maritime Delimitation Practices', *The Review of International Organizations* 20, (2024): p. 825; Ezgi Yildiz and Umut Yüksel, 'Understanding the Limitations of Behavioralism: Lessons from the Field of Maritime Delimitation', *German Law Journal* 23, (2022): p. 413.

[96] See Laurence R Helfer and Erik Voeten, 'International Courts as Agents of Legal Change: Evidence from LGBT Rights in Europe', *International Organization* 68, (2014): p. 77; Kanstantsin Dzehtsiarou, *European Consensus and the Legitimacy of the European Court of Human Rights* (Cambridge University Press, 2015); Jens T Theilen, *European Consensus between Strategy and Principle* (Nomos Publishers, 2021).

[97] See, e.g., Erik Voeten, 'The Politics of International Judicial Appointments: Evidence from the European Court of Human Rights', *International Organization* 61, (2007): p. 669.

[98] Jeffrey Kucik and Sergio Puig, 'The Appellate Body's Judicial Pathway: Precedent, Resistance and Adaptation', in *The Many Paths of Change in International Law*, edited by Nico Krisch and Ezgi Yildiz (Oxford University Press, 2023).

[99] See Tom Ginsburg, 'Political Constraints on International Courts', in *The Oxford Handbook of International Adjudication*, edited by Cesare P R Romano, Karen J Alter and Yuval Shany (Oxford University Press, 2014).

insulated from politics, change through the judicial path is shaped by a unique set of considerations compared to the more overtly political pathways.

The Private Authority Path

Change in this final modality originates from statements or reports by recognized private authorities without a clear affiliation to or mandate from states or international organizations. This includes formally private organizations, such as the ICRC or the Institut de Droit International, but also civil society organizations and expert groups that are assembled ad hoc. The authority of actors on this path can derive from various sources, including expertise, capacity, principles, and potentially inclusive procedures.[100] Often, however, interventions in change processes gain authority not only from the actors or processes behind them, but also from their substantive content.[101] The ICRC study on customary international humanitarian law, touched upon in Chapter 1, certainly benefited from the authority of the ICRC and the expert input in its drafting process, but it became an important reference point also because of the recognized quality and widespread acceptability of its findings.[102]

Private authority often carries less weight than actions on other paths: it may not bring about fully consolidated new understandings but may nevertheless help shape discourses in ways that lay the foundation for consolidation through other interventions in change processes. Take, for example, the 2006 'Watson Report' of Brown University's Watson Institute on fair and clear procedures in the UN sanctions regime.[103] In and of itself, it would not have sufficed to generate convergence around a new understanding of procedural requirements in the Security Council decision-making on sanctions. But because it responded to and inserted itself into a broader, partly inter-governmental process on the issue, it managed to establish itself as a reference point for contestation around existing Council practices.[104]

In some cases, private authority may go beyond that and itself generate, or significantly contribute to, the lasting change of established rules. International humanitarian law may be a notable example here, particularly given the unique role of the ICRC. The effect of private authority might be particularly strong when it addresses gaps that emerge from new demands—resulting, for example, from new

[100] On the sources of private authority in international affairs see Rodney Bruce Hall and Thomas J Biersteker, eds., *The Emergence of Private Authority in Global Governance* (Cambridge University Press, 2002).

[101] See Zarbiyev (n 53).

[102] See 'Change in Practice: Two Vignettes' in Chapter 1.

[103] Watson Institute, 'Strengthening Targeted Sanctions Through Fair and Clear Procedures' (Brown University, 2006).

[104] See, e.g., Thomas J Biersteker, 'Targeted Sanctions and Individual Human Rights', *International Journal* 65, (2010): p. 99.

technologies or shifts in values that are not, or are only insufficiently, addressed elsewhere. This may operate through solution-oriented interventions in specific issue areas and the production of technical manuals, standards, and regulations. The San Remo Manual on the International Law Applicable to Armed Conflicts at Sea, for example, draws much of its authority from the fact that it is 'the only comprehensive international instrument that has been drafted on the law of naval warfare since 1913'.[105]

Because of the typically limited formal authority of actors or institutions on the private authority path, its outcomes will often have a more fragile standing, relying even more heavily on recognition from the relevant community compared to interventions on other paths. The constant struggle for acceptance may also generate tighter constraints on the law-creating potential of such interventions. At the same time, the low threshold for making such interventions also facilitates normative experimentation. Outputs such as the Maastricht Principles on Extraterritorial Obligations of States in the Area of Economic, Social, and Cultural Rights—an ambitious document drawn up by a group of academics, human rights experts, and activists[106]—may well be able to formulate a vision for change more coherently than might be possible on other paths. As seen in this case and many others, if change attempts advanced through private authority generate uptake, at least among parts of the interpretive community, they may contribute to shifts in broader discourses.

4. Varying Dynamics

Juxtaposing the different paths of international legal change helps us not only to build a typology that structures our empirical inquiry but also to generate more fine-grained expectations about the dynamics and politics of change processes. This comparative perspective allows us to assess how different paths vary in terms of their accessibility, pace, and influence, as well as how they interact with broader institutional and geopolitical contexts. We have already hinted at some aspects of this in Chapter 1; here, we lay out broader conjectures about core differences between the various paths, identifying how they shape and are shaped by the actors, authorities, and mechanisms involved. We also present expectations as to the logics that pertain to different stages of change processes—selection, construction, and reception—highlighting the contingent and iterative nature of these stages. We emphasize that these stages are not always sequential but often overlap or repeat,

[105] Louise Doswald-Beck, 'San Remo Manual on International Law Applicable to Armed Conflict at Sea', *International Review of the Red Cross* 35, (1995): p. 583.
[106] See Olivier De Schutter and others, 'Commentary to the Maastricht Principles on Extraterritorial Obligations of States in the Area of Economic, Social and Cultural Rights', *Human Rights Quarterly* 34, (2012): p. 1084.

influenced by the strategic choices of change agents and the resistance of their opponents.

Paths in Contrast

The speed, ease, and outcomes of change processes inevitably depend heavily on the different paths available to them. We highlight here three factors we conjecture to be particularly relevant for accounting for this variation.

In the first place, such variation stems from differences in *access and influence* across the different paths. This is perhaps most clearly visible with respect to non-state actors who often do not have direct access to state-driven processes. Although multilateral fora vary in the degree of openness, the gulf between the relatively closed operation of the UN Security Council and the inclusiveness of environmental COPs is vast.[107] In contrast, some courts and tribunals give individuals and NGOs direct access, which, by many accounts, has been a key factor in these courts' ability to expand their terrain.[108] However, even among courts that provide such access, the degree of receptivity can vary significantly.[109] Not all influence of non-state actors is through formal channels, of course—especially corporations and business associations have used their lobbying power with states and their representatives to achieve favourable results in international negotiations.[110] States, too, exert varying degrees of influence across different paths. States are at the helm in the multilateral and state action paths, but less so in the others, and particularly judicial and private authority paths will often be less prone to direct influence by states. Especially from the perspective of powerful states, direct influence might be decreasing as we move across different paths. Traditional state action path is more amenable to the exercise of the tools of the powerful, whereas in judicial bodies or among private experts, influence—never entirely absent—typically needs to come in subtler ways.[111]

Consequential differences also exist as regards the *shape and pace* of the change process. Authorities on the different paths have different degrees of latitude to effect change. In the judicial and private ones—largely limited to the interpretation

[107] See Alan Boyle and Christine Chinkin, *The Making of International Law* (Oxford University Press, 2007), ch. 2; more broadly Jonas Tallberg and others, *The Opening Up of International Organizations: Transnational Access in Global Governance* (Cambridge University Press, 2013).

[108] See Karen Alter, *The New Terrain of International Law: Courts, Politics, Rights* (Princeton University Press, 2014).

[109] Heidi Nichols Haddad, *The Hidden Hands of Justice: NGOs, Human Rights, and International Courts* (Cambridge University Press, 2018); Ezgi Yildiz, 'Enduring Practices in Changing Circumstances: A Comparison of the European Court of Human Rights and the Inter-American Court of Human Rights', *Temple International & Comparative Law Journal* 34, (2020): p. 309.

[110] See Melissa J Durkee, 'The Business of Treaties', *UCLA Law Review* 63, (2016): p. 264.

[111] See also Nico Krisch, 'International Law in Times of Hegemony: Unequal Power and the Shaping of the International Legal Order', *European Journal of International Law* 16, (2005): p. 369.

of law rather than its creation—change will usually have to come through smaller steps. For example, courts may gradually expand the scope of existing treaty provisions over a series of rulings, incrementally shifting the understanding of the law without overtly creating new obligations. This process often unfolds subtly, with changes presented 'in disguise' as the identification of existing law, rather than an overt attempt to develop it further.[112] This does not mean that change is barred—language, and especially language in use, is heavily malleable—but change is likely to be more circumscribed. In the contrast between gradualist accounts and those focused on punctuated equilibria,[113] the more interpretive paths are generally more aligned with the former category. The paths on which open law creation is possible—state action and multilateral—in principle allow for bigger leaps, but whether this occurs in practice depends on the degree of convergence among states (and other actors) at a given moment. When interests align, this can result in the adoption of groundbreaking treaties or unanimous resolutions which have the potential to shift legal and normative baselines rapidly.[114]

Finally, we can expect a variation across different paths as regards the *weight* of their conclusions. In line with the foregoing, a resolution of a multilateral conference may be able to settle an issue without much more, and converging state action might also lead to decisive change. The challenge here often lies in generating such convergence, as more limited support from states may not entirely frustrate a change attempt but can leave it precariously balanced. Action on other paths—especially those involving non-state authorities—will typically require further support and consolidation. This may occur through repetition over time, confirmation by other paths and authorities, or affirmative reception by an interpretive community that gradually sets aside doubts and comes to take the envisioned change for granted.[115] What weight a particular path carries is not a foregone conclusion. However, as emphasized above, in some contexts, courts or institutions have come to be recognized as central reference points for change processes, but not in others. Weight is also relative—even weaker authorities may be very consequential on a given issue if other paths are silent. Especially on newly emerging issues on which opinions (in particular positions of states) are not fully formed, the potential for consequential action on non-state paths is likely to be greater.

[112] See Ezgi Yildiz, 'A Court with Many Faces: Judicial Characters and Modes of Norm Development in the European Court of Human Rights', *European Journal of International Law* 31, (2020): p. 73; Werner (n 4).

[113] See 'International Law between Stasis and Change' in Chapter 1.

[114] Andreas Motzfeldt Kravik, 'An Analysis of Stagnation in Multilateral Law-Making—and Why the Law of the Sea Has Transcended the Stagnation Trend', *Leiden Journal of International Law* 34, (2021): p. 935.

[115] On degrees of consolidation, see also 'Contestation and the Changing Paths of Change' in Chapter 7.

Table 2.1 below summarizes the main features of the different pathways and highlights how varying institutional and actor configurations shape the dynamics and impact of the legal change they generate.

While we neatly delineate distinct paths of international legal change, in practice, most issue areas are shaped by multiple, interacting pathways rather than a singular trajectory. As we elaborate in Chapter 3, most change processes involve the sequential or simultaneous activation of several paths. This multiplicity can create opportunities for change agents, as different paths may build momentum and reinforce one another. Yet it can also produce friction when competing interpretations emerge across paths. The interaction between multiple paths—often operating simultaneously and even across issue areas—shapes the politics of change in an increasingly fragmented and complex international legal order. As we explore in Chapter 6, this interplay can foster cross-path authority-building and reinforce legitimacy; but as Chapter 7 will show, it may also complicate norm consolidation in the face of overlapping jurisdictions and contesting actors.

Different Stages

The dynamics of change processes are bound to vary not only across different paths but also within any given path, depending on the stage in which a change process finds itself. We distinguish here between three ideal-typical stages of change processes to gain a clearer understanding of the actors and social and institutional dynamics at play. This distinction is primarily an analytical device, not a chronological structure, as will become clearer at the end of this section.

The first stage is the *selection* stage in which change agents choose and activate a pathway to realize their vision of change. Given the important differences in the dynamics across the various paths, this selection is highly consequential. It does not, of course, have to be a conscious 'selection' in the sense of a deliberative choice among alternatives—under certain circumstances, there may be one normalized, focal path for change on a given issue, and actors will not perceive a situation of choice.[116] In international law, however, such normalization is rare. Change agents are typically faced with a range of options, which often depend on their own nature—non-state actors, for instance, usually have options that are markedly different from those available to officials in a foreign ministry. Actors may also activate multiple pathways simultaneously to bolster their legitimacy claims or undermine the legitimacy of rival interpretations, while opposing agents—antipreneurs—might opt for a competing pathway to counter the change attempt.

[116] On actors' choices between different sites, see Joseph Jupille, Walter Mattli and Duncan Snidal, *Institutional Choice and Global Commerce* (Cambridge University Press, 2013), ch. 2. See also 'Complexity, Change and Cumulated Authority' and 'Paths of Least Resistance' in Chapter 6.

Table 2.1 Main features of paths in contrast

	State action	Multilateral	Bureaucratic	Judicial	Private authority
Character	Unilateral actions of states	Multiple states acting in international organizations or conferences	International organizations, officials, and bodies (secretariats, commissions, experts, etc.) beyond inter-governmental bodies	International courts, tribunals, quasi-judicial bodies	Private authorities, experts, academics, NGOs
Source of authority	States as primary subjects of international law	Collective state authority or authority of institutions that serve as multilateral fora	Bureaucratic, expert, or moral authority	Judicial or expert authority	Expertise; moral authority; authority of inclusive processes
Process	Accumulation of unilateral actions by states	Multilateral consensus-building within institutional fora	Clarification, interpretation, restatement of existing norms	Judgments, awards, advisory opinions; accumulation of precedent	Reports, statements, and studies by recognized private authorities
Scope of change	Broad scope; possibility of open law creation through customary international law, as well as interpretive impact through subsequent practice	Moderate to broad scope through resolutions and declarations on treaty-making, customary law, and interpretive processes	Limited to moderate; through interpretation of existing rules by the accumulation of expert reports, technical assessments, and bureaucratic activity	Limited to moderate: interpretation of existing law—scope dependent on the authority and centrality of the judicial body	Limited scope; typically producing peripheral change through interpretive impact
Accessibility	Only available to states; easier access for powerful states	Direct access for states; accessible to weaker state coalitions; for other actors, indirect access through lobbying and advocacy	Access through influence on institutions (diplomatic, budgetary, ideational, expert, etc.)	Limited access—depends on jurisdiction and standing; some allow individuals/NGOs via amicus curiae and, rarely, direct standing	Accessible to non-state actors, academics, NGOs, experts, typically through consultations, hearings, advocacy, etc.

The second stage is that of *construction*. Here, the actors and authorities associated with the particular pathway process the change attempt and generate statements about the status of the norm in question—confirming, refuting, finding a middle ground, or avoiding any clear position. This processing and position-taking may help create a new norm or clarify an existing one, and, in some instances, it may reject proposed new definitions and frustrate the change attempt altogether. The resulting statements are then leveraged by change agents to construct legitimacy claims for their proposals, whether to strengthen support for change or to justify efforts at rejection. If the selection stage is often dominated by activist modes of engagement with potentially a choice between different fora, the construction stage tends to follow different logics, depending on the kind of path and institution in question—along the lines sketched in the previous part.

The third stage is that of *reception*, where the outcome of the construction stage is appraised by the broader range of actors in the field; it is here that change attempts are accepted, partially accepted, or rejected—or held in suspense, when change is recognized as potential yet not complete or when disagreement keeps a norm development in abeyance. These actors will typically include especially state representatives—executive, legislative, and judicial—as well as international courts, scholars, and other experts. Whose voice counts in this process is determined by the specific field and community involved. As outlined above, fields differ in the range of actors they include, the strength of ties between them, and their respective social positions.[117] In some fields, for example, human rights law, civil society organizations will play a significant role; in others, less so. The social hierarchies that characterize a field are bound to be consequential in the process, and some actors' voices will be heard much louder than others. Moreover, actors in the reception stage will assess a proposed change based on its substance or its pedigree. The more the actors and institutions involved in the construction stage are recognized as authorities, the more likely others in the reception stage are to defer to them, even if this means setting aside their own preferred substantive outcomes. Yet, of course, actors in a field may not always be aligned either on substance or authority, and the reception may remain inconclusive and change attempts unsettled as a result.

Figure 2.1 below visualizes the three ideal-typical stages that structure change processes, helping us analytically disentangle the often entangled and iterative nature of norm change. While the arrows indicate a typical progression from one stage to the next, these stages are not necessarily sequential or clearly separated in practice. Change processes may move back and forth between stages, overlap, or even skip stages altogether. Feedback from the reception stage may come in while the construction phase is still underway; selection and construction stages may

[117] See section 2 above.

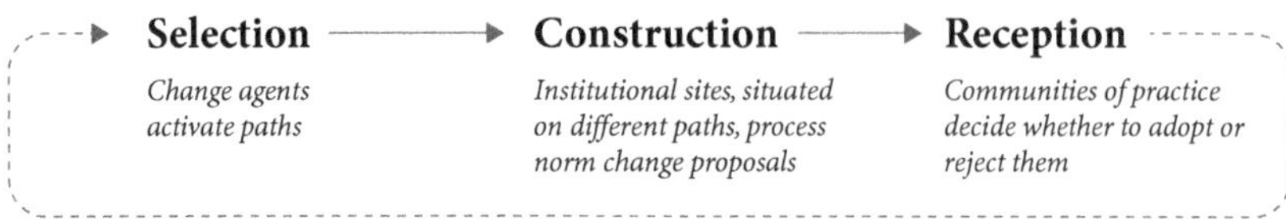

Figure 2.1 The selection-construction-reception framework

overlap; and change agents may also pursue new paths to build on ongoing construction processes in other fora. Moreover, the different stages may be repeated multiple times through different pathways in the overall change process, with change agents (or antipreneurs) building on the outcome of a previous cycle to pursue their aims in another.

A good illustration of these stages, unfolding in a relatively straightforward and linear fashion—which is not typical for most cases—is the process that led to the emergence of a right to water between the late 1990s and the early 2010s.[118] Here, activist change agents first targeted (*selection*) a UN expert body—the Committee on Economic, Social and Cultural Rights—and managed to generate a favourable General Comment by the Committee (*construction*). This led to significant positive reactions (*reception*), including recognition by companies and domestic courts, albeit not yet in a generalized way. Activists (and other change agents) then selected other bodies, for example, the UN Commission on Human Rights and, later, its successor, the Human Rights Council, to generate supportive action, such as the appointment of a special rapporteur on the issue. This paved the way for a more widespread (but still not undivided) reception among states and other actors and allowed change agents to target (another selection) the General Assembly and also the Human Rights Council. It was only after their adoption of resolutions recognizing the right to water as a human right (yet another instance of construction) that, eventually, reception became general and consolidated. Various cycles of the three stages—partly sequential, partly entangled—thus allowed for a gradual build-up of authority and eventually led to a changed legal landscape that is now no longer seriously contested.

5. Conclusion

International law is not carved in stone; it is shaped in motion. It evolves through battles over meaning that play out across institutions, courtrooms, and conference

118 See Nina Reiners, 'Despite or Because of Contestation? How Water Became a Human Right', *Human Rights Quarterly* 43, (2021): p. 329; see also Nina Reiners, *Transnational Lawmaking Coalitions for Human Rights* (Cambridge University Press, 2021); Madeline Baer, *Stemming the Tide: Human Rights and Water Policy in a Neoliberal World* (Oxford University Press, 2017).

halls. This chapter has provided us with some of the core elements of the process of international legal change introduced in Chapter 1. As we have seen, these revolve around social practices, in particular fields that generate authority and thereby establish paths on which change processes can travel. We have distinguished between five ideal-typical paths, each involving distinct actor constellations and dynamics, pointing to important implications regarding how the availability and selection of certain paths affect influence, accessibility, and the shape and pace of the change processes. This contrasts starkly with classical, doctrinal accounts of change in international law, and also with the largely statist approaches prominent among international relations scholars. It highlights the degree to which the formal categories used by international lawyers depend on—and are defined by—particular social practices, and it opens up the possibility of them taking on very different forms in different contexts.

What emerges is a view of international law not as a static set of rules, but as a living, evolving practice—one that changes not only through treaties and formal declarations, but through discursive shifts, institutional dynamics, and the work of actors bold enough to challenge inherited meanings and reimagine what the law can become. It is a picture of significant dynamism and gradual change: a social process in which states and other actors come together to make and remake rules, and in which structures and authorities emerge from the practices they engage in. It is of a multifaceted, variegated international law—with potentially different paths, actors, and marks of authority in different contexts. And it is not just a social, but also a heavily institutional picture, in the sense that much of what we think international law is about has to do with the institutions created and recognized in particular social settings. How and where change proceeds, and what actors and logics dominate in a given change process, depend heavily on the practices and institutions that have emerged over time in respective contexts.

The paths of international law we introduce here are primarily heuristic devices that allow us to trace similarities and differences in the frames in which change processes unfold across the many areas of international law. But they are guided by the intuition that change in international law is much more thickly embedded in social and institutional processes, and structured through common understandings and authorities, than the typical focus on inter-state law-making suggests. This reflects the conjecture, developed in Chapter 1, that change in international law often does not come through sudden moves, based on hard-fought agreement among many states, but instead through gradual processes of redefinition and meaning-making which, in the aggregate and over time, may converge to constitute major shifts.

The first two chapters of this book have set the scene for what comes next. They have sought to understand what is at stake in international legal change and developed a framework—one that enables us to address long-overlooked questions such as: When does change take root, and when does it wither? Who propels change and who stands in its way? How does international law evolve in a world of fragmented authority, contested norms, and competing actors? As we move forward, the next chapters will pursue these theoretical insights and questions in empirical case studies, assessing the extent to which the image we have advanced holds true. They will inquire into the variations across different areas of international law, the conditions under which change is more or less likely, the role of power, the impact of complexity and fragmentation, and the interplay between contestation and consolidation. Our analyses are based on a limited amount of empirical evidence, and they can naturally not claim to be fully conclusive or representative. But they rest on a far wider and richer basis than existing accounts, which typically centre on a small number of cases, often from the same issue area. While no single analysis can encompass all dimensions of such a multifaceted process, the broader and more comprehensive approach presented in this book provides us with rich insights into the actual 'paths' of international law—insights that reflect the messiness, politics, and potential of legal change.

3

The Many International Laws

A Comparison*

How is norm change processed in each subfield of international law? Does change occur in a more or less homogeneous manner across the field, or do its workings vary depending on a specific subfield? The discussion of the different paths in Chapter 2 has already pointed in the direction of the latter, and our case studies provide ample evidence of significant variation: paths, authorities, constraints, and temporalities differ across subfields of international law, sometimes to a striking extent. What might take decades to achieve in the law of the sea, for instance, might happen suddenly in international criminal law. Likewise, a blocked change attempt in international environmental law might find an easier route through international human rights law. Behind these contrasts lie different constellations of paths—diverse interplays among the state action, multilateral, bureaucratic, judicial, and private authority pathways.

Traditional accounts of change in international law, however, paint a more uniform picture. International legal theorists typically approach change through the doctrine of sources, which is thought to apply homogeneously throughout international law.[1] To them, no meaningful differences exist—treaties and custom are treaties and custom everywhere in the field, and conceding the opposite would risk opening the door to fragmentation.[2] Accordingly, institutions such as the International Law Commission (ILC) present a unified approach to sources, with only a minor allowance for variation.[3] More sophisticated accounts—for instance in international relations scholarship—have contributed greatly to understanding change in international law, often spotting diversity in change processes. Yet they also tend to fall short of observing how change works

* We are grateful to Dorothea Endres for her contributions to this chapter.

[1] ILC, 'Draft Conclusions on Identification of Customary International Law with Commentaries', by Sir Michael Wood, Special Rapporteur (2018) UN Doc A/73/10, pp. 5, 6.

[2] Pierre-Marie Dupuy, *L'unité de l'ordre juridique international: cours général de droit international public* (M Nijhoff, 2003).

[3] See ILC (n 1); ILC, 'Draft Conclusions on Subsequent Agreements and Subsequent Practice in Relation to the Interpretation of Treaties, with Commentaries', (2018) UN Doc A/73/10. Some variation is acknowledged for the law of international organizations, but it is kept to a minimum.

Change in International Law. Nico Krisch, Ezgi Yildiz, and Pedro Martínez Esponda, Oxford University Press.
 DOI: 10.1093/9780198918325.003.0003

at the level of subfields.[4] Dissenting voices may have grown louder over time, but they have not been able to change the prevailing approach.[5]

This chapter takes the diversity of international law into view by using the empirical insights gathered in our project. The aim is to provide a thick description and comparison of the particularities of change in the different subfields as a means to gain a richer understanding of how change happens throughout the field. This is done on the basis of the twenty-five case studies, focusing on specific instances of norm change across eight issue areas of international law: general international law (GIL), the law of the sea (LoS), international human rights law (IHRL), international humanitarian law (IHL), international criminal law (ICL), international environmental law (IEL), international trade law (ITL), and international investment law (IIL). In Chapter 4, we inquire further into specific factors that influence the success of change attempts on the different paths, and Chapters 5, 6, and 7 focus on particular aspects of the conditions of change: power, complexity, and contestation.

A first glimpse at the paths through which change is channelled is revealing. Figure 3.1 below shows the dominant pathways across all case studies. From the perspective of traditional sources doctrine, the state action and multilateral paths should be the main avenues for change—given their close association to state

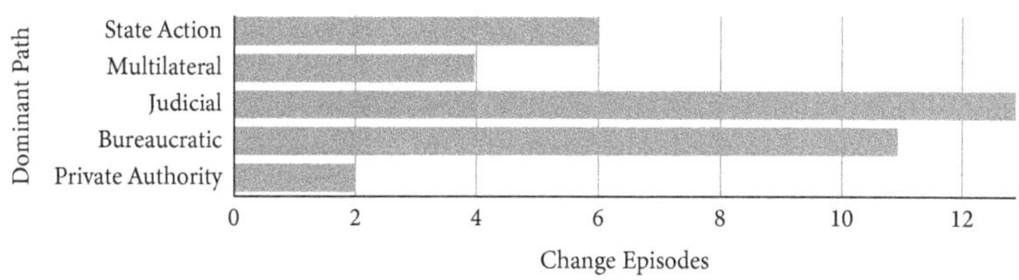

Figure 3.1 Dominant paths[a]

[a]This figure reflects the pathways that were coded as dominant in each of the project's case studies. This was done on the basis of a qualitative assessment of the role that the different paths had in each case, as well as the choices of norm entrepreneurs in their efforts to drive change. It is important to note that the number of paths coded as dominant exceeds the number of case studies, which is twenty-five. This is because, in some case studies, more than one path played a dominant role.

[4] Paul F Diehl and Charlotte Ku, *The Dynamics of International Law* (Cambridge University Press, 2010); Pierre-Hugues Verdier and Erik Voeten, 'Precedent, Compliance and Change in Customary International Law: An Explanatory Theory', *American Journal of International Law* 108, (2014): p. 389; Anette Stimmer, *The Politics of International Norms: A Rhetorical Approach* (Cambridge University Press, 2025).

[5] See, e.g., Samantha Besson, 'Sources of International Human Rights Law: How General Is General International Law?', in *The Oxford Handbook of the Sources of International Law*, edited by Samantha Besson and Jean d'Aspremont (Oxford University Press, 2017) and the other chapters in Part IV of the same volume.

agency and consent. Yet, our case studies suggest otherwise. The judicial and bureaucratic paths emerge as most prominent in practice, serving as one of the dominant paths in nearly half of our cases (thirteen and eleven cases, respectively). State action and multilateral pathways play a comparatively lesser role, appearing among the dominant paths in fewer than a quarter of our cases (six and four cases, respectively). Notably, it is very telling that much of international law's dynamism happens in and through courts and international bureaucratic bodies, more so than through the actual actions and statements of states or multilateral bodies. The private authority path, for its part, featured as dominant only in two cases. This might seem comparatively low, but it is still significant, especially considering the general lack of acknowledgement of this path in traditional accounts of change in international law.

Beyond this general outlook, when taking variation across issue areas into view, meaningful differences and cross-cutting patterns emerge. Figure 3.2 below captures the distribution of dominant paths by issue area, organized into three levels of prominence. It shows, very much in line with the general trend shown in Figure 3.1, that most issue areas tend to process change either through the judicial or the bureaucratic paths: ITL, ICL, and IIL have the former as primary path, while LoS, IHRL, and IHL have the latter as primary. Only IEL and GIL have different primary paths: multilateral and state action, respectively. But if one then moves to secondary paths of change, one realizes the true weight of the judicial pathway: except for GIL, in every issue area in which the judicial path was not primary, it functions as secondary. The bureaucratic path is also important but less prominent: aside from the three areas where it is primary, only in GIL does it feature as secondary, and in ITL and IEL as tertiary. The state action and multilateral paths are considerably less relevant, the former featuring in GIL as primary and in ICL as secondary, while the latter appears in IEL as primary and in ITL as secondary. The multilateral pathway, however, is more present as a tertiary pathway for LoS, IHRL, and IHL.

As we engage in the more detailed comparison of these areas in the following pages, we are guided by the framework developed in Chapters 1 and 2 of this book. This draws our attention towards the social practices through which paths of change are used and produced in a given field. We thus ask here not only about the paths themselves, but also the actors and communities that matter in a given area—in other words, the actors that recognize particular paths and give discursive weight to the interpretations emanating from them. We also, and especially, ask about the authority constellations prevalent in different fields: the institutions and actors that can de facto induce deference from a broader range of actors in the field. In some contexts, we are bound to find more centralized institutions; in others, a multiplicity of institutions populating a field and interacting in a less structured fashion; in yet others, we may find that states remain the core

Table 3.1 Relevant paths in different issue areas[a]

Issue area	Primary path	Secondary path	Tertiary path
ITL	Judicial	Multilateral	Bureaucratic
IEL	Multilateral	Judicial	Bureaucratic
LoS	Bureaucratic	Judicial	State action/Multilateral
ICL	Judicial	State action	X
GIL	State action	Bureaucratic	Judicial/Private authority
IHRL	Bureaucratic	Judicial	Multilateral
IIL	Judicial	State action	X
IHL	Bureaucratic	Judicial	Multilateral/state action

[a]The columns in this table reflect the frequency with which a path has been identified as dominant or present in each case study of the project's sample on the basis of the cases' specific trajectory. Where a path has been dominant in at least two out of three case studies per issue area, it is reflected here as primary. If a path has been dominant in one out of three case studies, it is identified as secondary. The paths that were present but not dominant are recorded in the 'tertiary path' column.

authorities with little beyond them. Finally, we also pay particular attention to the political dynamics prevalent in a given field and ask where the geopolitical incentives for or against change tend to lie, which (groups of) states are typically involved in change attempts, and what the stakes are in the issues around which change attempts occur.

In what follows, we focus on each subfield of international law, using these questions to structure our inquiry into each of them. This should allow us to provide a snapshot of the different path configurations that exist in each issue area. Before we turn to the areas, however, we need briefly to introduce the case studies that form the basis of the comparison.

1. The Case Studies: Methodology, Selection, Purpose

As explained above, the empirical core of our project consists of twenty-five in-depth case studies of individual norm change attempts beyond those focused exclusively on treaty-making. By 'individual norm change', we mean here change in specific rules of international law—i.e., concrete instances of rights, obligations, or other specific international normative provisions. In other words, we are interested in change at the micro level of particular norms, not (or not primarily) in systemic change in the international legal system. This is a key, distinctive element of our approach—as explained in Chapter 1, even broader transformations in international law tend to occur through gradual steps, and it is these steps that we seek to capture.

We selected these case studies in accordance with the following steps. First, we identified a larger class of cases (our population) through a thorough review of leading textbooks in the eight fields mentioned above: GIL, IHRL, IHL, ICL, ITL, IIL, IEL, and LoS.[6] In total, we collected 116 cases, and we briefly assessed the course and the outcome of each episode. Secondly, we listed ten to fifteen potential cases in each subfield, clearly demarking the time frame in which these change episodes materialized. This was an important step since our intention was to select cases from different time periods. For example, we made sure to include change episodes that materialized before and after the 2000s, and we included some episodes that are currently ongoing. Ensuring variation across time helped us diversify the number of relevant actors, power constellations, or the nature of the ideational environment.[7]

Our focused sample included four cases from GIL and three cases from the other fields.[8] In total, we selected twenty-five cases that illustrate the dynamics of change we observe in each field. We adopted a *typical* case research design and ensured our cases portrayed typical dynamics to be found in the respective subfield.[9] A typical case research design was suitable for the purposes of probing into the causal mechanisms at work, which was our main goal in this project.[10]

When selecting cases, we sought to ensure a variation in our dependent variable, namely the degree of success in change attempts (i.e., shift in the burden of argument measured by the extent to which justification is required for a new position[11]). Given that we identified the population of cases through an assessment of textbooks and mainstream literature, which tend to pay more attention to successful change episodes, our sample includes a greater proportion of successful change attempts.[12] This, however, does not pose a significant problem for our

[6] In addition to the classical works such as Malcolm D Evans, ed., *International Law*, 3rd ed. (Oxford University Press, 2010); Malcolm N Shaw, *International Law* (Cambridge University Press, 2017), we also looked at the specialized textbooks. We examined, for example, Lavanya Rajamani and Jacqueline Peel, eds., *The Oxford Handbook of International Environmental Law*, 2nd ed. (Oxford University Press, 2021); Donald R Rothwell and others, eds., *The Oxford Handbook of the Law of the Sea* (Oxford University Press, 2017); Dinah Shelton, ed., *The Oxford Handbook of International Human Rights Law*, Reprint ed. (Oxford University Press, 2015); Peter Muchlinski, Federico Ortino and Christoph Schreuer, *The Oxford Handbook of International Investment Law* (Oxford University Press, 2008); Andrew Clapham and Paola Gaeta, *The Oxford Handbook of International Law in Armed Conflict* (Oxford University Press, 2014).

[7] Jack S Levy, 'Case Studies: Types, Designs, and Logics of Inference', *Conflict Management and Peace Science* 25, (2008): pp. 1, 7.

[8] John Gerring and Lee Cojocaru, 'Selecting Cases for Intensive Analysis: A Diversity of Goals and Methods', *Sociological Methods & Research* 45, (2016): p. 392.

[9] Alexander L George and Andrew Bennett, *Case Studies and Theory Development in the Social Sciences*, 4th ed. (The MIT Press, 2005).

[10] Jason Seawright and John Gerring, 'Case Selection Techniques in Case Study Research: A Menu of Qualitative and Quantitative Options', *Political Research Quarterly* 61, (2008): pp. 294, 299–300.

[11] See 'Identifying Change', in Chapter 2.

[12] Our mean is 2.6 out of 4.

study as our sample still includes a sufficient number of unsuccessful cases to distil conditions of success.[13] These conditions will be the focus of Chapter 4.

Finally, a word on why we selected these specific eight issue areas and not others is in order. Undoubtedly, issue areas such as international organizations law, refugee law, space law, or diplomatic law could have provided interesting insights. However, even if the baseline approach to selecting our sample had a maximizing intent—attempting to cover as much ground as possible—the project's timeframe and human capabilities obliged us to narrow it down. Among the possible options, we selected GIL, IHRL, IHL, ICL, ITL, IIL, IEL, and LoS under three main criteria.

The first of these criteria is generality. Each of these eight issue areas is itself broad and encompasses a good number of possible sub-issue areas. For instance, one could think of the law on immunities as an issue area that was excluded in our sample, but in fact, different aspects of it are covered by our broader categories of GIL, IHRL, and ICL. The same could be said about the law of maritime delimitation or the law on state responsibility, which are covered in our sample under LoS and GIL, respectively. We sought to avoid niche issue areas and focused on categories that constitute fully-fledged subfields of international law.

The second criterion is representativeness. Our eight issue areas span diverse subfields of international law, both in terms of the object of regulation and of the legal and political dynamics that shape them. GIL, ITL, and LoS, for example, establish mostly rights and obligations that belong to states, even if they have very different regulatory purposes. IHRL, ICL, and IIL, in contrast, have greater acceptance of non-state actor entitlements and thus operate differently. Importantly, too, these eight issue areas work through a diverse set of institutional constellations, an element we expected to be key in conditioning norm change.

Finally, this selection of issue areas focuses on particularly salient aspects of international law, making them fertile ground for studying change. This salience helps to capture issue areas with significant dynamism and active contestation, thereby illuminating the political realities of the contemporary world rather than merely legal technicalities.

2. Change across Issue Areas

General International Law

General International Law (GIL), as its name suggests, is not strictly speaking an issue area of international law, but rather a set of norms based in custom that apply throughout international law. For the purpose of this project, GIL comprises the

[13] Levy (n 7), p. 9.

basic legal framework of international law, derived from the key structural principles of international law that coordinate interactions among states, such as sovereign equality or state responsibility. This being so, it is unsurprising that authority in GIL is not fixed upon any specific institution or institutional regime.[14] A multitude of authorities take part in the game of norm change in GIL—even if, paradoxically, few are available when it comes to attempting change. This leads to unevenness and discontinuity in the process of norm-making in GIL, as well as to uncertain outcomes.

The most authoritative institutions in GIL are state-dominated or exclusively accessible to states. The International Court of Justice (ICJ), the United Nations (UN) General Assembly, and to a certain extent the UN Security Council are the venues that are most capable of triggering, catalysing, or enabling change in GIL, although some of these vary between sub-issue areas.[15] This tilts the balance of law-making and law-shaping power heavily towards states.[16] Yet, even for states, these institutions are mostly inaccessible. Taking a matter before the ICJ requires, first and foremost, finding a jurisdictional basis to file a case against another state. This is exceptional, especially when it comes to truly controversial issues. At the General Assembly, in contrast, no such jurisdictional hurdles exist, but serious law-making attempts require intense diplomatic mobilization and broad support from states, including for requesting an advisory opinion to the ICJ. Such diplomatic mobilization is, of course, also necessary in the Security Council, although much depends on the five permanent members refraining from exercising their veto power. On most salient issues, this creates an almost insurmountable obstacle.

This lack of institutional availability is reflected in the case studies on GIL in this project. Contrary to what could have been expected at the outset, none of the GIL cases featured the ICJ as an important authority in the construction of norm change. Only in the case of self-defence against non-state actors (SD-NSA) did it play a role, albeit an antipreneurial one, countering change attempts pursued by states. The General Assembly, for its part, played only a very minor role in the case study concerning the concept of internationally wrongful act—taking note of the final outcome—and the Security Council also had some (limited) influence in only one of the cases—again, SD-NSA. This, of course, does not mean that change in

[14] Georges Abi-Saab, 'Interprétation et Auto-Interprétation. Quelques Réflexions Sur Leur Rôle Dans La Formation et La Résolution Du Différend International', in *Recht zwischen Umbruch und Bewahrung Völkerrecht, Europarecht, Staatsrecht: Festschrift für Rudolf Bernhardt*, edited by Ulrich Beyerlin and others (Springer Verlag, 1995), p. 15; Pierre-Marie Dupuy, 'The Danger of Fragmentation or Unification of the International Legal System and the International Court of Justice', *NYU Journal of International Law and Politics* 31, (1998): p. 791.

[15] This predominant role is confirmed by the works of the ILC on the topic of identification of customary law. See ILC (n 1), Commentary to conclusion 13, para. (4). See also Robert Jennings, 'The Role of the International Court of Justice', *British Yearbook of International Law* 68, (1997), pp. 1–63.

[16] Jan Klabbers, '(I Can't Get No) Recognition: Subjects Doctrine and the Emergence of Non-State Actors', in *Nordic Cosmopolitanism: Essays in International Law for Martti Koskenniemi* (Martinus Nijhoff, 2003), pp. 355–57.

GIL is not possible through these institutions, but only that their vast authority is in practice less crucial than generally thought when it comes to channelling legal change, precisely because of their limited accessibility. It suffices to think of very well-known examples such as the concept of *erga omnes* norms, brought to prominence by the ICJ in *Barcelona Traction*,[17] or the principles of decolonization as set by the General Assembly throughout the 1960s and 1970s,[18] to realize that change—and even systemic change—is indeed possible through these channels, but this is the exception rather than the rule.

The limited accessibility of these institutions leaves norm entrepreneurs in GIL—be they states or not—with little scope for manoeuvre, pushing change attempts to the periphery. Less central institutions with perhaps more limited but still considerable authority become then relevant.[19] The most obvious of these is the International Law Commission (ILC), which played a fundamental role in two cases: state-official immunity and the concept of international wrongful act.[20] In both, it provided an alternative to the more restricted and politicized multilateral and judicial pathways of the ICJ and the General Assembly. Being an expert body with no formal law-making capacities, the ILC lends itself to substantive discussions on controversial matters that are made possible because of its alleged technicality and apparent detachment from diplomatic concerns.[21] This lays the ground for the production of important norm-changing outputs vested with considerable institutional authority.[22] The best example of this is the Draft Articles on State Responsibility—the unavoidable reference on any question related to the law on state responsibility nowadays. But as the case of state-official immunities shows, achieving unanimity or even a majority at the ILC is not a given. Harnessing uptake by its members requires time and a good amount of compromise, and the requisite examination of the ILC's work at the GA's Sixth Committee gives states a weighty voice that sets the bar of success higher.[23]

[17] ICJ, *Barcelona Traction, Light and Power Company Limited (Belgium v Spain)* [1970] ICJ Rep 3, para. 34; see also Jörg Kammerhofer, 'Obligations Erga Omnes', in *Max Planck Encyclopedias of International Law* (Oxford University Press, 2024).

[18] Guy Fiti Sinclair, 'A Battlefield Transformed: The United Nations and the Struggle over Postcolonial Statehood', in *The Battle for International Law: South-North Perspectives on the Decolonization Era*, edited by Jochen von Bernstorff and Philipp Dann (Oxford University Press, 2019), pp. 257–77.

[19] Loveday Hodson, 'Women's Rights and the Periphery: CEDAW's Optional Protocol', *European Journal of International Law* 25, (2014): p. 561.

[20] Pedro Martínez Esponda, 'State Official Immunity', in *The Paths of International Law: Case Studies*, edited by Pedro Martínez Esponda and others (SSRN, 2023); Pedro Martínez Esponda, 'The Concept of Internationally Wrongful Act', in *The Paths of International Law: Case Studies*, edited by Pedro Martínez Esponda and others (SSRN, 2023).

[21] *Future Topic and Problems of the International Legislative Process Part V [1998] International Law Commission Fifty Years After: An Evaluation. Proceedings of the Seminar Held to Commemorate the Fiftieth Anniversary of the International Law Commission* (UN Publications, 2000), p. 111.

[22] Wouter Werner, 'The Making of Lawmaking: The ILC Draft Conclusions on the Identification of Customary Law', in *The Many Paths of Change in International Law*, edited by Nico Krisch and Ezgi Yildiz (Oxford University Press, 2023), pp. 129–49.

[23] Pemmaraju Sreenivasa Rao, 'International Law Commission (ILC)', in *Max Planck Encyclopedia of Public International Law* (Oxford University Press, 2017).

Another important peripheral venue that is often used in GIL is domestic courts.[24] Domestic courts are particularly relevant when non-state actors launch change attempts, as the state-official immunities and the effects doctrine cases show. *Pinochet* for the former and *Alcoa* for the latter are paradigmatic in this regard.[25] In both instances, domestic actors used the legal machinery of states on matters primarily concerning domestic law, but in doing so, they challenged prevalent understandings in international law, questioning international actors and pushing them to discuss new legal frameworks. However, and again, as these cases show, domestic courts are more useful when it comes to unsettling prevalent legal understandings and starting the process of legal change than they are in actually consolidating new rules. This is because their authority in GIL is generally limited, and they form part of a landscape of dispersed, diffuse authority.

Aside from domestic courts, other forms of authority sometimes play an important role in GIL. For instance, private associations, such as the *Institut de droit international*, and even academics on their own, can have an impact in supporting or rejecting change attempts. The case of self-defence against non-state actors provides a good example in this regard, where one professor, Olivier Corten, coordinated an influential statement by 243 international scholars opposing norm change.[26] But private forms of authority in GIL serve mostly the purpose of unsettling prevailing understandings around a norm and getting the process of change started. They do not normally become a main pathway on their own. Most expectations in GIL for norm change rest in the ICJ, the General Assembly, and the Security Council, despite their unavailability. However, as we explain in Chapter 6, peripheral institutions such as those with private authority are key in smoothing the way to more central sites.

The vacuum of authority left by the inaccessibility of central institutions in GIL, combined with the general lack of enforcement of international law, gives states an incentive to pursue their change interests on their own, without seeking institutional endorsement, through the state action pathway. This is the case especially with powerful states, which can often realize their change visions without any external endorsement. The US, in the case of the effects doctrine, and Israel, in the

[24] Antonios Tzanakopoulos, 'Domestic Courts in International Law: The International Judicial Function of National Courts', *Loyola of Los Angeles International & Comparative Law Review* 34, (2011): p. 133. See also ILC (n 1).

[25] Martínez Esponda, 'State Official Immunity' (n 20); Pedro Martínez Esponda, 'The Effects Doctrine of Jurisdiction', in *The Paths of International Law: Case Studies*, edited by Pedro Martínez Esponda and others (SSRN, 2023); UKHL. R v Bartle and the Commissioner of Police for the Metropolis and Others, ex parte Pinochet, 38 ILM 581 (HL 1999); UKHL. R v Evans and Another and the Commissioner of Police for the Metropolis and Others, ex parte Pinochet [1999] UKHL 17; US Circuit Court of Appeals. United States v Aluminum Co of America 148 F.2d 416 (US Circuit Court of Appeals, Second Circuit 1945).

[26] 'Plea Against the Abusive Invocation of Self-Defence as a Response to Terrorism', Centre de Droit International (June 2016), https://cdi.ulb.ac.be/wp-content/uploads/2016/06/A-plea-against-the-abusive-invocation-of-self-defence.pdf.

case of self-defence against non-state actors, are great examples of this.[27] In both instances, they implemented their views on international law unilaterally, even avoiding having multilateral discussions on these issues. The lack of broader institutional endorsement or argumentative credibility in these cases seems to have mattered less than the possibility of giving a legal justification—*any* justification—for a given course of action.[28] Similarly, states might be satisfied with destabilizing the understandings around a norm for a number of reasons, not least because it can reduce the legal constraints on a given strategic issue. We will return to questions of destabilized, unsettled norms in Chapter 7.

On issues that require broader coordination, change in GIL has a high threshold. Treaty-making is exceptional and requires huge diplomatic efforts. This is why, for instance, the ILC's Draft Articles on State Responsibility were, in the end, just put to the consideration of the General Assembly and not opened for a diplomatic conference, as had happened with the law of treaties or the law of the sea.[29] The failure of the United Nations Convention on Jurisdictional Immunities of States is also a case in point. Both matters had to navigate pathways with lower levels of politicization and formality, primarily through the ILC. To be sure, change and even counter-hegemonic change is possible through multilateral avenues—take, for instance, the momentous process of decolonization and the Declaration on Friendly Relations of 1970, which successfully travelled through the General Assembly[30]—but more often than not, the political capital for this is simply unreachable, obliging actors to redirect.[31]

These two phenomena—the incentive for unilateralism by the powerful and the difficulty of multilateral coordination for norm change—make GIL a field prone to norm ambiguity and discontinuities in norm consolidation.[32] States might actively evade authoritative institutional pronouncements—e.g., effects doctrine—or they

[27] Martínez Esponda, 'The Effects Doctrine of Jurisdiction' (n 25); Pedro Martínez Esponda, 'Self-Defense against Non-State Actors', in *The Paths of International Law: Case Studies*, edited by Pedro Martínez Esponda and others (SSRN, 2023).

[28] Fuad Zarbiyev, 'Of Bullshit, Lies and "Demonstrably Rubbish" Justifications in International Law', *Völkerrechtsblog* (18 March 2022), https://voelkerrechtsblog.org/of-bullshit-lies-and-demonstrably-rubbish-justifications-in-international-law/.

[29] ILC, 'Fourth Report on State Responsibility, by Mr James Crawford, Special Rapporteur (A/CN.4/517 and Add.1)' para. 23; For an analysis of strategies within the ILC, see Sandesh Sivakumaran, 'Beyond States and Non-State Actors: The Role of State-Empowered Entities in the Making and Shaping of International Law', *Columbia Journal of Transnational Law* 55, (2017); Fuad Zarbiyev, 'A Quiet Revolution in the Making? The Changing State Authority in Treaty Interpretation', in *The Many Paths of Change in International Law*, edited by Nico Krisch and Ezgi Yildiz (Oxford University Press, 2023).

[30] Samuel Moyn and Umut Özsu, 'The Historical Origins and Setting of the Friendly Relations Declaration', in T*he UN Friendly Relations Declaration at 50*, edited by Jorge E Viñuales (Cambridge University Press, 2020).

[31] Sundhya Pahuja, *Decolonising International Law: Development, Economic Growth, and the Politics of Universality* (Cambridge University Press, 2011), pp. 2–5.

[32] Pedro Martínez Esponda, 'Norm-Instability as a Strategy in International Lawmaking: The Case of Self-Defence against Non-State Actors', in *The Many Paths of Change in International Law*, edited by Nico Krisch and Ezgi Yildiz (Oxford University Press, 2023), p. 69.

might purposefully stay silent on an issue—e.g., self-defence against non-state actors. They might fiercely oppose change when it touches upon their interests but support it in other cases—e.g., state-official immunities. Or they might support a given normative outcome but be unwilling or unable to formalize it—e.g., the concept of internationally wrongful act. This shows that GIL rules and the practices around them mostly stay—or are kept—in a state of low precedential value, leaving room for contestation and setting a low argumentative and political burden for defiance.[33]

All of this underlines the obvious fact that states play a key systemic role in the dynamics of change in GIL.[34] But if this is true, it is certainly not the case that other actors are powerless.[35] The bureaucratic, judicial, and private authority pathways remain plausible options for non-state entrepreneurs. The case studies provide ample evidence of this. In the case of state-official immunities, a network of non-governmental organizations (NGOs) made frequent use of domestic courts to bring international criminals to trial, thereby successfully destabilizing the law on immunities. Academics also played a crucial role in gaining the upper hand at the ILC and pushing for change, even against the strong opposition of major global powers.[36] Likewise, in the case concerning the concept of internationally wrongful act, it is remarkable to what extent Roberto Ago, as an individual scholar, managed to channel his own views on state responsibility into the deliberations of the ILC.[37] Key to both cases was the ability of non-state actors to capitalize on broader, global ideational trends. In the case of state-official immunity, this was the powerful narrative against impunity in the 1990s, coupled with the mainstreaming of human rights and international criminal law. For the concept of internationally wrongful act, it was the rising acknowledgement of *erga omnes* and *jus cogens* norms—or, rather, the end of the bilateral paradigm of international obligations. Discursive openings in international society thus facilitate the use of alternative paths, helping to break the dominance of states in GIL law-making.

To sum up, change in GIL is marked by a series of features that are common to all international legal fields, but that are more visible and decisive here: the limited access to institutional authority, the need for depoliticised pathways of change, the

[33] This assessment speaks directly to Verdier and Voeten's approach to the force of customary international law as based in the precedential value of the practices around them. See Verdier and Voeten (n 4).

[34] This point is at the core of formalist accounts of norm-making and norm-transformation in international law, which tend to emphasize the role of states as 'primary subjects of the international legal system . . . possessing a general competence, [and] play[ing] a pre-eminent role in the formation of customary international law', or in the context of treaty interpretation, where the ILC has noted the 'primary role of the States parties to a treaty who are the masters of the treaty and are ultimately responsible for its application'. See ILC (n 1), Conclusion 4, para. (2); ILC (n 3), Conclusion 5, para. (10).

[35] Margaret E Keck and Kathryn Sikkink, *Activists Beyond Borders: Advocacy Networks in International Politics* (Cornell University Press, 2014), pp. 1–38.

[36] Martínez Esponda, 'State Official Immunity' (n 20).

[37] Martínez Esponda, 'The Concept of Internationally Wrongful Act' (n 20).

self-interest and zero-sum politics of state-dominated politics, and the importance of discursive openings for non-state norm entrepreneurs.

Law of the Sea

Law of the Sea (LoS) is one of the oldest and most structured fields of international law.[38] While the earliest developments in the field date back to the fifteenth century,[39] its central piece, the United Nations Convention on the Law of the Sea (UNCLOS), often described as 'a constitution for the oceans', was adopted in 1982.[40] With seventeen parts, 320 articles, and nine annexes, the UNCLOS is the result of a long multilateral treaty-making process aimed at formulating comprehensive rules for state rights and obligations in the sea. In addition to its comprehensive nature, this treaty also had a complicated, highly politicized negotiation history. In fact, it was not entirely clear whether it would ever come into force until the 1994 Implementation Agreement cleared some disagreements.[41] These two features, namely the UNCLOS's comprehensiveness and its complicated negotiation history, have led experts like Malcolm Evans to describe the possibility of change through renegotiating UNCLOS not only as practically inconceivable but also as a high-risk enterprise.[42] As a result, the dynamism in this field mainly comes from three main sources: expert-based solutions, legal interpretation, and initiatives led by peripheral authorities, although treaty-making through multilateral channels is not impossible, as proven by the 2023 High Seas Treaty.[43] Hence, in this field, change initiatives are often led and processed by secretariats, bureaucrats, and international courts, with the ICJ leading the charge instead of the International Tribunal of the Law of the Sea (ITLOS), the specialized tribunal under UNCLOS.[44] ITLOS—facing direct competition from the ICJ and arbitral

[38] Seline Trevisanut, 'The Future of the Oceans: The Role of Human Rights and International Environmental Law in Shaping the Law of the Sea', in *The Many Paths of International Law*, edited by Nico Krisch and Ezgi Yildiz (Oxford University Press, 2023).

[39] The origins of the field are traced to a Papal Bull of 1493, dividing the oceans between Spain and Portugal; see P Hoagland, J Jacoby and M E Schumacher, 'Law of the Sea', in *Encyclopedia of Ocean Sciences*, edited by John H Steele (Academic Press, 2001), p. 1481.

[40] Tommy T B Koh, 'A Constitution for the Oceans' (Remarks by the President of the Third United Nations Conference on the Law of the Sea, 1982)', https://www.un.org/depts/los/convention_agreements/texts/koh_english.pdf.

[41] Surabhi Ranganathan, *Strategically Created Treaty Conflicts and the Politics of International Law* (Cambridge University Press, 2014), p. 167.

[42] House of Lords, International Relations and Defence Committee, 'UNCLOS: Fit for Purpose for the 21st Century, Witness Statement from Sir Malcolm Evans' (20 October 2021), https://committees.parliament.uk/oralevidence/2853/pdf/.

[43] For a comprehensive assessment of change in LoS, see Rozemarijn Roland Holst, *Change in the Law of the Sea: Context, Mechanisms and Practice* (Brill Nijhoff, 2022).

[44] For example, in the context of continental shelf delimitation, out of twenty-six international rulings, only two belong to the ITLOS, fourteen to the ICJ, and ten to arbitral tribunals. For more, see Ezgi Yildiz and Umut Yüksel, 'The Defocalizing Effect of International Courts: Evidence from Maritime Delimitation Practices', *Review of International Organizations* 20, (2025): p. 825.

tribunals, which have been operational longer—has a relatively small docket and limited influence.[45] In all of these efforts, states appear to be catalysing multilateral, bureaucratic, or judicial efforts, yet they also often (although less visibly) channel private interests.[46]

This field has always dealt with questions of higher stakes, such as access to resources or control over maritime areas. These questions were at the centre of negotiations of the UNCLOS, which took place between 1973 and 1982 and included both developed and developing countries.[47] There was a series of heated debates, for example, around the limits of freedom at sea and access to resources, especially those that lie beyond national jurisdiction. The latter topic, in particular, almost brought negotiations to a halt because it revealed the irreconcilable differences between the interests of industrialized Western countries and the Global South.[48] Developing states, gathered under the banner of Group 77, acted as a solid block during the negotiations, which served as a fertile ground to test their ideas for the new international economic order (NIEO).[49] They managed to include the revolutionary concept of the common heritage of humankind into the treaty, despite the opposition from industrialized states.[50] Yet, they made compromises on other issues, such as allowing transit through straits or forgoing technology transfer and steady funding to the Enterprise—the stillborn independent mining organization under the UNCLOS.[51]

The deadlock in the negotiations left several questions unanswered. For example, while the essential details of the seabed mining regime were sketched out, the operational rules were left to the International Seabed Authority (ISA) to

[45] Jacob Katz Cogan, 'Competition and Control in International Adjudication', *Virginia Journal of International Law* 48, (2007): p. 411; Philippe Sands, 'Of Courts and Competition: Dispute Settlement under Part XV of UNCLOS', *Contemporary Developments in International Law*, (2016): p. 789. But see also Lan Ngoc Nguyen, *The Development of the Law of the Sea by UNCLOS Dispute Settlement Bodies* (Cambridge University Press, 2023).

[46] Marianthi Pappa, *Non-State Actors' Rights in Maritime Delimitation: Lessons from Land* (Cambridge University Press, 2021); Eduardo Guedes Pereira and Marianthi Pappa, 'The Relationship between Host Government Contracts for Oil and Gas Activities and Public Participation', in *Regulation of Extractive Industries: Community Engagement in the Arctic*, edited by Rachael Lorna Johnstone and Anne Merrild Hansen (Routledge, 2020); Felix Mallin and Mads Barbesgaard, 'Awash with Contradiction: Capital, Ocean Space and the Logics of the Blue Economy Paradigm', *Geoforum* 113, (2020): p. 121.

[47] Alan Beesley, 'The Negotiating Strategy of UNCLOS III: Developing and Developed Countries as Partners: A Pattern for Future Multilateral International Conferences', *Law and Contemporary Problems* 46, (1983): p. 183.

[48] David L Larson, 'Deep Seabed Mining: A Definition of the Problem', *Ocean Development & International Law* 17(4), (1986): p. 271.

[49] Elizabeth Borgese, 'The New International Economic Order and the Law of the Sea', *San Diego Law Review* 14, (1977): p. 584. See also Allan G Kirton and Stephen C Vasciannie, 'Deep Seabed Mining Under the Law of the Sea Convention and the Implementation Agreement: Developing Country Perspectives', *Social and Economic Studies* 51(2), (2002): pp. 63.

[50] Larson (n 48), p. 275.

[51] Aline Jaeckel, Jeff A Ardron and Kristina M Gjerde, 'Sharing Benefits of the Common Heritage of Mankind: Is the Deep Seabed Mining Regime Ready?', *Marine Policy* 70, (2016): p. 198.

determine.[52] When the ISA began its work in 1996, power constellations had already changed, and with less political pressure, the ISA could offer bureaucratic solutions by issuing technical-looking mining regulations that substantially shaped how the regime operates.[53] Led by the Secretariat and the Legal and Technical Commission (a legislative body of the ISA, composed of scientists and practitioners often linked with the industry), these mining codes effectively phased out site-banking rules for some minerals, namely polymetallic nodules and cobalt-rich crusts.[54] Yet, at the same time, the Secretariat acted as a gatekeeper and, despite repeated calls from member states, refused to end site-banking for other minerals.[55] This case nicely demonstrates that, while change attempts through multilateral negotiations can be arduous, bureaucratic solutions of a technical nature—especially when supported by scientists and private interests—can render legally or politically complicated change attempts more palatable.[56] The ISA, moreover, as an inter-governmental body created by states specifically for the purpose of providing governance solutions on matters regarding the seabed, is vested with an additional layer of influence. This mixture of technical expertise and a state-based mandate makes for an efficient form of authority in international law, not too different from that of the ILC or the human rights treaty bodies.[57]

Another question left unanswered was the method for continental shelf delimitation.[58] Once it became clear that the UNCLOS would enter into force with vague rules around continental shelf delimitation, the ICJ attempted to fill in the gaps left in the Convention.[59] More specifically, it began proactively devising a predictable yet flexible delimitation method starting with the 1993 *Jan Mayen* ruling.[60] In the 2009 *Black Sea* case, the ICJ went even further and introduced the three-stage approach by merging the principles of equidistance and equity—i.e., starting the delimitation exercise by drawing a median line between opposing coasts and

[52] Ezgi Yildiz, 'Revising the "Parallel System of Access" Rule for Seabed Mining', in *The Paths of International Law: Case Studies*, edited by Pedro Martínez Esponda and others (SSRN, 2023).

[53] ISBA, 'Considerations relating to the regulations for prospecting and exploration for hydrothermal polymetallic sulphides and cobalt-rich crusts in the Area' (29 May 2001) ISBA/7C/2.

[54] Site-banking is a part of the parallel system of access rule under the UNCLOS, according to which contractors would need to propose two areas of exploration of roughly equal value. They would mine one area and the other one would be reserved to be mined in the name of the international community.

[55] ISBA, 'Issues related to the possible alignment of the Authority's regulations on prospecting and exploration concerning the offer of an equity interest in a joint venture arrangement' (6 February 2018) ISBA/24/LTC/4, p. 2, s. 6.

[56] For a good critique of the current setup of the seabed regime, see Marc-Andrej Felix Mallin, 'From Sea-Level Rise to Seabed Grabbing: The Political Economy of Climate Change in Kiribati', *Marine Policy* 97, (2018): p. 244.

[57] Sivakumaran (n 29), p. 307.

[58] The rules around continental shelf delimitation are under UNCLOS's Articles 74(1) and 83(1).

[59] Ezgi Yildiz, 'The Equidistance Principle', in *The Paths of International Law: Case Studies*, edited by Pedro Martínez Esponda and others (SSRN, 2023).

[60] ICJ, *Maritime Delimitation in the Area between Greenland and Jan Mayen (Denmark v Norway)* (Judgment) [1993] ICJ Rep 38, para. 64.

correcting it as circumstances require.[61] Our study shows that this three-stage method is primarily acknowledged by other international courts and tribunals, and academics, yet it is not uniformly followed by all states.[62] On this issue, the ICJ's attempt to clarify and shape the law thus largely failed to move states' positions, which had often been defined at an earlier stage.

In addition to its high-stakes nature, the field is also open to changes brought by technological advancements and increased environmental concerns—admittedly not the main focus of UNCLOS.[63] Some of these concerns could only be processed by peripheral authorities, as we see in the case of the role of the Food and Agriculture Organization (FAO) in curbing and deterring illegal, unreported, and unregulated (IUU) fishing.[64] FAO had been involved in fisheries management since the late 1970s, and it specifically targeted the IUU problem in the late 1990s in response to an Australia-led initiative.[65] The FAO was the path of least resistance, becoming the catalyst when other pathways became frustrated—the most emblematic was the failure of Australia's proposal to amend the UNCLOS.[66] In particular, the FAO spearheaded the 2009 Agreement on Port State Measures to address IUU fishing to complement the UNCLOS, which only sets out obligations for the flag states and coastal states (mainly in the context of responding to pollution from vessels).[67] While this agreement only attracted eighty-four states—yet including great powers such as the US, China, and European countries—it served as a reference point for discussions to address IUU fishing.[68] The agreement also, to a certain extent, solidified the previously sporadic practice of states enforcing port state authority to battle IUU fishing, while falling short of fully consolidating this new understanding, with port state jurisdiction remaining 'permissive, not mandatory',[69] and serious enforcement gaps remaining.[70] More recently, it is

[61] ICJ, *Maritime Delimitation in the Black Sea (Romania v Ukraine)* (Judgment) [2009] ICJ Rep 61, para. 116.

[62] Ezgi Yildiz and Umut Yüksel, 'Understanding the Limitations of Behavioralism: Lessons from the Field of Maritime Delimitation', *German Law Journal* 23(3) (2022): p. 413; Yildiz and Yüksel (n 44).

[63] Benjamin K Sovacool and Kelly E Siman-Sovacool, 'Creating Legal Teeth for Toothfish: Using the Market to Protect Fish Stocks in Antarctica', *Journal of Environmental Law* 20, (2008): p. 15.

[64] Kevin Bray, 'A Global Review of Illegal, Unreported and Unregulated (IUU) Fishing' (2000) AUS:IUU/2000/6, http://www.fao.org/3/y3274e/y3274e08.htm#fn67. For our case study, see Ezgi Yildiz, 'The Emergence of Port State Measures Against IUU Fishing', in *The Paths of International Law: Case Studies*, edited by Pedro Martínez Esponda and others (SSRN, 2023).

[65] S M Garcia, 'Ocean Fisheries Management: The FAO Programme', in *Ocean Management in Global Change*, edited by Paolo Fabbri (Elsevier Applied Science, 1992), p. 399.

[66] CCAMLR, 'Report of the Twenty-first Meeting of the Commission' (21 October–1 November 2002), s. 8.62–8.73, https://www.ccamlr.org/en/ccamlr-xxi.

[67] Erik J Molenaar, 'Port State Jurisdiction', in *Max Planck Encyclopedias of International Law* (Oxford University Press, 2014).

[68] Erik J Molenaar, 'Port State Jurisdiction to Combat IUU Fishing: The Port State Measures Agreement', in *Recasting Transboundary Fisheries Management Arrangements in Light of Sustainability Principles*, edited by Dawn A Russell and David L VanderZwaag (Brill, 2011), pp. 369–86.

[69] Maria Gavouneli, *Functional Jurisdiction in the Law of the Sea* (Brill Nijhoff, 2007), p. 44.

[70] Gabriela A Oanta, 'Illegal Fishing as a Criminal Act at Sea', in *Crimes at Sea*, edited by K N Trapp and E Papastavridis (Brill, 2014).

noteworthy that the issue of IUU fishing was addressed through yet a different, peripheral path: the World Trade Organization (WTO) Agreement on Fisheries Subsidies, adopted at the 12th Ministerial Conference (MC12) on 17 June 2022, and which requires the acceptance by two-thirds of the WTO membership to enter into force.[71]

Overall, the centrality of the UNCLOS and its comprehensive yet outdated nature in an evolving field of regulation have largely informed the way change transpires in this field and pushed the change attempts to alternative paths[72]—including interpretive change, legal change of a technical nature endorsed by bureaucratic authorities, as well as complementary initiatives led by peripheral authorities.

International Human Rights Law

International human rights law (IHRL), more than other fields of international law, is structured around a multitude of conventional norms. The Universal Declaration of Human Rights (UDHR)—a non-binding instrument—has served as the basis on which a vast network of universal and regional treaties has come to populate the field during the second half of the twentieth century and the first decades of the twenty-first.[73] Some of these are broad universal conventions covering wide areas of human rights, some others are also universal but issue-specific and often with moderate authority, and yet others are regional but also often more authoritative and all-encompassing in substance. At first sight, then, IHRL is largely the product of intense, formal multilateral treaty-making with states in the driver's seat.

This image is, however, incomplete—if not misleading. The intricate network of human rights treaties provides only the skeleton of a much more complex legal field where most norm entrepreneurship takes place through other pathways, mainly the bureaucratic, judicial, and multilateral pathways. Authority in IHRL is dispersed and congregated around a multiplicity of actors and procedures with varying degrees of influence.[74] At the universal level, the UN provides the institutional framework of IHRL. This consists of three main institutional clusters. First,

[71] Mitchell Lennan and Stephanie Switzer, 'Agreement on Fisheries Subsidies', *International Journal of Marine and Coastal Law* 38, (2023): p. 161.

[72] Kate Purcell, *Geographical Change and the Law of the Sea* (Oxford University Press, 2019).

[73] UNGA Res 217 A (III), 'Universal Declaration of Human Rights' (10 December 1948) UN Doc Resolution 217 A (III); Jack Donnelly, *Universal Human Rights in Theory and Practice*, 3rd ed. (Cornell University Press, 2013), p. 92; Mark Mazower, 'The Strange Triumph of Human Rights, 1933-1950', *The Historical Journal* 47, (2004): p. 379; Edward Bates, 'History', in *International Human Rights Law*, edited by Daniel Moeckli, Sangeeta Shah and Sandesh Sivakumaran, 3rd ed. (Oxford University Press, 2018), pp. 18–19.

[74] See, e.g., Elizalde Pilar, 'A Horizontal Pathway to Impact? An Assessment of the Universal Periodic Review at 10', in *Contesting Human Rights: Norms, Institutions and PRACTICE*, edited by Alison Brysk and Michael Stohl (Edward Elgar Publishing, 2019).

there are the different treaty bodies—expert committees—created by states parties to each of the universal human rights treaties in order to oversee their implementation and provide interpretive guidance. Secondly, there is the inter-governmental UN Human Rights Council (HRC), which passes resolutions and conducts the Universal Periodic Review, as well as its subsidiary bodies, most notably the different special rapporteurs and working groups specializing in different rights and issues. And lastly, there is the UN High Commissioner for Human Rights and its Office, which not only performs a secretarial function vis-à-vis the treaty bodies and the HRC but also engages in substance and human rights diplomacy.[75]

In this configuration, while some authorities, such as the HRC, enjoy a more prominent place, others assume more peripheral roles. This is not entirely a disadvantage, however, as peripheral institutions tend to be less visible and thus below the radar in terms of political constraints; they are therefore often able to initiate or process change attempts of a more audacious nature. For example, in the development of the prohibition of violence against women, we can observe the catalysing force of the CEDAW Committee,[76] a peripheral institution.[77] Other, more central authorities walked on the path it opened and helped contribute to the solidification of the new norm protecting women from domestic violence.[78]

Furthermore, what sets this issue area apart from the other ones examined in this book is the presence of strong regional institutions.[79] In particular, regional human rights courts appear to be highly influential actors driving international legal change in most of the cases under study. They have typically undertaken this task by engendering judicial innovation[80] and by drawing on other regional and international courts' jurisprudence and thus entangling regional developments

[75] Jane Connors, 'United Nations', in *International Human Rights Law*, edited by Daniel Moeckli, Sangeeta Shah and Sandesh Sivakumaran, 3rd ed. (Oxford University Press, 2018); Miloon Kothari, 'From Commission to the Council: Evolution of UN Charter Bodies', in *The Oxford Handbook of International Human Rights Law*, edited by Dinah Shelton (Oxford University Press, 2013).

[76] Neil A Englehart and Melissa K Miller, 'The CEDAW Effect: International Law's Impact on Women's Rights', *Journal of Human Rights* 13, (2014): p. 22. For our case study, see Ezgi Yildiz, 'The Protection of Women from Domestic Violence', in *The Paths of International Law: Case Studies*, edited by Pedro Martínez Esponda and others (SSRN, 2023).

[77] Loveday Hodson, 'Women's Rights and the Periphery: CEDAW's Optional Protocol', *European Journal of International Law* 25, (2014): p. 561.

[78] Neil A Englehart, 'CEDAW and Gender Violence: An Empirical Assessment', *Michigan State Law Review*, (2014): p. 265; Ronagh J A McQuigg, 'The Responses of States to the Comments of the CEDAW Committee on Domestic Violence', *The International Journal of Human Rights* 11, (2007): p. 461; see also Natalie R Davidson, 'Everyday Lawmaking in International Human Rights Law: Insights from the Inclusion of Domestic Violence in the Prohibition of Torture', *Law & Social Inquiry* 47, (2022): p. 205.

[79] Wayne Sandholtz and Adam Feldman, 'The Trans-Regional Construction of Human Rights', in *Contesting Human Rights: Norms, Institutions and Practice*, edited by Alison Brysk and Michael Stohl (Edward Elgar Publishing, 2019), p. 83.

[80] Laurence R Helfer and Erik Voeten, 'International Courts as Agents of Legal Change: Evidence from LGBT Rights in Europe', *International Organization* 68, (2014): p. 77; Ezgi Yildiz, 'A Court with Many Faces: Judicial Characters and Modes of Norm Development in the European Court of Human Rights', *European Journal of International Law* 31, (2020): p. 73.

into a more universal web.[81] The case on the right to the truth brings this to the forefront.[82] This seemingly new right is fundamentally rooted in the context of enforced disappearances in Latin America, and it initially concerned only the forensic evidence related to the disappeared persons.[83] Yet, over time, it grew out of this limited context and came to include wider truth recovery in transitional justice settings.[84] This expansion was largely driven by civil society activists, and this emerging right was carefully constructed first in the jurisprudence of the UN Human Rights Committee and the Inter-American Commission on Human Rights, as well as the Inter-American Court of Human Rights during the 1970s and 1980s.[85] It is upon these foundations that this new right was later recognized in Europe in the late 1990s and 2000s—a development dubbed as 'Latin-Americanization of the European system'.[86]

Civil society actors have been at the forefront of most change attempts in this field[87]–through advocacy campaigns, individual complaints before human rights bodies, or through other mechanisms that call for states, international organizations, and corporations to respect human rights.[88] Civil society actors also tend to build coalitions in order to push for legal change.[89] While sometimes successful, as we see in the above-mentioned case of the right to the truth, such attempts do not always translate into fully accepted norm change. For example, in the struggle for introducing human rights obligations owed directly by corporations, the

[81] Niccolò Ridi, 'The Shape and Structure of the "Usable Past": An Empirical Analysis of the Use of Precedent in International Adjudication', *Journal of International Dispute Settlement* 10, (2019): p. 200.

[82] Pedro Martínez Esponda and Ezgi Yildiz, 'Right to the Truth', in *The Paths of International Law: Case Studies*, edited by Pedro Martínez Esponda and others (SSRN, 2023).

[83] Iosif Kovras, 'Explaining Prolonged Silences in Transitional Justice: The Disappeared in Cyprus and Spain', *Comparative Political Studies* 46, (2013): pp. 730, 733. See also Melanie Klinkner and Howard Davis, *The Right to the Truth in International Law: Victims' Rights in Human Rights and International Criminal Law* (Routledge, 2020).

[84] William A Schabas, 'Time, Justice, and Human Rights: Statutory Limitation on the Right to Truth?', in *Understanding the Age of Transitional Justice*, edited by Nanci Adler (Rutgers University Press, 2018).

[85] Patricia Naftali, 'Crafting a "Right to Truth" in International Law: Converging Mobilizations, Diverging Agendas?', *Champ pénal/Penal field* XIII, (2016); Yasmin Naqvi, 'The Right to the Truth in International Law: Fact or Fiction?', *International Review of the Red Cross* 88, (2006): p. 245.

[86] Christina M Cerna, 'The Inter-American System for the Protection of Human Rights', *Florida Journal of International Law* 16, (2004): pp. 195, 202.

[87] See, e.g., Heidi Nichols Haddad, *The Hidden Hands of Justice: NGOs, Human Rights, and International Courts* (Cambridge University Press, 2018); Mitali Jahan, 'How Legal Change Happened through Effective Policy Advocacy in Bangladesh: Adoption of the Domestic Violence Law', *Asian Journal of Women's Studies* 23, (2017): p. 401; Leonie M Huijbers and Claire M S Loven, 'Pushing for Political and Legal Change: Protecting the Cultural Identity of Travellers in the Netherlands', *Journal of Human Rights Practice* 11, (2019): p. 508.

[88] See, e.g., George Andreopoulos, 'Better Late than Never? The Evolving Responsibility of International Organizations', in *Contesting Human Rights: Norms, Institutions and Practice*, edited by Alison Brysk and Michael Stohl (Edward Elgar Publishing, 2019); Neli Frost, 'Transnational Corporations as Agents of Legal Change: The Role of Corporate Social Responsibility', *Cambridge International Law Journal* 5, (2016): p. 502.

[89] Nina Reiners, *Transnational Lawmaking Coalitions for Human Rights* (Cambridge University Press, 2021).

resistance faced by the original bid for binding obligations has provoked a shift towards less formal (although discursively powerful) standards such as the UN Guiding Principles on Business and Human Rights.[90]

Also crucial for understanding change in IHRL is the discursive and ideational force traditionally underlying human rights. This element often carries change attempts past political and institutional hurdles by gathering social legitimacy and creating strong political incentives for states and other actors not to block change, something especially visible during the post-Cold War period. Actively opposing the development of human rights norms is, for most states, especially in the West, costly and compromising.

This might be less so in the current context of increasing political backlash against human rights and other progressive narratives.[91] Indeed, in the last fifteen years, countries with historically poor democratic records like Russia, China, or Egypt have progressively grown more audacious in their strategies of discarding human rights and in their efforts to develop alternative and more authoritarian narratives.[92] Another trend in this direction has been the backlash in the form of non-compliance and national reassertion within the Council of Europe, a long-established regional system of human rights.[93] But perhaps the most consequential backlash against human rights has been the stance of the US vis-à-vis human rights during the first and second Trump administrations. The US government's long-standing reluctance to engage seriously with IHRL in international fora has intensified, manifesting not only in withdrawal from institutions like the HRC, but also more crucially in the decision to defund and vilify human rights agencies at all levels. All of these developments have put pressure on institutions to appear less like norm entrepreneurs and have emboldened states to elude human rights narratives ever more publicly.[94]

Yet, the discursive force of IHRL remains significant. Open defiance of human rights norm entrepreneurship by states is still rare. States wishing to spoil or block

[90] Dorothea Endres, 'Direct Human Rights Obligations of Corporations', in *The Paths of International Law: Case Studies*, edited by Pedro Martínez Esponda and others (SSRN, 2023).

[91] Nayyeri M Populism, 'Backlash Morality and Immigrants', *International Journal of Law in Context* 21, (2025): pp. 58–79.

[92] Leslie Vinjamuri, 'Human Rights Backlash', in *Human Rights Futures*, edited by Stephen Hopgood, Jack Snyder and Leslie Vinjamuri (Cambridge University Press, 2017), pp. 114–16. See also Tom Ginsburg, 'Authoritarian International Law?', *American Journal of International Law* 114, (2020): p. 221.

[93] Mikael Madsen, 'From Boom to Backlash? The European Court of Human Rights and the Transformation of Europe', *iCourts Working Paper Series*, no. 211 (2020): p. 15, https://papers.ssrn.com/sol3/papers.cfm?abstract_id=3681925; Mikael Rask Madsen, Pola Cebulak and Micha Wiebusch, 'Backlash against International Courts: Explaining the Forms and Patterns of Resistance to International Courts', *International Journal of Law in Context* 14, (2018): p. 197; Ezgi Yildiz, *Between Forbearance and Audacity: The European Court of Human Rights and the Norm Against Torture* (Cambridge University Press, 2023).

[94] Wayne Sandholtz, 'Resurgent Authoritarianism, Rights, and Legal Change', in *The Many Paths of Change in International Law*, edited by Nico Krisch and Ezgi Yildiz (Oxford University Press, 2023).

substantive norm change usually do it through silence, lack of endorsement, or legal technicality. This was visible in the attitude of most African and Asian states in the case of the right to the truth—who simply never endorsed the emergence of this right—and in the position of Global North countries on human rights obligations of corporations—with a continued insistence that only states can be direct bearers of obligations under IHRL.

Another reflection of the discursive force of IHRL can be found in the way norm entrepreneurs in other fields often resort to human rights in order to boost their arguments. This proved to be a highly successful strategy in a number of our cases: for instance, in the cases on the human right to a healthy environment, state official immunity, or rape as a war crime.[95] These strategies of discourse mobilization across issue areas are dealt with in more detail in Chapter 6.

International Humanitarian Law

International humanitarian law (IHL) is grounded in the idea that even wars are subject to rules and limitations.[96] This was traditionally understood as concerning mainly conflicts between states, meaning in turn that law-making in IHL was seen, since its inception and for over a century, essentially as a matter of diplomatic conferences and multilateral treaty-making.[97] Indeed, IHL originated and evolved mostly through these means from the early Geneva Conventions of 1864—concerned with the protection of people vulnerable in times of war[98]—to the Hague Conferences around the turn of the century—focused on the means of warfare[99]—all the way to the merger of both branches with the adoption of the Geneva Conventions of 1949 and later their Additional Protocols (APs) in 1977.[100] In a sense, this pace meant that treaties would regularly be 'updated' on the basis of the experiences of prior conflicts, making the law somewhat lag one war behind.[101]

[95] Dorothea Endres, 'The Human Right to a "Good" Environment', in *The Paths of International Law: Case Studies*, edited by Pedro Martínez Esponda and others (SSRN, 2023); Martínez Esponda, 'State Official Immunity' (n 20); Dorothea Endres, 'Rape as a War Crime', in *The Paths of International Law: Case Studies*, edited by Pedro Martínez Esponda and others (SSRN, 2023).

[96] Marco Sassòli, *International Humanitarian Law: Rules, Controversies, and Solution as to Problems Arising in Warfare* (Edward Elgar Publishing, 2019), p. 5.

[97] While early efforts to codify rules governing the conduct of war are visible in the domestic sphere (for example in the Lieber Code during the American Civil War) it is clear from those early times that there existed a perceived need among the international community to address the issue through international law-making. See Emily Crawford and Alison Pert, *International Humanitarian Law* (Brill Nijhoff, 2018), ch. 3.

[98] Sassòli (n 96), p. 7.

[99] ibid pp. 8 and 10.

[100] ibid pp. 10–11; François Bugnion, 'Law of Geneva and Law of The Hague', *International Review of the Red Cross* 83, (2005): pp. 901, 905.

[101] Sassòli (n 96), pp. 9–10.

The adoption of the APs in 1977, however, marked an important shift in the norm change dynamics of IHL, away from treaty-making.[102] An important element to explain this is that the actor constellation changed considerably, bringing the newly independent states to the negotiation table.[103] These had a number of concerns with which Western powers did not necessarily agree, notably the status of national liberation movements. The result was an increase in the political hurdles for treaty-making, as reflected by the 'acrimony, uncertainty, and tension' of the negotiations of the APs throughout three years, in contrast to the relative ease with which the Geneva Conventions had been adopted in 1949.[104] A sign of this was that, even if the APs were ratified by a majority of states, key actors like the US, India, Turkey, or Israel refused to ratify them—signalling that future treaty-making in IHL would very likely be yet more cumbersome.

But in addition to changes in geopolitics, the nature of war started changing, too. International armed conflict never ceased to occur, but it became less common, giving way to markedly non-international or mixed armed conflicts—often non-international armed conflicts with foreign states intervening. This arguably made it clearer to states that IHL was on the verge of applying to issues they considered within their domestic realm, raising politically sensitive questions on how to conduct operations within their own territories and against domestic actors to whom they were unwilling to extend combatant privileges. States—both Northern and Southern—gradually lost their incentives to engage in treaty-making, perceiving that they had more to lose than to win in negotiating IHL treaties.[105] This became particularly evident in the conceptualization of the US-led 'war on terror', which was purposefully kept outside the traditional logic of IHL.[106] Likewise, the avoidance of clear rules on issues such as combatant immunity and direct participation in hostilities exemplifies the impasse of treaty-making in IHL.[107]

[102] Giovanni Mantilla, 'From Treaty to Custom: Shifting Paths in the Recent Development of International Humanitarian Law', *Leiden Journal of International Law* 37, (2024): p. 359.

[103] Amanda Alexander, 'International Humanitarian Law, Postcolonialism and the 1977 "Geneva Protocol I"', *Melbourne Journal of International Law* 17, (2016): p. 15; Eyal Benvenisti, 'The Birth and Life of the Definition of Military Objectives', *International and Comparative Law Quarterly* 71, (2022): p. 269; Emma Stone Mackinnon, 'Contingencies of Context Legacies of the Algerian Revolution in the 1977 Additional Protocols to the Geneva Conventions', in *Contingency in International Law: On the Possibility of Different Legal Histories*, edited by Ingo Venzke and Kevin Jon Heller (Oxford University Press, 2021).

[104] Giovanni Mantilla, *Lawmaking under Pressure: International Humanitarian Law and Internal Armed Conflict* (Cornell University Press, 2020), p. 131.

[105] ibid pp. 133–34.

[106] Lisa Hajjar, 'International Humanitarian Law and "Wars on Terror": A Comparative Analysis of Israeli and American Doctrines and Policies', *Journal of Palestine Studies* 36, (2006): p. 21.

[107] Dorothea Endres, 'Direct Participation in Hostilities', in *The Paths of International Law: Case Studies*, edited by Pedro Martínez Esponda and others (SSRN, 2023); Emily Crawford, *Identifying the Enemy* (Oxford University Press, 2015).

Subsequent legal change therefore shifted onto less formal paths, especially customary law and expert-based guidance.[108] Actors, such as the International Committee of the Red Cross (ICRC) or UN-sponsored mechanisms, have become crucial norm entrepreneurs and, at the same time, institutional focal points vested with considerable authority. They operate mostly by means of expert-based studies and guidelines interpreting treaty rules.[109] Thus, the bureaucratic pathway has become crucial for the development of IHL. The ICRC—formally a private Swiss association vested with important mandates under IHL treaties—enjoys a unique position of authority, acting as an international organization, an enabler and driver of state conferences, a source of expert-based documents, and a lobbyist.[110] Moreover, it assumes an active role in norm entrepreneurship through its efforts on identifying customary international law and other outputs which are influential among the constituencies[111]—even if military practice varies in the recognition and implementation of these outputs.[112] The case concerning rules on the direct participation in hostilities, again, evidences the strengths and limits of the ICRC's law-changing capacity.[113]

But other important law-making efforts happen through alternative mechanisms operating more in the periphery. The best example of these is the attempts to develop rules for the conduct of hostile cyber-operations.[114] Two groups of experts convened under the aegis of the North Atlantic Treaty Organization (NATO) have produced a series of guidelines on this question—the *Tallinn Manuals*—and, in parallel to this, two processes have been set in motion at the UN; the Group of Governmental Experts on Advancing Responsible State Behaviour in Cyberspace in the Context of International Security, where government-appointed experts sit in their personal capacity, and the Open-Ended Working Group on the Developments in the Field of Information and Telecommunication in the Context

[108] This is not to say that treaty-making came to a standstill. Indeed, several Conventions have seen the light after the 1970s. See Sassòli (n 96), pp. 13–14. The point is that treaty-making ceased to be the dominant pathway for legal change.

[109] Anton O Petrov, *Expert Laws of War: Restating and Making Law in Expert Processes* (Edward Elgar Publishing, 2020).

[110] Marco Sassòli, Antoine A Bouvier and Anne Quintin, eds., *Un Droit dans la Guerre? Cas, Documents et Supports d'enseignement Relatifs à la Pratique Contemporaine du Droit International Humanitaire* (Comité International de la Croix-Rouge 2012), pp. 561–95; David P Forsythe, *The Humanitarians: The International Committee of the Red Cross* (Cambridge University Press, 2005).

[111] Sandesh Sivakumaran and Marko Milanovic, 'Assessing the Authority of the ICRC Customary IHL Study', *International Review of the Red Cross* 104, (2022): p. 1856.

[112] For the role of military manuals in particular see Charles Garraway, 'The Use and Abuse of Military Manuals', *Yearbook of International Humanitarian Law* 7, (2004): p. 425; Josef Teboho Ansorge and Tarak Barkawi, 'Military Manuals', in *Making Things International 2: Catalysts and Reactions* (University of Minnesota Press, 2016).

[113] Endres (n 107); Dapo Akande, 'Clearing the Fog of War?', *International & Comparative Law Quarterly* 59, (2010): p. 180; Emily Camins, 'The Past as Prologue: The Development of the "Direct Participation" Exception to Civilian Immunity', *International Review of the Red Cross* 90, (2008): p. 853.

[114] Nina Kiderlin, 'The Rules of Cyber Warfare', in *The Paths of International Law: Case Studies*, edited by Pedro Martínez Esponda and others (SSRN, 2023).

on International Security, which is composed of states. Very tellingly, however, the outcomes have received only partial support, not only by states but also by the ICRC, showing how divided positions are on the matter and how several militarily powerful states, like Russia or China, for instance, have little interest in seeing this change attempt move forward.

In contrast to other issue areas, courts play a relatively peripheral role in IHL, but they are nevertheless influential.[115] An example of this is the case study on the relation between human rights and humanitarian law, where the ICJ played a catalysing role in determining the content of the *lex specialis*.[116] Courts appear to be most influential when IHL is coupled with other issue areas, in particular ICL and IHRL—entanglements which are especially visible in non-international armed conflicts, where domestic courts often find themselves balancing norms from these different fields.[117] Such entanglements are also apparent in the jurisprudence of the International Criminal Tribunal for the former Yugoslavia (ICTY), the International Criminal Tribunal for Rwanda (ICTR), the hybrid tribunals for Cambodia, Lebanon, and Sierra Leone, and more recently the International Criminal Court (ICC), which, in dealing with international crimes, have interpreted a number of IHL rules. A clear example is the *Tadic* case with regard to the boundaries of non-international armed conflict and the applicability of war crimes in them.[118] These interactions of IHL with other fields have contributed considerably to the development of IHL in the last three decades.

A last point worth mentioning is the fragmentation of communities of practice in IHL. Every case study conducted for the project in this field evidences the extent to which discussions on the rules of IHL tend to divide two epistemic camps: 'humanitarian' lawyers on the one side, emphasizing human dignity and human rights as the central business of IHL, and 'military' lawyers on the other side, focusing on

[115] For the role of the International Court of Justice see Marko Milanovic, 'The Lost Origins of Lex Specialis: Rethinking the Relationship between Human Rights and International Humanitarian Law', in *Theoretical Boundaries of Armed Conflict and Human Rights*, edited by Jens David Ohlin (Cambridge University Press, 2016); Paola Gaeta, 'The Interplay Between the Geneva Conventions and International Criminal Law', in *The 1949 Geneva Conventions: A Commentary* (Oxford University Press, 2015).

[116] Dorothea Endres, 'The Relationship between IHRL and IHL', in *The Paths of International Law: Case Studies*, edited by Pedro Martínez Esponda and others (SSRN, 2023); A Guellali, 'Lex Specialis, Droit International Humanitaire et Droits de l'homme: Leur Interaction dans les Nouveaux Conflits Armés, '*Revue Générale de Droit International Public* 111, (2007): p. 539; Dorothea Endres, 'Whose International Law Is Changing? The Practice of Fragmented Communities Constructing Legal Change', in *The Many Paths of Change in International Law*, edited by Nico Krisch and Ezgi Yildiz (Oxford University Press, 2023).

[117] Sandesh Sivakumaran, *The Law of Non-International Armed Conflict* (Oxford University Press, 2012), p. 2.

[118] Naz K Modirazeh, 'Folk International Law: 9/11 Lawyering and the Transformation of the Law of Armed Conflict to Human Rights Policy and Human Rights Law to War Governance', *Harvard National Security Journal* 5, (2014): p. 225; Paola Gaeta and Abhimanyu George Jain, 'Individualisation of IHL Through Criminal Responsibility for War Crimes and Some (Un)Intended Consequences', in *The Individualization of War*, edited by Dapo Akande and Jennifer Welsh (Oxford University Press, 2021).

military necessity and the practicalities of armed conflict.[119] These two communities tend to have different understandings of the same concepts—*lex specialis*, or participation in hostilities, for example—which is made possible by the scarcity of institutions with overarching authority in the field. The result is often normative instability—uncertainty or lack of consensus on how a rule applies or what its concrete meaning is—which hinders the operation and implementation of IHL and leads to contested, unsettled norm change. While this is not unknown to other fields of international law, in IHL it is particularly pronounced.

International Criminal Law

International Criminal Law (ICL) has, for the most part, emerged and developed in historically brief yet contextually unique moments of crisis, followed by relatively long periods of inaction and, at times, regression.[120] While precursors can be found far back in history,[121] two such moments stand out in the modern history of ICL. The first was the end of the Second World War, with the Allied powers still aligned and in a position to impose the creation of the Nuremberg and Tokyo tribunals on the defeated Axis powers.[122] The second one, more relevant for contemporary ICL, was the end of the Cold War; a context involving political realignments at the global scale coupled with the quick rise of human rights and the 'fight against impunity' as dominant narratives of global justice.[123] The result was not only the establishment of ad hoc tribunals—the ICTY, ICTR, and several hybrid criminal courts—but also, and remarkably, the creation of a permanent court: the ICC, whose purpose was precisely to lock-in a universal system of international criminal justice. Also noteworthy in this second moment is the proliferation of domestic attempts to prosecute international crimes through exercises of universal jurisdiction since 1995.[124] More recent developments point to

[119] Endres, 'Whose International Law Is Changing?' (n 116), p. 267.

[120] See Hilary Charlesworth, 'International Law: A Discipline of Crisis', *Modern Law Review* 65, (2002): p. 377; Carsten Stahn, 'Evolution, Revolution or New Culture? The Changing Anatomy of International Criminal Justice (and Some of Its Curiosities)', *International Criminal Law Review* 15, (2015): pp. 1122, 1126–27.

[121] Robert Kolb and Damien Scalia, eds., *Droit International Pénal: Précis*, 2nd ed. (Helbing Lichtenhahn, 2012), pp. 27–33.

[122] Robert Cryer, *An Introduction to International Criminal Law and Procedure*, 3rd ed. (Cambridge University Press, 2014), pp. 115–25; M Sharīf Basyūnī, *Introduction to International Criminal Law*, 2nd rev. ed. (Martinus Nijhoff, 2013), pp. 29 and 1047–58; Kevin Jon Heller, *The Nuremberg Military Tribunals and the Origins of International Criminal Law* (Oxford University Press, 2011).

[123] Stahn (n 120), pp. 1122, 1124; Andrew Clapham, 'Préface', in *Immunités et violations graves des droits humains: vers une évolution structurelle de l'ordre juridique international?*, edited by Annyssa Bellal (Bruylant, 2011); Michel Cosnard, 'Les immunités du chef d'état', in *Le chef d'Etat et le droit international: colloque de Clermont-Ferrand* (A Pedone, 2002).

[124] Cherif Bassiouni, *Introduction to International Criminal Law*, 2nd rev. ed. (Martinus Nijhoff, 2013), pp. 29 and 1072–75; Antonio Cassese and Mireille Delmas-Marty, *Juridictions Nationales*

what could be a third moment in ICL, characterized by the multipolar geopolitics of the last five years. In particular, the Special Tribunal for the Crime of Aggression against Ukraine, created through an agreement between the Council of Europe and Ukraine in 2025 and which has the unique mandate to prosecute individuals bearing "greatest responsibility for the crime of aggression against Ukraine", could be an indication of this further inflection.[125] The unprecedented expansion of ICL seen in the 1990s gradually came to an end throughout the 2000s in a context of important contestation around the prosecutorial policies of the ICC, lack of membership by global powers, political opposition to and lack of interest in the creation of further ad hoc tribunals, and backlash against the use of universal jurisdiction. Despite all of this, however, the aim of transforming ICL into a fixed legal regime in less than two decades had by then largely been accomplished. This transformation took place primarily through the multilateral pathway. States felt the political need to respond to serious and widely broadcast crises like the genocides in Bosnia and Rwanda through international criminal justice. This is especially visible for the ad hoc tribunals of the 1990s—the ICTY and the ICTR—which were created through Chapter VII resolutions by the UN Security Council. Their statutes were the work of expert commissions set up by the UN Secretary General, but their approval and establishment were owed to the strong political will of members of the Security Council at that specific time in history—something unthinkable before the fall of the Berlin Wall or today. In the case of the ICC, the Rome Statute was the product of intense NGO activism, focused multilateral negotiations, and exceptional political alignment—despite strong contestation by the US and other major powers.[126]

But multilateralism is only the means through which institutions are set up in ICL. Once these are in place, the judicial pathway comes to the centre stage. Among the constituencies of ICL—judges, prosecutors, lawyers, scholars—courts have become the key sources of authoritative meaning.[127] Jurisprudence is therefore crucial in the development of ICL rules. The most important leaps in terms of normative development have been the product of institutions like the ICTY, the ICTR, and the ICC. Their case law has proven crucial in many regards: giving content to concrete norms through interpretation, but also opening interpretive avenues and settling structural normative quandaries in ways that would very likely

et Crimes Internationaux (Presses Universitaires de France, 2002); Fannie Lafontaine and William A Schabas, 'National Jurisdictions', in *International Criminal Law* (Cambridge University Press, 2016).

[125] Claus Kreß, 'On Recent Events Concerning the Crime of Aggression', *Journal of International Criminal Justice* 23, Issue 3-4 (2025), p. 405.

[126] John Washburn, 'The Negotiation of the Rome Statute for the International Criminal Court and International Lawmaking in the 21st Century', *Pace International Law Review* 11, (1999): p. 361; Nora Stappert, 'Practice Theory and Change in International Law: Theorizing the Development of Legal Meaning Through the Interpretive Practices of International Criminal Courts', *International Theory* 12, (2019): p. 33.

[127] Stappert (n 127).

not have been possible through alternative pathways. Legal change is therefore built into ICL mostly through the articulation of precedents and the reliance on the authority of previous pronouncements.[128]

The ICTY is paradigmatic of this. Despite its limited mandate, it served as a channel for hugely influential norm developments going well beyond its jurisdictional sphere, and even beyond ICL.[129] Two of the three ICL cases in the project reflect this: the inclusion of rape into the catalogue of war crimes and the applicability of war crimes to non-international armed conflict feature the ICTY as a central institutional channel for norm change.[130] Similar influential developments stemmed from the ICTR and the ICC. At the same time, attempts to influence broader norms of general international law, like those concerning attribution of non-state actor behaviour to states—the debate between 'overall' and 'effective' control in the ICTY and the ICJ—have mostly been unsuccessful.[131] With the clear exception of IHL, the authority of ICL courts outside their field is admittedly low.[132]

Now, behind the façade of institutional identity, courts often reflect the entrepreneurism of other actors. The initiative and interests of judges, prosecutors, and external activists have a succinct force in directing legal change.[133] One prominent example is the construction of the 'ideal victim' as a strategic device to channel legal change, most visibly seen in the case of the mainstreaming of sexual violence into ICL jurisprudence.[134] This is particularly evident in the way in which rape emerged as a war crime, which relied on a combination of individual efforts from within and without the tribunals and the court, and the focus on women as victims and men as perpetrators.[135] But the power of certain actors—notably prosecutors—to steer the direction of judicial institutions has also led to significant criticisms of selectivity,

[128] ibid.

[129] Alexandra Huneeus, 'International Criminal Law by Other Means: The Quasi-Criminal Jurisdiction of the Human Rights Courts', *American Journal of International Law* 107, (2013): p. 1; Cherif Bassiouni, 'The History of Universal Jurisdiction and Its Place in International Law', in *Universal Jurisdiction: National Courts and the Prosecution of Serious Crimes under International Law*, edited by Stephen Macedo (University of Pennsylvania Press, 2004).

[130] Endres, 'Rape as a War Crime' (n 95); Nina Kiderlin, 'War Crimes in Non-International Armed Conflicts', in *The Paths of International Law: Case Studies*, edited by Pedro Martínez Esponda and others (SSRN, 2023).

[131] Stefan Talmon, 'The Responsibility of Outside Powers for Acts of Secessionist Entities', *The International and Comparative Law Quarterly* 58, (2009): p. 493.

[132] Hortensia D T Gutierrez Posse, 'The Relationship between International Humanitarian Law and the International Criminal Tribunals', *International Review of the Red Cross* 88, (2006): p. 65.

[133] Masahiro Kurosaki, 'The Fight against Impunity for Core International Crimes: Reflections on the Contribution of Networked Experts to a Regime of Aggravated State Responsibility', in *Experts, Networks and Institutional Change* (Cambridge University Press, 2017); Stahn (n 120), pp. 1122, 1129; Heidi Nichols Haddad, *The Hidden Hands of Justice: NGOs, Human Rights, and International Courts* (Cambridge University Press, 2018), pp. 109–62.

[134] Christine Schwöbel-Patel, *Marketing Global Justice: The Political Economy of International Criminal Law* (Cambridge University Press, 2021), pp. 127–50.

[135] Pam Spees, 'Women's Advocacy in the Creation of the International Criminal Court: Changing the Landscapes of Justice and Power', *Journal of Women in Culture and Society* 28, (2003): p. 1233; Phillip Weiner, 'The Evolving Jurisprudence of the Crime of Rape in International Criminal Law', *Boston College Law Review* 54, (2013): p. 1207; Janet Halley, 'Rape at Rome: Feminist Interventions in

claiming that courts target only certain groups of people and ignore other equally culpable parties.[136] In fact, much backlash against the ICC traditionally stemmed from its focus on African defendants, which raised deep questions about double standards and intervention.[137] This backlash, in turn, might in the long run have unchained norm change processes, as hinted by several shifts in the prosecutorial strategies of the ICC's prosecutors in recent years.[138]

More explicit than in other issue areas is the entanglement between the national and international spheres of ICL.[139] This is clearly reflected in the logic of subsidiarity, manifested in the Rome Statute and underlying the entire field. The principle allocates the task of prosecuting international crimes primarily to the states that exercise territorial or personal jurisdiction over international criminals. This jurisdictional distribution, and thus the entanglement of national and international law, has nonetheless been the object of dispute. As the case study on universal jurisdiction shows, several states—mostly European—have attempted to set up domestic legal frameworks to prosecute international crimes over individuals who do not fall under their territorial or personal jurisdiction.[140] This push for universal jurisdiction has been led especially on the state action pathway. However, the backlash felt by legislators, judges, and prosecutors when attempting to try nationals of major global powers has been enormous, forcing norm entrepreneurs to readjust their strategies and adopt a more limited version of universal jurisdiction—requiring the physical presence of the accused and the existence of some form of connection between the prosecuting state and the crime.[141] For the same reason, attempts to endorse universal jurisdiction through the multilateral, bureaucratic, and international judicial pathway have so far been unsuccessful.

In sum, change in ICL is characterized by acute sensitivity to geopolitical momentum as well as by a concentration of authority around courts, making the judicial pathway the central avenue for change. Actors such as prosecutors and civil society are able to achieve change by seeking judicial endorsement and by generating jurisprudential threads. Change can also be achieved through other pathways, as in the creation of international tribunals in the past and today,

the Criminalization of Sex-Related Violence in Positive International Criminal Law', *Michigan Journal of International Law* 30, (2008): p. 1.

[136] Asad G Kiyani, 'The Three Dimensions of Selectivity in International Criminal Law', *Journal of International Criminal Justice* 15, (2017): p. 624.

[137] Henry Lovat and Shaina Western, 'Behind Backlash: The ICC and "African Backlash" in Context', GCILS Working Paper Series no. 11 (2021).

[138] See, e.g., ICC-OTP, 'Strategic Plan 2019-2021, by M. Fatou Bensouda, Prosecutor', (2019).

[139] James Stewart and Asad Kiyani, 'The Ahistoricism of Legal Pluralism in International Criminal Law', *American Journal of Comparative Law* 65, (2017): p. 393.

[140] Nina Kiderlin and Pedro Martínez Esponda, 'Universal Jurisdiction', in *The Paths of International Law: Case Studies*, edited by Pedro Martínez Esponda and others (SSRN, 2023).

[141] Luc Reydams, *Universal Jurisdiction: International and Municipal Legal Perspectives* (Oxford University Press, 2004).

potentially through attempts at codifying crimes against humanity, which have so far transited mostly through the bureaucratic and multilateral paths.[142] Lastly, it is relevant to say that ICL as a field is entangled with other fields and with domestic institutions, allowing for increased dynamism in change processes.

International Environmental Law

The environment, as an object of regulation, involves three crucial traits largely shaping how the field of international environmental law (IEL) operates and conditioning how and through which pathways legal change materializes: the intense need for inter-state cooperation, the management of future risk, and the inclusion of technical progress. IEL is confronted with challenges that one state alone cannot solve, such as the effects of climate change or the management of cross-border rivers.[143] The field also seeks to manage risks that have not yet materialized, which introduces an element of scientific uncertainty. The extinction of endangered species or the depletion of the ozone layer are clear examples. Finally, and related to the second point, developments in IEL are guided by scientific discoveries, and the field itself is adaptive to rapid technical progress and technological innovation.[144] While bestowing a dynamic character to the field, this feature sometimes gives the impression that decisions and solutions in this field are of a technical, rather than a political or normative, nature.[145] As a result, on the surface, the suspension of political or normative concerns opens up space for more technocratic solutions, but in reality, as our case studies reflect, it is hardly possible to disentangle the political and normative from the technical.

A first element reflecting these dynamics is the fact that the field's historical development revolves around conferences and climate summits.[146] These structures—distinctive of IEL—are multistakeholder mechanisms through which states interact with international organizations, scientific experts, and, crucially, a large number of civil society organizations, producing normative outputs that become key elements of the field.[147] The Stockholm Conference of 1972 and the

[142] Leila Nadya Sadat, *Forging a Convention for Crimes against Humanity* (Cambridge University Press, 2011). See also ILC, 'Draft Articles on Prevention and Punishment of Crimes Against Humanity', (2019) UN Doc A/74/10.

[143] Anita M Halvorssen, 'The Origin and Development of International Environmental Law', in *The Origin and Development of International Environmental Law*, edited by Alam Shawkat and others (Routledge, 2013).

[144] Ulrich Beyerlin and Thilo Marauhn, *International Environmental Law* (Hart Publishing, 2011), p. 284.

[145] Theodore M Porter, *Trust in Numbers*, reprint ed. (Princeton University Press, 1996).

[146] Beyerlin and Marauhn (n 144), pp. 1–30; Edith Brown Weiss, 'The Contribution of International Environmental Law to International Law: Past Achievements and Future Expectation—The Evolution of International Environmental Law', *Japanese Yearbook of International Law* 54, (2011): p. 1.

[147] Brown Weiss (n 146), p. 5; Linda Malone and Scott Pasternack, *Defending the Environment: Civil Society Strategies to Enforce International Environmental Law* (Island Press, 2006).

Rio Conference in 1992 are paradigmatic here. While the former crystallized modern IEL as an autonomous field of international law, the latter solidified many of the principles and rules of the field,[148] including the notion of sustainable development.[149] Their concluding documents, the United Nations Stockholm Declaration on Human Environment and the Rio Declaration on Environment and Development, have had far-reaching influence on the development of IEL, both substantively and institutionally.[150]

The field is also populated by a more inclusive group of norm entrepreneurs. Its late birth date sets it apart from other issue-areas insofar as it is the only area in which newly independent states participated from the outset and immediately took part in the creation of the institutions structuring the field. This is reflected in structural aspects of the field, as for instance the fact that the notion of development did not come as an afterthought but, on the contrary, was directly linked to core principles of the field.[151] Civil society organizations and other non-state actors have also been crucial in the trajectory of IEL. This has been the case from the outset: an unprecedented participation of civil society organizations—250 NGOs were accredited—took part in the 1972 Stockholm Conference, having significant influence not only on the proceedings but also on the outcome. Since then, a large number of civil society organizations have taken part in conferences and played a significant role in environmental norm-making.[152]

Another key feature of IEL is the absence of central authorities and the resulting regime complexity: no single institution has the authority, let alone the formal competence, to issue hard or soft norms capable of inducing deference among all the actors across the field. A general authoritative pronouncement capable of influencing actors in IEL across the board, like the ICJ's advisory opinion on climate change issued in 2025,[153] is highly exceptional. Rather, international environmental agreements often overlap or operate in parallel to each other and have influence mostly within their own, limited communities of practice. They often

[148] UNGA, 'Rio Declaration on Environment and Development', (3–4 June 1992) UN Doc A/CONF.151/26 (Vol I); Brown Weiss (n 146), pp. 4–10.

[149] Sumudu Atapattu, *Emerging Principles of International Environmental Law* (Brill/Nijhoff, 2007), p. 7; Brown Weiss (n 146), p. 10.

[150] Most importantly, the 1972 Convention for the Prevention of Marine Pollution by Dumping of Wastes and Other Matters (adopted 29 December 1972) 1046 UNTS 120; the 1972 Convention for the Protection of World Cultural Heritage (adopted 16 November 1972) 1037 UNTS 151; the 1973 Convention on International Trade in Endangered Species of Wild Flora and Fauna (adopted 3 March 1973) 993 UNTS 243 (CITES).

[151] Peter H Sand, 'Origin and History', in *The Oxford Handbook of International Environmental Law*, edited by Lavanya Rajamani and Jacqueline Peel, 2nd ed. (Oxford University Press, 2021), pp. 56–57.

[152] Kal Raustiala, 'The "Participatory Revolution" in International Environmental Law', *Harvard Environmental Law Review* 21, (1997): p. 537; Elisabeth Corell and Michele M Betsill, 'NGO Influence in International Environmental Negotiations: A Framework for Analysis', in *International Environmental Governance* (Routledge, 2008).

[153] ICJ, *Obligations of States in respect of Climate Change* (Advisory Opinion) [2025] ICJ Rep 2025.

have their own system of monitoring and reporting, their own secretariat, and often their own separate financing facility.[154] This is a form of polycentric governance in the sense that authority and decision-making are exercised in different, formally independent sites that nonetheless operate on the basis of shared normative understandings—the principles of IEL and of general international law more broadly.[155] In terms of law-making, this allows for very dynamic norm development and particularly meandering trajectories, with many open doors for change agents, but very few pathways which are powerful enough to achieve overarching norm change on their own. In this context, change attempts in IEL tend to follow four main patterns: technical change through appendices to framework conventions, reliance on abstract but ubiquitous principles, spill-overs to neighbouring fields, and processes led by non-state actors.

The first of these patterns consists of the use of protocols and annexes to conventions to attempt change, coupled with law-making by conferences of the parties (COPs) or meetings of the parties (MOPs), moving beyond their original mandate.[156] This emphasizes the importance of the more informal and flexible solutions provided by the multilateral pathway, in addition to the involvement of private authorities such as experts and NGOs. The case study concerning the adoption of the notion of sustainable use in the CITES regime is an example of this. The divide between Southern African nations pushing for sustainable use and a preservationist group of mostly developed, Global North countries was resolved in favour of the former through a technical procedure adopted by the COP.[157] Instead of a lengthy treaty amendment process, this involved the introduction of new classification criteria and the reorganization of the species listed in different annexes.[158]

The second pattern visible in IEL change attempts, namely the reliance on principles, is the borrowing of overarching norms from national law into conferences and other venues. The precautionary principle, originating in German and Swedish law, is a good example of this.[159] Much like other principles, such as the 'polluter pays principle', the precautionary principle spread fast, functioning

[154] Brown Weiss (n 146), p. 7.

[155] Stephan Mark, Graham Marshall and Michael McGinnis, 'An Introduction to Polycentricity and Governance', *Governing Complexity: Analyzing and Applying Polycentricity*, edited by Andreas Thiel, William A Blomquist and Dustin E Garrick (Cambridge University Press, 2019).

[156] Beyerlin and Marauhn (n 144), pp. 265–80; Sand (n 151), pp. 56–58. See also Jutta Brunnée, 'COPing with Consent: Law-Making Under Multilateral Environmental Agreements', *Leiden Journal of International Law* 15, (2002): p. 1.

[157] Daniel Bodansky, 'The United Nations Framework Convention on Climate Change: A Commentary', *Yale Journal of International Law* 18, (1993): p. 451; Nele Matz-Lück, 'Framework Conventions as a Regulatory Tool', *Goettingen Journal of International Law* 1, (2009): p. 439.

[158] Peter H Sand, 'Whither CITES? The Evolution of a Treaty Regime in the Borderland of Trade and Environment', *European Journal of International Law* 8, (1997): p. 29.

[159] Meinhard Schröder, 'Precautionary Approach/Principle', in *Max Planck Encyclopedias of International Law* (Oxford University Press, 2014).

as a 'substantive principle' in the sense of being more of an actual norm than an abstract aspirational principle.[160] However, while this in-between nature makes principles ubiquitous, it also renders them hollow and unstable. This is precisely the case with the precautionary principle: despite its ubiquity—it has travelled to various subfields of IEL such as oceans, seabed, environment, watercourses, climate change, and biodiversity, as well as other fields of international law like human rights, trade, and investment[161]—the principle's legal nature and content are still uncertain while its impact is debated.[162]

The third widespread pattern is the interaction with other fields. Change attempts in IEL draw significant dynamism by establishing links to neighbouring fields, in particular human rights law, the law of the sea, trade and investment law, and security law.[163] IEL also exports changes to other fields—often 'greening' them—and flows through other forums to be fully realized, as in the case study on the emergence of a human right to a healthy environment.[164] In this case, several norm entrepreneurs turned to human rights institutions such as the UN treaty bodies after IEL institutions had initially failed to show receptiveness to their change attempts.[165] Once human rights precedents had been created, however, IEL institutions reconsidered and helped to consolidate the change.

International Trade Law

International trade law (ITL) as a field is structured around two sets of institutions. First, quite obviously, is the WTO, which in terms of membership, institutional complexity, and interpretive relevance has been the most prominent of the two, at least from its creation in 1994 to the crisis of the WTO's Appellate Body

160 In particular, 'no harm' and 'polluter pays' principles. Beyerlin and Marauhn (n 144), p. 59.

161 David L VanderZwaag, 'The ICJ, ITLOS and the Precautionary Approach: Paltry Progressions, Jurisprudential Jousting', *University of Hawai'i Law Review* 35, (2013): p. 617.

162 Ezgi Yildiz, 'The Precautionary Principle: Ubiquitous Yet Hollow and Marginal', in *The Paths of International Law: Case Studies*, edited by Pedro Martínez Esponda and others (SSRN, 2023); Patricia Birnie, Alan Boyle and Catherine Redgwell, *International Law and the Environment* (Oxford University Press, 2009), pp. 154–64.

163 Beyerlin and Marauhn (n 144), pp. 241–314.

164 See, e.g., Endres, 'The Human Right to a "Good" Environment' (n 95); Nina Kiderlin, 'General Exceptions under GATT Article XX', in *The Paths of International Law: Case Studies*, edited by Pedro Martínez Esponda and others (SSRN, 2023); Kiderlin and Martínez Esponda (n 140); Kiderlin (n 130); Endres, 'The Relationship between IHRL and IHL' (n 116).

165 For an overview on the activities of the UN Special Rapporteur on human rights and the environment, see https://www.ohchr.org/en/special-procedures/sr-environment. John H Knox and Ramin Pejan, 'Introduction', in *The Human Right to a Healthy Environment*, edited by John H Knox and Ramin Pejan (Cambridge University Press, 2018), p. 3. See also Dorothea Endres, 'Conceptualizing Legal Change as "Norm-Knitting" through the Example of the Environmental Human Right', *Leiden Journal of International Law* 36(4), (2023): p. 879.

in 2019.[166] Then, in parallel to the WTO regime, there exist over 350 regional or bilateral trade agreements,[167] many of which have emerged or been strengthened as a response to the stagnation of negotiations at the WTO since 2000, and which often address issues going beyond trade strictly speaking, as for instance investment or political cooperation between states—sometimes through the creation of major regional free trade areas.[168] These agreements, at least until 2019, operated in a mostly fragmentary way, having little normative interaction among each other or the WTO, and receiving less attention in ITL literature.[169] This contrasts with other fragmented legal fields, for example, IHRL, where regional courts and commissions regularly interact with each other and with the universal UN bodies, and are deemed central in the normative development of the field. In view of this, and of our project's main focus on change until 2020, our attention centres on the WTO regime.

Having made this caveat, ITL, seen as WTO law, is remarkable for its degree of isolation and centralization. Its legal sources are all based on the General Agreement on Tariffs and Trade (GATT) and the Uruguay Round agreements, and the WTO institutional framework encompasses most of what goes on in the field in terms of disputes, interpretation, and enforcement. Links are sought from the inside out but only seldomly: the WTO institutions and community perceive and treat their field largely as a self-contained regime,[170] even if they have publicly pretended otherwise.[171] The Appellate Body (AB) is seen—or at least was seen until its demise—as holding interpretive primacy.[172] This embeddedness in the WTO means that legal change in ITL travels fundamentally through the judicial path and, at least historically but less so nowadays, through the multilateral avenues of rounds of trade negotiations and ministerial conferences.

[166] Gregory Messenger, *The Development of World Trade Organization Law: Examining Change in International Law* (Oxford University Press, 2016), pp. 47–80.

[167] According to the WTO webpage, there were 373 regional trade agreements (multi- and bilateral) as of January 2025. See https://www.wto.org/english/tratop_e/region_e/region_e.htm.

[168] Malebakeng Agnes Forere, *The Relationship of WTO Law and Regional Trade Agreements in Dispute Settlement: From Fragmentation to Coherence*, vol 50 (Kluwer Academic, 2015), pp. 4–6.

[169] Joseph Weiler and Joseph H H Weiler, *The EU, the WTO, and the NAFTA: Towards a Common Law of International Trade?* (Oxford University Press, 2001); Thomas Cottier, 'The Common Law of International Trade and the Future of the World Trade Organization', *Journal of International Economic Law* 18, (2015): p. 3.

[170] See, e.g., the rejection by the AB of the precautionary principle: WTO Appellate Body, *European Communities—EC Measures Concerning Meat and Meat Products (Hormones)* (1998) WT/DS26/AB/R, para. 125.

[171] WTO Appellate Body, *US—Standards for Reformulated and Conventional Gasoline* (1996) WT/DS2/AB/R, para. 17; WTO Appellate Body, *US—Import Prohibition of Certain Shrimp and Shrimp Products* (1998) WT/DS58/AB/R, paras. 154–57.

[172] Gregory Shaffer, Manfred Elsig and Sergio Puig, 'The Extensive (but Fragile) Authority of the WTO Appellate Body', *Law & Contemporary Problems* 79, (2016): p. 237; Robert Howse, 'The World Trade Organization 20 Years On: Global Governance by Judiciary', *European Journal of International Law* 27, (2016): p. 9.

This reflects the fact that trade has historically been understood as essentially a matter of inter-state relations, in contrast, for instance, to the international investment regime, where private actors play a more direct role.[173] Governments in ITL function as focal points for domestic economic actors and interests, particularly in liberal democracies where chambers of commerce, trade unions, and associations of exporters and importers are important domestic political players and have considerable leverage with executive and legislative branches.[174] This has led to the development of domestic bureaucratic structures and governmental trade expertise to coordinate these interests and channel them into foreign trade policy. In planned economies, states play an even more important role in determining trade interests themselves and translating them into foreign trade policy.[175] Whether in market or planned economies, these aggregated domestic interests interact and reach compromises in the legal space of ITL—all through the representation of states. States are, therefore, at least formally, in the driving seat of change in international law.

Unsurprisingly, then, ITL has a long tradition of multilateral negotiation, which has yielded a highly codified field. An array of understandings having conventional status exist below the broad aegis of the GATT, the General Agreement on Trade in Services (GATS), the Trade-Related Aspects of Intellectual Property Rights Agreement (TRIPs), the Agreement on Subsidies and Countervailing Measures (SCM), the Anti-Dumping Agreement (AD Agreement), and the Agreement on the Application of Sanitary and Phytosanitary Measures (SPS Agreement). Even trade tariffs are the result of thorough inter-state bargaining. This degree of detail in conventional binding norms has perhaps no parallel in international law. It is, of course, the result of a particular political and ideological constellation that arose after the end of the Cold War. Coupled with significant pressure from the US and the EU, this constellation brought about a highly institutionalized multilateral trade regime with global scope.[176]

Yet, multilateralism in trade law has stalled considerably since the Doha Round started in 2001. The most relevant trade agreements in force today date back to the 1990s, and little multilateral norm-making has happened since then. The clearest explanation behind this is that the emergence of China, India, and several other rising powers has shifted the geopolitical equilibrium that gave birth to the WTO in 1994.[177] More broadly, however, there has been a dispute in the

[173] Michael John Trebilcock and Robert Howse, *The Regulation of International Trade*, 3rd ed. (Routledge, 2005), pp. 7, 8; Joanne Gowa and Soo Yeon Kim, 'An Exclusive Country Club: The Effects of the GATT on Trade, 1950-94', *World Politics* 57, (2005): p. 453.

[174] Peter Rosendorff, 'Domestic Politics and International Disputes (Chapter 8)', in *The Oxford Handbook of the Political Economy of International Trade*, edited by Lisa L Martin, 1st ed. (Oxford University Press, 2015).

[175] Daniel Yuichi Kono, 'Authoritarian Regimes', in *The Oxford Handbook of the Political Economy of International Trade*, edited by Lisa L Martin, 1st ed. (Oxford University Press, 2015), pp. 298–312.

[176] See John H Barton and others, *The Evolution of the Trade Regime: Politics, Law, and Economics of the GATT and the WTO* (Princeton University Press, 2006).

[177] See Amrita Narlikar, *International Trade and Developing Countries: Bargaining Coalitions in GATT and WTO* (Routledge, 2004); Matthew Stephen, 'Contestation Overshoot: Rising Powers,

trade community between neoliberal market liberalization and other social goals, and no compromise has been found so far. This stagnation of multilateralism is reflected in the failure of the Doha Round of trade negotiations.[178] Originally meant to accommodate the development interests of emerging and underdeveloped economies, the US and its Western allies refused to concede on key issues they thought risked putting them in a disadvantaged position.[179] The political bodies of the WTO have also failed to issue guidance on a range of contested issues, leaving important political disputes unsettled.[180]

The consequence of this multilateral lethargy was the rise of the judicial pathway as the main avenue for norm change in ITL.[181] At the time of the foundation of the WTO in 1994, considerable energy was set on reshaping and strengthening the mechanisms of dispute settlement that existed during the GATT era. The main outcomes of this institutional reinvention were the proper judicialization of the procedures and the creation of the AB through the Dispute Settlement Understanding.[182] This institution provided what other branches of international law lack: an institutional focal point capable of authoritatively establishing homogeneous interpretations of formal agreements.[183] Since then, and until not long ago, the AB became the necessary pivot of norm change in the international trade system. No discussion on any legal aspect of ITL could escape the authority of the AB, and no argument running against its jurisprudence could go very far.[184] Like no other authority in international law, the AB became the centre of gravity of its issue area.

The central role of the AB may have also contributed to the collapse of the system.[185] Since 2016, the US has upheld a policy of blocking the appointments of new AB members, to the point that today, the AB has no members left and has

NGOs, and the Failure of the WTO Doha Round', in *Contested World Orders*, edited by Matthew Stephen and Michael Zürn (Oxford University Press, 2019).

[178] Mitsuo Matsushita and others, *The World Trade Organization: Law, Practice, and Policy*, 3rd ed. (Oxford University Press, 2015), pp. 26, 27.

[179] Sungjoon Cho, 'The Demise of Development in the Doha Round Negotiations', *Texas International Law Journal* 45, (2010).

[180] Nicolas Lamp, 'Arrested Norm Development: The Failure of Legislative-Judicial Dialogue in the WTO', *Leiden Journal of International Law* 38, (2025): p. 570.

[181] Ingo Venzke, *How Interpretation Makes International Law: On Semantic Change and Normative Twists* (Oxford University Press, 2012), pp. 148–49.

[182] ibid.

[183] See, e.g., Richard H Steinberg, 'Judicial Lawmaking at the WTO: Discursive, Constitutional, and Political Constraints', *American Journal of International Law* 98, (2004): p. 247; Joost Pauwelyn, 'The Rule of Law without the Rule of Lawyers? Why Investment Arbitrators Are from Mars, Trade Adjudicators from Venus', *American Journal of International Law* 109, (2015): p. 761; Shaffer, Elsig and Puig (n 174).

[184] Venzke (n 181), p. 149. See also Shaffer, Elsig and Puig (n 172).

[185] Simon Lester, 'Ending the WTO Dispute Settlement Crisis: Where to from Here?', International Institute for Sustainable Development, (2 March 2022), https://www.iisd.org/articles/united-states-must-propose-solutions-end-wto-dispute-settlement-crisis.

ceased functioning.[186] This has provoked an unprecedented impasse in WTO dispute settlement whereby a party losing a procedure before a panel 'appeals into the void' of a non-functioning AB, thus prolonging disputes indefinitely. The US stance is, in part, a reaction to a perceived overreach of the institution in its case law and a string of rulings unfavourable to its interests.[187] At a deeper level, however, some argue that the AB's 'deviation from some of the basic tenets' of the neoliberal trade agenda of the Uruguay Round led to a conflict between this institution and the Western (especially US) trade policy elite.[188] Other authors see it more as a predictable effect of the shift in the geopolitics of trade and the improvement of the legal capacity—and consequently norm entrepreneurship—of rising economic powers, namely China, India, and Brazil.[189] The AB has been politically sensitive in responding to contestation and non-compliance,[190] but in the polarized context of global trade wars, responsiveness to one party is read as the rejection of others. Either way, this is a stark example of how an institutional system that is incapable of finding political equilibrium in its norm-change structures might collapse. One consequence is a shift in focus towards regional and mega-regional trade and investment agreements.

This shift from the multilateral pathway to the judicial pathway is reflected in the case studies conducted in this project on ITL. The earliest of these, the case on the Enabling Clause and the Generalized System of Preferences, is marked by the multilateral mobilization of developing states within the GATT and other fora like UNCTAD, with a very limited role of (quasi-)judicial institutions.[191] During this phase—prior to the creation of the WTO and its judicialized structure—developing countries saw it as the only option to act in coordination and to confront developed countries through multilateral diplomacy. In contrast, in the case of the general exceptions under GATT Article XX, norm entrepreneurs sought to obtain through dispute settlement and the AB what they had failed to obtain through negotiations during the Uruguay Round, namely an expansion of the grounds for exceptions to the basic GATT rules.[192] The judicial pathway proved very useful in this attempt.

[186] Mark A Pollack, 'Trump as a Change Agent in International Law: Ends, Means, and Legacies', in *The Many Paths of Change in International Law*, edited by Nico Krisch and Ezgi Yildiz (Oxford University Press, 2023), p. 61.

[187] See Office of the United States Trade Representative, 'Report on the Appellate Body of the World Trade Organization' (2020) https://ustr.gov/sites/default/files/enforcement/DS/USTR.Appellate.Body.Rpt.Feb2020.pdf.; James Bacchus and Simon Lester, 'The Rule of Precedent and the Role of the Appellate Body', *Journal of World Trade* 54, (2020): p. 183.

[188] Howse (n 172).

[189] Gregory C Shaffer, *Emerging Powers and the World Trading System: The Past and Future of International Economic Law* (Cambridge University Press, 2021), pp. 14–20.

[190] Jeff Kucik and Sergio Puig, 'The Appellate Body's Judicial Pathway: Precedent, Resistance, and Adaptation', in *The Many Paths of Change in International Law*, edited by Nico Krisch and Ezgi Yildiz (Oxford University Press, 2023), p. 249.

[191] Pedro Martínez Esponda, 'Differentiated Treatment in the GATT System', in *The Paths of International Law: Case Studies*, edited by Pedro Martínez Esponda and others (SSRN, 2023).

[192] Kiderlin (n 164).

And finally, in the case study concerning subsidies, China set out to change the definition of the term 'public bodies' in the Subsidies and Countervailing Measures (SCM) Agreement, with some degree of success—although triggering a political confrontation with the US that ended up in the AB's crisis.[193] Here again, the judicial pathway provided a means of change that would have been entirely impossible through the multilateral path. At the same time, it might be that the shortcomings of the judicial avenue in addressing political confrontation explain the backlash in the WTO system.

A last point worth stressing is that WTO law has been especially the target of norm-making activities in other fora, particularly along the lines of the contestation between market liberalization and other social goals. The Cartagena Protocol on Biosafety in the SPS context, the UNESCO Convention on Cultural Diversity, and WHO declarations on essential medicines in the TRIPS context are examples of this.[194] These developments suggest that, even if the structure of ITL is particularly anchored in the WTO regime and change in the core rules requires either multilateral or judicial action, some change in the periphery is also feasible under certain circumstances. The implications of trade in other domains are vast, and therefore change initiatives in other issue areas aimed at having an impact on ITL are not uncommon. The receptiveness of WTO institutions to these initiatives, and particularly the AB, however, has been uneven—while the AB professed not to read ITL 'in clinical isolation' from other areas of international law, it has often found ways of insulating itself from developments in other fields.[195]

International Investment Law

International investment law (IIL) has several features that make it unique and that manifest in the way its rules change. These include marked power asymmetries, highly dispersed institutional authority, a clear preference for the judicial pathway, and a general lack of transparency of decision-making and law-generating processes. Admittedly, these features are not unknown to other issue areas of international law; change in IIL does not radically differ from change in the rest of

[193] Nina Kiderlin, 'Subsidies and the Definition of "Public Bodies"', in *The Paths of International Law: Case Studies*, edited by Pedro Martínez Esponda and others (SSRN, 2023).

[194] Joost Pauwelyn, *Conflict of Norms in Public International Law* (Cambridge University Press, 2003); Margaret A Young, *Trading Fish, Saving Fish: The Interaction between Regimes in International Law* (Cambridge University Press, 2011).

[195] Rostam J Neuwirth, 'The 'Culture and Trade Debate' Continues: The UNESCO Convention in Light of the WTO Reports in China—Publications and Audiovisual Products: Between Amnesia or Déjà Vu?', *Journal of World Trade* 44, (2010): p. 1333; Aaron Cosbey and Petros C Mavroidis, 'Heavy Fuel: Trade and Environment in the GATT/WTO Case Law', *Review of European, Comparative & International Environmental Law* 23, (2014): p. 288.

international law. Yet, these attributes are particularly acute in IIL, and their impact on norm change is very visible.

The first key feature of change in IIL has to do with its origin as a regime. Like no other area of international law, IIL is the product of the imagination and interests of private actors. Facing the end of colonialism and the spread of nationalization in the newly independent countries, the business community in the Global North started imagining ways to protect its investments in the Global South.[196] Western men closely linked to the business community, like Hermann Abs, Hartley Shawcross, or Eugene Black, devised a system of investment protection based on the ideas of arbitral investor-state dispute settlement, full compensation for expropriation, and a number of additional safeguards, which today constitute the basis of IIL.[197] These proposals failed to transit into international law through the multilateral path, basically because a multilateral treaty on these issues became impossible with the Cold War and the clustering of developing countries around the new international economic order (NIEO) and the non-aligned movement. However, the Western business community managed to channel the project through the bilateral foreign policy of several capital-exporting countries and certain international institutions such as the Organisation for Economic Co-operation and Development (OECD)—the state action and bureaucratic pathways.[198] This strategy proved effective in dodging the hurdles of multilateralism and yielded the fragmentary network of bilateral investment treaties (BITs) and free trade agreements (FTAs) that we know today.

For change in international law, this had two crucial implications. The first one is that the rules of IIL are based on significant power asymmetries. While a great deal of thought went into devising these rules in a way that favoured the interests of investors, the receiving side—capital-importing states of the Global South—took a rather passive attitude in accepting them. They entered into BITs and FTAs mostly without asking questions, partly because of a lack of expertise but also because of acute short-termism and a lack of awareness of longer-term consequences. This locked in a bilateral conventional regime that has proven considerably resilient to revision by Global South countries.[199] In fact, most systemic changes in recent

[196] Stephan W Schill, *The Multilateralization of International Investment Law* (Cambridge University Press, 2009), p. 35.

[197] UNCTAD, 'Draft Convention on Investments Abroad (Abs–Shawcross Convention), International Investment Instruments: A Compendium—Volume V, p. 395, https://www.international-arbitration-attorney.com/wp-content/uploads/137-volume-5.pdf. See articles I, II, and III. See Quinn Slobodian, *Globalists: The End of Empire and the Birth of Neoliberalism* (Harvard University Press, 2018).

[198] Kate Miles, *The Origins of International Investment Law: Empire, Environment and the Safeguarding of Capital* (Cambridge University Press, 2013), pp. 71–121. See also on the origins of the ICSID Convention Taylor St John, *The Rise of Investor-State Arbitration: Politics, Law, and Unintended Consequences* (Oxford University Press, 2018).

[199] M Sornarajah, *Resistance and Change in the International Law on Foreign Investment* (Cambridge University Press, 2015), pp. 389–93; see also Andrew T Guzman, 'Why LDCs Sign Treaties That Hurt Them: Explaining the Popularity of Bilateral Investment Treaties', *Virginia Journal of International*

years have come from Global North states realizing that they too can see their policies and public budgets compromised by arbitral awards,[200] even if arbitral decisions continue to favour them significantly more than Global South states.[201] The capacity of developing countries to manoeuvre against IIL has been very limited, at least until countries like China and India started playing a more active and weighty role in the global economy.[202]

The second important implication concerns the legal nature of the regime. As mentioned above, the failure of a multilateral treaty drove capital-exporting countries and Western elites to opt for bilateral treaties and for ad hoc dispute settlement. The result was a widespread network of BITs and FTAs—that is, fixed and very abstract conventional rules, the interpretation of which is fundamentally in the hands of a single type of institution: arbitral tribunals. This makes institutional authority a very limited resource in IIL, and one entirely focused on the judicial pathway. When one looks for authorities to back a given interpretation of a rule, few options other than arbitral jurisprudence are available. More importantly, perhaps, this source of authority is extremely unstable, given the ad hoc nature of the tribunals, the absence of formal *stare decisis*, and the general lack of proper instances of appeal, as well as mechanisms for settling jurisprudential conflicts.

For legal change, all of this means that, short of treaty amendment, arbitrators hold a quasi-monopoly of authority in IIL. Moreover, most arbitrators are Western men sharing similar professional biases and understandings of the discipline.[203] No real way of accessing the system exists for non-state actors other than claimant companies—who, needless to say, are the least interested in changing the regime.[204] It is interesting to see in this regard the reaction—or lack of it—of sixty-three states to a letter sent by several UN Special Rapporteurs with a call for the inclusion of human rights in the discussions of UNCITRAL's Working Group III on Investor-State Dispute Settlement Reform in 2019.[205] Out of those sixty-three states, only six replied, and only one seriously engaged with the substance of

Law 38, (1997): p. 639; Beth A Simmons, 'Bargaining over BITs, Arbitrating Awards: The Regime for Protection and Promotion of International Investment', *World Politics* 66, (2014): p. 12.

200 Anthea Roberts, 'Incremental, Systemic, and Paradigmatic Reform of Investor-State Arbitration', *American Journal of International Law* 112, (2018): p. 410.

201 Malcolm Langford and Daniel Behn, 'Managing Backlash: The Evolving Investment Treaty Arbitrator?', *European Journal of International Law* 29, (2018): p. 551.

202 Shaffer (n 189), pp. 19, 20.

203 See e.g., Sergio Puig, 'Social Capital in the Arbitration Market', *European Journal of International Law* 25, (2014): p. 387.

204 See, e.g., Anthea Roberts, 'Power and Persuasion in Investment Treaty Interpretation: The Dual Role of States', *American Journal of International Law* 104, (2010): p. 179; Anthea Roberts, 'Clash of Paradigms: Actors and Analogies Shaping the Investment Treaty System', *American Journal of International Law* 107, (2013): p. 45.

205 United Nations Commission on International Trade Law, 'Possible Reform of Investor-State Dispute Settlement (ISDS). Note by the Secretariat' (2019) UN Doc A/CN.9/WG.III/WP.166, para. 7.

the letter's concern—by defending the exclusion of human rights from IIL with a highly formalistic argument.[206]

The nature of IIL also means that precedents are highly unstable, so even if a norm entrepreneur manages to break in and have his or her interpretation endorsed by an arbitral tribunal, nothing binds other tribunals to follow the same route. A great example of this is the case of the definition of investment.[207] There, the academic initiative to include the economic development of the host state as a (restrictive) element of the definition of investment found relative success in being adopted by the *Salini* arbitral tribunal. Yet, after *Salini*, the uptake of this element has been highly irregular,[208] and the same can be said of many other issues in IIL. The cases where a broad change in the jurisprudence is visible—the case studies on indirect expropriation and Fair and Equitable Treatment (FET) illustrate this[209]—require not only good arguments to reach arbitrators but also influential states to step in and revise their model BITs or use the few interpretive means at their hands to uphold a given position. This was the case, for instance, with the revision of the indirect expropriation clauses in the BIT and FTA models by Canada and the US in 2004, or with the NAFTA Free Trade Commission's interpretive note of 2001, limiting FET to the 'customary international law minimum standard of treatment of aliens'.[210] And even in these cases, achieving a true shift in the burden of argument took many more years and arbitral awards. Change in IIL, therefore, happens when the jurisprudence of arbitral tribunals on a given point starts forming clear interpretive threads that become impossible for subsequent tribunals to ignore and come to form part of the so-called 'common law of international investment'.[211]

A further point that is worth stressing about change in IIL is the general lack of transparency that exists in the field and its implications. First of all, even in law faculties, investment is often seen as a very technical regime, more linked to private law than to public concerns. This draws attention away from IIL's potential for constraining virtually any policy of a state. Thus, democratically relevant decisions risk technification and delocalization. And in addition to this, the degree of judicialization of the field and the fact that decision-making is conducted by ad hoc arbitral tribunals that dissolve after the conclusion of a case—as opposed to

[206] 'Informe Del Estado Mexicano (En relación con la Comunicación Conjunta OL MEX 3/19)', (24 January 2020), https://spcommreports.ohchr.org/TMResultsBase/DownLoadFile?gId=35129.

[207] Dorothea Endres, 'The Definition of Investment', in *The Paths of International Law: Case Studies*, edited by Pedro Martínez Esponda and others (SSRN, 2023).

[208] ibid.

[209] Pedro Martínez Esponda, 'The Doctrine of Police Powers in Indirect Expropriation' in *The Paths of International Law: Case Studies*, edited by Pedro Martínez Esponda and others (SSRN, 2023); Pedro Martínez Esponda, 'The Development of Fair and Equitable Treatment', in *The Paths of International Law: Case Studies*, edited by Pedro Martínez Esponda and others (SSRN, 2023).

[210] NAFTA Free Trade Commission, 'Notes of Interpretation of Certain Chapter 11 Provisions', http://www.sice.oas.org/tpd/nafta/commission/ch11understanding_e.asp.

[211] M C Porterfield, 'An International Common Law of Investor Rights', *University of Pennsylvania Journal of International Economic Law* 27, (2006): p. 79.

standing institutions—make it difficult to hold anyone politically and legally accountable for socially harmful outcomes. This means that the political and ideational constraints that shape how international law changes in other fields are less present here.

This links back to a point made above: IIL has up to now been remarkably resilient to critique and even impervious to backlash. The lack of transparency, plus the fact that the substance of the field is embedded in a network of over 2,800 BITs, makes overarching change close to impossible. Thus, for instance, the scepticism that led countries like Bolivia, Ecuador, Venezuela, South Africa, India, and Indonesia to denounce the International Centre for the Settlement of International Disputes (ICSID) Convention and/or terminate or amend most of their BITs never really evolved into a larger movement of detraction at the global scale.[212] As Waibel, Kaushal, Chung, and Balchin correctly anticipated in 2010, 'the investment regime [survived] this hiccup, just like others in the past'.[213] Another illustration is provided by the failed negotiations of the OECD-sponsored Multilateral Agreement on Investment during the 1990s. While public awareness and civil society mobilization managed to derail the process completely in a remarkably short period of time, this backlash hardly did anything to the existing regime of IIL.[214] Moreover, as Alschner has recently shown, the endeavour by many states to redesign investment treaties—for instance by limiting the scope of indirect expropriation or even excluding fair and equitable clauses—has not led to meaningful changes in the way treaties are interpreted in investment arbitration.[215] The same can be said of attempts at change using arguments from other fields, notably IHRL. The tendency by investment tribunals here has been to exclude exogenous norms through narrow interpretations of their jurisdiction or of the applicable law.[216]

Despite this resilience, IIL currently faces significant broader change attempts.[217] Several multilateral reform processes are underway, including UNCTAD's Investment Policy Framework for Sustainable Development; the

[212] Anastasiya Ugale and Vanina Sucharitkul, 'Backlash in Investment Arbitration (Wiki Note)', *Jus Mundi*, (23 December 2024), accessed 23 June 2022, https://jusmundi.com/en/document/wiki/en-backlash-in-investment-arbitration.

[213] Michael Waibel and others, 'The Backlash Against Investment Arbitration: Perceptions and Reality', *The Backlash Against Investment Arbitration*, edited by Michael Waibel and others (Kluwer Law International, 2010), p. 5.

[214] Catherine Schittecatte, 'The Politics of the MAI: On the Social Opposition of the MAI and Its Role in the Demise of the Negotiations', *Journal of World Investment & Trade* 1, (2000): p. 329.

[215] Wolfgang Alschner, *Investment Arbitration and State-Driven Reform: New Treaties, Old Outcomes* (Oxford University Press, 2022). See also Langford and Behn (n 205).

[216] Dorothea Endres, 'The Human Side of Protecting Foreign Investment', *Transnational Legal Theory* 12, (2021): pp. 249, 261; Filip Balcerzak, 'Investor–State Arbitration and Human Rights', *Investor–State Arbitration and Human Rights* (Brill Nijhoff, 2017), pp. 100–26; Moshe Hirsch, 'Social Movements, Reframing Investment Relations, and Enhancing the Application of Human Rights Norms in International Investment Law', *Leiden Journal of International Law* 34, (2020): p. 127.

[217] Iva Grgić, 'The Future of Investor–State Dispute Settlement: Reforming Law, Practice and Perspectives for a Fast-Changing World', *ICSID Review - Foreign Investment Law Journal*, (2025).

Proposals for Amendment of the ICSID Rules, and the emergence of UNCITRAL's Working Group III, referred to above.[218] It is yet to be seen to what extent they will succeed, particularly with regard to substantive rather than merely procedural issues.[219] Other challenges stem from particular (groups of) countries. Arguably the main example is the creation of the European Union's Investment Court System (ICS) which, if successful, could transform dispute settlement in IIL. The rise of China as an economic superpower, and the alternative paradigm of investment protection sought in its Belt and Road Initiative, forecast change as well. For now, however, it is safe to assume that, with 306 pending cases at ICSID alone, and more than 2800 bilateral investment treaties (BITs) still in place, traditional IIL will not lose its relevance any time soon.[220]

3. Conclusion

The paths of change in international law vary heavily across issue areas. This chapter has analysed this variation in greater detail, with four main points standing out.

The first and perhaps most evident difference between issue areas concerns the authority structures in each field, a point that has been touched upon in Chapter 2 when introducing authority constellations as one of the groups of factors that may determine the outcomes of norm change attempts.[221] In fields where authority tends to gravitate around centralizing institutions, change can be more orderly and follow somewhat more linear trajectories than in fields with diffuse authority settings.[222] The WTO's AB in ITL was an example of this form of authority until its recent paralysis, as is the ISA in issues concerning the ocean's seabed beyond national jurisdiction, different institutions in some of IEL's sub-regimes, such as CITES, and the ICTY and ICTR for some time during the 1990s in ICL. But this is exceptional in international law.[223] Most fields have a myriad of institutions enjoying different degrees of authority and accessibility, often competing with each other, which makes legal change a matter of interpretive accumulation—with

[218] Daniel Behn, Ole Kristian Fauchald and Malcolm Langford, *The Legitimacy of Investment Arbitration: Empirical Perspectives* (Cambridge University Press, 2022), pp. 7, 8.

[219] For a discussion on the matter, see Anthea Roberts and Taylor St John, 'The Originality of Outsiders: Innovation in the Investment Treaty System', *European Journal of International Law* 33, (2023): p. 1153.

[220] 'Pending Cases | ICSID' <https://icsid.worldbank.org/cases/pending> accessed 29 January 2026; 'Home | UNCTAD Investment Policy Hub' <https://investmentpolicy.unctad.org/> accessed 29 January 2026.

[221] See 'Paths of Change' in Chapter 2.

[222] For empirical evidence on this point, see 'Findings II: Regression Analysis' in Chapter 4.

[223] For a discussion on regime complexity in international law, see Karen Alter and Kal Raustiala, 'The Rise of International Regime Complexity', *Annual Review of Law and Social Science* 14, (2018): p. 329.

an inevitably protracted and often unstable shape.[224] GIL, IHL, and IIL are paradigmatic of this: change attempts in these fields tend to take longer and lead to less consolidated outcomes in the context of the case studies conducted for our project. Yet other fields like IHRL have a more complex institutional architecture, with universal institutions working in parallel with regional courts and commissions, sometimes complementing each other's work and sometimes diverging in interpretative approaches. In Chapter 7, we will explore further the lack of consolidation that comes with this authority layout, the continuing role of contestation it facilitates, and the consequences of both for change (and the paths of change) in international law.

Secondly, some issue areas have a marked preference for certain paths. In fields like ITL, ICL, and IIL, the judicial path is particularly prominent, while LoS, IHRL, and IHL strongly feature the bureaucratic path in addition to the judicial path. Judges, bureaucrats, and experts are thus crucial vectors of change in international law. Together with the relatively low use of the multilateral and state action paths, this points to the fact that norm entrepreneurs often resort to the judicial and bureaucratic paths as a means for translating their norm change attempts into technicality or legalism, thereby evading the political hurdles of their issue areas. Also noteworthy is that some issue areas are expansive and tend to spill over into other issue areas, as for instance IHRL, ICL, and IEL. This means that pathways often get entangled and have reciprocal effects. A product of the bureaucratic path in one issue area, for example, might have implications in the multilateral or judicial path of other issue areas. The human right to a healthy environment is a good illustration of this dynamic. The implications of this complexity for international legal change will come into clearer view in Chapter 6.

Thirdly, differences are also prominent in terms of the actors that take part in norm change and venture into norm entrepreneurship in different regimes. While some issue areas are dominated by states, again like ITL but also LoS, others leave less prominent roles to states and place other actors—civil society, international bureaucracies, businesses—in the driver's seat. This is very visible in fields like IHRL, IHL, and IIL. Civil society, international bureaucrats and experts are the main agents of IHRL, while states have a more passive role in supporting or rejecting their change attempts. IHL, for its part, prominently features the ICRC, a unique institution that serves as a focal point for change but that is also active in pushing for change. And in IIL, businesses and industrial groups have considerable influence in norm change mainly through the appointment of

[224] For example, focusing on global environmental governance, some have identified the authority landscape there as 'polycentric'. See Tanya Heikkila, Sergio Villamayor-Tomas and Dustin Garrick, 'Bringing Polycentric Systems into Focus for Environmental Governance', *Environmental Policy and Governance* 28, (2018): p. 207.

arbitrators—a function they share with states—and through their influence on the foreign policies of their home states as well as in multilateral fora like UNCITRAL. Multistakeholder configurations, too, can play important roles in fields like IEL, where different actors have a direct say in the production of normative outputs, as the final documents of environmental conferences and summits make evident.

Lastly, very different political frameworks and background settings operate in each issue area. Certain fields observe entrenched and very public confrontations among groups of states which often perceive the stakes involved to be of a zero-sum nature. ITL exemplifies this very well, along the cleavage between developed and developing states or the competition between China and the US. But LoS and, in certain settings, IEL do too: the continental shelf and CITES cases are good examples. Change in these circumstances often requires recourse to technicism or legalism. In yet other fields, political cleavages are less visible but equally—or more—pervasive. IHL, on the one hand, has been largely paralysed since the 1979 Additional Protocols, at least on the multilateral pathway. Only expert (re)interpretations and interactions with other fields, such as ICL and IHRL, have brought about tangible change here. Fields like ICL, on the other hand, have been largely dependent on political momentum in very intense and short periods of time following moments of crisis. Change in these instances becomes suddenly available and develops very quickly. In contrast, under some conditions, incentives are created for states to pursue change individually, without seeking institutional endorsement—mostly when states are capable of implementing their legal positions in a unilateral fashion. In these instances, norms are purposefully left unstable for long periods of time. This was visible in GIL in the cases concerning self-defence against non-state actors and the effects doctrine. Moreover, under some circumstances, there exist ideational hurdles that constrain the possibilities of states to object to norm change, as often happens in IHRL, where states tend to be rather passive and mostly reactive.

The paths of international law or the constellations of paths in the different issue areas we have surveyed here are remarkably distinct. In terms of paths, authorities, actors, and background understandings, the institutional and social differentiation of the field has led to semi-autonomous areas that are hard to subsume under the umbrella of one international law, except perhaps in a very formal sense. Interactions between the different areas are frequent, but even if we do not go so far as to see the areas as 'systems' in a strong sense,[225] they do tend to process many of the interactions through their own frames and institutions, leading to significant divergences in orientation. The frictions many feared as a result of the fragmentation of international law in the early 2000s may not have come to

[225] Andreas Fischer-Lescano and Gunther Teubner, 'Regime-Collisions: The Vain Search for Legal Unity in the Fragmentation of Global Law', *Michigan Journal of International Law* 25, (2004): pp. 999, 1007.

pass, and many institutions have found ways of responding to, and sometimes accommodating, the positions of others.[226] But divergences certainly continue, especially between economic law, on the one hand, and human rights, as well as environmental law, on the other. And given the different paths on which international law travels in its different areas, such divergences may well increase over time. Today's international law is not one, but many.

[226] Anne Peters, 'The Refinement of International Law: From Fragmentation to Regime Interaction and Politicization', *International Journal of Constitutional Law* 15, (2017): pp. 671, 671–72.

4

Conditions for Successful Legal Change

Under what conditions does international law change? In the previous chapters, we have provided a thicker description of the actual processes of change in international legal rules, and we have seen how they differ across international legal subfields. We have also begun to identify factors that appear to play a particular role in those subfields, especially with a view to different political dynamics and varying constellations of actors and authorities.

Our concern throughout has been with shifts in authoritative legal understandings over time. In recent years, particularly in the context of renewed great power contestation, some of the most visible legal developments have taken overtly disruptive forms, marked by deliberate erosion, obstruction, or hollowing out of established legal commitments and institutions. While the actual effects of these attempts are yet to be seen, this chapter (and the book for that matter) does not seek to explain their immediate or short-term impact. Instead, it focuses on the general conditions under which change efforts consolidate into widely accepted understandings within relevant legal communities.

On this basis, we pursue a more systematic inquiry into the conditions of change, focusing on change attempts undertaken mainly since the 1970s and extending into the 2020s. This inquiry points to a contrast between two broader accounts of what drives change. The first, 'statist', account is dominant in both international relations and international law. It centres on state interactions and emphasizes the importance of state support, especially from powerful states, while acknowledging the relevance of certain norm properties. The second, 'institutionalist', account places greater emphasis on institutions and authorities. It views support from the surrounding authority constellation as a key determinant of a change attempt's success and as a factor that also shapes the influence of other variables. Here, we lay out this second account in more detail, drawing on insights from historical and discursive institutionalism, which have—as intimated in Chapters 1 and 2—many close links with our broader understanding of international law as a process and social practice.

These two broader accounts lead to different expectations about the paths, pace, and factors behind change, and in this chapter, we specify these expectations and draw on data from our case studies to get a better understanding of which of the expectations hold. The factors we take into view are clustered into four groups: the

Change in International Law. Nico Krisch, Ezgi Yildiz, and Pedro Martínez Esponda, Oxford University Press.
 DOI: 10.1093/9780198918325.003.0004

role of states, norm properties, authority constellations, and ideational openings, all of which are linked to different theoretical approaches to norms, law, and change in the international order. We do not, of course, expect any single factor or group of factors to explain fully the outcome of change processes on its own. Rather, we are interested in the different weights they may have in bringing about (or hindering) the success of change attempts overall.

In the next step, we use these expectations to guide our analysis of the data from our research project. As briefly outlined in the previous chapter, our empirical analysis is grounded in a systematic study of twenty-five cases, chosen to represent a range of change attempts outside formal treaty-making processes. Based on qualitative accounts of the processes leading to change (or the lack thereof), we have coded the presence or absence of various potentially relevant factors and created a dataset. We then have analysed this dataset, first through descriptive methods and subsequently through regression analysis using ordinary least squares (OLS) regression. The relatively small number of cases limits what can be achieved through quantitative tools, but by combining statistical analysis with an in-depth qualitative examination of case studies, our study is able to provide a more comprehensive assessment of the dynamics influencing change in international law than was previously available.

The findings from our analysis hold several key insights. The first is that states matter less than most observers would expect. State support has limited relevance, and it is only state opposition that emerges as a significant factor in influencing change outcomes. Perhaps yet more surprisingly, the role of great powers appears less central than traditional accounts might suggest, challenging the commonly held view that the position of major powers is usually decisive for the success of international legal change. In contrast, the role of institutional authority appears more significant—the presence of focal authorities in a given field increases the likelihood of success significantly, and it does so even in the face of state opposition. This underscores the importance of authority constellations in change processes and suggests that the institutionalist account we develop here has considerable purchase.

The picture we paint is not deterministic—we do not aim to explain everything about change processes: only certain conditions that may facilitate or hinder change. A full understanding of any given change process would need to take into view the contingencies of every individual case in a much more concrete way.[1] Our account necessarily operates with a certain parsimony, trying to see patterns and generalities—given the inherent variety of the many practices that constitute

[1] See Ingo Venzke, 'The Path Not Taken: On Legal Change and Its Context', in *The Many Paths of International Law*, edited by Nico Krisch and Ezgi Yildiz (Oxford University Press, 2023); see also Ingo Venzke and Kevin Jon Heller, eds., *Contingency in International Law: On the Possibility of Different Legal Histories* (Oxford University Press, 2021).

international legal change, a full account might not be realistic or even desirable.[2] We thus necessarily downplay some of the particularities of the cases, but we hope that our approach allows us to move towards a better understanding of the contours of a bigger picture of the dynamics of international law.

This chapter proceeds as follows. First, we develop the contrast between statist and institutionalist accounts (section 1) and use it to derive factors and expectations to guide our empirical analysis (section 2). In section 3, we introduce our methodology. Next, we delve into the empirical examination of change processes, with a descriptive analysis (section 4), followed by a regression analysis (section 5) and an analysis of interaction effects (section 6). We conclude by reflecting on the broader implications of our study for understanding change in international law.

1. Towards an Institutionalist Account

General accounts of change in international law (and international norms more broadly) tend to focus on states and their positions, as well as on the types of norms that their change attempts propose and relate to. However, these accounts downplay aspects that, on the basis of our theoretical framework, would appear potentially very relevant, namely factors related to institutions, authority, and broader ideational contexts. Shifting the focus to the latter helps us to develop richer expectations as to the circumstances in which change attempts are likely to be successful. Here, we set out the contrasting approaches in order to provide a basis for our analysis in the following sections.

From States and Norms . . .

The positions of states stand, unsurprisingly, at the centre of most accounts of change in international norms, whether legal or otherwise. This is only natural from the perspective of international lawyers, given the focus on states' views and practices in traditional doctrine. As discussed in Chapter 1, the emergence of a new customary rule from a legal-doctrinal perspective depends on the convergence of the *opinio iuris* and practice of states. Similarly, whether subsequent practice results in a changed interpretation of a treaty also hinges on the convergence of

[2] See, e.g., Friedrich Kratochwil, 'Practices and a "Theory" of Action? Some Conceptual Issues Concerning Ends, Reasons and Happiness', in *Conceptualizing International Practices: Directions for the Practice Turn in International Relations*, edited by Alena Drieschova, Christian Bueger and Ted Hopf (Cambridge University Press, 2022).

state positions.[3] From this standpoint, other factors or actors are merely ancillary. International organizations, for example, can serve as a forum for member states to express their positions, and thus, they can facilitate the creation of custom, but they do not play an independent role beyond that of a 'participant' in the relevant processes.[4]

A focus on state positions is also typical for most international relations scholars, given the (still) largely statist focus of the discipline. International relations literature, in a rationalist mould, approaches norms and rules as a function of state preferences—this is most clearly expressed in work on the rational design of treaties and formal institutions.[5] The (relatively rare) rationalist treatment of other change processes, such as customary international law, largely replicates a picture of matching reciprocal preferences.[6] Realist approaches naturally pay less attention to law, but for them, international law matters primarily when it aligns with the preferences of powerful states.[7]

Constructivist approaches paint a different, more social picture of the process by which international (legal) norms come about. However, they also tend to focus on state positions. In Martha Finnemore and Kathryn Sikkink's influential model of norm dynamics, for instance, norm entrepreneurs play a central role in the early stages, but their work only comes to fruition if they mobilize a sufficient number of states to reach a tipping point that can then lead to a norm cascade that brings the remaining states to the table.[8] Likewise, Wayne Sandholtz's cycles of change have a clear structure built around norm tensions, but the move from one cycle to the next largely depends on the 'broad support' of states.[9]

For constructivists, state positions themselves are not exogenous to international interactions, and they are shaped by different factors—particularly ideational ones. Existing law and, in particular, the structure of legal arguments and

[3] See, e.g., ICJ, *North Sea Continental Shelf Cases (Federal Republic of Germany v Denmark; Federal Republic of Germany v Netherlands)* [1969] ICJ Rep 3, para. 74; ILC, 'Draft Conclusions on Identification of Customary International Law with Commentaries', (2018) UN Doc A/73/10.

[4] See, e.g., ILC, 'Draft Conclusions on Identification of Customary International Law with Commentaries', Conclusion 12 and Commentary on Conclusion 12 (2018) UN Doc A/73/10, pp. 147–49.

[5] See, e.g., Kenneth W Abbott and others, 'The Concept of Legalization', *International Organization* 54, (2000): p. 401; Barbara Koremenos, *The Continent of International Law: Explaining Agreement Design* (Cambridge University Press, 2016).

[6] See Pierre-Hugues Verdier and Erik Voeten, 'Precedent, Compliance, and Change in Customary International Law: An Explanatory Theory', *American Journal of International Law* 108, (2014): p. 389.

[7] See Richard H Steinberg, 'Wanted—Dead or Alive: Realism in International Law', in *Interdisciplinary Perspectives on International Law and International Relations: The State of the Art*, edited by J L Dunoff and M A Pollack (Cambridge University Press, 2012).

[8] Martha Finnemore and Kathryn Sikkink, 'International Norm Dynamics and Political Change', *International Organization* 52, (1998): p. 887. Tipping points are also central to the more rationalist account of Verdier and Voeten (n 6).

[9] Wayne Sandholtz, 'International Norm Change', Oxford Research Encyclopedia of Politics, 2017, https://oxfordre.com/view/10.1093/acrefore/9780190228637.001.0001/acrefore-9780190228637-e-588.

rules are among these factors.[10] In norm change processes, a key factor often highlighted is the presence of adjacent norms—existing norms that are conceptually or functionally related and can serve as points of connection for norm entrepreneurs seeking to legitimize new claims. These adjacent norms help embed emerging ideas within established normative frameworks, increasing their resonance and chances of acceptance. Drawing on the ideational strength of an existing framework, change agents can thus increase the standing of their own proposal (and present it as a continuation rather than as a rupture).[11]

... to Institutions, Authorities, and their Ideational Contexts

Our approach builds on these accounts, but it takes them further to emphasize the broader social context in which change takes place. This leads in a somewhat different direction—one that gives institutions, authority, and ideational contexts a more prominent place. In this approach, state positions also matter, but alongside other factors and potentially with lesser weight.

That authority, and especially institutional authority, would matter in norm change processes might seem evident from the practice-based account we introduced in Chapter 2. In our understanding, authority is a socially constructed relation that allows an actor to elicit deference from others, and it is established through recognition within a community of practice. This recognition grants the authority holder the power to influence, based not only on formal delegation but also on expertise, moral principles, or procedural legitimacy. If international law is indeed a social practice, social attributes such as authority, hierarchy, or capital are bound to play an important role.[12] They are, of course, contingent, and as we have observed in Chapter 3, different fields generate their own authorities—in some fields, these may be institutions; in others, particular experts; in others, merely states.

The importance of authority constellations for norm change is also obvious for students of historical sociology or historical institutionalism. For them, the shape of existing processes and institutions is central to understanding how change

[10] See, e.g., Michael Byers, *Custom, Power and the Power of Rules: International Relations and Customary International Law* (Cambridge University Press, 1999).

[11] See Wayne Sandholtz and Kendall W Stiles, *International Norms and Cycles of Change* (Oxford University Press, 2009), pp. 331–32.

[12] Nora Stappert, 'Practice Theory and Change in International Law: Theorizing the Development of Legal Meaning through the Interpretive Practices of International Criminal Courts', *International Theory* 12, (2020): p. 33; Tanja Aalberts and Ingo Venzke, 'Moving Beyond Interdisciplinary Turf Wars: Towards an Understanding of International Law as Practice', in *International Law as a Profession*, edited by Jean d'Aspremont and others (Cambridge University Press, 2017); Ezgi Yildiz, 'Enduring Practices in Changing Circumstances: A Comparison of the European Court of Human Rights and the Inter-American Court of Human Rights', *Temple International & Comparative Law Journal* 34, (2020): p. 309.

unfolds and what shape it takes.[13] For example, in the historical institutionalism literature on gradual change which we have drawn upon in Chapter 1, the type and direction of change processes are heavily conditioned by decision-making power within an existing institution—which will determine whether change can be pursued internally or must be routed through other avenues.[14] The 'institutions' in historical institutionalism are not necessarily formal organizations. Rather, they are typically broader regimes with recognized rules governing decision-making and the processes through which change can be effectuated. In this regard, they are very much akin to the different constellations of paths we have identified in the previous chapter, as characteristic of various areas of international law.

This institutional dimension typically occupies no central place in the literature on international legal change. In the norm change literature, institutions are usually ubiquitous but theoretically secondary—they appear as organizational platforms or sites in which other actors (mostly states) interact to shape norms.[15] For example, in Mona Lena Krook and Jacqui True's widely cited study of the life cycle of gender equality norms, almost all of the story revolves around the United Nations, with different bodies—from the Commission on the Status of Women to the United Nations Development Programme and the Security Council—playing key roles in furthering norm development. The authors note that '[t]he UN thus remains a crucial actor in teasing out the contours and meanings of gender equality norms, introducing opportunities but also possible limitations in their effects'.[16] However, their process-oriented account of the norm life cycle has little place for institutions and focuses instead on the character of the norms at issue, their internal contradictions, and the influence of competing norms.[17]

This relative neglect of authority and institutions may partly stem from the fact that most existing accounts seek to construct timeless models, whereas institutions—at least formal ones—are relatively recent developments. Nonetheless, authority and institutions have begun to feature more prominently in some areas of the literature, particularly in recent debates on norm contestation.[18] With more specific attention to law, Paul Diehl and Charlotte Ku's *Dynamics of*

[13] See Wolfgang Streeck and Kathleen Thelen, eds., *Beyond Continuity: Institutional Change in Advanced Political Economies* (Oxford University Press, 2005); Orfeo Fioretos, 'Historical Institutionalism in International Relations', *International Organization* 65, (2011): p. 367.

[14] ibid.

[15] See, e.g., the treatment in Finnemore and Sikkink (n 8), pp. 899–901; Beth A Simmons and Hyeran Jo, 'Measuring Norms and Normative Contestation: The Case of International Criminal Law', *Journal of Global Security Studies* 4, (2019): p. 18; Michal Ben-Josef Hirsch and Jennifer M Dixon, 'Conceptualizing and Assessing Norm Strength in International Relations', *European Journal of International Relations* 27, (2021): p. 521.

[16] Mona Lena Krook and Jacqui True, 'Rethinking the Life Cycles of International Norms: The United Nations and the Global Promotion of Gender Equality', *European Journal of International Relations* 18, (2012): pp. 103, 122.

[17] ibid p. 123.

[18] See Antje Wiener, *Contestation and Constitution of Norms in Global International Relations* (Cambridge University Press, 2018).

International Law makes potential space for institutions and authorities through the notion of an 'operating system' of international law—a system that specifies which actors and processes produce new law.[19] Likewise, Mark Raymond's *Social Practices of Rule-Making* places emphasis on the procedural rules on norm-making that emerge in international society; these rules, variable as they are, might specify institutional roles, although these do not come out strongly in his cases, and he largely falls back on classical legal doctrines.[20]

These insights, combined with our reconstruction of the different paths of international law in Chapters 2 and 3, help us to develop a more robust institutional account—one that acknowledges that the 'institutions', 'operating systems', or secondary rules of international law do not consist merely of rules but of a conglomerate (some might say an 'assemblage') of rules and actors, especially actors with authority in a given field. Where an actor's authority to interpret (or even change) the law is recognized, it is likely to play an important role in change processes, as we have seen in many of the cases of change examined so far. Think of the role of the World Trade Organization (WTO) Appellate Body (in its day) for the development of world trade law:[21] where an authority is focal in a given context, it may be decisive for the success or failure of change attempts. But even where authority is diffuse (as is the case in most fields of international law), we can expect it to shape change processes—and to calibrate the importance of other factors, especially the role of states.

Our broadly institutionalist frame points us towards another important yet often overlooked direction—one linked to the ideational contexts that favour or disfavour change. In classical historical institutionalism, 'critical junctures' and other forms of crises occupy a central place as they open up opportunities to disrupt the path dependence of institutions.[22] Historical institutionalism alone cannot typically explain how these developments come about, and even the more recent endogenous accounts of gradual change do not place this question at the centre of their analysis.

In recent years, another institutionalism—'discursive institutionalism', which we drew upon in Chapter 2—has emerged to fill some of this gap. Particularly suited to account for discursive practices, such as law, discursive institutionalism points to the role of ideas and ideational environments in creating space for institutional

[19] Paul F Diehl and Charlotte Ku, *The Dynamics of International Law* (Cambridge University Press, 2010), p. 37.

[20] Mark Raymond, *Social Practices of Rule-Making in World Politics* (Oxford University Press, 2019), ch. 5, but also the short discussion of authority on pp. 248–50.

[21] See Gregory Shaffer, Manfred Elsig and Sergio Puig, 'The Extensive (But Fragile) Authority of the WTO Appellate Body', *Law and Contemporary Problems* 79, (2016): p. 237; Robert Howse, 'The World Trade Organization 20 Years On: Global Governance by Judiciary', *European Journal of International Law* 27, (2016): p. 9.

[22] See Giovanni Capoccia and R Daniel Kelemen, 'The Study of Critical Junctures: Theory, Narrative, and Counterfactuals in Historical Institutionalism', *World Politics* 59, (2007): p. 341.

change.[23] Space for broader change—whether through critical junctures or smaller scale openings—is often generated by linking with and mobilizing ideas.

When trying to understand why certain change attempts succeed at a given moment, we thus have to pay attention to ideational contexts, and especially openings in existing ideational environments that might enable normative change. This point may seem obvious when looking at actual cases of change. For example, the criminalization of acts in non-international armed conflict, which in the 1990s benefited heavily from a broader anti-impunity discourse that change agents could connect with.[24] However, accounts of international legal change and international norm change have typically not placed much weight on the ideational context, aside from acknowledging the role of norm entrepreneurs in generating new ideas and frames.[25] Here we take into view, more broadly, the context that enables such strategies—specifically, the ideational openings that may make it possible to attract support for new norm proposals.

Understanding international law as a social, discursive practice thus allows us to shift the emphasis when it comes to explaining processes of international legal change. It also helps us to make sense of and reflect insights from many actual cases in which institutions, authorities, and ideational openings play a significant—and sometimes a dominant—role. This might suggest, quite in contrast with the typical, statist picture, that the different paths of change in international law are not merely auxiliary to the interplay of states but may, under certain circumstances, take their place. In any event, the contrast developed here gives us broader tools to account for variation in change processes across issue areas and historical periods.

2. Factors behind Change: Expectations

We are now in a position to formulate more clear-cut expectations that help to structure our inquiry into the relevant factors behind legal change. In the following, we lay out a number of hypotheses concerning such factors, clustered around the broader themes developed in the previous sections—the role of states, norm properties, authorities and institutions, and ideational contexts. These hypotheses are not definitive statements but are instead meant to allow for a systematic exploration of different explanations, which requires us to pitch competing accounts against each other without taking a side. Our empirical tests will then either confirm or challenge these expectations, enabling us to evaluate their relevance and impact more rigorously. By systematically testing these hypotheses, we aim to uncover the underlying mechanisms behind legal change, providing

[23] See Vivien A Schmidt, 'Discursive Institutionalism: The Explanatory Power of Ideas and Discourse', *Annual Review of Political Science* 11, (2008): p. 303.

[24] See Nina Kiderlin, 'War Crimes in Non-International Armed Conflicts', in *The Paths of International Law: Case Studies*, edited by Pedro Martínez Esponda and others (SSRN, 2023).

[25] See Finnemore and Sikkink (n 8), pp. 896–99.

insights into the change processes at work and the conditions under which successful change episodes are more or less likely.

The Role of States

In line with a statist understanding of international law and politics, state positions on change processes are typically thought to be the single most important factor in explaining change outcomes. As discussed above, most accounts start from the assumption that change does not take place without state support or against significant state opposition.[26] Along these lines, change in treaties and customary international law (and norms in general) is thought to require broad support from states (or state parties, in the case of treaties).[27] There is, however, not always agreement on what 'broad' might mean: while legal-doctrinal approaches often see widespread to unanimous support as necessary, the focus among international relations scholars is often on support from a critical mass of states.[28] In any event, if the focus on states in these accounts is correct, we would expect the following hypotheses to hold:

> Hypothesis 1a: As the breadth of state support widens, the rate of successful change outcomes increases.
>
> Hypothesis 1b: As the breadth of state opposition widens, the rate of successful change outcomes decreases.

An even stronger rendering of these expectations—reflecting standard legal-doctrinal requirements—might conceive of broad state support not just as a facilitating factor but indeed as a necessary (and potentially even sufficient) condition for change. We will return to this point below.

Not all states are equal—differences among states in terms of political, economic, or social capital are vast, which, by all accounts, play an important part in international politics.[29] Realist approaches, in particular, emphasize the outsized role great powers play in international law-making and legal change,[30] and critical scholars have long pointed to the special attention paid to the practice of powerful

[26] Finnemore and Sikkink (n 8); Pierre-Hugues Verdier and Erik Voeten, 'How Does Customary International Law Change? The Case of State Immunity', *International Studies Quarterly* 59, (2015): p. 209; Margarita H Petrova, 'Naming and Praising in Humanitarian Norm Development', *World Politics* 71, (2019): p. 586.

[27] See, e.g., Anthea Elizabeth Roberts, 'Traditional and Modern Approaches to Customary International Law: A Reconciliation', *American Journal of International Law* 95, (2001): p. 757; Finnemore and Sikkink (n 8); Verdier and Voeten (n 6), p. 389; Verdier and Voeten (n 26); Sandholtz (n 9).

[28] Finnemore and Sikkink (n 8). Tipping points are also central to the more rationalist account of Verdier and Voeten (n 6).

[29] Roland Paris, 'The Right to Dominate: How Old Ideas About Sovereignty Pose New Challenges for World Order', *International Organization* 74, (2020): p. 453.

[30] Steinberg (n 7).

countries in the identification of customary international law.[31] Constructivists, too, regard this practice as central: for Wayne Sandholtz and Kendall Stiles, for example, '[t]he adherence of major powers to an emergent norm is most critical', and 'agreement among the leading powers of the time' lies behind most successful cases of norm change.[32] This may be the result of persuasion but also of compulsion. Powerful states tend to have tools to pressure smaller states into supporting or resisting change.[33] Against this background, we would indeed expect that major power support facilitates change attempts and perhaps even more so that opposition by major powers would stop such attempts in their tracks. However, not all observations point in the same direction. Some studies have found great powers to be relatively unsuccessful in influencing the development of customary law, and others see norm change occurring despite (and at times because of) great power opposition.[34] In order to test which of these expectations are upheld in our study, we posit the following hypotheses:

> Hypothesis 1c: The existence of major power support increases the chances of successful change attempts.

> Hypothesis 1d: The existence of major power opposition decreases the chances of successful change attempts.

In this chapter, we inquire into the role of states and great powers in international legal change in broad strokes across our cases. In Chapter 5, we return to the theme of power in more detail to unpack the ways in which powerful states do—and do not—influence change processes.

Norm Properties

A second group of factors relates to the characteristics of the norms in question. As we have briefly mentioned above, constructivist international relations scholars often argue that change attempts are more likely to materialize if they successfully build on the 'adjacency' to existing norms.[35] Such adjacency claims present new

[31] See B S Chimni, 'Customary International Law: A Third World Perspective', *American Journal of International Law* 112, (2018): p. 1.

[32] Sandholtz and Stiles (n 11), p. 333.

[33] See Renee de Nevers, 'Imposing International Norms: Great Powers and Norm Enforcement', *International Studies Review* 9, (2007): p. 53.

[34] See Stephen Toope, 'Powerful but Unpersuasive? The Role of the United States in the Evolution of Customary International Law', *United States Hegemony and the Foundations of International* Law, edited by M Byers and G Nolte (Cambridge University Press, 2003); Petrova (n 26). See also Byers (n 10).

[35] See Finnemore and Sikkink (n 8); Sandholtz and Stiles (n 11), pp. 331–32; Elizabeth Baisley, 'Reaching the Tipping Point? Emerging International Human Rights Norms Pertaining to Sexual

ideas as a continuation of existing understandings, thereby lowering the cost of innovation and dressing change more as a matter of technical adjustment than as a consequential shift.[36] They also help change agents to side-step the need for formal law-making or acquiring state consent. Following this literature, we also test the influence of norm adjacency claims:

> Hypothesis 2a: Change attempts that build on existing norms are more likely to lead to more successful change outcomes.

In contrast, change initiatives facing *rival* norms might face greater difficulty in becoming the reference point for relevant actors or solidifying as the dominant understanding.[37] Rival norms create greater ambiguity and thus increase the justificatory burden necessary for a change attempt. The existence of an opposing or rival norm might thus destabilize change attempts.[38] For example, the equidistance principle, codified in the 1958 Convention on the Continental Shelf, was on its way to solidifying as a customary norm and acquiring a default rule status for maritime delimitation exercises and agreements. This was undercut when the International Court of Justice introduced a rival norm, based on 'equitable principles', in its 1969 *North Sea Continental Shelf Cases* ruling. This endorsement licensed actors who wished to deviate from the equidistance principle, preventing its full solidification as the default rule.[39] In order to test the effect of rival norms more broadly, we propose the following hypothesis:

> Hypothesis 2b: Change attempts that are confronted with an opposing norm are less likely to lead to successful outcomes.

The types of norms sought by change agents may also have a bearing on the change outcomes. This is not accounted for in the existing literature, but while observing our case studies, we noticed a qualitative difference between two groups of norms—*permissive* norms, which expand the range of possible actions

Orientation and Gender Identity', *Human Rights Quarterly* 38, (2016): p. 134; Miriam Bradley, 'Unintended Consequences of Adjacency Claims: The Function and Dysfunction of Analogies between Refugee Protection and IDP Protection in the Work of UNHCR', *Global Governance: A Review of Multilateralism and International Organizations* 25, (2019): p. 620.

[36] Ezgi Yildiz and Isabel Silagy, 'Norms, Legitimacy, and Compliance: Between International Law and Politics', *The Oxford Handbook of Norms Research in International Relations*, edited by Sassan Gholiagha, Phil Orchard, and Antje Wiener (Oxford University Press, 2025).

[37] Ezgi Yildiz and Umut Yüksel, 'The Defocalizing Effect of International Courts: Evidence from Maritime Delimitation Practices', *The Review of International Organizations* 20, (2024): 825.

[38] Nico Krisch, Francesco Corradini and Lucy Lu Reimers, 'Order at the Margins: The Legal Construction of Interface Conflicts over Time', *Global Constitutionalism* 9, (2020): p. 343.

[39] Ezgi Yildiz and Umut Yüksel, 'Understanding the Limitations of Behavioralism: Lessons from the Field of Maritime Delimitation', *German Law Journal* 23, (2022): p. 413; Yildiz and Yüksel (n 37).

for individual states, and *collaborative* norms, which require a collective effort of states in implementation. Norms in the former group might require a lower threshold of support to be operational and to shift the justificatory burden in their favour; they may also not require full consolidation to to influence state practice. Actors invoking such norms argue for and benefit from these norms' existence without necessarily seeking the norms' full consolidation or broad acceptance. For example, the effects doctrine in jurisdiction—a permissive norm that relaxes jurisdictional limits—has long played a significant role in legal discourse despite the fact that it was supported by only a limited group of (admittedly powerful) actors.[40] Collaborative norms, however, require more buy-in and positive uptake from relevant stakeholders for them to show effect and to shift the burden of argument that they exist or have changed. The port state obligation to curb illegal, unreported, and unregulated fishing is an example of such a norm whose successful implementation necessitates broad agreement.[41] To test if these differences do indeed result in different change outcomes, we propose the following hypothesis:

> Hypothesis 2c: Change attempts around permissive norms are more likely to lead to successful outcomes compared to change attempts around collaborative norms.

Authority Constellations

While most accounts of international legal change focus to a large extent on states and their positions, we have suggested in the previous section that we should shift—or at least expand—our gaze towards institutions and authority constellations. In a social, discursive practice with many paths on which change can travel, the success of change attempts may depend on authorities other than states—at least in areas where such authority is widely recognized.

If this institutionalist approach has purchase, we can expect the constellation of authority in an area to have a significant effect on the course, pace, and outcome of change processes. We distinguish here primarily between focal and peripheral authority layouts. The more recognized and central an authority is in a given field, the more likely norm entrepreneurs are to gravitate towards it when seeking to change the existing understanding of a given norm.[42] Antipreneurs, too, will focus

[40] Pedro Martínez Esponda, 'The Effects Doctrine of Jurisdiction', in *The Paths of International Law: Case Studies*, edited by Pedro Martínez Esponda and others (SSRN, 2023).

[41] See Ezgi Yildiz, 'The Emergence of Port State Measures Against IUU Fishing', in *The Paths of International Law: Case Studies*, edited by Pedro Martínez Esponda and others (SSRN, 2023).

[42] See also Joseph Jupille, Walter Mattli and Duncan Snidal, *Institutional Choice and Global Commerce* (Cambridge University Press, 2013), p. 9.

their effort on it when seeking to prevent such change. Focal authorities—central institutions with medium or strong authority—are also likely to appear as gatekeepers, enabling change through their support but also able to thwart it through their resistance. The WTO Appellate Body may have occupied such a place (as long as it was operative) for norms about global trade, especially during the deadlock of political negotiations in the Doha Round.[43] However, as we saw in Chapter 3, most areas of international law are characterized not by focal institutions, but by diffuse authority. They are typically populated by a range of peripheral institutions—such as the CEDAW Committee—that occupy more marginal spaces and have limited authority.[44] Such peripheral, often specialized, institutions tend to be more open to new change proposals and setting new agendas, but their statements will usually fall short of solidifying a given change attempt—at least on their own. In areas with peripheral authority, change is then likely to come about only through the cumulation of authority from a variety of institutions and actors, and it is less likely to lead to full consolidation. To test whether our expectations around focal and peripheral authorities hold true, we propose the following:

> Hypothesis 3a: Change attempts that are processed or endorsed by focal authorities are more likely to be successful.

Authority constellations vary not only in their focality, but also in their scope. In international law and global governance today, multiplicity and complexity are defining features, and change agents often pursue paths that lead them across different issue areas. On the one hand, this may facilitate change attempts, as it creates new pathways and avenues for broader challenges.[45] On the other hand, growing institutional proliferation, fragmentation, and regime complexity can also generate friction and stagnation—a recurrent theme in the literature on these phenomena.[46] In particular, the existence of multiple institutions across different regimes may produce contradictory interpretations that prevent change attempts from reaching full consolidation.[47] As a result, change attempts that are limited to a specific regime or field may have a higher chance of success. Within single domains, actors and institutions are often more closely aligned, the number of participants

[43] Shaffer, Elsig and Puig (n 21).

[44] See Loveday Hodson, 'Women's Rights and the Periphery: CEDAW's Optional Protocol', *European Journal of International Law* 25, (2014): p. 561.

[45] Krisch, Corradini and Reimers (n 38).

[46] Karen Alter and Kal Raustiala, 'The Rise of International Regime Complexity', *Annual Review of Law and Social Science* 14, (2018): p. 329; Karen J Alter, 'The Promise and Perils of Theorizing International Regime Complexity in an Evolving World', *Review of International Organizations* 17, (2022): p. 375; Daniel W Drezner, 'The Power and Peril of International Regime Complexity', *Perspectives on Politics* 7, (2009): p. 65; Stephanie C Hofmann, 'Overlapping Institutions in the Realm of International Security: The Case of NATO and ESDP', *Perspectives on Politics* 7, (2009): p. 45.

[47] See, e.g., Drezner (n 46); Alter and Raustiala (n 46); Alter (n 46).

required for change is smaller, and the risk of encountering conflicting norms is reduced. This can be formulated as follows:

> Hypothesis 3b: Change attempts within a specific regime or field are more likely to be successful than those that travel to other regimes.

In Chapter 6, we will return to the question of authority constellations—with a particular focus on institutional complexity—to better understand on which paths change travels and how the universe of available paths conditions the success of change attempts.

Ideational Openings

Change is typically facilitated by crises and critical junctures, which serve as windows of opportunity, by easing structural constraints and enabling agents to sidestep existing limitations without much resistance.[48] More broadly, as intimated in the previous section and in line with expectations from historical and discursive institutionalism, change in international law is also likely to benefit from ideational openings that are less conspicuous. Both cognitive and moral shifts create opportunities for actors to argue for a change in the governing rules.[49] We can thus expect that openings in the ideational environment can have a considerable influence on the fate of a change attempt. Developments in human rights or international criminal law, for instance, operated in a very favourable ideational environment during the 1990s, which resulted in a number of successful instances of norm development, such as the emergence of the state obligations to protect women from domestic violence or the inclusion of rape within the umbrella of war crimes.[50] We, therefore, hypothesize that there might be a positive correlation between openings in the ideational environment and successful change outcomes. In other words:

> Hypothesis 4: The existence of ideational openings increases the likelihood of successful change outcomes.

[48] Hillel David Soifer, 'The Causal Logic of Critical Junctures', *Comparative Political Studies* 45, (2012): pp. 1572, 1573; Paul Pierson, *Politics in Time: History, Institutions, and Social Analysis* (Princeton University Press, 2004); Capoccia and Kelemen (n 22).

[49] Vivien A Schmidt, 'The State and Political Economic Change: Beyond Rational Choice and Historical Institutionalism to Discursive Institutionalism', in *State, Globalization and Multilateralism: The Challenges of Institutionalizing Regionalism*, edited by Mario Telò (Springer Netherlands, 2012); see also Wiener (n 18).

[50] Ezgi Yildiz, 'The Protection of Women from Domestic Violence', in *The Paths of International Law: Case Studies*, edited by Pedro Martínez Esponda and others (SSRN, 2023); Dorothea Endres, 'Rape as a War Crime', in *The Paths of International Law: Case Studies*, edited by Pedro Martínez Esponda and others (SSRN, 2023).

Interaction Effects

These four sets of factors are likely to influence the likelihood of successful change—how and to what extent they do so will be the focus of our analysis in the following sections. Some may also represent necessary conditions; for example, state support is often considered indispensable in the existing literature. But beyond that, the factors are likely to interact—the importance of one category may depend on the presence or absence of factors in another. Norm adjacency is likely to play a greater role in certain institutional contexts (for example, in courts) but may be less important when significant ideational openings are present or when there is broad state support for change. Conversely, widespread state support might be less critical if a strong focal institution exists or if a critical juncture creates an opportunity for change. In this vein, the failure of states to reach a collective agreement on norm adaptation through the political bodies of the WTO did not necessarily block change altogether; rather, it redirected those efforts towards the organization's dispute settlement system, which had already accumulated considerable authority.[51] The different factors are thus likely to be mutually reinforcing, but to a certain extent, they may also serve as substitutes for one another. In section 6, we will examine some of these interaction effects in greater detail.

The authority constellation, the openness of the ideational environment, and, by association, the range of obstacles and hurdles a change attempt might encounter are also likely to depend significantly on timing. In our cases, we expect that norm development in the 1980s—still shaped by the dynamics of the Cold War—differed markedly from the post-Cold War period, characterized by unipolarity and a more dominant ideological consensus. By contrast, the shift towards multipolarity and increased contestation after 2000 probably reintroduced greater friction. To account for these temporal dynamics, our analysis includes a period variable that distinguishes the decades during which each change attempt was primarily initiated and carried forward.

3. Methodology: Cases and Measurement

Coding and Measurement

As explained in Chapter 3, we selected twenty-five cases systematically to examine the conditions under which international legal change occurs outside formal treaty-making processes, using a typical case research design to probe the causal

[51] See Nicolas Lamp, 'Arrested Norm Development: The Failure of Legislative-Judicial Dialogue in the WTO', *Leiden Journal of International Law* 38, (2025): p. 570.

mechanisms at work.[52] In assessing these case studies, we followed clear and consistent guidelines. First, we wrote in-depth case studies by analysing relevant primary and secondary resources and relying on occasional background interviews. Each case study had a more or less similar length (about twenty to thirty pages) and a similar narrative structure, wherein we traced the chronology and different stages of change episodes and focused on the role of actors—including states, institutions, or experts—the type of norms, and the scope, ambition, and timing of change attempts, and the receptivity of the ideational environment. The case studies are published and openly accessible.[53] Secondly, we coded each case narrative, attributing values on an ordinal scale based on intensity and on a binary scale (0 = absence; 1 = presence of the factors of concern). Each case was coded by two coders who had to agree on each classification in order to ensure inter-coder reliability.[54] In cases of disagreement, a third coder was invited to weigh in.

Our measure of a successful change outcome is different from what is proposed by traditional, doctrine-based accounts that focus entirely on state positions and set a high threshold for state support to appraise successful change attempts, as we discussed in Chapter 2.[55] In order to be able to capture change that occurs outside of established doctrinal categories, we define our dependent variable (successful change outcomes) using a 10-point scale of discursive shift, the distribution of which is shown in Figure A3 in the Appendix. For ease of analysis, we collapse this 10-point scale into five categories ranging from '0' to '4': 0 means 'no discursive shift', 1 means 'low discursive shift', 2 means 'medium discursive shift', 3 means 'high discursive shift', and 4 means 'full discursive shift'. This aggregation reduces sparsity in individual categories while preserving the ordinal structure of the outcome variable.

The degree of discursive shift variable is directly associated with the justificatory burden for a given change attempt. When the discourse fully shifts, for example, the burden of argument for the new position is non-existent or minimal. This implies that the change attempt is fully accepted and internalized by the relevant communities of practice, such that advancing this new understanding requires little to no justification. When the discourse has not fully shifted, by contrast, there is a higher justificatory burden to explain and defend a position as settled law.

We base our assessment of the degree of discursive shift on the opinion of the specific communities of practice operating in each subfield. We have garnered such an opinion through a review of the secondary sources, such as seminal textbooks, specialized books, articles, and references in official documents, such as

[52] For a detailed explanation on case selection strategy, see 'The Case Studies: Methodology, Selection, Purpose' in Chapter 3.

[53] Pedro Martinez Esponda and others, eds., *The Paths of Change in International Law: Case Studies* (SSRN, 2023).

[54] Cliodhna O'Connor and Helene Joffe, 'Intercoder Reliability in Qualitative Research: Debates and Practical Guidelines', *International Journal of Qualitative Methods* 19, (2020): p. 1.

[55] See 'Actors, Practices, Authority: The Social Frame of Change' in Chapter 2.

UN General Assembly resolutions, judicial decisions, or expert reports. Cases we classify as full discursive shift cases are typically those that are considered firmly consolidated and uncontested norms by the experts in a field, and those frequently figure in official documents of international bodies. High discursive shift cases are widely accepted and recognized norms without significant contestation. Cases coded as medium or low discursive shift cases demonstrate these characteristics on a decreasing scale. Medium discursive shift cases attract relatively notable academic and institutional endorsement, but they remain subject to contestation. Low discursive shift cases, by contrast, receive limited academic or institutional endorsement and face substantial open contestation. Cases coded as no discursive shift are highly contested or (partially or fully) rejected within legal academia and do not figure much in official documents produced by international institutions.

In our study, we looked for factors that could explain the variation we observed in the outcome variable in light of the expectations we listed above. We coded the *breadth of state support* on a scale from 0 to 3: '0' indicates no support or silence; '1' signifies support from limited regions or groups; '2' implies support from the majority of regions or groups with some parts opposing or remaining silent; and '3' denotes near-universal support without any opposition. The *breadth of state opposition* similarly measures the spread of state opposition as an ordinal variable with values ranging from 0 to 3: '0' means there is no opposition or silence, '1' implies there is opposition from limited regions or groups, '2' represents opposition from the majority of regions or groups with some parts holding out (supporting or remaining silent); and '3' means opposition from virtually all without any support. We also coded the existence of *major power support and opposition* as binary variables (non-existence having the value of '0' and existence having the value of '1'). Our definition of great powers is adopted from the list of major powers proposed by the Correlates of War project.[56]

We also looked at the extent to which the norm in question builds on existing norms and understandings. Our *degree of norm adjacency* variable is an ordinal variable ranging from 0 (no adjacency) to 1 (loosely builds on) and 2 (clearly builds on). The *existence of an opposing norm* or *rival norm* is a binary variable: '0' indicates that there is no existing norm that can destabilize the change attempt, while '1' means there is an opposing norm that could potentially undermine and destabilize it. The *norm type* is another binary variable created by looking at whether a given norm is collaborative, thus requiring the involvement and buy-in from many actors for it to become operational (with the value of 0). Alternatively, the norm

[56] The list includes countries such as the US, Russia, China, Germany, the United Kingdom, France, Germany, and Japan. For more, see Correlates of War Project, 'State System Membership List, v2016', https://correlatesofwar.org (2017). We also considered the direct involvement of the European Union as a major power intervention.

may be permissive which gives individual actors more latitude to use the destabilization of existing understandings as a justification (with the value of 1).

In line with our conjectures about potential factors behind change, we also analysed the authority structure in a given case—especially whether the *institutional authority* activated to process a change attempt was peripheral or focal. We coded this variable as a binary variable, with peripheral having the value of 0 and focal having the value of 1. The focal or peripheral nature of a given authority is assessed differently in each field. Some authorities that appear to be focal in a subfield may only be peripheral for international law in general, as we discussed in Chapter 3. When coding, we identified field-specific attributes of a given institutional authority. Moreover, we coded whether a *change attempt is confined to a specific regime or a field* (with the value of 0) or whether it spills into different fields and institutions and uses paths and authorities from other areas (with the value of 1).

Finally, we also examined the factors related to the ideational environment and timing of the change attempt. We coded the shifts in the ideational environment as a binary variable with '0' signifying that there is no or only a narrow ideational opening, '1' meaning there is a broad ideational opening (including critical junctures—discursive turning points that have a profound impact on the ideational environment).[57] In addition, we focused on *the timing of the change attempt* (i.e., the period when the change attempt was constructed) and created a categorical variable that distinguishes between change attempts occurring before the 1990s, during the 1990s, and in the post-2000s period.

4. Findings I: Descriptive Analysis

What drives international legal change? After laying out potential factors and hypotheses, we now turn to exploring the empirical evidence as it emerges from our cases. We begin by presenting descriptive graphs showing the bivariate relationship between different explanatory factors and our outcome variable: the degree of discursive shift. The values are presented in percentages and encoded using a graded shading scale, ranging from light shading (no discursive shift) to dark shading (full discursive shift). These graphs are intended to provide an initial exploration and visual representation of the data, highlighting potential patterns and trends. They do not communicate definitive answers as to which factors are most influential but rather serve as a starting point for deeper analysis, guiding our subsequent empirical tests and helping to identify areas where further investigation is warranted.

[57] Giovanni Capoccia, 'Critical Junctures', in *The Oxford Handbook of Historical Institutionalism*, edited by Orfeo Fioretos and others (Oxford University Press, 2016).

The Role of States

As far as the role of states is concerned, our cases show both expected and surprising patterns. When we look at the relationship between the breadth of state support and change outcome in Figure 4.1, we find that cases that receive full state support (support from virtually all states without any opposition) all reflect a full discursive shift.[58] We also find that cases with broad state support (that is, support from most regions with pockets of opposition or silence) tend to be more successful overall, whereas cases that receive limited state support seem to be the least successful. This picture largely aligns with statist expectations, but it does not, by itself, establish state support as the defining factor, since states may be more likely to express support in cases that are likely to succeed.

Interestingly, we also find instances of high and full discursive shifts occurring even in cases with limited state support, indicating that successful change is possible without broad state endorsement. As such, while state support is a significant factor, it appears that it is not the sole determinant of success; this challenges the widely held belief that broad state backing is essential for driving legal change.

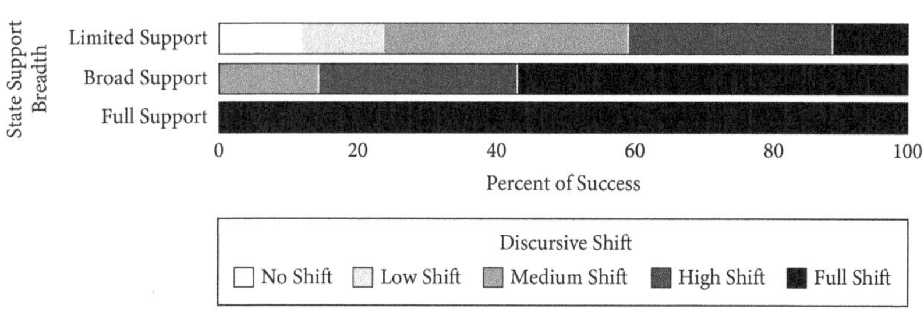

Figure 4.1 The relation between the breadth of state support and change outcomes

The breadth of state opposition is similarly distributed; as expected, however, it has an inverse relationship with change outcomes (Figure 4.2).[59] While cases that receive no or limited state opposition are more likely to be successful overall, the existence of broad opposition reduces these chances. The cases with broad state opposition are relatively less successful. However, we do observe positive change outcomes even in the presence of broad state opposition—almost two-thirds of the cases resulted in medium or high discursive shifts. Contrary to typical expectations, this suggests that even when facing substantial resistance, change is not entirely precluded. This observation runs counter to the common assumption that

[58] It should be noted that there are no observations under the 'no support' category and as a result that category is not shown in this graph.

[59] The state opposition category does not show the 'full opposition' category since there are no observations falling under this category in our study.

state opposition is an insurmountable barrier to change. Among those cases, however, we do not observe a full discursive shift; broad state opposition may thus not hinder change altogether, but it may pose obstacles to its full consolidation.

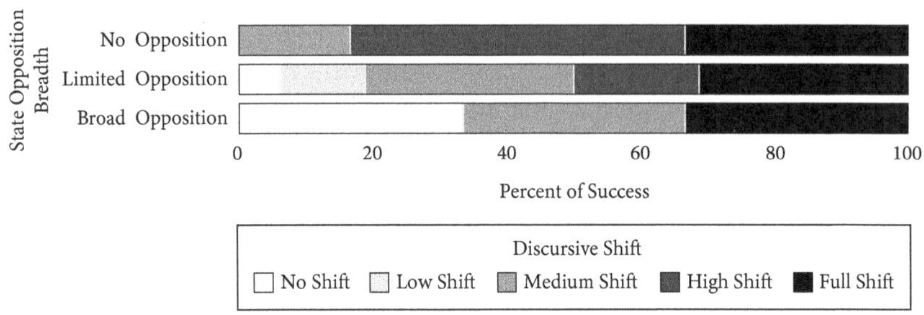

Figure 4.2 The relation between the breadth of state opposition and change outcomes

Taken together, our findings confirm that state support and opposition are closely associated with change outcomes. Nevertheless, they also reveal counterintuitive dynamics and challenge the common assumption that broad state support is a necessary condition for change and that state opposition is sufficient to derail change. Instead, it appears that there is a significant number of cases where change occurs with limited or without state support, indicating that change can sometimes unfold in relative independence from state positions.

Another key factor frequently raised in the literature is the power of the change-sponsoring or change-endorsing states. Not all states possess the same amount or kind of political, economic, or social capital, and such power differentials play an important role in international politics. To what extent does the support or opposition from great powers influence change outcomes, then? Figure 4.3 demonstrates the link between the two.

Rather surprisingly, as the left-hand panel suggests, the influence of major power support does not appear to be notable: the percentage of successful cases with high or full discursive shift remains roughly the same, at nearly 60%, regardless of

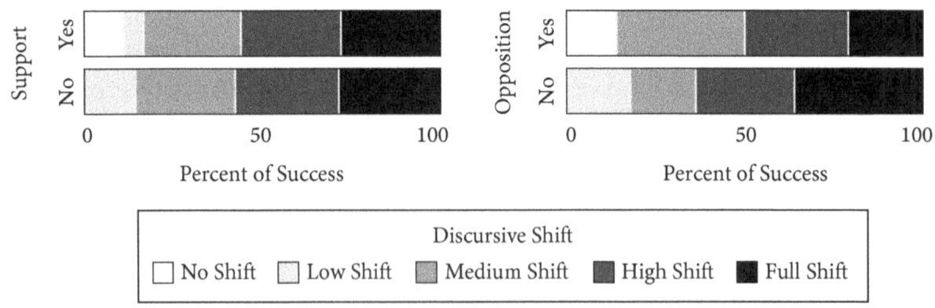

Figure 4.3 The relation between major power support and opposition and change outcomes

whether such support is present. The impact of major power opposition appears to be modest but observable. While approximately 62% of cases without major power opposition appear to achieve high or full shift, only around 50% of cases facing major power opposition seem to be successful. It is important to bear in mind, however, that major power support and opposition are not mutually exclusive; the same case may (and often does) attract both support and opposition from different major powers, potentially blurring the overall patterns observed here. Nonetheless, the data indicate that successful instances of change frequently occur even in the face of major state opposition, with half of such cases resulting in high or full discursive shift. Viewed in combination, these patterns suggest that the role of great powers in shaping international legal change is neither uniform nor decisive, but conditional and context-dependent, at least on the paths of change we take into focus in this book. We return to this point in greater detail in Chapter 5.

Norm Properties

Norm properties are frequently regarded as consequential for the success of change attempts, but we do not initially find much support for this. In particular, as Figure 4.4 suggests, norm adjacency claims may not present a significant advantage, according to the patterns observed in our sample. It appears that nearly 65% of the successful change attempts do not have any adjacency claims, whereas change attempts that clearly seem to build on existing understandings tend to be less successful, with only around 45% of such attempts obtaining high or full discursive shifts. This observation appears to run counter to the common expectation that norm adjacency claims usually accompany successful change attempts. While it is not possible to dive deeper into the reasons behind this counterintuitive observation here, one can imagine that norm adjacency claims come with benefits and disadvantages. Adjacency claims can surely help certain change attempts by concealing their innovative nature. This was the case, for example, in the case of the emergence of a right to truth on the basis of existing norms, such as the prohibition of torture and inhuman or degrading treatment, and the victimhood of the family of the disappeared persons.[60] However, adjacency claims can also sometimes be constraining and render norms vulnerable to the spillover of underlying resentment or opposition. The precautionary principle illustrates this dynamic. This principle built upon and co-emerged with governments' obligation to regulate the environment and enjoyed broad political support in the 1970s and 1980s, in places

[60] Ezgi Yildiz and Pedro Martínez Esponda, 'The Right to Truth', in *The Paths of International Law: Case Studies*, edited by Pedro Martínez Esponda and others (SSRN, 2023); Ezgi Yildiz, *Between Forbearance and Audacity: The European Court of Human Rights and the Norm Against Torture* (Cambridge University Press, 2023).

like the US, before the tides turned and deregulation became the norm—in particular during the neo-liberal Reagan/Thatcher era.[61] Growing scepticism towards environmental regulation may also have shaped perceptions of the precautionary principle itself, which could help explain how an otherwise ubiquitous concept remains politically unsettled.[62]

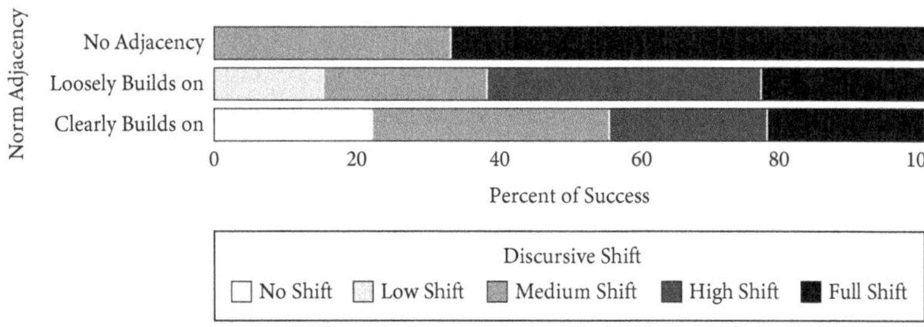

Figure 4.4 Norm adjacency claims and change outcomes

As Figure 4.5 suggests, successful change outcomes may be more common when there are no opposing norms, with full discursive shifts occurring in close to 38% of such cases in our sample. However, the presence of a rival norm does not appear to preclude meaningful change. Even with a rival norm, full discursive shifts occur in nearly 18% of cases, and high discursive shifts in about 34%, together making up just over half of the outcomes observed. For example, in the domain of maritime delimitation, equitable principles emerged as a rival approach challenging the default status of the equidistance principle as the method of continental shelf delimitation. While this challenge is likely to have undercut the popularity of equidistance, it did not completely eradicate it either.[63]

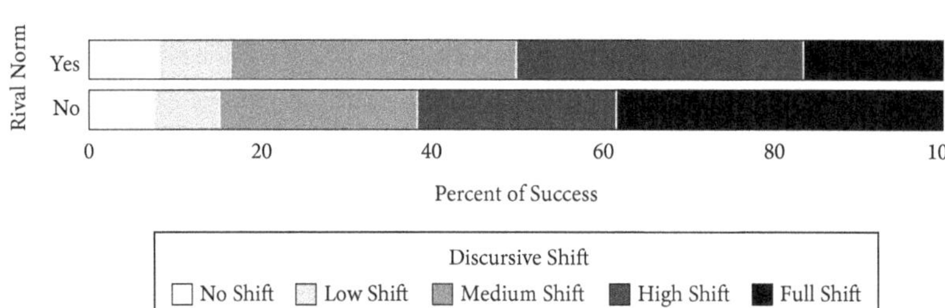

Figure 4.5 Rival norms and change outcomes

[61] Daniel Bodansky, 'The Precautionary Principle in US Environmental Law', in *Interpreting the Precautionary Principle*, edited by Timothy O'Riordan and James Cameron (Routledge, 2013), p. 205.

[62] Ezgi Yildiz, 'The Precautionary Principle', in *The Paths of International Law: Case Studies*, edited by Pedro Martínez Esponda and others (SSRN, 2023).

[63] Yildiz and Yüksel (n 37); Yildiz and Yüksel (n 39).

When comparing collaborative and permissive norms in Figure 4.6, some variation in the rate of success becomes apparent. While overall nearly 62% of change attempts involving collaborative norms seem to achieve either full or high discursive shifts, about 50% of change attempts involving permissive norms result in full or high discursive shifts. Interestingly, change attempts around collaborative norms appear to have a higher rate of successful outcomes (around 28%) and a higher rate of unsuccessful change outcomes, with 18% of change attempts resulting in no discursive shift. For permissive norms, while there are no change attempts resulting in no discursive shift, a higher percentage of change outcomes (around 50%) seem to achieve low to medium discursive shifts. This observation aligns with our initial expectations around permissive norms: actors invoking permissive norms might benefit from the destabilization of existing understandings without needing to consolidate these norms fully to be able to benefit from them effectively.

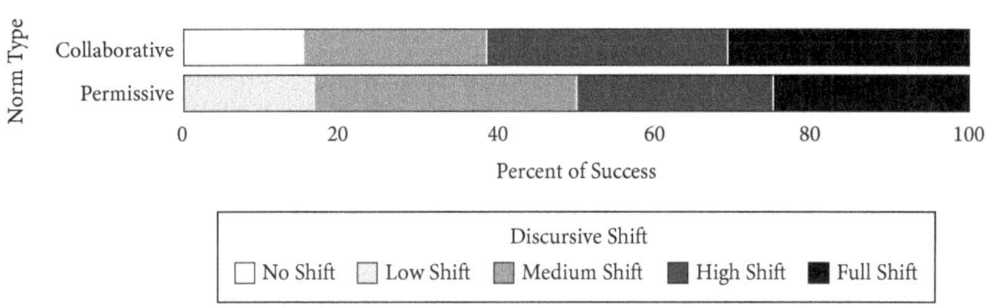

Figure 4.6 The link between norm types (collaborative or permissive) and change outcomes

Authority Constellations

Another notable bivariate relation between one of our independent variables and our outcome variable can be seen in Figure 4.7, which depicts the link between authority types and change outcomes. It seems that all change attempts involving intervention from a focal authority resulted in at least a medium discursive shift, with nearly 45% resulting in a full discursive shift. In contrast, change attempts relying on statements from peripheral authorities appear to be less successful, with only around 15% securing a full discursive shift and nearly 25% resulting in either no discursive or low discursive shift. The highest percentage of observations in this category (nearly 60%) falls somewhere between medium and high discursive shifts. This seems to support our theory around the role of focal authorities in converging existing understandings and providing reference points for all actors to follow.

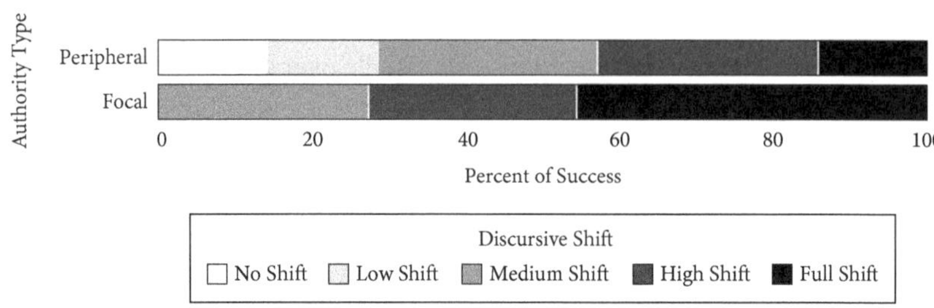

Figure 4.7 Link between authority types (focal and peripheral) and change outcomes

Success also seems to be conditioned by whether a change attempt takes place within a distinct regime. As Figure 4.8 shows, change attempts within a distinct regime appear to secure nearly 48% full discursive shift, while this number is much smaller (only around 18%) for change attempts that take place in multiple regimes. Although the rate of unsuccessful change attempts is roughly equal for both modalities of change, most change attempts that occur in more than one regime appear to result in either low or medium shifts (48%). For change attempts that are contained within a single regime, the majority (nearly 70%) seem to result in a high or full discursive shift. This pattern may indicate that change efforts focused on a single regime can more effectively mobilize resources, align stakeholders, and create cohesive narratives, leading to more substantial discursive shifts. In contrast, attempts spanning multiple regimes might face greater resistance due to the need to navigate diverse discourses, competing interests, and varied institutional frameworks, which could dilute change attempts' overall impact and lead to less significant shifts. However, it is important to note that these observations are based on a descriptive analysis—as we will see below, the multiple regression analysis tells a rather different story.

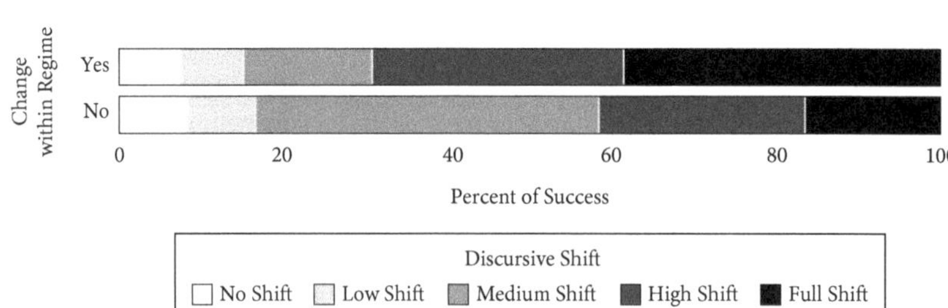

Figure 4.8 Location of change attempt and change outcomes

Ideational Openings

The openness of the ideational environment might be expected to be consequential in a discursive practice such as international law, but our findings are not very clear-cut in this respect (see Figure 4.9). Broad ideational openings—also including cases of critical junctures—seem to be more associated with full shift (nearly 30%), whereas narrow openings appear to be associated with low and medium shift (about 42%). But interestingly, the only instances of no shift (around 18%) occur in the context of broad ideational opening. Therefore, this picture does not point to a strong relationship between the width of the ideational opening and the degree of successful change outcomes.

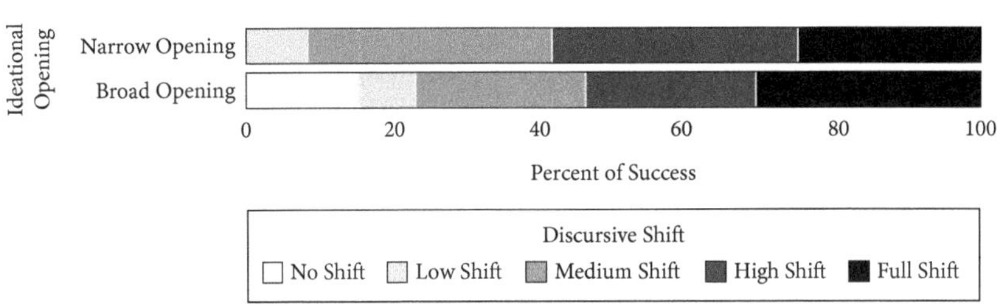

Figure 4.9 Link between degrees of ideational openings and change outcomes

While these figures illustrate the main characteristics of our sample and highlight bivariate relationships, they do not enable a comprehensive assessment of the combined influence of all four groups of factors. Bivariate analyses can only reveal simple associations between two variables at a time, potentially overlooking the combined and interactive effects of multiple variables. To assess the relationship between these factors and the degree of discursive shift, we use a simple OLS regression. This approach allows us to adjust for the presence of other variables and estimate the association between each factor and our outcome variable, while holding other factors constant. It thus provides a more nuanced understanding of the dynamics at play than the bivariate relationships described above.

5. Findings II: Regression Analysis

Our regression model incorporates four sets of explanatory factors—state roles, norm characteristics, authority dynamics, and ideational openings—and tests how they relate to the likelihood of successful change within our sample. As explained above, our sample is relatively small, and the results we present here should be assessed against this backdrop. While this limitation prevents us from presenting definitive results, our exploratory analysis reveals interesting insights potentially relevant to understanding broader trends.

In this study, we test two models to compare the explanatory power of traditional accounts with our approach: Model 1 tests only the traditional explanations commonly found in international law and international relations scholarship, namely the variables related to the role of states and norm characteristics. Model 2 includes our variables, which go beyond the role of states and norm characteristics and include authority constellations, norm types (permissive versus collaborative), and ideational openings. We listed all the factors expected to have an influence on the outcome variable, and we created a period variable to control for time in each model.

The complete regression results are reported in Table A1 in the Appendix. Below, we present a coefficient plot that provides a visual summary of these results, making it easier to interpret the estimates and their statistical significance, assessed at the conventional 0.05 level in the social sciences.

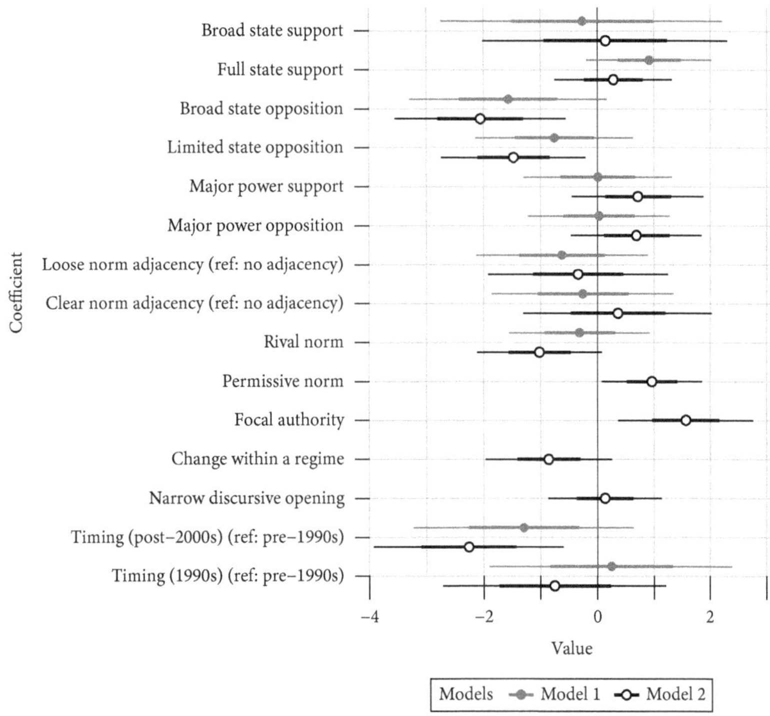

Figure 4.10 Coefficient plot depicting the results of an OLS regression with the degree of discursive shift as the dependent variable (Table A1 in the Appendix demonstrates the results)

Figure 4.10 displays the results of an OLS regression using the two models described above.[64] Model 1 is depicted in grey, and Model 2 is depicted in black.

[64] Despite the modest sample size (n = 25), the regression results appear robust and well-specified (see Appendix for details). Diagnostic tests confirm that key assumptions hold: residuals are

Horizontal bars in grey and black indicate each variable's regression estimates and associated confidence intervals. For the purposes of this assessment, we should focus on the thin bars, which reflect the 95% confidence intervals ($p < 0.05$).[65] In these plots, the vertical line at zero represents the null hypothesis—the assumption that there is no relationship between a variable and the outcome. Variables whose confidence intervals do not cross this line are considered statistically significant, with p-value of 0.05 or lower. In such cases, we can reject the null hypothesis and conclude that there is evidence of a relationship. Conversely, if a confidence interval (shown with the thin band) crosses the vertical line at zero, we cannot reject the null hypothesis. This suggests that the variable does not have a statistically significant relationship with the outcome. The direction of the relationship is indicated by the side of the zero line on which the coefficient is placed: variables positioned to the left of the zero line (with negative values) are negatively correlated with the outcome variable (i.e., the degree of discursive shift), whereas variables positioned to the right (with positive values) are positively correlated with it, controlling for all other variables included in the model.

Model 1 (shown in grey), which includes only commonly known explanations such as state support and opposition and norm adjacency, has no variables significant at the 0.05 level.[66] This suggests that these traditional explanations may not be as strongly linked to change outcomes as often assumed. Despite this, it is worth mentioning that one variable—broad state opposition—achieves statistical significance, albeit at the less stringent 0.10 level (see Table A1 in the Appendix). Because its p-value is above 0.05, there is only weak evidence against the null hypothesis of no relationship. In other words, in this instance, there is only limited statistical support for the claim that broad state opposition is associated with successful change outcomes, all else being equal.

approximately normal (Jarque–Bera, $p = 0.29$), variance is constant (studentized Breusch–Pagan, $p = 0.35$), the linear functional form is appropriate (Ramsey RESET, $p = 0.85$), and all variance inflation factors are below 2. Robustness checks excluding influential observations (Cook's Distance, leverage, studentized residuals) yield substantively consistent results, with stable signs and magnitudes for key predictors (see Table A3 in Appendix). We also ran a robustness check using the 10-point scale version of the dependent variable, which produced substantively similar results (see Table A6 in the Appendix).

[65] Confidence intervals tell us how precise a measurement is. It serves as another way to communicate probability. 95% confidence level means we can expect that 95 out of 100 times an observation will fall between the upper and lower values specified by the interval. In Figure 4.10, the thick bars represent the default 68% confidence intervals (±1 standard error), offering a quick visual sense of the estimate's precision, while the thin bars represent the 95% confidence intervals (±2 standard errors), which are typically used to assess statistical significance. These intervals follow the default settings of the multiplot command in R, which automatically displays both 68% and 95% confidence intervals. For more on confidence intervals, see Marshall A Taylor, 'Visualization Strategies for Regression Estimates with Randomization Inference', *The Stata Journal* 20, (2020): p. 309.

[66] As explained above, the threshold for significance is 0.05. In this model, there is one variable, broad state opposition that is statistically significant at alpha level 0.10, which falls under this threshold. See Table A1 in the Appendix.

Model 2, which builds upon the traditional explanations by incorporating our additional variables, demonstrates substantially greater explanatory power compared to Model 1, with the R^2 increasing from 0.646 to 0.847 and the adjusted R^2 from 0.346 to 0.593 (see Table A1 in the Appendix). This enhanced model provides a more comprehensive understanding of norm change in international law. The inclusion of new variables allows us to capture dynamics that were overlooked in the more conventional analyses. Notably, several of the variables introduced in Model 2—namely, broad state opposition, limited state opposition, rival norm, permissive norm, and focal authority—emerge as statistically significant within our model, with other factors held constant.[67] The significance of these variables suggests that they are meaningfully associated with variation in the outcomes of norm change processes and that relying solely on traditional explanations such as state support and norm adjacency might be limiting.

Our comprehensive model accounts for a large share of the observed variation in the dependent variable. It confirms several of our hypotheses while contradicting others. One of the most important findings concerns the role of states. We can find some evidence for Hypothesis 1a and Hypothesis 1b, namely that the breadth of state support is positively correlated, and the breadth of state opposition is negatively correlated with the rate of successful change outcomes, controlling for other factors. However, of these two variables, only the breadth of opposition appears to be statistically significant. Compared to no state opposition, limited state opposition is negatively related to change outcomes, and this negative association increases as the breadth of state opposition widens.

What we find here indicates that, in our sample, broad (or even limited) state opposition is associated with lower rates of successful change, whereas state support, on its own, is not a reliable indicator of change attempts' success. The greater importance of state opposition—as opposed to support—also underscores the role of states more as blockers than as drivers in legal change processes.

Another notable finding concerns the role of great powers. While great power support appears to have a positive association with change outcomes, this relationship is not statistically significant. Hence, we do not have enough evidence to confirm Hypothesis 1c. Similarly, great power opposition does not have a statistically significant association with the level of discursive shift, contrary to Hypothesis 1d. As discussed earlier in the chapter, one possible explanation for these null results is that support and opposition from major powers frequently co-occur in the same cases, thereby diluting the association between each and the outcome variable. This pattern, foreshadowed by the descriptive statistics, runs directly counter to standard expectations about the decisive role of the powerful driving legal change.[68] We will further investigate the role of power in Chapter 5.

[67] All these variables have a p-value (significance value) of 0.05 with the exception of 'rival norms' and 'permissive norms' with a p-value of 0.10.

[68] See also our more detailed discussion in Chapter 5.

Interestingly, our analysis finds no support for Hypothesis 2a, which concerns the influence of norm adjacency claims—a widely shared expectation in the constructivist international relations literature. Contrary to the predictions of Hypothesis 2a, we find that norm adjacency claims, regardless of their degree, do not have a statistically significant relationship with change outcomes. In fact, clear norm adjacency is negatively correlated with the outcome variable, indicating that claims closely aligned with existing understandings tend to coincide with lower levels of successful change in our sample. These findings are consistent with the patterns observed in the descriptive statistics presented above.

We find some evidence for Hypothesis 2b—the existence of rival norms has a negative, statistically significant relationship with the rate of successful change attempts, consistent with our prediction. Another factor that is related to norm characteristics with a statistically significant association is the norm type. In contrast with the interpretation of the descriptive statistics in the previous section, the regression analysis indicates that change attempts involving permissive norms are positively associated with higher rates of success. This finding aligns with Hypothesis 2c. As explained above, self-licensing permissive norms require a lower threshold to be invoked, acknowledged, and used by states, and that usage might lead to broader recognition even in the absence of widespread state endorsement.

A statistically significant association is also present between our variable related to the type of authority and the outcome variable. As we predicted under Hypothesis 3a, change attempts processed or endorsed by focal authorities achieve higher rates of success, keeping all else constant. This finding underscores the importance of focal authorities' involvement in successful outcomes. In our sample, this is particularly visible in cases concerning international criminal law, trade law, and the law of the sea, where specialized judicial and non-judicial institutions occupy a central position within their respective fields.

When it comes to the location of change processes, our expectations under Hypothesis 3b did not find support, as the location of change attempts did not have a statistically significant association with change outcomes. Additionally, we found that pursuing change attempts within a single regime is negatively correlated with successful outcomes, all else being constant. This unexpected finding stands in contrast with what appeared from the descriptive statistics. And it suggests that, while specialized focus can be beneficial in certain contexts, change attempts might benefit from engagement with multiple regimes—something not fully accounted for in the regime complexity literature. Institutions and pathways situated in other regimes, outside the one where change is being pursued, may serve as paths of least resistance and help to overcome obstacles to change by offering their endorsements. We will explore this dynamic in greater depth in Chapter 6.

The degree of openness in the ideational environment shows some association with change outcomes in our sample, but this relationship is not statistically significant, contrary to what we expect under Hypothesis 4. One possible reason is that the number of cases featuring broad ideational openings (including critical junctures) was limited in our sample. Future studies could build on this intuition and further examine the potential influence of varying degrees of ideational openness.

Finally, we included a period variable as a control, distinguishing between the pre-1990s, the 1990s, and the post-2000s periods. The pre-1990s period serves as the reference category. Compared to the pre-1990s, change attempts initiated in the 1990s have a negative association with discursive shift outcomes, but this relationship is not statistically significant. This suggests that while there is some evidence of a trend towards lower success rates in the 1990s, the difference could be due to random variation, and there is no strong evidence of a systematic change. By contrast, change attempts initiated in the post-2000s period show a statistically significant negative relationship with discursive shift outcomes at the 0.05 level. This suggests that, relative to efforts launched before 1990, more recent initiatives have been less likely to be accompanied by successful discursive shifts. This could be because some of these cases are still ongoing and need more time until they reach full consolidation. However, the post-2000s period also features a different political configuration, including a renewed great power rivalry, reflected, for example, in the creation of the BRICS group (a coalition of Brazil, Russia, India, China, South Africa, and a growing number of other countries). Change attempts thus faced higher resistance in this period, which may have frustrated their success. We will return to this theme in greater detail in Chapter 7.

Taken together, our analysis points to several factors that are associated with successful change outcomes in our sample. Among them is the constraining effect of state opposition, although notably, neither broad state support nor great power influence, whether in favour of or against change, shows a statistically significant association with our dependent variable. By contrast, the analysis shows a positive association between focal authorities in charge of or supporting change processes and successful outcomes. It thus highlights the relevance of authority constellations that played an important role in our expectations. In addition, our analysis underscores the importance of factors related to norm characteristics, but different from those that have received the most attention in the existing literature. In particular, rival norms tend to coincide with lower rates of successful outcomes, whereas change attempts involving self-licensing permissive norms are more often associated with successful outcomes, all else being equal.

Our findings are suggestive. They do not allow us to draw definitive conclusions due to the small sample size, which limits the generalizability of our results. In addition, our focus on cases outside of classical treaty renegotiation processes may place less emphasis on the kinds of state-based, traditional explanations that are often highlighted in the literature. Further research with larger samples will be necessary to confirm these preliminary findings and to provide more robust evidence on the relationships explored in this study.

6. Assessing Interactions and Predictions

The different factors are likely to have an effect not just on their own but also in interaction with others. As set out at the beginning of this chapter, we expect the additional factors we propose—namely the authority type, the openness of the ideational environment, as well as norm types or the existence of rival norms—to have an accelerating or moderating effect on other well-established factors related to the role of states and norm adjacency. The new factors can also interact with each other in conditioning change prospects.

In this section, we explore these possible interaction effects. In order to measure them, we calculated predicted values by looking at the interaction between our variables of interest.[69] Each predicted value in the interaction is represented by the point located at the centre of the lines, which shows the range of uncertainty or variability around that prediction (see Figure 4.11). To understand whether there is a significant interaction effect, we compare these points across different categories on the x-axis.[70] This assessment further emphasizes the importance of our newly proposed factors and their moderating effect. We run several models with interaction between traditionally accepted variables—namely, state support/opposition, major power support/opposition, and norm adjacency—with our proposed explanatory factors and plot predicted values for our outcome variable based on them.

Of the several models tested, the interaction between authority type and state opposition was statistically significant overall (see Table A2 in the Appendix).[71] This suggests that the type of institutional authority can moderate the effect of state opposition. Change attempts processed by focal authorities and facing only limited state opposition show the highest predicted discursive shift. Figure 4.11 portrays the predicted value of our outcome variable based on a model with an interaction between the authority type (either focal or peripheral) and the breadth of state opposition (the degrees of state opposition ranging from 'no opposition' to 'broad opposition'[72]) on our outcome variable, the degree of discursive shift. Focal

[69] We used the cat_plot function, which helps display predicted values for categorical variables, with each point representing the estimated value for a specific category or combination of categories. The lines extending from each point show the range of uncertainty around these predictions, represented with confidence intervals. By examining the position of the points and the overlap of the lines, one can assess differences between categories and determine if these differences are statistically significant. In this case, we looked at three-way interaction between variables of interest and our outcome variable, the degree of discursive shift.

[70] Lines are the error bars that indicate the estimated errors and give a sense of the precision of the measurement. They represent the lower outer limit.

[71] In these models, our dependent variable, degree of discursive shift is a numerical variable whereas our interacting variables are categorical. We find that the only statistically significant interaction (at the 0.10 level) is between focal authority and limited state opposition.

[72] Note that broad opposition is the highest value in our variable as none of the cases we studied faced full state opposition.

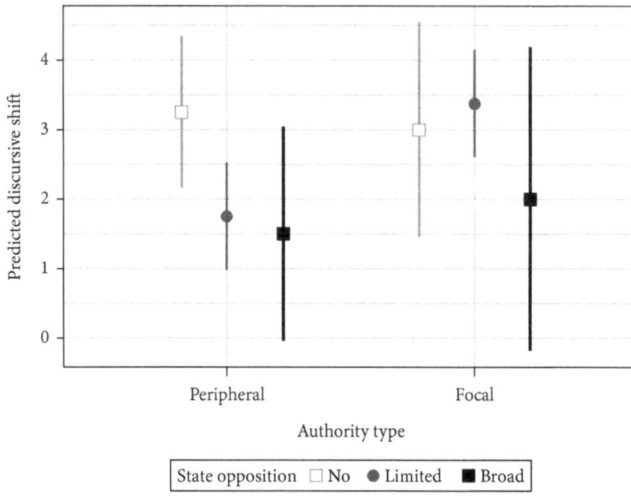

Figure 4.11 The interaction between authority type and breadth of state opposition

and peripheral authorities differ in the way they process and endorse change attempts when confronted with state opposition. When there is no state opposition (lightest grey), peripheral authorities have a slightly higher predicted discursive shift than focal authorities. With limited opposition, focal authorities have a higher predicted discursive shift. Under broad opposition, focal authorities still have a higher point estimate than peripheral authorities, but the wide confidence intervals suggest considerable uncertainty around this difference.

Focal authorities thus seem to countervail and mitigate state opposition. This finding is in line with our authority-based account elaborated in Chapter 2 and the beginning of the present chapter. We observe the positive influence of focal authorities in the case of individual criminal responsibility in non-international armed conflicts, for example. This new understanding was anchored around the endorsement issued in the *Tadic* decision of the International Criminal Tribunal for the Former Yugoslavia (ICTY), a pivotal reference point in the field.[73] This ruling drastically shifted the burden of argument in favour of establishing individual criminal responsibility and helped to squash opposing views. This is yet another finding that is consistent with Hypothesis 3a and our expectation that change attempts endorsed by focal authorities are more likely to be successful. This is the case even when there is visible (albeit limited) state opposition.

[73] Nina Kiderlin, 'War Crimes in Non-International Armed Conflict', in *The Paths of International Law: Case Studies*, edited by Pedro Martínez Esponda and others (SSRN, 2023).

7. Conclusion

This chapter has built on the actor-, practice-, and authority-focused account introduced in Chapter 2 to distil explanatory factors driving, propelling, or blocking change in international law. The social frame of change we drew in Chapter 2 around paths of change and the authority structures located on or overseeing these paths served as an inspiration to develop theoretically and empirically derived expectations going beyond what the existing literature typically focuses on. Alongside widely acknowledged explanatory elements such as the role of states and the strength of norm adjacency claims, we have explored additional factors such as the type of institutional authority and openings in the ideational environment. We have assessed each factor's individual and combined effect and explained how these four different groups of factors may be mutually reinforcing but, in certain circumstances, also potential substitutes for one another, relying on statistical analysis.

The most consistent and statistically significant association with successful outcomes in our study is the presence of focal authorities—central institutions with recognized authority in a given field. Their support is generally associated with higher discursive shift and with weaker observed effects of state opposition (see Table A2 in the Appendix). These findings point to a potentially constructive and enabling role of authority structures, which is often downplayed in existing literature where institutions are treated primarily as passive forums for state interaction. Our analysis brings these actors to the centre and reveals that, in many cases, focal authorities are present in successful change processes, including those marked by considerable resistance from states.

In contrast, state support, a pillar of traditional explanations, does not have a statistically significant relationship with successful change attempts. While broad state opposition is associated with lower predicted success, instances of successful change are still observed in some cases where focal authorities are involved (see Table A2 in the Appendix). This asymmetry between support and opposition suggests that states matter less as drivers of change than as potential veto players or sources of friction. State opposition appears to operate primarily by slowing, narrowing, or destabilizing processes of legal consolidation rather than by preventing change altogether.

The political salience of focal authorities and state opposition is also visible in contemporary patterns of institutional contestation. For example, President Trump's memorandum of 7 January 2026 directs executive agencies to take immediate steps to withdraw US participation and support from a wide set of international bodies (explicitly targeting, among others, UN entities and legal and scientific institutions such as the International Law Commission, the UN Framework Convention on Climate Change, and the Intergovernmental Panel on Climate Change).[74] Rather than advancing a coherent substitute legal project, this mode of contestation operates by challenging existing institutions and practices. The fact that these efforts are directed at institutions themselves underscores that their authority is not merely epiphenomenal, but a central object of political struggle in periods of heightened contestation—an observation that aligns with other studies of politicization and backlash.[75] This also indicates that state opposition, especially during the current period, manifests primarily as a strategy of institutional erosion without a corresponding attempt at legal construction.

Against this backdrop, our findings on great powers are also important but they require careful interpretation. While great power influence has long been assumed to be decisive in both international law and international relations scholarship, we find no significant relationship between great power support or opposition and change outcomes in our sample. This does not suggest that powerful states are irrelevant. Rather, it indicates that their influence may be exercised less through direct sponsorship or veto of legal change than through indirect strategies aimed at contesting, weakening, or withdrawing from authoritative rules and institutions. Their greatest weight is likely to be felt on other paths than the ones we focus on here—in treaty-making, for example—and in their ability to ignore and circumvent the law. Understanding power in these terms invites a rethinking of how influence operates in legal change processes—a task we undertake in Chapter 5.

Beyond the role of states and authority constellations, our findings also prompt a reassessment of widely held expectations about norm characteristics. In particular, we find no support for the view that norm adjacency claims facilitate successful change, which is a common expectation in constructivist literature. Instead, our analysis points to the importance of norm type: change attempts involving permissive or self-licensing norms are more often associated with successful outcomes, whereas collaborative norms face higher thresholds for acceptance and operationalization, making them more difficult to consolidate. In addition, we have found that the existence of rival norms is negatively associated with the rate of successful change attempts. Rival norms create competing narratives and expectations, which can fragment support and hinder the adoption of new practices or policies.

[74] The White House, 'Presidential Memoranda: Withdrawing the United States from International Organizations, Conventions, and Treaties that Are Contrary to the Interests of the United States' (7 January 2026), https://www.whitehouse.gov/presidential-actions/2026/01/withdrawing-the-united-states-from-international-organizations-conventions-and-treaties-that-are-contrary-to-the-interests-of-the-united-states/.

[75] See, e.g., Michael Zürn, Martin Binder and Matthias Ecker-Ehrhardt, 'International Authority and Its Politicization', *International Theory* 4, (2012): p. 69; Erik Voeten, 'Is the Public Backlash against Globalization a Backlash against Legalization and Judicialization?', *International Studies Review* 24, (2022): p. c015.

Taken together, these findings support the institutionalist account introduced at the start of this chapter. They affirm the importance of authority constellations in shaping change processes and show that legal transformation is not simply the product of state will, especially not that of the most powerful states. Instead, this institutionalist lens helps explain why change occurs in some cases and not others and opens new avenues for understanding legal transformation through non-traditional pathways. It invites scholars and practitioners alike to pay closer attention to who speaks with authority in international law, how new understandings gain traction, and when ideational environments create openings to shift the burden of argument towards a particular interpretation of the law. While this chapter advances the debate on the drivers of international legal change, it also highlights the need for further research as our limited sample size precludes sweeping generalizations. Nonetheless, the patterns we identify are robust enough to warrant closer attention and to challenge existing paradigms. Future studies can build on these insights by expanding the empirical base, refining measurement strategies, and probing more deeply into the dynamics uncovered here.

5

Beyond Might? Varieties of Power in Legal Change

Power, both as an analytical tool and a constitutive force, has long been considered an 'integral part of all political relationships' in international relations.[1] Similarly, power holds a central place in international law and manifests in the ability to craft and interpret rules, set agendas, and influence the behaviour of other actors.[2] It is, therefore, intuitive to attribute a significant role to power dynamics when analysing the politics of international law and legal change. After all, it seems natural to expect that those who hold power are the ones making decisions and imposing their change visions on others. Similarly, it is reasonable to assume that the powerful establish the rules of the game and set the parameters within which others must operate, leaving the powerless with limited room to manoeuvre. According to this logic, while small windows of opportunity may exist for the powerless to initiate change, substantial and transformative change is typically the domain of those with material power.[3]

Recent episodes of great power contestation reinforce this intuition. Open challenges to international legal commitments, attacks on multilateral institutions, and efforts to hollow out established regimes are often taken as evidence that material power ultimately prevails and that international law bends (or breaks) under pressure. Yet, whether such moments amount to genuine legal change is far from self-evident, as we explained in Chapter 1. We treat such episodes as potential catalysts for discursive change, but we do not equate rupture or violation with legal change unless it is followed by sustained shifts in justificatory practice. Periods of disruption may unsettle existing norms without necessarily reconfiguring the underlying understandings of what the law requires. Whether they remain transient blips or harden into more durable shifts in legal practice is difficult to arbitrate in real time and depends on how other actors respond, resist, or adapt, and on whether

[1] K J Holsti, 'The Concept of Power in the Study of International Relations', *Background* 7, (1964): pp. 179, 192.

[2] William W Burke-White, 'Power Shifts in International Law: Structural Realignment and Substantive Pluralism', *Harvard International Law Journal* 56, (2015): p. 1; Nico Krisch, 'International Law in Times of Hegemony: Unequal Power and the Shaping of the International Legal Order', *European Journal of International Law* 16, (2005): p. 369; Oona A Hathaway, 'Between Power and Principle: An Integrated Theory of International Law', *The University of Chicago Law Review* 72, (2005): p. 469.

[3] See, e.g., China Miéville, *Between Equal Rights: A Marxist Theory of International Law* (Brill, 2005).

Change in International Law. Nico Krisch, Ezgi Yildiz, and Pedro Martínez Esponda, Oxford University Press.
 DOI: 10.1093/9780198918325.003.0005

alternative interpretations become stabilized within relevant communities of practice. It is precisely this gap between disruption and discursive (re)settlement that renders the role of power in legal change more complex and analytically more interesting than conventional accounts suggest.

In the project that gave rise to this book, we, too, initially assumed that material power would play a dominant role (even if, as intimated in Chapter 1, not necessarily the same across the different paths of international law).[4] However, our comparative case analysis has revealed a more nuanced picture. While material power is undoubtedly significant, its influence is often tempered by other factors, and it is often ideationally, institutionally, and procedurally constrained or enabled. Moreover, as we laid out in Chapter 4, the analysis has underscored that powerful states, while significant in obstructing change, do not usually dictate outcomes in international law. Their support or opposition is often not the (only) decisive factor shaping the outcome of change attempts. This chapter seeks to provide an account that helps to explain this surprising finding.

For this account, we unpack the notion of power—a notoriously multifaceted concept that extends well beyond its common association with material resources. We especially emphasize 'ideational power' as key to understanding the role of power in the discursive practice of international law. This draws on scholarship on discursive institutionalism, which has emphasized that power manifests not only in material forms but also in ideational and relational dimensions, where the ability to shape norms, construct narratives, and frame arguments becomes a potent tool of influence.[5]

Power is then not merely the capacity of actors to impose their will on others but also their ability to frame issues, mobilize coalitions, and leverage receptive authority structures to their own benefit. In this vein, we advocate for a greater focus on what we term *discourse mobilization*—a strategic process whereby change agents use ideational frames, institutional practices, and procedural rules to persuade, socialize, normalize, or elicit deference. Discourse mobilization not only serves as a form of legal justification for change but also depends on and generates political power.[6] We thus demonstrate how change agents harness ideational power through these interconnected strategies, and we illustrate how these strategies can obscure or diminish the role of material power while shaping diverse forms and outcomes of power in practice. Our findings and grounded assessment of gradual change processes help us challenge the traditional emphasis on material

[4] See 'The Politics of Change' in Chapter 1.

[5] Martin B Carstensen and Vivien A Schmidt, 'Power through, over and in Ideas: Conceptualizing Ideational Power in Discursive Institutionalism', *Journal of European Public Policy* 23, (2016): p. 318; Thomas Schultz, 'International Law in the Minds: On the Ideational Basis of the Making, the Changing, and the Unmaking of International Law', *Leiden Journal of International Law* 37, (2024): p. 649.

[6] Ian Hurd, 'The Permissive Power of the Ban on War', *European Journal of International Security* 2, (2017): pp. 1, 14.

power by taking into clearer view the use of ideational power—a more pliable yet often equally commanding force.

This approach also helps us to shed further light on the dynamics of the paths of change that stand at the centre of our exploration of the change processes in international law. Not all paths are equally open to ideational power and to discourse mobilization in particular. Each institutionalizes discursive elements differently, suggesting that ideational power plays a more prominent role on the more interpretive paths—such as bureaucratic, judicial, and private-authority pathways—and a lesser role in more overtly state-centred, law-making ones. Treaty-making, in particular, is likely to be more susceptible to material power, as its dominant logic is often one of bargaining rather than arguing. This may also explain why classical power politics—less visible in the informal, incremental change processes we examine here—reassert themselves more forcefully during treaty-making episodes that mark foundational moments or broader institutional transitions.

In this chapter, we first situate our inquiry within broader debates on power, drawing on the insights from existing accounts to examine how power is generated, mobilized, and manifested in legal contexts (section 1). We then explain how material power features in our empirical analysis, paying particular attention to material power's obstructive qualities (section 2). To capture other ways in which power may manifest in legal change, we present the main mechanisms and strategies of discourse mobilization, with a focus on the use of ideational frames, of institutions and authority, and of procedural rules and opportunities. We pay particular attention to how different paths of change shape the role and reach of ideational power (section 3).

1. Conceptualizing Power in International Law

International law has been typically studied through the lens of material power, albeit through markedly divergent approaches. Classical legal thought often downplays the role of power and conceives law as 'a set of neutral rules' applied objectively[7] and even-handedly to the weak and the strong alike.[8] In contrast, the (legal) realists that became influential after the Second World War significantly deviated from this perspective;[9] instead, they viewed law as 'politics by other means'.[10] Representing this line of thinking—in particular, realism as an account of world

[7] Rosalyn Higgins, 'Policy Considerations and the International Judicial Process', *International & Comparative Law Quarterly* 17, (1968): p. 58.

[8] Rosalyn Higgins, 'The Identity of International Law', in *Themes and Theories*, edited by Rosalyn Higgins (Oxford University Press, 2009).

[9] Shirley V Scott, 'International Law as Ideology: Theorizing the Relationship between International Law and International Politics', *European Journal of International Law* 5, (1994): p. 313.

[10] Richard H Steinberg and Jonathan M Zasloff, 'Power and International Law', *American Journal of International Law* 100, (2006): p. 64.

politics—Hans Morgenthau describes power and state interests as the source of international law and the balance of power as the reason why states refrain from violating the law.[11] The popularity of this view waxed and waned, but it never fully disappeared. For example, it found its contemporary expression in other realist works, such as the one by Jack Goldsmith and Eric Posner, who argue that international law's appeal and potential are limited by 'the configurations of state interests and the distribution of state power'.[12] Others, like William Burke-White, for example, have built on these insights to highlight how international law reflects power shifts.[13] Interestingly, both Third World Approaches to International Law (TWAIL) and critical perspectives echo these points by depicting international law as a tool that serves the interests of powerful states and actors.[14] TWAIL scholars argue that international law has historically been shaped by colonial legacies and continues to perpetuate global inequalities by reinforcing the dominance of Western states and marginalizing the Global South.[15] Similarly, critical perspectives contend that international law, rather than being a neutral and objective framework, is deeply embedded in existing power structures, serving to legitimize and perpetuate the *status quo*.[16]

Realism gives significant weight to the role of great powers. Indeed, if all that matters is state power, and the expectation is that *might makes right*, then it is logical to anticipate that great powers will have a major role in determining the course of change in international law. For example, Detlev Vagts highlights how hegemony enables states to use international organizations to magnify their authority, avoid inconvenient obligations by declining to commit to certain treaties, and selectively endorse rules that align with their interests while rejecting those that do not.[17] But do great powers really benefit from their advantageous position within the international system?[18] While scholars like Jack Goldsmith and Eric Posner contend that they do, pointing to the example of the US and the ways in which it resisted and weakened international law in the post-Cold War period,[19]

[11] Hans J Morgenthau, 'Positivism, Functionalism, and International Law', *American Journal of International Law* 34, (1940): p. 260.

[12] Jack L Goldsmith and Eric A Posner, *The Limits of International Law* (Oxford University Press, 2006), p. 225.

[13] Burke-White (n 2).

[14] Ntina Tzouvala, *Capitalism as Civilisation: A History of International Law* (Cambridge University Press, 2020); Umut Özsu, *Completing Humanity: The International Law of Decolonization, 1960–82* (Cambridge University Press, 2023).

[15] Makau Mutua, 'What Is TWAIL?', *Proceedings of the ASIL Annual Meeting* 94, (2000): p. 31; Luis Eslava and Sundhya Pahuja, 'Beyond the (Post)Colonial: TWAIL and the Everyday Life of International Law', *Verfassung und Recht in Übersee/Law and Politics in Africa, Asia and Latin America* 45, (2012): p. 195.

[16] Anthony Carty, 'Critical International Law: Recent Trends in the Theory of International Law', *European Journal of International Law* 2, (1991): p. 66; Nigel Purvis, 'Critical Legal Studies in Public International Law', *Harvard International Law Journal* 32, (1991): p. 81.

[17] Detlev F Vagts, 'Hegemonic International Law', *American Journal of International Law* 95, (2001): pp. 843, 846.

[18] Krisch (n 2).

[19] Goldsmith and Posner (n 12).

others like Thomas Franck argue that the international system is not governed by a logic of '*La loi, c'est moi*' and that the law has not lost its compliance pull even in the face of resistance from powerful states.[20] A middle view argues that international law's place is secured not by absolute deference to power but by its ability to reflect the demands of powerful states alongside the aspirations for justice held by the broader international community.[21]

While realist and critical perspectives have illuminated the role of power in shaping international law, their focus often remains on material dimensions of power. However, power is an amorphous or 'polymorphous' concept, and its study extends beyond these traditional paradigms.[22] Drawing on a range of approaches—from Weberian perspectives, which define power as the ability to compel action,[23] to Foucauldian views that emphasize power's constitutive and productive effects—scholarship has increasingly focused on how power operates not only to constrain but also to create.[24]

Michael Barnett and Raymond Duvall, for instance, define power as the 'production, in and through social relations, of effects that shape the capacities of actors to determine their circumstances and fate' and emphasize the different forms of power other than material power, which is often associated with capability and capacity.[25] They distinguish forms of power along two analytical dimensions: 'the kinds of social relations through which power works' and 'the specificity of social relations through which effects are produced', and propose a fourfold taxonomy.[26] Compulsory power is similar to the traditional definitions of power and implies direct control over the actions of others. Institutional power manifests itself as indirect control over socially distant others, mediated through institutional rules and positions.[27] Structural power translates as the co-constitution of capacities of actors, based on the notion that actors' capabilities and interests are directly shaped by their social positions.[28] Finally, productive power shifts attention beyond structures and relates to the constitution of all social subjects in and through

[20] Thomas M Franck, 'The Power of Legitimacy and the Legitimacy of Power: International Law in an Age of Power Disequilibrium', *The American Journal of International Law* 100, (2006): p. 88.

[21] Krisch (n 2).

[22] Michael Barnett and Raymond Duvall, 'Power in International Politics', *International Organization* 59, (2005): pp. 39, 40.

[23] Stefano Guzzini, 'The Concept of Power: A Constructivist Analysis', *Millennium* 33, (2005): p. 495. Yet Weber himself acknowledged the limitations of this definition for social theory; see Stefano Guzzini, 'On the Measure of Power and the Power of Measure in International Relations' (2009) DIIS Working Paper 2009:28, 9 https://www.econstor.eu/handle/10419/44660 (accessed 25 September 2022). For further discussion, see Max Weber, *Wirtschaft Und Gesellschaft* (Mohr Siebeck, [1922], 1980).

[24] For a comprehensive overview of different traditions, see, e.g., Steven Lukes, *Power: A Radical View*, 2nd ed. (Palgrave Macmillan, 2004).

[25] Different forms include compulsory power, institutional power, structural power, and productive power. For more, see Barnett and Duvall (n 22), pp. 39, 43.

[26] ibid p. 48.

[27] ibid.

[28] ibid pp. 52–55.

discursive practices.[29] Bringing together different traditions to study power, this taxonomy provides a helpful road map for exploring the various manifestations of power in world politics.

The ability to shape actors and their beliefs has also been named 'ideational power'. In the tradition of discursive institutionalism, Martin Carstensen and Vivien Schmidt describe ideational power as actors' capacity 'to influence other actors' normative and cognitive beliefs through the use of ideational elements'.[30] According to them, actors may generate such an effect in three main ways: the capacity to persuade through reasoning and argument (power through ideas), the capacity to dominate understandings (power over ideas), and the capacity to structure thoughts and institutionalize ideas (power in ideas).[31] This definition, and discursive institutionalism more broadly, resonates with our approach; as already pointed out in Chapter 2, (international) law itself is a discursive practice, making insights from discursive institutionalism particularly relevant.

A key premise of our approach is that international law operates, in many of its aspects, as a discursive and argumentative practice.[32] Rather than viewing legal outcomes solely as products of material power or strategic bargaining, we emphasize that actors seek to persuade relevant audiences of the legal validity of their positions. This discursive character is most evident in judicial proceedings, but it also extends to processes of law-making and legalization, whether through treaty-making or more informal mechanisms.[33] Building on scholars like Ian Johnstone, we view international law as a 'fundamentally discursive process',[34] created intersubjectively 'through a process of justificatory discourse'.[35] Even when arguments are strategic or insincere, the very act of framing a position in legal terms reflects an attempt to persuade within a shared normative structure.[36]

The emphasis on discursive construction does not imply an absence of constraints or structures. As Martti Koskenniemi highlights, persuasive legal arguments must adhere to certain markers of legitimacy. To be effective, arguments must align with the norms and interpretative practices of international law,

[29] ibid pp. 55–57.

[30] Carstensen and Schmidt (n 5), p 320. See also Vivien A Schmidt, 'Discursive Institutionalism: The Explanatory Power of Ideas and Discourse', *Annual Review of Political Science* 11, (2008): p. 303; Vivien A Schmidt, 'Taking Ideas and Discourse Seriously: Explaining Change through Discursive Institutionalism as the Fourth "New Institutionalism"', *European Political Science Review* 2, (2010): p. 1.

[31] Carstensen and Schmidt (n 5), pp. 321–24.

[32] Martti Koskenniemi, *From Apology to Utopia: The Structure of International Legal Argument* (Cambridge University Press, 2005).

[33] Nicole Deitelhoff, 'The Discursive Process of Legalization: Charting Islands of Persuasion in the ICC Case', *International Organization* 63, (2009): p. 33; Ingo Venzke, 'Understanding the Authority of International Courts and Tribunals: On Delegation and Discursive Construction', *Theoretical Inquiries in Law* 14, (2013): p. 381.

[34] Ian Johnstone, *The Power of Deliberation: International Law, Politics and Organizations* (Oxford University Press, 2011), p. 22.

[35] ibid.

[36] ibid.

drawing on recognized legal sources rather than relying solely on moral, political, or policy-based reasoning.[37] The constraints that come with this blend of formulaic rigour and inherent discursiveness are real but also susceptible to negotiation. At the same time, they delineate a particular social field—one in which technically skilled legal actors are especially well-positioned to influence norm creation and policy development.[38]

These techniques distinguish legal practices from others, and they help to constitute international law as a social field. In Bourdieu's framework, fields are structured social spaces with their own rules and power dynamics, where agents compete for various forms of capital, including social and cultural capital.[39] Applying this to international law, we see how actors make use of their social capital—such as credibility, expertise, and authority within communities of practice—to shape discursive practices and advance legal change.

Discursive power thrives in settings where technical knowledge, normative evaluation, and legitimacy are paramount and political considerations are often obscured behind procedural rules and technicalities. Actors' social capital, which enables them to elicit deference from others, is not a priori dependent on their material resources. In any event, the field of international law enables actors to compete effectively by deploying persuasive arguments, framing, or socialization strategies that resonate with the norms and expectations of a given community of practice.

Given that ideational power is particularly relevant to a discursive practice like international law, it is Carstensen and Schmidt's first dimension—'power through ideas'—that speaks most directly to the change processes we examine. In these processes, agents employ power in practice[40] and pursue change attempts deliberately. As we try to show in greater detail in section 3, they do so through particular efforts at discourse mobilization, by grounding their legal claims within established ideational frames, institutions, and procedures with a view to establishing their vision as the dominant one. This process may involve actors with authority exercising 'power over ideas'. Where such change efforts succeed, new interpretations of the law become anchored within the relevant community of practice, and come to constitute 'power in ideas'.

[37] Martti Koskenniemi, 'Methodology of International Law', *Max Planck Encyclopedias of International Law*, 2007, https://opil.ouplaw.com/display/10.1093/law:epil/9780199231690/law-9780199231690-e1440.

[38] See Pierre Bourdieu, 'La force du droit: Eléments pour une sociologie du champ juridique', *Actes de la recherche en sciences sociales* 64, (1986): p. 3.

[39] Pierre Bourdieu, *Distinction: A Social Critique of the Judgement of Taste* (Harvard University Press, 1984); Pierre Bourdieu and Loïc J D Wacquant, *An Invitation to Reflexive Sociology* (University of Chicago Press, 1992).

[40] Rebecca Adler-Nissen and Vincent Pouliot, 'Power in Practice: Negotiating the International Intervention in Libya', *European Journal of International Relations* 20, (2014): p. 889.

Discourse mobilization, we argue, as a tool of ideational power, is likely to be particularly important for instances of gradual change—as opposed to treaty-making episodes, where material power tends to be more explicit. Indeed, treaty-making episodes are more akin to bargaining—a form of interaction that usually revolves around a set of preferences, identities, and expectations.[41] Actors, usually diplomats or politicians, come to the table with instructions from the capital and negotiate in a way that maximizes pre-defined interests. Bilateral negotiations are particularly subject to a logic of consequences—strategic bargaining or (reciprocal) concessions, where material power can be especially influential. Gradual change episodes, by contrast, involve a greater fluidity of ideas and the adaptability of actors, as they are much more prone to changing calculations in light of external circumstances and emerging trends. By employing discourse mobilization, change agents can elicit support from authorities, such as expert networks, international organizations, or influential legal bodies, to position their arguments as authoritative and legitimate. This process enables actors to alter the discursive landscape subtly, gaining traction even in the face of broad state opposition. Rather than relying on coercive or bargaining strategies, change agents can turn to authority constellations and discourse mobilization to reshape the normative and cognitive structures underpinning legal and policy.

2. Material Power in International Legal Change

What is the role of material power in international legal change processes? Can change happen in the absence of support from or even despite the opposition of the powerful? A central part of age-old governance questions, power is usually assumed to be key to determining who governs and whose agenda and world vision prevails. As we pointed out at the outset, many think the same of international law. Yet the assumption that material power drives change in international law deserves closer scrutiny.

In this chapter, we interrogate the centrality of material power in the episodes of international legal change we analysed in our case studies. We assess the degree to which change episodes were created or propelled by the (materially) powerful by paying more attention to how power manifests.[42] What we observe is that material power does not explain most instances of change in international legal norms, at least outside of treaty-making episodes. This has two concrete implications, which are observable in our case studies.

[41] Nicole Deitelhoff and Harald Müller, 'Theoretical Paradise: Empirically Lost? Arguing with Habermas', *Review of International Studies* 31, (2005): p. 167.

[42] See also the approach in Adler-Nissen and Pouliot (n 40).

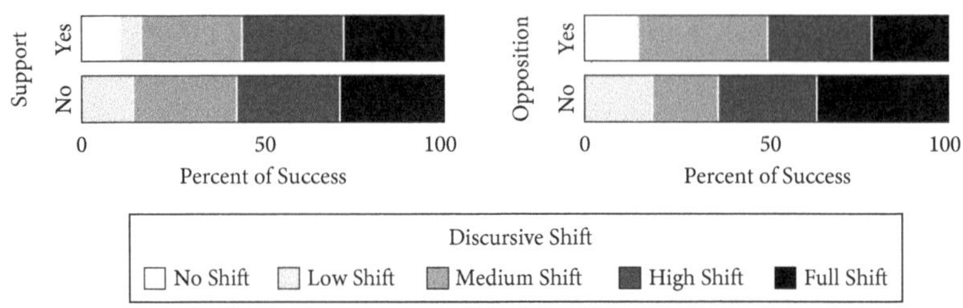

Figure 5.1 The percentage of success with major power support and opposition (reprinted)

First, we observe—as already pointed out in Chapter 4—that the existence of major power support does not have a significant effect on the success of change attempts, measured as the degree of discursive shift.[43] Our analysis shows that even in the absence of major power backing, successful legal change can still occur through other mechanisms, such as strong support from focal authorities.

As Figure 5.1 shows, a nearly equal percentage of change episodes achieve successful outcomes with or without major power *support* (as we see on the left-hand side of the panel). When we look at the impact of major power *opposition*, we see that change attempts that receive major power opposition are slightly less successful—the percentage of cases achieving a full shift or high shift decreases by around 20% (as we see on the right-hand side of the panel). This picture indicates that great powers may play a larger role in obstructing change rather than propelling it. Nevertheless, it also highlights that the effect of both their support and opposition is limited—more limited than would be expected.

However, we should also note that major power support and opposition do not operate in isolation. As a matter of fact, when we look at our sample, we see that a majority of cases (thirteen out of twenty-five) attract both great power support and opposition. Five cases receive *only* great power support, and one case receives *only* great power opposition. Table 5.1 below contains a list of cases that receive support or opposition from at least one great power, indicated with a '✓', while those that do not receive any support or opposition are left empty.[44]

In our regression analysis, as reported in Chapter 4, we analysed the influence of major power support and opposition alongside other variables to gain a clearer understanding of their effect. After controlling for various factors, we did not find statistically significant evidence that major power support or opposition

[43] As detailed in 'Methodology: Cases and Measurement' in Chapter 4, this measurement captures the extent to which discourse changes around a given issue, reflecting whether change attempts are accepted and incorporated into the prevailing normative frameworks.
[44] There are six cases in which major powers neither support nor oppose the initiative.

Table 5.1 Cases with great power support and opposition

Case names	**Major Power Support**	**Major Power Opposition**
CITES and the Definition of Conservation	✓	✓
Concept of Internationally Wrongful Act	✓	✓
Continental Shelf Delimitation Rules	✓	
Cyber Warfare Rules	✓	✓
Deep Seabed Mining Rules	✓	
Definition of Investment		
Direct Participation in Hostilities		
Domestic Violence (Protection of Women)		
Effects Doctrine of Jurisdiction	✓	✓
Fair and Equitable Treatment	✓	
General Exceptions–GATT Article XX	✓	
Human Right to a Healthy Environment		
Police Powers in Indirect Expropriation	✓	✓
Obligations of Corporations (Human Rights)	✓	✓
Port State Measures Against IUU Fishing	✓	✓
Precautionary Principle	✓	✓
Rape as a War Crime		
Relationship Between IHRL and IHL		✓
Right to Truth		
Special & Differential Treatment Treatment in the GATT System	✓	✓
Self-defence against Non-state Actors	✓	
State Official Immunity	✓	✓
Subsidies and the Definition of Public Bodies	✓	✓
Universal Jurisdiction	✓	✓
War Crimes in in Non-International Armed Conflicts	✓	✓
Total (N=25)		

determined change outcomes.[45] Given the limited number of cases (and especially of cases with only major power support or opposition), the results of this analysis should be treated with some caution. Nonetheless, they align with the patterns observed in the descriptive statistics above and strongly suggest that the presence of major power support or opposition alone does not account for the outcomes we observe.

Many of our cases—as in many cases of legal change in general—involve both major power support and opposition and it is possible that, in such instances, material power neutralizes itself, allowing other factors to play a more decisive role in shaping the course and success of change attempts. This effect seems evident in several cases where great powers counter one another. While such dynamics can leave change attempts in an unsettled grey zone with limited traction, they do not necessarily prevent successful change if other enabling factors are present.

The cases in our sample exemplify these different dynamics well. The limited effect of great power support is on display in the case of self-defence against non-state actors.[46] The claim of self-defence as a legal basis for the use of force against non-state actors has consistently been invoked by Israel since the 1970s, with only a limited number of other states—including the US—invoking it sporadically during the 1980s and 1990s. After the 9/11 terrorist attacks and the war against ISIS a decade later, other powerful states like the UK, France, and Germany came to invoke it, too, and no major power opposed the claim. Nevertheless, the doctrine remains highly contested, both by a number of states[47] as well as in ICJ rulings[48] and within academic circles.[49] Major power support alone did not guarantee success here.

[45] See 'Findings II: Regression Analysis' in Chapter 4, section 5.

[46] Pedro Martínez Esponda, 'Self Defense Against Non-State Actors', in *The Paths of International Law: Case Studies*, edited by Pedro Martínez Esponda and others (SSRN, 2023). Pedro Martínez Esponda, 'Norm-Instability as a Strategy in International Law-Making: The Case of Self-Defence against Non-State Actors', in *The Many Paths of Change in International Law*, edited by Nico Krisch and Ezgi Yildiz (Oxford University Press, 2023).

[47] An example of strong opposition to self-defence against non-state actors is Mexico and Brazil's stance on this matter as expressed at the United Nations Security Council (UNSC). See the records of UNSC Meetings 8262 (17 May 2018) S/PV.8262 at https://documents.un.org/doc/undoc/pro/n18/151/80/pdf/n1815180.pdf, and UNSC Meetings 8395 (9 November 2018) S/PV.8395 at https://documents.un.org/doc/undoc/pro/n18/368/63/pdf/n1836863.pdf. The voices denouncing self-defence against non-state actors increased with the African Union's recent announcement of its common position, which maintains that the right of self-defence can only be invoked when responding to an armed attack attributable to a state. Mohamed Helal, 'Common African position on the application of international law to the use of information and communication technologies in cyberspace, and all associated communiques adopted by the peace and security council of the African Union', Ohio State Legal Studies Research Paper No. 823, (2024), http://dx.doi.org/10.2139/ssrn.4714756.

[48] ICJ, *Legal Consequences of the Construction of a Wall in the Occupied Palestinian Territory* (Advisory Opinion) [2004] ICJ Rep 136.

[49] Olivier Corten, 'A Plea Against the Abusive Invocation of Self-Defence as a Response to Terrorism', *EJIL: Talk!*, 14 July 2016, https://www.ejiltalk.org/a-plea-against-the-abusive-invocation-of-self-defence-as-a-response-to-terrorism/.

Cases with both major power support and opposition also show heavily varied outcomes, thus suggesting that the opposing forces might cancel each other out. Sometimes, this results in unsettled states of the law, as in the case of the precautionary principle in international environmental law.[50] This principle originated in the domestic law of some European countries, and it was mainly Germany that, throughout the 1980s, started to advocate for its inclusion in international environmental instruments. These include the 1982 World Charter for Nature, the 1992 Río Declaration, and treaties in different but related fields, such as the law of the sea, human rights, and investment.[51] But this acknowledgement remains limited and, at best, scattered. At a general level, the status of the precautionary principle—especially as customary international law—is highly controversial and thus doubtful.[52] A crucial factor behind this lack of consolidation is the historical reluctance of the US to accept the precautionary principle as binding, especially since the Reagan administration. The US considered the principle an 'approach' rather than a rule, and it voted against the World Charter for Nature, failed originally to endorse the Río Declaration, and is not a party to many of the binding instruments that mention the precautionary principle. Similarly, in the context of trade law and the World Trade Organization (WTO), the US has been vocal about its opposition. Even in the face of strong EU advocacy in its favour, the principle has thus remained unstable.

Another example of cases with opposing great powers, although with a slightly different trajectory, is the treatment of subsidies under WTO law.[53] Since its accession, China has advocated for a change in the understanding of a 'public body'—a key term in subsidy law—with the aim of creating more space for its subsidy practices. Despite the fervent opposition of the US and European states, the Appellate Body (AB) moved towards the Chinese position in 2010. For the following years, most of the community of world trade lawyers—and also most governments that were critical of the AB's move on substance—considered the law as settled around the new interpretation. It was only when the US began its broader attack on WTO dispute settlement—which was partly fuelled by anger over the subsidy

[50] Ezgi Yildiz, 'The Precautionary Principle: Ubiquitous Yet Hollow and Marginal', in *The Paths of International Law: Case Studies*, edited by Pedro Martínez Esponda and others (SSRN, 2023).

[51] David L VanderZwaag, 'The ICJ, ITLOS and the Precautionary Approach: Paltry Progressions, Jurisprudential Jousting', *University of Hawai'i International Law Review* 35(2), (2013): pp. 617.

[52] See P Birnie, A Boyle and C Redgwell, *International Law and the Environment* (Oxford University Press, 2009), pp. 154–64.

[53] Nina Kiderlin, 'Subsidies and the Definition of "Public Bodies"', in *The Paths of International Law: Case Studies*, edited by Pedro Martínez Esponda and others (SSRN, 2023). Nina Teresa Kiderlin, 'World Trade Law and the Rise of China: Struggles over Subsidy Rules', in *The Many Paths of Change in International Law*, edited by Nico Krisch and Ezgi Yildiz (Oxford University Press, 2023).

jurisprudence itself—that the AB and the panels, from 2018 on, began to take steps back towards the earlier understanding.[54]

However, in other cases, the coexistence of major power support and opposition did not prevent the eventual consolidation of change attempts. This is illustrated by the way in which international criminal law was reshaped in the 1990s, largely through the action of the ad hoc tribunals.[55] The recognition that war crimes could take place in non-international armed conflict and not in international armed conflict exclusively—which was supported by the US and European governments—succeeded despite the fact that, as late as the Rome Conference to establish the International Criminal Court in 1998, important states such as China, India, and Turkey opposed the shift. As a result of action on the judicial and bureaucratic pathways and of the eventual ICC Statute, the consolidation of the change soon ceased to be in question.

The influence of great powers on change processes often depends not only on *who* supports or opposes a proposal but also *when* that support or opposition occurs. The opposition of China and India in the case concerning war crimes in non-international armed conflict mentioned in the previous paragraph, for example, may have mattered significantly more a decade later (also because they may have been able to assemble a broader coalition then). Likewise, the opposition of Western countries—and especially the US—would probably have been more consequential during the 1990s and early 2000s. This latter dynamic is also evident in the fate of efforts by some developing states and civil society organizations to impose human rights obligations on corporations—an initiative that powerful (Northern) states successfully watered down and obstructed to a great extent.[56] This particular initiative was first advanced by the UN Sub-Commission on Human Rights. In 2003, building on the work of an expert group, the Sub-Commission adopted the 'Norms on the Responsibilities of Transnational Corporations and Other Business Enterprises with Regard to Human Rights'.[57] However, this document, which explicitly established that corporations were bound by international human rights law, was loudly opposed by Western powers within the UN Commission on Human Rights—and duly rejected.[58] In response, a second initiative was launched in 2005 at the now Human Rights Council and led by John Ruggie. This process culminated in the successful adoption of the UN

[54] See also Dukgeun Ahn, 'Why Reform Is Needed: WTO "Public Body" Jurisprudence', *Global Policy* 12, (2021): p. 61.

[55] Nina Kiderlin, 'War Crimes in Non-International Armed Conflicts', in *The Paths of International Law: Case Studies*, edited by Pedro Martínez Esponda and others (SSRN, 2023).

[56] Dorothea Endres, 'Direct Human Rights Obligations of Corporations', in *The Paths of International Law: Case Studies*, edited by Pedro Martínez Esponda and others (SSRN, 2023).

[57] Giovanni Mantilla, 'Emerging International Human Rights Norms for Transnational Corporations', *Global Governance* 15, (2009): p. 279; John G Ruggie, 'The Social Construction of the UN Guiding Principles on Business & Human Rights', Harvard Kennedy School Faculty Research Working Paper Series 8, no. RWP17-030 (2017), https://www.hks.harvard.edu/publications/social-construction-un-guiding-principles-business-human-rights.

[58] UNCHR Res 11 (2004) UN Doc E/CN.4/2004/L.73/Rev1.

Guiding Principles on Business and Human Rights in 2011. These, however, were framed as constituting only a 'normative framework and corresponding policy guidance',[59] and they explicitly made a distinction between the *duty* of states to protect against human rights abuses by third parties and the corporate *responsibility* to respect human rights. This diluted outcome was welcomed by the US, the EU, and other powers. Subsequent efforts by developing countries and civil society organizations to revive the push for establishing human rights obligations for companies through a legally binding instrument negotiated under UN auspices have—partly because of the continued resistance of Northern countries—not borne fruit, even after a decade of work.[60]

In this particular case, the opposition of the US and European governments managed to derail a change attempt carried out by others. However, as we have seen throughout the different cases described above and throughout this book, neither does the support from great powers significantly help change efforts, nor does the opposition from great powers necessarily frustrate them. In many cases, with major powers pitched against one another, their efforts cancel each other out—and the success of change attempts is influenced far more by other factors.

3. From Ideas to Action: Mechanisms and Strategies of Discourse Mobilization

How do we account for the limited effect of material power in international legal change? We return here to the discussion of different forms of power in section 1 and try to understand better how an alternative form of power—ideational power—is used effectively by actors seeking to shift legal rules and understandings in an incremental fashion.

In a discursive practice such as international law, discourse mobilization is a key vehicle for bringing ideational power to bear, and this section explores how discourse mobilization can translate ideational power into actionable change. There are four main mechanisms through which change agents use discourse mobilization to make an impact on broader audiences. *Persuasion* involves convincing others to adopt a particular idea, belief, or norm through rational arguments, evidence, or appeals to emotion. It is an active process where actors use communication strategies to influence others' preferences and viewpoints.[61] *Socialization*

[59] John G Ruggie, *Just Business* (Norton & Company, 2013), ch. 2.

[60] Andrés Felipe Lopez Latorre, 'In Defence of Direct Obligations for Businesses Under International Human Rights Law', *Business and Human Rights Journal* 5, (2020): p. 56; Marco Fasciglione, 'A Binding Instrument on Business and Human Rights as a Source of International Obligations for Private Companies: Utopia or Reality?', *Legal Sources in Business and Human Rights* (Brill Nijhoff, 2020).

[61] Thomas Risse, '"Let's Argue!": Communicative Action in World Politics', *International Organization* 54, (2000): p. 1.

entails the process of integrating individuals or states into a community by teaching them the norms, values, and practices of that community. Through repeated interactions, actors learn to conform to these expectations and internalize them as appropriate behaviour.[62] *Normalization*, or *internalization*, is the process of making certain ideas, norms, or practices appear natural, self-evident, or taken for granted. It works by embedding specific expectations into daily life and social discourse, thereby limiting the range of acceptable alternatives and making it difficult to question or resist these norms.[63] *Deference to authority* involves accepting and adhering to norms, rules, or directives not because they align with one's interests or beliefs but because they emanate from a recognized authority figure or institution. Such deference may be driven by perceptions of legitimacy, fear of sanctions, or the desire to maintain stability and order.[64]

Discourse mobilization can rely on certain tools and constructs in order to generate the results that change agents envisage. Here, we focus on three means: *ideational frames* (involving emerging and dominant discourses),[65] *institutions and authority* (encompassing institutions, networks, and communities of practice), and *procedures* (procedural rules and principles that regulate the rules of access and participation). Although these are deeply interconnected and they often reinforce one another in practice, we analyse them separately to better understand the unique role each plays in enabling discourse mobilization. By tracing these elements, we avoid collapsing power with agency or structure.[66] Rather, we show how the interaction between the two constrains and enables varieties of power.

Who is best placed to access ideational power through discourse mobilization? To be sure, ideational power is related to material power. Material power can assist actors directly by enhancing their leverage through coercion, concessions, or trade-offs. It can also operate indirectly, by enabling access to or control over institutions that can produce, shape, or rubber-stamp arguments benefiting the materially powerful. What is more, material power can also help stronger actors form alliances and build consensus around the ideas they put forward. Hence, all things

[62] Brian Greenhill, 'The Company You Keep: International Socialization and the Diffusion of Human Rights Norms', *International Studies Quarterly* 54, (2010): p. 127; Jeffrey T Checkel, 'International Institutions and Socialization in Europe: Introduction and Framework', *International Organization* 59, (2005): p. 801.

[63] Ryan Goodman and Derek Jinks, 'Incomplete Internalization and Compliance with Human Rights Law', *European Journal of International Law* 19, (2008): p. 725.

[64] Richard Friedman, 'On the Concept of Authority in Political Philosophy' in *Authority*, edited by Joseph Raz (New York University Press, 1990); Ian Hurd, 'Legitimacy and Authority in International Politics', *International Organization* 53, (1999): p. 379.

[65] Erving Goffman, *Frame Analysis: An Essay on the Organization of Experience* (Northeastern University Press, 1986).

[66] Stefano Guzzini, 'Structural Power: The Limits of Neorealist Power Analysis', *International Organization* 47, (1993): pp. 443, 465.

being equal, materially powerful actors are likely to have a better shot at discourse mobilization.[67]

Material power does not, however, translate automatically into ideational power, because the latter requires interlocutors to engage in persuasion, socialization, normalization, or deference (to authority).[68] In such contexts, ideas are not fixed but malleable; actors can be convinced or constrained by a weightier or more reasonable argument. Discourse mobilization involves a common attempt to reach 'a reasoned consensus' that is independent of the initial motivations.[69] In this sense, it differs from bargaining, where actors negotiate based on fixed preferences using threats, concessions, and rewards (a logic of consequences).[70] Instead, in discursive contexts, plausibility and justifiability also matter (a logic of argument).[71] As a result, such settings create openings for materially less powerful actors, such as small states or non-state actors, to boost their position.[72] Through discourse mobilization, the weak or the underprivileged can wield ideational power by advancing legally persuasive discourses that have a purchase within the community or by gaining support or endorsement from authorities in the respective field. Indeed, as Chaïm Perelman explains, effective argumentation must build on premises already accepted by its audience, relying on what is acknowledged as true, normal, probable, or valid.[73] In this regard, moral and ethical argumentation often resonates more strongly with community values, while hard power, coercion, or threats might have the opposite effect.[74]

Discourse mobilization also plays a critical role in alliance-building—a key ingredient in the success of many change efforts. Change agents seek like-minded actors or allies to recruit to their cause and build a growing consensus around their proposals. Socialization, acculturation, in-group, and out-group formation are useful pathways to diffuse one's argument and ensure buy-in from a larger group of actors.[75] Building alliances also signals consensus and diminishes the chances of opposition since it is costlier to go against a group of like-minded actors. Alliances—both of an inter-governmental and transnational kind—played

[67] Risse (n 61), p. 16.

[68] One can argue that the game of persuasion is largely driven by the logic of argumentation—whereby actors keep their preferences open and shape their identities and interests in the course of their interaction with one another. They can change during argumentation and actors that commit to an argument or a deal as a rhetorical action may get to (or be forced to) believe in that argument There are two other logics that Thomas Risse talks about: logic of consequentialism (shaped by interests, identities, and preferences), logic of appropriateness (shaped by social norms around how one should behave). See more, ibid p. 22.

[69] Deitelhoff and Müller (n 41), p. 172.

[70] ibid p. 170.

[71] ibid p. 171.

[72] Risse (n 61), p. 33.

[73] Chaïm Perelman, *The Idea of Justice and the Problem of Argument* (Routledge & Kegan Paul 1963), p. 156.

[74] Deitelhoff and Müller (n 41), p. 171.

[75] Greenhill (n 62); Checkel (n 62); Goodman and Jinks (n 63).

a significant role in many of our cases, ranging from efforts to tackle illegal, unreported, and unregulated (IUU) fishing to the establishment of the right to truth.[76]

Material power is not absent from the discursive practice of international law, but other forms of power are also—and sometimes more—consequential. In the following, we focus on three constructs that stand, as mentioned above, at the centre of efforts at using ideational power through discourse mobilizations.

Power and Ideational Frames

Ideational frames are important constructs that determine which arguments can legitimately be made and present a sort of 'external authority for competing validity claims'.[77] The persuasiveness of an argument depends in large part on its alignment with such frames. Therefore, skilled change agents know how to anchor legal change proposals into existing narratives that are dominant within a particular community of practice.[78]

The importance of connecting with such frames was very visible in our case studies, especially in those involving human rights or other highly moralized issues. The recognition of war crimes in non-international armed conflict or of rape as a war crime are clear examples. In these cases, the atrocities committed in the Balkans and Rwanda during the 1990s received significant visibility in global media. This, combined with the widespread appeal of narratives emphasizing the fight against impunity and the importance of human rights among politicians, diplomats, international officials, and the broader public, helped legitimize the revision of rigid legal norms and categories.[79]

The struggle to carve out exceptions to state official immunity for international crimes in domestic courts followed a similar trajectory. However, in this context, the appeal to ending impunity clashed with a competing frame centred on

[76] Ezgi Yildiz, 'Port State Measures Against IUU Fishing', in *The Paths of International Law: Case Studies*, edited by Pedro Martínez Esponda and others (SSRN, 2023); Ezgi Yildiz, 'The Right to Truth', in *The Paths of International Law: Case Studies*, edited by Pedro Martínez Esponda and others (SSRN, 2023). See also Nina Reiners, *Transnational Lawmaking Coalitions for Human Rights* (Cambridge University Press, 2021); Nina Reiners, 'Transnational Lawmaking Coalitions as Change Agents in International Law', in *The Many Paths of Change in International Law*, edited by Nico Krisch and Ezgi Yildiz (Oxford University Press, 2023).

[77] Deitelhoff and Müller (n 41), p. 174.

[78] ibid p. 172; see also Moshe Hirsch, 'Social Movements, Reframing Investment Relations, and Enhancing the Application of Human Rights Norms in International Investment Law', *Leiden Journal of International Law* 34, (2021): p. 127; Andrea Bianchi and Moshe Hirsch, *International Law's Invisible Frames: Social Cognition and Knowledge Production in International Legal Processes* (Oxford University Press, 2021).

[79] Dorothea Endres, 'Rape as a War Crime', in *The Paths of International Law: Case Studies*, edited by Pedro Martínez Esponda and others (SSRN, 2023); Dorothea Endres, 'Direct Participation in Hostilities', in *The Paths of International Law: Case Studies*, edited by Pedro Martínez Esponda and others (SSRN, 2023).

sovereign equality. This latter frame gained prominence in the 2010s and has, so far, constrained efforts to advance accountability measures that challenge official immunity—and, by extension, the broader push for legal change. However, frames can also arise quickly, for example, as a result of an overpowering appeal after critical junctures that suspend previously held hesitations and resistance towards new understandings. To some extent, this was the case for the use of self-defence against non-state actors in the aftermath of 9/11, where the US saw no opposition to its invocation of UN Charter Article 51 against Al-Qaeda and even managed to pass a resolution in the UN Security Council recognizing it.[80]

To be sure, there might be more than one community of practice, with distinct values and frames, operating within a particular field or around an issue area.[81] Such multiplicity is further compounded when change attempts travel across different issue areas, navigating the complex web of rules and institutions that characterize international politics today, as we will explore further in Chapter 6. In such cases, an argument that resonates strongly within one community of practice may not have the same impact in others, creating a need for actors to tailor their arguments to align with multiple, and sometimes conflicting, frames. This selective framing can involve emphasizing different aspects of the issue, strategically using language that bridges the divide, or downplaying elements that might cause friction. Consequently, the ability to navigate and adapt to these diverse frames becomes crucial for achieving broader appeal. While the fit may occasionally be natural, it more often requires deliberate and careful crafting to reconcile competing perspectives. For example, in the attempt to counter intellectual property protections for essential medicines, change agents were able to generate resonance in the fields of global health and human rights, but a much greater effort was necessary to connect with economic frames dominant in the WTO context (and success there eventually was the result of institutional dynamics and alliance formation).[82]

Actors who can access dominant ideational frames can claim moral authority and social capital, which helps them to make their argument resonate with the rest of the community that operates in light of these frames. However, these dominant ideational frames are not 'neutral' or necessarily 'moral'—they are often shaped and propagated by materially powerful actors according to their vision of the world. From Marxist and critical perspectives, the ruling class's control over material resources extends to the production of ideas and ideologies, making dominant

[80] Pedro Martinez Esponda, 'Self Defense Against Non-State Actors', in *The Paths of International Law: Case Studies,* edited by Pedro Martinez Esponda and others (SSRN, 2023).

[81] Dorothea Endres, 'Whose International Law Is Changing? The Practice of Fragmented Communities Constructing Legal Change', in *The Many Paths of Change in International Law*, edited by Nico Krisch and Ezgi Yildiz (Oxford University Press, 2023).

[82] Laurence Helfer, 'Pharmaceutical Patents and the Human Right to Health: The Contested Evolution of the Transnational Legal Order', in *Transnational Legal Orders*, edited by Terence C Halliday and Gregory Shaffer (Cambridge University Press, 2015).

frames the intellectual manifestations of their material power.[83] In this view, the ideational and material are deeply intertwined. In the international law context, this is nowhere nearly as obvious as in economic law. For example, the unbound interpretation, during the 1990s and early 2000s, of indirect expropriation as almost equivalent to direct expropriation (requiring full compensation regardless of the purpose of regulatory measures affecting an investment) did not meet with much contestation, as this principle was inherently compatible with the neoliberal ideology prevalent at the time.[84]

While materially powerful actors may have the upper hand in creating ideational frames, others can tap into these frames to pursue their own visions—although the scope of their pursuits may be constrained by the existing structures. Weaker actors can thus successfully initiate change attempts by drawing on dominant ideational frames. The emergence of the right to truth in human rights, for example, is historically the result of two pivotal civil society struggles which occurred at different times, in different parts of the world, and drew on distinct aspects of then-emerging liberal frames.[85] Its success, as Patricia Naftali describes, is primarily explained by the capacity of the narrative of truth to 'accommodate a plurality of causes'.[86] The first of these causes was linked to the fight against enforced disappearance in the context of the military dictatorships in Latin America throughout the 1960s, 1970s, and 1980s. The second important civil society movement that found an anchor in the right to truth was the struggle against amnesties for serious violations of human rights and humanitarian law throughout the 1990s.[87] Human rights activists denounced the impunity that amnesties sometimes implied and thus focused on the human rights questions that they gave rise to. This led to a turn towards accountability in human rights activism, marked by the emergence of the field of 'transitional justice'—a framework to which the narrative of truth is central.[88] Hence, the right to truth has organically grown by associating itself with the larger anti-impunity and transitional justice movements, but also with a broader emphasis on transparency rooted in a liberal good governance logic.

Ideational frames can also help to counter visions of the materially powerful. We see this most vividly in the case of the emergence of the sustainable use principle within the Convention on International Trade in Endangered Species (CITES)

[83] Umut Özsu, 'An Anti-Imperialist Universalism? *Jus Cogens* and the Politics of International Law', in *International Law and Empire: Historical Explorations*, edited by Martti Koskenniemi and others (Oxford University Press, 2017), p. 295; Susan Marks, *The Riddle of All Constitutions: International Law, Democracy, and the Critique of Ideology* (Oxford University Press, 2003).

[84] Pedro Martínez Esponda, 'The Doctrine of Police Powers in Indirect Expropriation', in *The Paths of International Law: Case Studies*, edited by Pedro Martínez Esponda and others (SSRN, 2023).

[85] Ezgi Yildiz, 'The Right to Truth', in *The Paths of International Law: Case Studies*, edited by Pedro Martinez Esponda and others (SSRN, 2023).

[86] Patricia Naftali, 'Crafting a "Right to Truth" in International Law: Converging Mobilizations, Diverging Agendas?', *Justice penale internationale* XIII, (2016), https://doi.org/10.4000/champpenal.9245.

[87] ibid para. 7.

[88] ibid para. 7.

regime.[89] In this case, states from the Global South could generate change despite the resistance of more powerful countries from the Global North. CITES is a conservation treaty aiming at regulating the trade in species of wild animals and plants to prevent their extinction.[90] Its text reflects a strong allegiance to preservationism (i.e., the total cessation of trade in endangered species), and the small number of state parties in the early years shared this vision. Yet as time passed and the membership diversified, the sustainable use principle (i.e., the use of a portion of endangered species to fund and facilitate the conservation of the rest of their population) gained traction. While the preservationist bloc was mainly made up of wealthy developed nations, the sustainable use bloc consisted of 'cash-poor but resource-rich developing nations'.[91] The latter camp wanted to bring the CITES regime in line with the sustainable use logic and, as a corollary, to increase the volume of regulated trade in some endangered species.[92] To this aim, they could connect with the shifting ideational environment and the emergence of the sustainable development principles embedded in the 1992 Río Declaration. Their argument prevailed despite strong resistance from Northern and Western countries, especially the US. As a result of the mobilization led primarily by Southern African countries, the Convention's orientation shifted from preservation to a 'sustainable use-based conservation philosophy' in the mid-to-late 1990s.[93] Although the change was expressed in merely technical rules and guidelines (i.e., classification criteria) and amendments to the Appendices, it fundamentally transformed the CITES regime.

As these examples show, ideational frames are not all that stable, but they provide opportunities for the powerful and less powerful to mobilize their change visions. Importantly, the availability of such frames does not always privilege (neo-) liberal projects alone. For example, recently, legal change initiatives of an autocratic nature have also gathered momentum.[94] Actors with sufficient power to resist dominant ideologies have pursued their interests by cultivating an 'ideational ecology' among like-minded allies, portraying themselves as 'counter-hegemonic' and producing new authoritarian-leaning frames in the process.[95]

[89] Ezgi Yildiz, 'CITES and the Changing Definition of Conservation', in *The Paths of International Law: Case Studies*, edited by Pedro Martínez Esponda and others (SSRN, 2023).

[90] Jess Hemmings, 'Does CITES Conserve Biodiversity', *Asia Pacific Journal of Environmental Law* 7, (2002): pp. 95, 108–09.

[91] Quoted in Catharine L Krieps, 'Sustainable Use of Endangered Species under Cites: Is It a Sustainable Alternative', *University of Pennsylvania Journal of International Economic Law* 17, (1996): pp. 461, 484.

[92] Saskia Young, 'Contemporary Issues of the Convention on International Trade in Endangered Species of Wild Fauna and Flora (CITES) and the Debate over Sustainable Use', *Colorado Journal of International Environmental Law and Policy* 14, (2003): pp. 167, 173.

[93] Michael J Hickey, 'Acceptance of Sustainable Use within the Cites Community', *Vermont Law Review* 23, (1998): pp. 861.

[94] Tom Ginsburg, 'Authoritarian International Law?', *American Journal of International Law* 114, (2020): p. 221.

[95] B S Chimni, 'Epilogue: Fragmentary Thoughts on Informal Change', in *The Many Paths of Change in International Law*, edited by Nico Krisch and Ezgi Yildiz (Oxford University Press, 2023).

Power, Institutions, and Authority

Institutions often offer benign settings for actors to harness and employ ideational power. When interactions are embedded within institutions, they are guided by common norms, shared understandings, and established procedures, which facilitate access to collective experiences and commonly accepted argumentative references.[96] Such structures can help to counterbalance power asymmetries since, ideally, all the participants can reach and employ existing understandings and references. Especially non-hierarchical and open set-ups that give voice to the less powerful can be effective in countering power imbalances and creating an inclusive space for negotiation and argumentation among all relevant participants.

Furthermore, institutions often come with authority—a core element in processes of discourse mobilization. Authority has been important throughout this book—we made a claim for its centrality in Chapter 2, traced variations in the structure of authority across international legal fields in Chapter 3, and presented our findings on its relevance in Chapter 4. As we have seen, the authority structure prevailing in a given issue area is one of the most significant factors behind the success of change attempts. In areas with a focal authority, such attempts are considerably more likely to lead to a discursive shift. Even in settings characterized by a diffuse authority constellation, the gradual accretion of support from authoritative actors is one of the key mechanisms to boost change proposals' appeal. This is because authorities can elicit deference, and their statements—whether in favour of or against a proposed change—can significantly shape the positions of other actors within the field. Deference to authority often has ideational roots—arising from moral, ethical, or technical credibility, or from the gradual normalization of certain actors as authoritative within a given field.[97] This deference, in turn, shapes which visions of change gain traction and legitimacy.[98] The path to success is conditioned by the kinds of authorities change agents can recruit or convert to their causes.

We see this dynamic at play in the case of women's rights groups' success in mobilizing different institutions to create a new state obligation to protect women from domestic violence. In making domestic violence a public matter that required states' positive intervention, they were aided by existing institutions that were ideologically close to their cause.[99] What first gave them ground to internationalize their efforts to counter domestic violence was the UN Decade for Women and the World Conferences on Women—an achievement which was possible due to

[96] Deitelhoff and Müller (n 41), p. 173.

[97] See 'Actors, Practices, Authority: The Social Frame of Change' in Chapter 2.

[98] Anne-Marie Slaughter, 'A Global Community of Courts Focus: Emerging Fora for International Litigation (Part 2)', *Harvard International Law Journal* 44, (2003): p. 191.

[99] Ezgi Yildiz, 'The Protection of Women from Domestic Violence', in *The Paths of International Law: Case Studies*, edited by Pedro Martínez Esponda and others (SSRN, 2023).

lobbying of women's rights activists and the Committee on the Status of Women (CSW).[100] These conferences allowed activists to build a large coalition and anchor a new framing. Once they raised awareness at the international level, they began creatively constructing a new state obligation to protect women from domestic violence by forming an alliance with the Committee on the Elimination of All Forms of Discrimination Against Women (CEDAW).[101] To do so, they used analytical hooks in existing norms such as the prohibition of torture, the right to life, and positive obligations. The CEDAW Committee used this ideational frame and assumed a role 'at the forefront of' the construction of the positive obligation to protect women from domestic violence.[102] Neil Englehart argues that the CEDAW Committee 'acted more quickly than the CSW, even in the absence of a specific mandate from ECOSOC', despite the fact that the issue did not initially fall within the confines of the Convention text.[103] Empowered by the procedures that enabled it to issue general comments, the CEDAW Committee brought this new obligation within the confines of the Convention and made an intervention that was 'more timely, more aggressive, and more binding than the more modest efforts of other UN organizations'.[104] Born out of ideological proximity between the women's rights group and the CEDAW Committee,[105] this symbiotic alliance benefited both sides, amplifying their power.[106] At the time, the CEDAW Committee was considered a peripheral institution—it was not viewed 'as part of the UN human rights framework, but of the UN activities on women's affairs, which the UN secretariat in Vienna dealt with'.[107] The Committee was located in New York, away from Geneva-based human rights institutions.[108] Yet, as Loveday Hodson argues, the CEDAW's audacity in pushing for this new obligation was aided by its peripheral place away from the spotlight.[109] However, as a UN body established to monitor a widely ratified convention, the CEDAW Committee could lend the new interpretation a certain degree of authority—one that activists could then build upon

[100] Dorothy Q Thomas and Michele E Beasley, 'Domestic Violence as a Human Rights Issue', *Human Rights Quarterly* 15, (1993): pp. 36, 44.

[101] On alliances with UN human rights treaty bodies, see Reiners (n 76); Nina Reiners, 'States as Bystanders of Legal Change: Alternative Paths for the Human Rights to Water and Sanitation in International Law', *Leiden Journal of International Law* 37, (2024): p. 22.

[102] Neil Englehart, 'CEDAW and Gender Violence: An Empirical Assessment', *Michigan State Law Review* (2014): pp. 265, 268.

[103] ibid.

[104] ibid.

[105] Women members are often a minority in the case of other human rights treaty bodies.

[106] Yakın Ertürk and Bandana Purkayastha, 'Linking Research, Policy and Action: A Look at the Work of the Special Rapporteur on Violence against Women', *Current Sociology* 60(2), (2012): p. 144.

[107] Susanne Zwingel, 'From Intergovernmental Negotiations to (Sub)National Change', *International Feminist Journal of Politics* 7, (2005): pp. 400, 404.

[108] ibid p. 404.

[109] Loveday Hodson, 'Women's Rights and the Periphery: CEDAW's Optional Protocol', *European Journal of International Law* 25, (2014): pp. 561, 561–78.

in their efforts to broaden the uptake of their change attempt, which ultimately proved successful.

The opportunities for discourse mobilization vary depending on the authority layout—whether authority is dispersed or concentrated in a focal institution—but even more so on the types of paths available in a given context. While all paths of international law are vehicles through which actors shape or present arguments, each path has its particular strengths and weaknesses when it comes to discourse mobilization and ideational power. Skilled change agents activate the right path at the right moment and ride the wave generated by one path to remove roadblocks laid on other paths or to create a spill-over influence. Change agents then also often start with the path of least resistance and move towards the path of greatest influence, as we trace in Chapter 6.

What are the unique qualities of each path and its institutions for discourse mobilization efforts? The state action path is not particularly discursive in nature—its grounding in individual state action makes it more prone to unilateral action or hard political tactics such as bargaining, rather than actual persuasion, socialization, normalization, or invocation of authority structures. The multilateral path, in contrast, is more consensus-oriented, and it presents states' collective views, serving a confirmatory role. Resolutions and declarations from multilateral fora tend to be powerful elements in international legal discourses, especially if they emanate from sites which—like the UN General Assembly or the UN Human Rights Council in its field—are recognized as authoritative. The judicial path, for its part, is geared towards distilling legal arguments and determining the state of the law. Using it requires the employment of discursive tools to sway judges or arbitrators. It is also often particularly authoritative when it comes to debates on legal issues; statements of courts tend to serve as reference points for other actors. Somewhat similarly, the bureaucratic and private authority paths usually allow actors to embed their arguments in technical knowledge and interpretive proposals. While the resulting pronouncements may not, on their own, be decisive in driving change, their authority can significantly shape the subsequent development of legal discourse. Opportunities to wield ideational power vary significantly depending on the nature of the institutions and authorities along a given path. The more 'discursive' the setting—particularly in interpretive bodies such as courts—the more ideational tools tend to matter. At the same time, the more authoritative an institution is, the more actors can draw on its pronouncements to support future discourse mobilization efforts.

Our case studies provide an interesting window into the ways in which different paths (or a combination of paths) can be employed for discourse mobilization efforts. The case on the effects doctrine of jurisdiction, for example, shows the limited discourse mobilization capacity of the state action path. Here, the US unilaterally implemented its vision on antitrust jurisdiction based on the effects doctrine without any serious efforts at broader international legal change and without attempting to use other pathways. Despite an increasing convergence around this approach since the 1990s, it has not found broader institutional validation, and effects-based jurisdiction is still today not generally recognized.[110]

In contrast, in the case concerning the concept of internationally wrongful acts, change was sparked in the expert-based forum of the UN International Law Commission (the bureaucratic path) but then mobilized through several other pathways, including the judicial one with the International Court of Justice, and eventually widely accepted by states and the broader community of practice.[111] Here, discourse mobilization is evident in two ways: first, in the ability of the Special Rapporteur of the International Law Commission (ILC), Roberto Ago, to persuade other members to adopt his interpretive approach; and, secondly, in the use of the ILC articles by various actors as an authoritative reference point. This shaped discourses around state responsibility and eventually led to a consolidation of the new approach.

Authority and institutions are tools available to all types of actors, but they are especially vital for those with limited material power. Less powerful actors can creatively navigate the different paths of change to amplify their ideational influence. In contrast, materially powerful states often rely on other strategies. They tend to pursue their change vision using the state-action path and attempt to introduce change through shortcuts. However, as the effects doctrine case study illustrates, this approach does not always produce a full discursive shift—sometimes leaving their proposals in limbo, without sufficient support to generate a widely recognized change in the law.[112] This may, in fact, not matter much to states with greater material capability, as the space they gain by destabilizing prior understandings is often sufficient for their aims (a point we will return to in Chapter 7). The limited use of more discursive paths by powerful states—perhaps because these paths appear more resistant to their influence—may help explain why material power is not the primary driver of change in the cases we examine.

Power and Procedures

Discourse mobilization often depends on procedures that define how decision-making processes unfold and can thus create space for discursive engagements. Procedural norms often appear to be routine or mundane details, but they play a key role in suspending or propelling change attempts. They help actors reach equilibrium and confront or resolve deadlocks, yet they can also cement and lock

[110] Pedro Martínez Esponda, 'The Effects Doctrine of Jurisdiction', in *The Paths of International Law: Case Studies*, edited by Pedro Martínez Esponda and others (SSRN, 2023).

[111] Pedro Martínez Esponda, 'The Concept of Internationally Wrongful Act', in *The Paths of International Law: Case Studies*, edited by Pedro Martínez Esponda and others (SSRN, 2023).

[112] Pedro Martínez Esponda, 'Norm-Instability as a Strategy in International Law-Making: The Case of Self-Defence against Non-State Actors', in *The Many Paths of Change in International Law*, edited by Nico Krisch and Ezgi Yildiz (Oxford University Press, 2023).

in power and hide it under the guise of routine and technicality. They can also obscure innovation and dress legal change proposals as pure technicalities that are inevitable consequences of standard operations. Wouter Werner provides an interesting account of the ILC's use of draft conclusions to codify the law 'as it is'—while also including a significant number of points that develop the law further.[113]

Procedural norms are secondary norms.[114] They are themselves ideational constructs, although they operate at a more abstract level than behavioural norms whose creation they govern. Often embedded in institutional frameworks, they allocate roles and shape possibilities for participation. A case in point is the increasingly elaborate procedural norms governing the negotiation of multilateral environmental agreements and participation in conferences of the parties, which now allow for the involvement of thousands of non-state actors.[115] In public settings like these, the potential for discursive mobilization is bound to be higher than in negotiations among interested governments behind closed doors.

But procedures do more than simply open or close discursive space—they are themselves sites of contestation and creativity. Strategic actors can use procedural leverage not just to enable participation, but to smuggle in substantive change under the cover of technicality. When routine processes are reinterpreted or stretched, they can unlock new possibilities, disrupt prevailing legal understandings, and reframe debates. In this sense, procedural rules are not neutral. By controlling who participates, how arguments must be framed, and what counts as legitimate interpretation, procedures mediate the relationship between ideational and material power. They can level the playing field—or tilt it further. Attending to these dynamics allows us to see how power flows through the formalities of law, not just its grand pronouncements. And it reminds us that even seemingly mundane procedural choices can decisively shape the conditions under which legal change is pursued, resisted, or realized. Indeed, in the above-mentioned CITES example, the seemingly standard procedure of animal classification became the battlefront for renegotiating the scope of the CITES Convention by linking it to a different ideational frame.[116] Formally amending or renegotiating treaties is often too difficult, so change agents frequently pursue change through the back door—using standard procedures to introduce what appears to be a technical adjustment but in fact amounts to a shift in fundamental norms and principles.

[113] Wouter Werner, 'The Making of Lawmaking: The ILC Draft Conclusions on the Identification of Customary Law', in *The Many Paths of Change in International Law*, edited by Nico Krisch and Ezgi Yildiz (Oxford University Press, 2023).

[114] Mark Raymond, *Social Practices of Rule-Making in World Politics* (Oxford University Press, 2019).

[115] Bas Arts, 'Non-State Actors in Global Environmental Governance: New Arrangements Beyond the State', in *New Modes of Governance in the Global System: Exploring Publicness, Delegation and Inclusiveness*, edited by Mathias Koenig-Archibugi and Michael Zürn (Palgrave Macmillan UK, 2006).

[116] Yildiz (n 89).

We can observe these dynamics at play in the refashioning of the rules governing deep seabed mining operations.[117] The question of who would benefit from the resources of the deep sea became divisive during the Third United Nations Conference on the Law of the Sea. Developing countries, organized under the Group of 77 (G-77), pushed for the application of the common heritage of humankind principle and preferred a strong international institution (the International Seabed Authority, ISA) with an operating arm (the Enterprise) to extract resources and distribute benefits equally.[118] On the other end of the spectrum, Western countries with seabed mining capacity and those that were involved in seabed mining consortia were pursuing a more market-oriented approach. The eventual compromise established a parallel system of access. To qualify for a mining licence, a sponsoring state would be required to secure one area for its contractor while setting aside another area of roughly equal resource for exploration and exploitation by the Enterprise—a practice known as site-banking. But Western states, unconvinced by this scheme, initiated an alternative approach and passed domestic legislation allowing seabed mining outside of the international legal regime.[119] To overcome these countries' unwillingness to sign the UN Convention on the Law of the Sea (UNCLOS), the G-77 opened itself to renegotiations; these finally led to the 1994 Implementation Agreement, which allowed the regime to become operational, even if this meant reducing some of the safeguards for the common heritage approach.[120]

A yet further shift in favour of markets came about through arcane procedures for adopting and implementing regulations in the ISA. In the years after its inception, the ISA largely followed the parallel-system-of-access model under the UNCLOS in the mining regulations for exploring polymetallic nodules (PMNs). When later asked to develop mining regulations for lesser-known minerals—polymetallic sulphides (PMSs) and cobalt-rich crusts (CRCs)—the ISA changed course. Led by the Secretariat, the ISA partially departed from the original site-banking scheme and moved closer to a market model. That meant including a future equity interest as an option alongside site-banking in PMS and CRC regulations adopted by the Council and the Assembly in 2010. The ISA did not take this shift further—when the Council later made a request to align the mining codes and to include the equity interest option also in the PMNs regulations, the Secretariat signalled that such a step would require a formal amendment of the Convention.[121]

[117] Ezgi Yildiz, 'Revising the "Parallel System of Access" Rule for Seabed Mining', in *The Paths of International Law: Case Studies*, edited by Pedro Martínez Esponda and others (SSRN, 2023).

[118] For more, see Isabel Feichtner, 'Sharing the Riches of the Sea: The Redistributive and Fiscal Dimension of Deep Seabed Exploitation', *European Journal of International Law* 30, (2019): p. 601.

[119] Surabhi Ranganathan, *Strategically Created Treaty Conflicts and the Politics of International Law* (Cambridge University Press, 2014), pp. 147–211.

[120] David Anderson, 'Resolution and Agreement Relating to the Implementation of Part XI of the UN Convention on the Law of the Sea: A General Assessment', *ZaöRV* 55, (1995): pp. 275, 276. Yoshifumi Tanaka, *The International Law of the Sea* (Cambridge University Press, 2012), pp. 179–82.

[121] ISA Secretariat (6 February 2018) ISBA/24/LTC/4, p. 2, § 6.

However, the shift in the rules for PMSs and CRCs is significant. It demonstrates how proponents of a more market-oriented model were able to use formal institutional procedures to gain traction for their vision and accomplish what they had been unable to achieve through treaty negotiations.

As these examples show, in contexts where formal treaty change is out of reach, actors strategically exploit procedural norms not merely as fallback options but as stealth avenues of influence. Formal procedures—such as those embedded in judicial or multilateral processes—or technical procedures that dominate bureaucratic or private authority settings can be harnessed to reframe legal interpretations or to delay and redirect outcomes. Procedures thus serve as access points for ideational power in the form of apolitical routines. But when captured or manipulated, they can also function as tools of material domination cloaked in neutrality. In this way, procedural rules become key battlegrounds for legal change—sites where power is exercised less visibly, but no less decisively.

Discourse mobilization can take many forms, but it is more readily facilitated in certain settings. In this section, we have traced some of these routes, focusing on opportunities to draw on ideational frames, leverage institutional authority, and utilize procedural rules to create space for argument. On the more discursive, interpretative paths of change in international law, such mobilization encounters a relatively favourable environment, allowing actors to exert ideational power in ways that can sometimes circumvent the need for material power. Power, thus, circulates differently within and through these institutions. Therefore, it is unsurprising that powerful countries tend to be reluctant to agree to judicial dispute settlement and are often critical of an active role of international organizations and expert bodies.

4. Conclusion

The story of legal change cannot be told without giving an account of power—or the varieties of power in practice. In contrast to what traditional accounts would have led us to expect, we have not found that great powers play a preponderant role in generating gradual change. They are, however, at times more effective in obstructing change proposals put forward by other actors, in hollowing out existing norms and institutions, or in contesting (up to the point of disabling) certain paths of change. We will return to such contestation in Chapter 7. What emerges prominently in this chapter are the limitations of material power and the importance of ideational power—actors' ability to mobilize ideas—when it comes to positively effecting shifts in international legal discourses. By recognizing the interplay of material and ideational power, this chapter provides a heuristic framework for understanding how international law evolves as both a product and a mediator of power in global politics.

Ideational power, unlike material power, is inherently malleable, and it is accessible to both the weak and the strong, depending on how it is cultivated. Actors must actively build ideational power through discourse mobilization techniques, which involve anchoring arguments in widely accepted ideational frames, securing endorsements from focal authorities, and assembling diverse coalitions of support. These strategies rely on mechanisms such as persuasion, socialization, normalization, and deference to authority. But discourse mobilization requires more than just the right strategies—it demands skill and careful choreography to make arguments persuasive, appealing, and authoritative to a broader audience. Success often hinges on aligning arguments with the norms and beliefs of a given community while obtaining backing from influential sources. While materially powerful actors may have an advantage in accessing these resources, their efforts still depend on strategic execution. Without finesse and expertise—and a willingness to connect with normative views held by others—the powerful will often succeed in disrupting existing norms but struggle to translate that disruption into consolidated legal change. Conversely, less powerful actors, such as small states or transnational advocacy networks, can leverage discourse mobilization to amplify their influence. By effectively connecting their arguments to resonant ideational frames and strategically engaging with authority structures, these actors can gain legitimacy and increase their chances of driving meaningful change.

The parallel workings of material and ideational power reflect a dual nature of international law as 'both an instrument of power and an obstacle to its exercise'.[122] In fact, powerful states often find it challenging to muster the ideational power necessary to generate broad-based change within established legal frameworks, which can prompt them to act solo—either by using destabilization tactics, carving out exceptions, or simply choosing not to comply with international norms. They also pursue change by other means—substituting international law with informal rules or domestic law to establish clearer hierarchies and exercise more direct control.[123]

One important caveat to our findings is that they are based on a micro-level analysis of informal legal change episodes within a relatively limited timeframe, primarily focusing on change episodes that materialized in the post-1990s period. As such, these findings may not fully capture how change dynamics unfold over longer historical periods. Material power may indeed play a more significant role during treaty-making or foundational moments in international law, and it will often have a bearing on ideational frames over time—the emergence of a liberal and neo-liberal international law during the twentieth century is undoubtedly in part a result of the distribution of material power.

[122] Krisch (n 2), p. 371.
[123] ibid.

However, our analysis in this book demonstrates that change also takes place through iterative and discursive processes that operate beyond the immediate reach of the materially powerful. In these contexts, ideational power seems particularly effective, as it can reshape the discursive terrain, amplify an actor's influence, and generate lasting transformations, even for those who may lack material strength. As we have seen, some of the paths of change in international law—especially the more interpretive judicial, bureaucratic, or private authority pathways—lend themselves particularly well to discourse mobilization and the effective use of ideational power. In contrast, treaty-making and state action paths are more susceptible to material power and less open to discourse mobilization. This vindicates our conjecture in Chapter 1 that we need a comparative analysis of the politics of international law across the different paths of change—and between legal and other forms of change—to appreciate the significant variation in the role and impact of material power. The structure and discursive openness of a given path play a crucial role in shaping which forms of power are available and effective. Understanding the differentiated affordances of each path allows us to explain not just *whether* change occurs, but *how* it is brought about and by whom.

Ideational power through discourse mobilization is no magic bullet—it also operates within existing constraints and does not erase hierarchies. But it opens doors that material power would open only for the powerful. It enables actors to punch above their weight, to shift narratives, and to remake legal terrain from within. When deployed skillfully, it does not just change the law—it changes who gets to speak, who gets heard, and whose vision of change takes root. In the evolving landscape of international law, it is not always the mightiest who prevail, but those who know how to move minds, mobilize frames, and work the paths of change to their advantage.

6
Paths of Least Resistance
Legal Change amid Institutional Complexity

The account of change we develop in this book is in many respects an 'institutionalist' account. As we have seen in the previous chapters, institutional authority is central to change processes: the presence and type of authority in a given field condition the success of change attempts, authorities calibrate the role state support and opposition play, and they also affect the way in which material power can make itself felt in international legal change. The paths of change in international law often lead through authorities and institutions.

Yet institutions and authorities in the global order do not come alone. As Chapter 3 has shown, most issue areas in international law are characterized by a multiplicity of paths, centred on states, international organizations, courts, or experts. This contrasts with the typical imagery of institutionalists who tend to convey a unitary image, focusing on institutions dominant in a given context and thus able to condition the interactions of actors. In historical institutionalism, for example, institutions often become anchored in a field through processes of increasing returns and positive feedback, which make them difficult to displace, except in moments of crisis that unsettle the status quo. As long as they are so anchored, they structure the ways in which change can be achieved.[1]

This imagery originates in domestic politics, but even there it is typically inadequate to capture the relations of multiple, related institutions, better framed in terms of 'institutional assemblages'.[2] A unitary image is even less fitting in the international sphere, where concentrated authority and single institutions are usually elusive. Institutionalization has led to proliferation and multiplicity in many areas, with 'regime complexity' becoming a central theme in international relations scholarship and 'fragmentation' emerging as a key aspect of contemporary international law.[3]

[1] Paul Pierson, *Politics in Time: History, Institutions, and Social Analysis* (Princeton University Press, 2004).

[2] Johannes Gerschewski, 'Explanations of Institutional Change: Reflecting on a "Missing Diagonal"', *American Political Science Review* 115, (2021): p. 218.

[3] Karen J Alter and Kal Raustiala, 'The Rise of International Regime Complexity', *Annual Review of Law and Social Science* 14, (289): p. 329; Harlan Grant Cohen, 'Fragmentation', in *Concepts for International Law*, edited by Jean d'Aspremont and Sahib Singh (Edward Elgar Publishing, 2018).

Change in International Law. Nico Krisch, Ezgi Yildiz, and Pedro Martínez Esponda, Oxford University Press.
 DOI: 10.1093/9780198918325.003.0006

What does such complexity imply for international legal change? One possible answer is stagnation—in the midst of many paths and authorities, many would expect that political conflict translates into inter-institutional conflict in which a push for change in one site is undone by resistance to change in another. This would be in line with the friction and incoherence many observers have identified as a likely consequence of regime complexity in general,[4] and such friction and stagnation also appear in some of our cases. However, as we show in this chapter, they are not the dominant result: in many cases, we instead observe legal change *through* multiplicity as change agents successfully navigate, and make use of, the complex of paths and institutions in and across different legal fields.

To understand this process, we need to take into view not only the multiple authorities and their relations with one another, but especially the ways in which actors engage with them.[5] In this chapter, we thus explore the relation between institutional complexity and international legal change by zooming in on patterns of engagement by actors as they emerge from our cases. Unlike many accounts of the consequences of complexity which focus on institutional competition and forum-shopping—with a binary choice between one or the other institution—we observe here dynamics which often involve multiple institutions and follow a 'path of least resistance'. Actors operate under conditions of bounded rationality, and not all paths will always be available to them. Within these limits, however, actors often pursue paths that offer them the greatest chance of success—often in or through peripheral institutions—knowing that with each successful step, the likelihood of success in the next step increases. Change attempts then bear fruit if, over time, they can muster sufficient support, either from multiple authorities or focal authorities (where they exist). Where authorities diverge, these attempts usually lead to situations of legal uncertainty.

This result, we suggest, is due to the particularities of (legal) norm processes. Rather than being decided in any one forum, these processes tend to unfold over time and involve the iterative generation of support for new norm proposals. The more such support comes from recognized authorities, the more these proposals gain authority themselves—which makes it more likely that a broader range of actors will accept and support them going forward. This sequencing brings us back to the historical-institutionalist framework we introduced earlier in the book—gradual change is best understood if we take processes of path-dependence (here generated through social processes around authority) into view.[6]

[4] See Karen J Alter and Sophie Meunier, 'The Politics of International Regime Complexity', *Perspectives on Politics* 7, (2009): p. 13.

[5] See also Christian Kreuder-Sonnen and Michael Zürn, 'After Fragmentation: Norm Collisions, Interface Conflicts, and Conflict Management', *Global Constitutionalism* 9, (2020): p. 241; Nico Krisch, 'Entangled Legalities in the Postnational Space', *International Journal of Constitutional Law* 20, (2020): p. 476.

[6] See 'International Law between Stasis and Change' in Chapter 1.

In this chapter, we begin by explicating the broader framework for understanding legal change under conditions of complexity (section 1) and then show how this leads actors to seek paths of least resistance, conditioned by the expected receptivity of certain paths to a particular change attempt (section 2). We also show how such strategies often involve moving across different areas of international law, thus making use of the ever-greater complexity in global governance (section 3). But while such moves facilitate change attempts, their success is by no means guaranteed. If change efforts are frustrated, or if the paths of international law promise too little success from the outset, change agents may pursue other avenues for change: paths that take them outside of international law, towards informal, unilateral, or non-normative tools (section 4). The account we develop here, focused as it is on institutional receptivity and resistance, can thus also help to shed more light on the pressures on international law and its (tenuous) place in contemporary global governance.

1. Complexity, Change, and Cumulated Authority

Regime complexity has arguably become 'the signature feature of twenty-first-century international cooperation'.[7] Defined as 'an array of partially overlapping and nonhierarchical institutions that includes more than one international agreement or authority',[8] regime complexes are not altogether new,[9] but they have found much greater attention since the early 2000s across many areas of global governance.[10] International lawyers, meanwhile, pursued a related phenomenon—that of 'fragmentation', typically deriving from the growth of new subfields with their own institutions, especially courts. The initial concern was that these bodies might come to contrasting conclusions and therefore put the unity and coherence of international law at risk.[11] This fragmented, complex state of affairs is also reflected in our cases: more than three-quarters of them are characterized by a diffuse

[7] Alter and Raustiala (n 3), p. 345.

[8] ibid p. 333.

[9] See Orfeo Fioretos and Stephanie Hofmann, 'Global Complexity in Time: Structures, Agency, and Experiences', in *Experiencing Worlds of Complexity: Creative Agency and Global Governance in Time* (manuscript), edited by Orfeo Fioretos and Stephanie Hofmann.

[10] See, e.g., Kal Raustiala and David G Victor, 'The Regime Complex for Plant Genetic Resources', *International Organization* 58, (2004): p. 277; Laurence R Helfer, 'Regime Shifting: The TRIPS Agreement and New Dynamics of International Intellectual Property Lawmaking', *Yale Journal of International Law* 29, (2004): p. 1.

[11] See the overview of the debate in Anne Peters, 'The Refinement of International Law: From Fragmentation to Regime Interaction and Politicization', *International Journal of Constitutional Law* 15, (2017): p. 671.

authority layout, and in the other ones, focal authorities typically exist alongside a number of other institutions with secondary weight.[12]

In both international law and international relations, observers were initially concerned about the consequences of such complexity for order, stability, and governance. Risks of opportunism, increased conflict, and weakened compliance with international norms were a mainstay of early accounts.[13] These 'anxieties'[14] have over time given way to more nuanced accounts that emphasize the many ways in which friction is avoided or contained by practices of accommodation or pragmatic navigation and highlight the fact that 'entangled legalities' are a common rather than an aberrational phenomenon.[15] Even in the context of institutional complexity and fragmentation, 'interface conflicts' are not a natural given. They arise only if activated by societal or political actors, and the extent to which they cause friction depends on whether they are managed in cooperative or non-cooperative ways, and whether, over time, actors come to converge or diverge over the meaning of norms or the relevant site of governance of a particular issue. Whether we are more likely to see friction or accommodation seems to depend, in part, on the origins of such interface conflicts—as stemming from strategic creation or inadvertent overlaps. It also depends on their reach, especially on whether they span more than one sphere of authority and thus potentially reflect a greater divergence in institutional orientations and worldviews of associated actors.[16]

From the perspective of (legal) change, the greater openness and potentially disruptive consequences of complexity and fragmentation appear in a somewhat different light. Many commentators continue to highlight the risk of irresolution—if competing norms emerge, or existing norms find diverging interpretations in different institutions, law is uncertain, consolidation undermined, and the rule of law endangered. They accordingly analyse the ways in which such risks can be contained, especially through interpretive tools geared towards systemic integration.[17] Yet they often overlook the extent to which such irresolution also creates space for transformation. International legal norms are typically difficult to change or amend in formal ways, but complexity allows for an easier generation of competing understandings. When different norms stand formally alongside each other,

[12] Out of our twenty-five cases, we observed a diffuse authority layout in nineteen and a focal authority in six cases. On the distinction between focal and diffuse authority, see 'Factors behind Change: Expectations' in Chapter 4.

[13] See the symposium on Alter and Meunier (n 4).

[14] Martti Koskenniemi and Päivi Leino, 'Fragmentation of International Law? Postmodern Anxieties', *Leiden Journal of International Law* 15, (2002): p. 553.

[15] See Philippa Webb, *International Judicial Integration and Fragmentation* (Oxford University Press, 2013); Peters (n 11); Kreuder-Sonnen and Zürn (n 5); Nico Krisch, ed., *Entangled Legalities beyond the State* (Cambridge University Press, 2021).

[16] See Kreuder-Sonnen and Zürn (n 5) and also the other contributions to the symposium on 'After Fragmentation', *Global Constitutionalism* 9, no. 2 (2020).

[17] See, e.g., Mads Andenas and Eirik Bjorge, eds., *A Farewell to Fragmentation: Reassertion and Convergence in International Law* (Cambridge University Press, 2015); Peters (n 11).

the focus often shifts to the implementation stage, where actors need to create relations between the norms, often producing new meanings in the process.[18] This is true for unintentional norm conflicts, created by inadvertent inconsistencies generated in different fora or at different points in time. But complexity is also often generated intentionally, through strategic inconsistencies or direct treaty conflicts, with the aim of facilitating legal change—either by promoting new fora and norms to govern a particular issue or by destabilizing existing understandings.[19]

This latter perspective corresponds with historical institutionalist approaches to gradual change. If institutions themselves are relatively stable and hard to change—whether because of formal rules, normalization, or increasing returns—change will often be pursued through turning to (or layering on) other institutions or rules.[20] Movement can then emerge from interaction between different institutions. Historical institutionalists have thus begun to reflect institutional complexity by depicting institutions not as singular but instead as forming 'institutional assemblages' which generate interspaces and thus fertile ground for agency and endogenous change.[21] They have also pointed to 'the interplay of multiple institutions as a source of both tensions and opportunities' and as 'a possible source of dynamics which studies focused exclusively on a single institution are unlikely to capture'.[22]

Such dynamics may have their limits—multiplicity may hinder, rather than facilitate, large-scale ruptures and radical institutional change.[23] But it is likely to favour the more gradual change processes we focus on in this book: if such gradual change is expected to emerge 'in the "gaps" or "soft spots" between the rule and its interpretation or the rule and its enforcement',[24] regime complexity and fragmentation certainly open up such gaps and soft spots. Where interpreters can point to a norm or interpretation already in place in one context, they will typically find it easier to move to such an understanding also in another context. This has been the logic, for example, of attempts at rule-making in non-trade contexts—in

18 Alter and Meunier (n 4), pp. 15–17.

19 See Helfer (n 10); Surabhi Ranganathan, *Strategically Created Treaty Conflicts and the Politics of International Law* (Cambridge University Press, 2014); Nico Krisch, Francesco Corradini and Lucy Lu Reimers, 'Order at the Margins: The Legal Construction of Interface Conflicts over Time', *Global Constitutionalism* 9, (2020): p. 343.

20 See Chapter 2 and James Mahoney and Kathleen Thelen, 'A Theory of Gradual Institutional Change', in *Explaining Institutional Change: Ambiguity, Agency, and Power*, edited by J Mahoney and K Thelen (Cambridge University Press, 2010), pp. 16–18.

21 Gerschewski (n 2), 230; Patrick Emmenegger, 'Agency in Historical Institutionalism: Coalitional Work in the Creation, Maintenance, and Change of Institutions', *Theory and Society* 50, (2020): pp. 607, 620–21; Joseph Jupille and James A Caporaso, *Theories of Institutions* (Cambridge University Press, 2022), p. 43.

22 Pierson (n 1), p. 136.

23 Orfeo Fioretos, 'Historical Institutionalism in International Relations', *International Organization* 65, (2011): pp. 367, 391.

24 Mahoney and Thelen (n 20), p. 14.

environmental, cultural, or health fora—to facilitate change in the interpretation of World Trade Organization (WTO) rules.[25]

Observers of regime complexity in international relations and international law often downplay this effect because they frame institutional choice in binary terms and do not capture the interaction effects between different sites. Actors' choices when faced with multiple institutions are often understood in terms of forum-shopping, similar to the choice claimants face between different available judicial fora for the resolution of an individual case.[26] In such cases, selecting one forum means excluding other fora altogether. Yet in most governance contexts, and especially in processes of (legal) norm change, such a binary picture is inadequate—even if some actors choose a certain site, other sites typically remain available and potentially consequential for the process. For example, when in the early 2000s developing country governments sought to protect access to essential medicines against the patent protections of the Agreement on Trade-Related Aspects of Intellectual Property Rights (TRIPS Agreement), their turn to human rights institutions and the World Health Assembly did not remove the TRIPS Agreement and the WTO from the picture. Instead, it was meant to generate pressure and a feedback effect on world trade institutions to change their interpretation of the TRIPS Agreement—a strategy that was (partially) successful with the WTO's 2001 Doha Declaration and the adoption, two years later, of a generalized waiver.[27] Activating one institution is then not a binary choice but instead a move in a broader sequence.

The importance of such sequences becomes clearer when we consider the currency in which much legal change is traded. Discursive change processes in international law centre on questions of authority. A change attempt needs to garner sufficient support from actors with authority ('authorities') for it to gain authority itself as the dominant, most accepted understanding. As we saw in Chapter 2, authority is socially constructed, is relational and relative—its strength depends on the intensity of social recognition in a particular context—and is not exclusive.[28] Where an actor or text has authority, it is treated with deference in the sense that actors give it weight even if it may not align with their own ideas or preferences. As a result, authority can be cumulated, and a change attempt that is successful on several paths will typically carry greater weight among a larger audience (but that weight can also diminish when different authorities diverge in their assessment).

[25] See Helfer (n 10); Nico Krisch, *Beyond Constitutionalism: The Pluralist Structure of Postnational Law* (Oxford University Press, 2010), ch. 6. On different legal approaches to deal with such attempts, see Joost Pauwelyn, *Conflict of Norms in Public International Law* (Cambridge University Press, 2003).

[26] See Laurence R Helfer, 'Forum Shopping for Human Rights', *University of Pennsylvania Law Review* 148, (1999): p. 285; Joseph Jupille, Walter Mattli and Duncan Snidal, *Institutional Choice and Global Commerce* (Cambridge University Press, 2013).

[27] See Helfer (n 10); Frederick M Abbott, 'The WTO Medicines Decision: World Pharmaceutical Trade and the Protection of Public Health', *American Journal of International Law* 99, (2005): p. 317.

[28] See 'Actors, Practices, Authority: The Social Frame of Change' in Chapter 2; Nico Krisch, 'Liquid Authority in Global Governance', *International Theory* 9, (2017): p. 237.

Such cumulation of authority does not replicate the operation of precedent in a strict sense—in our cases, we are also often not concerned with judicial decisions—but the two mechanisms are similar in that past decisions have relevance for future ones.[29] This points to an important role for path dependence in processes of international legal change. When it comes to the generation of authority, a statement in favour of a given change attempt by one authority will normally increase the likelihood that other authoritative actors will come to the same conclusion. The same holds true, vice versa, for statements that reject that change attempt—these will make it more likely that other authorities will equally reject it. The mechanism behind such path dependence is not a rationalist one, as with increasing returns, but instead a social one which relies on the (relative) deference of actors to authority.[30] For example, the International Court of Justice (ICJ) regularly bolsters its own authority by drawing on the work of the (widely recognized) International Law Commission (ILC) of the United Nations (and vice versa).[31] In this vein, the adoption by the ILC of a particular approach to state responsibility centred on 'internationally wrongful acts'—based on the violation of a norm and excluding the requirement of damage—made it more likely that the ICJ would approach the issue in the same way.[32]

The scope of this dynamic does, however, have important limitations. For one, authority is relative not just in the sense of coming in degrees, but also in that of being relational.[33] Deference to a certain authority will thus often be limited to certain relations and audiences—to other actors, it might matter little or not at all. As a result, triggering institutions in one area may not have much effect in another—a theme we will return to in greater detail in section 3.

Path dependence is also limited in a second respect, namely when authority is overstretched. If statements in favour of change go too far in the eyes of some actors, they may trigger reactive sequences through politicization, contestation, and backlash.[34] Backlash processes in international law have been widely observed

[29] See Alec Stone Sweet, 'Path Dependence, Precedent, and Judicial Power', in *On Law, Politics, and Judicialization*, edited by M Shapiro and A Stone Sweet (Oxford University Press, 2002); also Rosalyn Higgins, *Problems and Process: International Law and How We Use It* (Clarendon Press, 1995), pp. 2–3.

[30] See, e.g., James Mahoney, 'Path Dependence in Historical Sociology', *Theory and Society* 29, (2000): p. 507; Michael Zürn, 'Historical Institutionalism and International Relations: Strange Bedfellows?', in *Historical Institutionalism and International Relations: Explaining Institutional Development in World Politics*, edited by Thomas Rixen, Lora Anne Viola and Michael Zürn (Oxford University Press, 2016), pp. 201–11.

[31] See, e.g., Stephen M Schwebel, 'The Inter-Active Influence of the International Court of Justice and the International Law Commission', in *Liber Amicorum 'In Memoriam' of Judge José María Ruda*, edited by Calixto A Armas Barea and others (Brill, 2000); Omri Sender, *International Law-Making by the International Court of Justice and International Law Commission: Partnership for Purpose in a Decentralized Legal Order* (Cambridge University Press, 2024).

[32] See Pedro Martínez Esponda, 'The Concept of Internationally Wrongful Act', in *The Paths of International Law: Case Studies*, edited by Pedro Martínez Esponda and others (SSRN, 2023).

[33] See also the discussion in David A Lake, 'Relational Authority and Legitimacy in International Relations', *American Behavioral Scientist* 53, (2009): p. 331.

[34] Michael Zürn, Martin Binder and Matthias Ecker-Ehrhardt, 'International Authority and Its Politicization', *International Theory* 4, (2012): p. 69.

in recent years, in particular with a view to international courts.[35] Strong reactions of (some) states to decisions of the International Criminal Court (ICC), the WTO Appellate Body, and regional human rights courts, as well as regional integration courts have been at the centre of attention here. Typically, though, the threshold for such backlash is relatively high—where international courts and quasi-judicial bodies are firmly established as authorities, states will often go along with their decisions even if they are unhappy with them in substance. The WTO Appellate Body's contested subsidy jurisprudence, for example, was recognized as reflecting world trade law even by most opposing states—until US discontent contributed to its decision to block further Appellate Body appointments and stop the organ from continuing its work.[36] Another recent example is the attitude by several European states vis-à-vis the European Court of Human Rights' (ECtHR) jurisprudence with regard to challenges posed by immigration. While states have expressed strong discontent on this issue, they are trying to change the direction of the Court rather than engaging in simple non-compliance or withdrawal—though some governments have warned that they may consider pulling out of the Court if it does not adjust its stance.[37] Such contestation potentially affecting the very paths on which international law travels will come into focus in Chapter 7.

Despite these limitations, the multiplicity of institutions and paths of change offers significant opportunities to change agents. In contrast to the typically rigid forms of change in international law, competing approaches in different sites can help to create greater space for movement. And by activating different authorities, change agents can build support and accumulate authority over time, potentially leading to the eventual consolidation of a new rule or interpretation.

2. Paths of Least Resistance

Which paths then do change processes travel on? Most areas of international law and politics today are characterized by a certain degree of institutional complexity, albeit with variations, and many problems concern more than one issue area and thus touch upon yet greater complexity. Change agents typically face a choice when

[35] See, e.g., Karen J Alter, James T Gathii and Laurence R Helfer, 'Backlash against International Courts in West, East and Southern Africa: Causes and Consequences', *European Journal of International Law* 27, (2016): p. 293; Mikael Rask Madsen, Pola Cebulak and Micha Wiebusch, 'Backlash against International Courts: Explaining the Forms and Patterns of Resistance to International Courts', *International Journal of Law in Context* 14, (2018): p. 197.

[36] Nina Kiderlin, 'Subsidies: A Changing Approach to "Public Bodies"', in *The Paths of International Law: Case Studies*, edited by Pedro Martínez Esponda and others (SSRN, 2023); Mark A Pollack, 'International Court Curbing in Geneva: Lessons from the Paralysis of the WTO Appellate Body', *Governance* 36, (2023): p. 23.

[37] Lena Riemer, 'From "Original Intentions" to "Unforeseeable Change of Circumstances": The 2025 Escalation of Pressure Towards the ECtHR' (*EJIL: Talk!*, 5 January 2026), at: https://www.ejiltalk.org/fromoriginalintentionstounforeseeablechangeofcircumstances/ accessed 2 February 2026.

it comes to the paths to pursue—and opponents may have a similar choice when trying to counter change. In this section, we build on the insights about cumulated authority outlined above to develop a basic model for the direction of change processes in international law centred on the receptivity or resistance of different paths to change attempts.

Choice, Receptivity, and Resistance

Perhaps the most prominent attempt to understand institutional choice in the global arena in recent years has been the 'Use—Select—Change—Create' (USCC) model proposed by Joseph Jupille, Walter Mattli, and Duncan Snidal. The model starts from an image of actors whose rationality is heavily bounded, and who, as a result, can be expected to *use* standard paths of change first before turning to alternatives—by *selecting* other available avenues, *changing* existing ones, or *creating* new ones.[38] Whether they move to these other avenues depends in this model on whether the default option produces a satisfactory, although not necessarily an ideal, result. If it does not, actors will explore alternatives which are typically fraught with greater uncertainty and potentially also greater transaction costs. A relative path dependence is here generated through psychological mechanisms and leads to a certain (limited) stability of the institutional status quo. The strategic element is relatively pronounced in this account, but the emphasis on bounded rationality brings the USCC model closer to social understandings of world politics.[39]

The core variable in the USCC model is the receptivity of certain institutions to a particular change attempt. The flipside of receptivity is resistance—and it is such resistance that stands at the centre of recent attempts to account for gradual change processes in historical institutionalism. In trying to understand which type of change (and by extension, which path) will become dominant, historical institutionalists point to two factors—the degree of veto possibilities and the space for (i) discretion and (ii) reinterpretation. The assumption here is that actors will seek change inside a given institution, typically through 'displacement'—the formal replacement of an existing rule with a new one. If this is rendered difficult, in particular because of too many veto points, actors are expected to turn to 'conversion'—the changed enactment of existing rules through strategic reinterpretation—if existing rules allow for sufficient discretion and there are institutional mechanisms to facilitate such conversion. If this is not the case,

[38] Jupille, Mattli and Snidal (n 26).

[39] On linkages with other institutionalisms, see Joseph Jupille, Walter Mattli and Duncan Snidal, 'Dynamics of Institutional Choice' in *International Politics and Institutions in Time*, edited by Orfeo Fioretos (Oxford University Press, 2017), pp. 131–36.

change agents are likely to turn to alternative forms, especially by 'layering' new rules (often produced in different settings) onto existing ones, thus changing the overall landscape, sidelining existing rules, and potentially also feeding back into the understanding of those rules themselves.[40]

With their emphasis on receptivity and resistance, both these strands highlight a core element behind the paths we observe in our cases. In several of them, frustrated efforts in a key institution led change attempts to spread out to other sites. The development of the right to a healthy environment, which we have encountered at various points in the previous chapters, is a good example. While already mentioned in the 1972 Stockholm Declaration, its further recognition stagnated in universal environmental conferences, and it was left out of the Rio Declaration and the agreements coming out of the 1992 Rio Conference. Instead, proponents of the right turned to other avenues, and they found early success in expert-led processes, in General Assembly resolutions, in regional instruments such as the Protocol of San Salvador, and in national courts. The acceptance broadened further, including in regional human rights jurisprudence, but it took until the 2010s for a concerted effort to generate recognition in a universal frame—in UN human rights institutions—and eventually to bear fruit in a widely supported General Assembly resolution in 2022.[41]

Many of our cases also reflect the emphasis on focal institutions in the USCC model (and in historical institutionalist approaches more generally). Where focal institutions are receptive, change usually happens through them—examples include the WTO Appellate Body (in its day) or the International Seabed Authority.[42] But similar observations abound in other contexts, too; perhaps most prominently in European human rights law, where the ECtHR has effectively established itself as a central institution over time; other actors often concentrate their change attempts on it.[43]

But where focal authorities resist change attempts, this is not necessarily the end of the matter. Change agents then often turn to other, secondary paths, insofar as these exist and are available to them—or attempt to create new paths. This is especially striking in areas in which traditional paths of law-making proved no

40 Mahoney and Thelen (n 20).

41 Dorothea Endres, 'The Human Right to a "Good" Environment, in *The Paths of International Law: Case Studies*, edited by Pedro Martínez Esponda and others (SSRN, 2023); Elena Cima, 'The Right to a Healthy Environment: Reconceptualizing Human Rights in the Face of Climate Change', *Review of European, Comparative & International Environmental Law* 31, (2022): p. 38; UNGA Res 76/300 (28 July 2022) UN Doc A/Res/76/300.

42 Kiderlin (n 36); Ezgi Yildiz, 'Revising the "Parallel System of Access" Rule for Seabed Mining', in *The Paths of International Law: Case Studies*, edited by Pedro Martínez Esponda and others (SSRN, 2023).

43 See Laurence R Helfer and Erik Voeten, 'International Courts as Agents of Legal Change: Evidence from LGBT Rights in Europe', *International Organization* 68, (2014): p. 77; Mikael Madsen, 'The Challenging Authority of the European Court of Human Rights: From Cold War Legal Diplomacy to the Brighton Declaration and Backlash', *Law and Contemporary Problems* 79, (2016): p. 141.

longer viable, at least from the perspective of certain change agents. The failure of early multilateral efforts at reaching an agreement on investment protection and the strong contestation of this project at the UN during the 1960s and 1970s led capital-exporting states to conclude bilateral agreements instead.[44] Likewise, the difficulty of moving towards new multilateral negotiations on international humanitarian law, fuelled especially by discontent among Northern countries with the process leading up to the Additional Protocols, made change agents turn to international courts and expert-led processes. This resulted in new rules via the reshaping of international criminal law—for example, on rape or crimes in non-international armed conflicts—as well as the development of customary international law *qua* restatement in the International Committee of the Red Cross's Study on Customary International Humanitarian Law.[45] Similarly, the inability of states to move forward with WTO negotiations during the Doha Round shifted the focus of actors towards the dispute settlement system, casting the Appellate Body as a focal authority but also potentially overburdening it and eventually engendering its demise.[46]

The image of focal paths, from which actors depart only if they face too much resistance, is compelling, but it does not tell the whole story. This is, in the first place, because most fields do not possess a central, default path or a focal authority. As discussed in Chapter 3, the recognition of specialized paths of international legal development varies widely across issue areas and geographical and institutional contexts—sometimes a particular path will stand out, while at other times various paths will stand alongside each other without a clear priority. Only in about a quarter of our cases did change processes operate in the presence of a focal authority. Moreover, as we have also seen, not all paths are available to all actors. Some actors, especially governments, typically have a greater range of options than, say, civil society groups which can access only a restricted set of fora, and sometimes only indirectly. Multilateral negotiations may be the dominant path in some areas—for example, environmental law—but they are only indirectly accessible to non-governmental organizations (NGOs).

Change processes in international law also differ from the USCC model in that they are often not confined to one path but can instead take place on multiple ones simultaneously (or sequentially). As we have already seen in the previous section, institutional choice here is not binary—the choice of one forum

[44] See 'International Investment Law' in Chapter 3; Taylor St. John, *The Rise of Investor-State Arbitration: Politics, Law, and Unintended Consequences* (Oxford University Press, 2018).

[45] See 'International Humanitarian Law' in Chapter 3; Giovanni Mantilla, 'From Treaty to Custom: Shifting Paths in the Recent Development of International Humanitarian Law', *Leiden Journal of International Law* 37, (2024): p. 1.

[46] See 'International Trade Law' in Chapter 3; Nicolas Lamp, 'Arrested Norm Development: The Failure of Legislative-Judicial Dialogue in the WTO', *Leiden Journal of International Law* 38, (2025): p. 570.

does not exclude others, and decisions by one institution also do not normally settle the matter definitively. Instead, actors can pursue their efforts in a variety of contexts and thus build support (and cumulate authority) for their aims gradually and over time. Many change agents are aware of this fact, and in twenty-four of our twenty-five cases, more than one type of path was activated, with an average number of activated types of paths per case above three. In addition, in some cases, multiple authorities within the same type of path were brought into play.

Multiplicity is thus a core element of change processes in international law—even in areas with a focal authority, we see more than one type of path being used. Just as in the USCC model and standard imageries of historical institutionalists, the receptivity/resistance of authorities on the different paths seems to play an important role, but unlike in those models, the activation of various paths alongside each other constitutes not so much an exception as the rule.

From the Periphery to the Centre

Three important conclusions follow from our discussion thus far regarding the direction of processes of legal change: change agents will typically seek receptive institutions; they can activate several institutions; and success on one path will often make success on other paths more likely, thus facilitating the cumulation of authority over time.

Many actors involved in international legal change processes are complex organizations—governments, NGOs, business associations, etc.—and they usually make conscious choices about the direction of their efforts. But their rationality will be bounded—they do not have all the relevant information about the different paths, and they will often have preconceived ideas about which of them may offer success and which may not.[47] Moreover, as we have just seen, not all paths are equally available or accessible to every actor.

In this light, we can expect change agents often to pursue a staged approach. Such an approach first targets, among the available paths, one that holds a promise of receptivity, even if it is less central or does not come with the greatest possible authority. If successful in the first step, a change agent would then seek endorsements from an institution with greater authority, which, recognizing the support gained along the previous path, can now be expected to be more receptive to the change attempt. If necessary, this would be, repeated so as to reach a sufficient combined authority for actors in the relevant field to recognize a change in the legal norm. If setbacks occur on this route, we expect actors to work around such resistance

[47] See also Jupille, Mattli and Snidal (n 26), pp. 31–37.

and seek out more receptive paths to strengthen their viewpoint again. Typically, in such an approach, actors move from the periphery to the centre—from more receptive but potentially more marginal institutions towards more central ones with higher thresholds for success. They thus take a 'path of least resistance', which ultimately, if not countered by rival interpretations, can lead to change through reception by actors in the broader field. Each step on the way would build on the outcome of the previous one, expanding influence and scope with each iteration if the institutional structure of the respective field so allows, and thus accumulating authority over time. This general pattern is captured, in a stylized form, in Figure 6.1.

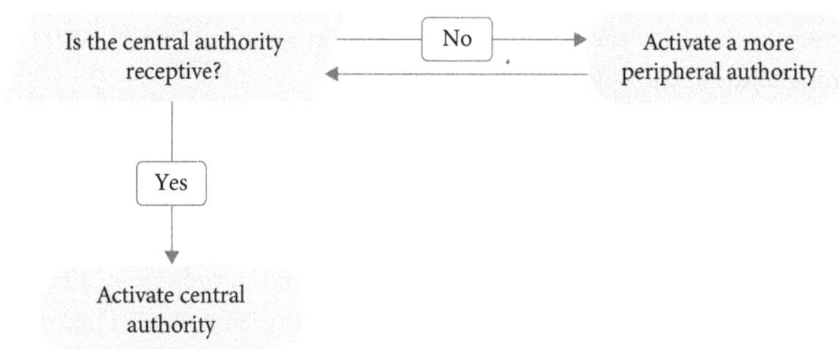

Figure 6.1 Paths of least resistance

A good example of this pattern is the development of the positive obligation of states to prevent violence against women.[48] The need for action against domestic and gender-based violence became part of international discourse throughout the UN Decade for Women in the 1970s and 1980s, but it was initially not framed in legal or human rights terms. The push for a binding state obligation did not at first find much resonance in the intergovernmental sites central to the struggle for gender equality, namely the Commission on the Status of Women, and the international conferences on the issue, especially the 1985 Nairobi conference. It was instead channelled through a more receptive body—the Committee on the Elimination of Discrimination against Women (CEDAW Committee), an international expert body set up under the 1979 Convention on the Elimination of All Forms of Discrimination against Women (CEDAW). In a General Recommendation adopted in 1989, the CEDAW Committee began to affirm that a positive obligation of states resulted from the other rights provided for in the

[48] Ezgi Yildiz, 'The Emergence of the Positive Obligation to Protect Women from Domestic Violence', in *The Paths of International Law: Case Studies*, edited by Pedro Martínez Esponda and others (SSRN, 2023). See also Natalie R Davidson, 'Everyday Lawmaking in International Human Rights Law: Insights from the Inclusion of Domestic Violence in the Prohibition of Torture', *Law & Social Inquiry* 47, (2022): p. 205.

Convention, and it reiterated and strengthened that position three years later.[49] On the back of this stance, similar language—although in hortatory form—came to be included in the General Assembly's 1993 Declaration on the Elimination of Violence against Women.[50] After that, the path towards consolidation led through the adoption of specialized agreements and judicial interpretations in the Inter-American, the African, as well as the European human rights systems, and through a widespread inclusion by states in their internal legislation.[51] It culminated in the Human Rights Council's 2016 recognition not only of the general principle but also of particular implications of states' positive obligation to protect women from gender-based violence.[52] The following year, the CEDAW Committee could thus conclude that the prohibition of gender-based violence had attained the status of customary law and list the ensuing obligations, in an update to its 1989 General Recommendation, with significant specificity.[53]

That this case centres on human rights is not coincidental—the periphery-centre pattern is perhaps best visible in the human rights field, just because it contains so many different sites and actors at the universal level, with receptivity for different kinds of causes. The development of the human right to a healthy environment, implicating a wide variety of regional and peripheral institutions before moving towards global recognition, is another case in point.[54] The emergence of the right to water and sanitation is also a good example, in which activists deliberately targeted, in a first step, receptive members of the UN Committee on Economic, Social and Cultural Rights (CESCR). When the Committee had taken a clear stance, the cumulation of authority continued in a variety of venues before moving into more central sites and eventually achieving support from the UN Human Rights Council (HRC) and the General Assembly.[55]

Yet we can observe similar trajectories in other areas as well. On cyber security, for example, Western states sought to influence the development of international legal rules not only through their own statements and manuals, but also through the creation of an international expert group that elaborated the Tallinn Manuals, thus preparing the ground for the UN process that began a few years later. Because

[49] UN Committee on the Elimination of Discrimination against Women, 'General Recommendation No 12: Violence against Women' (1989) UN Doc A/44/38; UN Committee on the Elimination of Discrimination against Women, 'General Recommendation 19: Violence against Women' (1992) UN Doc/A/47/38.

[50] UNGA Res 48/104 (20 December 1993), art. 4.

[51] For an overview, see Yildiz (n 48).

[52] UNHRC Res 32/19 (1 July 2016) UN/A/HRC/Res/32/19, adopted without a vote.

[53] UN Committee on the Elimination of Discrimination against Women, 'General Recommendation 35: Gender-based Violence against Women' (26 July 2017) CEDAW/C/GC/35.

[54] See text accompanying note 41.

[55] Nina Reiners, *Transnational Lawmaking Coalitions for Human Rights* (Cambridge University Press, 2021); Nina Reiners, 'States as Bystanders of Legal Change: Alternative Paths for the Human Rights to Water and Sanitation in International Law', *Leiden Journal of International Law* 37, (2024): p. 22.

of significant contestation around the issue, however, the UN process has not met with much success thus far.[56] Another, particularly striking illustration is the creation of port state rights and obligations to combat illegal, unregulated, and unreported (IUU) fishing mechanisms in light of ineffective flag state control.[57] Australia was, with a number of allies, a particularly active proponent of measures against IUU fishing throughout the 1990s and 2000s, but its attempts to establish stronger enforcement did not generate sufficient traction in the context of the Convention on the Conservation of Antarctic Marine Living Resources or in the Convention on International Trade in Endangered Species (CITES), and its own action against IUU fishing by arresting vessels in the Southern Ocean suffered setbacks in the International Tribunal for the Law of the Sea (ITLOS). Australia encountered more receptivity in the Food and Agriculture Organization of the UN (FAO). The FAO was not a central site in the law of the sea but had already been active with respect to fisheries for several decades. Its 1999 ministerial declaration on IUU fishing generated momentum and led to action in the UN through a report of the Secretary-General and then a General Assembly resolution of the same year. More concretely, it paved the way for an FAO-generated plan of action on IUU fishing, a significant part of which focused on port-state measures.[58] The 2001 Plan established a responsibility of port states to control whether ships seeking to enter their ports had been engaged in IUU fishing, or else deny them entry. The Plan was endorsed by the UN General Assembly and engendered further, gradual steps, in particular a Model Scheme on Port State Measures, which found support by the 2006 Review Conference of the UN Fish Stocks Agreement as 'the international minimum standard for port state control'. It also served as the basis for the Port State Measures Agreement adopted by the FAO Conference in late 2009, which entered into force in 2016 and is now ratified by eighty-four countries and the European Union. This has not led to a consolidated new norm under customary international law, but it has clarified the rights of port states vis-à-vis IUU fishing, made it possible to argue for port state obligations, and provided support for port states intent on taking more far-reaching measures.[59]

These cases concern contexts of diffuse authority, and in areas with a focal authority, we observe a somewhat different picture—although one which also reflects 'paths of least resistance'. As we have already seen, many existing models expect change efforts to be concentrated on a focal authority if it exists, and to switch

[56] See Nina Kiderlin, 'The Rules of Cyber Warfare', in *The Paths of International Law: Case Studies*, edited by Pedro Martínez Esponda and others (SSRN, 2023); Christian Henderson, 'The United Nations and the Regulation of Cyber-Security', in *Research Handbook on International Law and Cyberspace*, edited by Nicholas Tsagourias and Russell Buchan (Edward Elgar Publishing, 2021).

[57] See Ezgi Yildiz, 'The Emergence of Port State Measures Against IUU Fishing', in *The Paths of International Law: Case Studies*, edited by Pedro Martínez Esponda and others (SSRN, 2023).

[58] FAO, 'International Plan of Action to Prevent, Deter and Eliminate Illegal, Unreported and Unregulated Fishing' (IPOA-IUU) (2001) https://www.fao.org/3/y1224e/Y1224E.pdf.

[59] Yildiz (n 57).

elsewhere only if the results are unsatisfactory. This is certainly true in some instances, especially where the focal institution promises to be sufficiently receptive. The development of rape as a war crime through the ad hoc criminal tribunals and then the ICC may fall into this category, as well as the attempt of different countries (and companies) to adjust the rules for deep seabed mining through the International Seabed Authority.[60]

Yet even where a focal authority exists, change agents do not always target it exclusively. In the previous section, we have encountered instances in which frustrations with a focal authority have led actors to move towards (or even create) other avenues—just recall the shift from negotiations to dispute settlement in the WTO around the Doha Round.

Change agents may not wait for such frustration—they may instead activate other paths even before turning to a focal authority. They know that if they access a particular path prematurely, they may face a rejection of their change attempt, which is difficult to reverse later. If, however, they prepare the ground carefully and build up sufficient authority prior to accessing that same path, their success chances are significantly higher. Lawyers engaged in strategic litigation and cause lawyering know how important it is to pave the way for successful court decisions through media campaigns and political action.[61] The institutional complexity in the international arena allows for further possibilities for preparatory, sequential build-up. Change agents thus often begin by preparing the ground on secondary paths, hoping to increase their chances of success before the focal authority itself. They may, for example, target UN Special Rapporteurs or the Parliamentary Assembly of the Council of Europe—or indeed national institutions and courts—to generate greater receptivity in the ECtHR.[62] But they may also see promise in institutions in other issue areas, which may be more sympathetic to their views. This introduces a further element of complexity to which we turn now.

3. Sideways Moves: Cumulation across Issue Areas

The logic of 'paths of least resistance', with a gradual move towards more central authorities, is even more obvious when we take into view institutional complexity not only within a given issue area, but also across different spheres of authority.[63]

[60] See Dorothea Endres, 'Rape as a Crime in Times of War/Armed Conflict', in *The Paths of International Law: Case Studies*, edited by Pedro Martínez Esponda and others (SSRN, 2023); Yildiz (n 42).

[61] See Helen Duffy, *Strategic Human Rights Litigation: Understanding and Maximising Impact* (Bloomsbury Publishing, 2018), pp. 242–50.

[62] On the importance of sequencing and the use of multiple fora, see ibid pp. 250–56.

[63] On the distinction, see also Kreuder-Sonnen and Zürn (n 5).

Institutions from different issue areas are often concerned with the same problem, but typically come at it from different perspectives. This increases the risk of friction, but it also presents opportunities for change agents. Where they seek to shift understandings of a norm towards a different set of values, they will often encounter resistance from the institutions guarding the existing regime. Dispute settlement panels in trade resisted the embrace of environmental considerations for a long time, just as the World Bank kept out human rights considerations according to a strict interpretation of the political prohibition clause in the Articles of Agreement.[64] Regimes are not only conglomerates of norms, but also of associated institutions, actors, and communities that are often held together by particular ways of seeing the world, privileging certain assumptions about values, priorities, and causal links over others.[65] This brings us back to the role of communities of practice in processes of legal change, already highlighted in Chapter 2.[66] Around different regimes, we often find distinct communities that typically process change attempts differently.

Where change agents can activate a path from a different sphere of authority, they may find more receptive institutions (and communities) in the hope of overcoming the limitations of change in a given regime. This 'sideways' move is, again, an attempt to find a path of less resistance, with the aim of building up sufficient authority to influence the norm development in the regime concerned. This also puts into perspective the notion of focal authorities, which are often focal only within a particular context—say, the WTO Appellate Body for trade in its day—but peripheral when seen from another sphere of authority. Authority is relative in this sense, too—actors in different areas have different notions of authority; they pray to different gods.

The general pattern of sideways moves is captured in Figure 6.2. We have already come across several such cases in this chapter. In the essential medicines case, actors attempting to limit TRIPS disciplines successfully activated institutions from the fields of health and human rights law to generate support for their endeavour. In the IUU fishing case, it was the move to the FAO that helped to increase momentum for a change in the understanding of the rights and obligations of port states. And in the case of the right to a healthy environment, it was precisely the shift from environmental to human rights paths that made it possible gradually to anchor such a right in international legal discourses.

[64] See, e.g., Joanne Scott, 'International Trade and Environmental Governance: Relating Rules (and Standards) in the EU and the WTO', *European Journal of International Law* 15, (2004): p. 307; Galit Sarfaty, *Values in Translation: Human Rights and the Culture of the World Bank* (Stanford University Press, 2012).

[65] See also Michael Waibel, 'Interpretive Communities in International Law', in *Interpretation in International Law*, edited by Andrea Bianchi, Daniel Peat and Matthew Windsor (Oxford University Press, 2014); Andrea Bianchi, 'Epistemic Communities', in *Concepts for International Law*, edited by Jean d'Aspremont and Sahib Singh (Edward Elgar Publishing, 2019).

[66] See 'Actors, Practices, Authority: The Social Frame of Change' in Chapter 2.

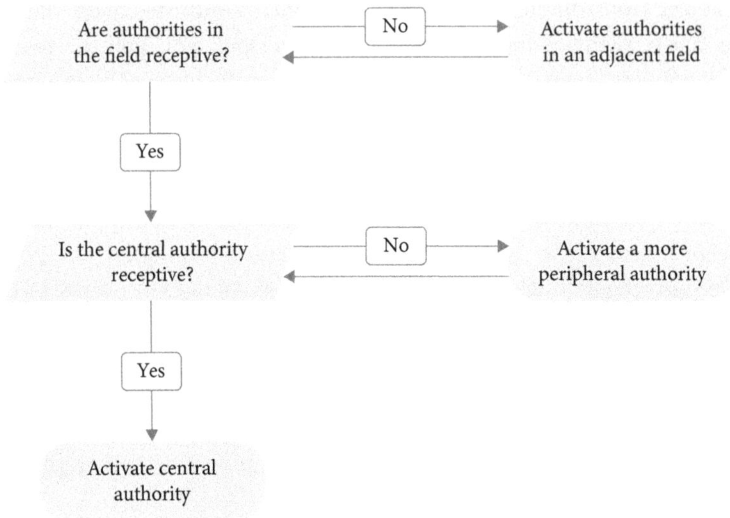

Figure 6.2 Paths across different fields

Probably the most emblematic example concerns the trade-environment nexus. The focus here was for a long time on the limits placed by GATT Article XX on national measures to protect the environment.[67] This issue came into relief most vividly in the *Tuna-Dolphin* cases in the early 1990s, in which GATT panels rejected US measures requiring particular catch methods for imported tuna with a view to protecting dolphins from being caught as well.[68] Environmental activists perceived the GATT regime as inimical to their concerns, and they pursued their cause in more receptive environmental fora, as reflected in the Brundtland Report's call for the GATT 'to integrate environment and development concerns into international trading arrangements',[69] attempts by the UN Environmental Programme (UNEP) to engage with the GATT,[70] and the 1992 Rio Declaration's emphasis on making international trade, environmental protection, and development goals compatible.[71] This helped to generate movement within the trading system, at least on a broad rhetorical level, as in the 1994 Ministerial Decision on

[67] Nina Kiderlin, 'General Exceptions under GATT Article XX and the Incorporation of Non-trade Considerations into Decision-making', in *The Paths of International Law: Case Studies*, edited by Pedro Martínez Esponda and others (SSRN, 2023).

[68] GATT Panel Report, *United States—Restrictions on Imports of Tuna* (3 September 1991) WT/DS21/R, unadopted, GATT BISD 39S/155; GATT Panel Report, *United States—Restrictions on Imports of Tuna* (16 June 1994) WT/DS29/R, unadopted.

[69] UNGA 'Report of the World Commission on Environment and Development: Our Common Future' (1987) UN Doc A/42/427, para. 2.4.

[70] See, e.g., GATT document (25 November 1988) L/6437.

[71] See UNGA 'Report of the United Nations Conference on Environment and Development' (12 August 1992) UN Doc A/CONF.151/26, Principle 12.

Trade and Environment, which embraced the aim 'to coordinate the policies in the field of trade and environment' and set up a Committee on Trade and Environment to work in this direction.[72] While the Committee struggled to find consensus on a new approach to Article XX,[73] the newly created WTO Appellate Body signalled greater openness. In its 1998 *Shrimp-Turtle* decision, the AB found US measures to restrict imports for shrimp caught with methods endangering sea turtles to violate the GATT, but it did so primarily on procedural grounds and accepted them as justified in principle.[74]

This stance suggested responsiveness and some success in the attempt to influence the trade regime by way of action in environmental fora. The Appellate Body also stressed that, as a matter of principle, the GATT was 'not to be read in clinical isolation from public international law'.[75] In a similar vein, other international courts and quasi-courts came to take into account norms and developments in other issue areas, which mitigated existing anxieties about fragmentation and helped spur diagnoses of a 'refinement' of international law dealing with a more variegated legal landscape.[76] It led, for example, the ICJ to state that it 'ascribe[d] great weight' to findings of the UN Human Rights Committee,[77] or investment tribunals to find that a bilateral investment treaty 'does not represent . . . a set of rules defined in isolation without consideration given to rules of international law external to its own rules'.[78]

Overall, this reflected an approach geared towards systemic integration in international law.[79] The ILC's study group on the issue of fragmentation placed particular emphasis on this approach in its attempt to distil principles for relating different sets of norms to one another.[80] Such integrative rhetoric did not, however, always correspond with actual results in practice: in the trade-environment context, the greater openness did not generally translate into actual successes

[72] WTO, Ministerial Decision on Trade and Environment (15 April 1994) https://www.wto.org/english/tratop_e/envir_e/issu5_e.htm.

[73] See Kiderlin (n 67), p. 680.

[74] WTO Appellate Body, *United States—Import Prohibition of Certain Shrimp and Shrimp Products* (12 October 1998) WT/DS58/AB/R (98-3899).

[75] WTO Appellate Body, *United States—Standards for Reformulated and Conventional Gasoline (US—Gasoline)* WT/DS2/AB/R, adopted 20 May 1996.

[76] Peters (n 11). See also Andenas and Bjorge (n 17).

[77] ICJ. Case Concerning Ahmadou Sallio Diallo (Republic of Guinea v Democratic Republic of the Congo) [2010] ICJ Rep 639, para. 66.

[78] ICSID. Urbaser SA and Consorcio de Aguas v Argentina (Award of 8 December 2016) ICSID Case No ARB/07/26, para. 1189.

[79] See, e.g., Webb (n 15); Campbell McLachlan, *The Principle of Systemic Integration in International Law* (Oxford University Press, 2024).

[80] ILC, 'Conclusions of the Work of the Study Group on the Fragmentation of International Law: Difficulties Arising from the Diversification and Expansion of International Law' (2006) UN Doc A/61/10, para. 251. But see also the emphasis on pluralism alongside coherence in ILC, 'Report of the Study Group of the International Law Commission', finalized by Martti Koskenniemi (13 April 2006) UN Doc A/CN.4/L.682.

for environmental causes,[81] and the findings of UN human rights treaty bodies were also at times dismissed by the ICJ despite its coherence-seeking approach in principle.[82]

The continuing distance between regimes—and corresponding limits for 'sideways moves'—is most clearly on display in the interplay between human rights institutions and investment tribunals.[83] Activists for a stronger responsiveness to human rights concerns in international investment protection—frustrated by the reluctance of investment tribunals—turned to international human rights institutions to gain validation for their attempt at reinterpreting investment rules—an attempt with great relevance, especially for social rights, like the right to water, but also for indigenous rights. As a result, bodies such as the CESCR or the UN Working Group on Business and Human Rights urged that the formulation and interpretation of investment agreements take into account universally accepted human rights.[84] The arbitral tribunals in the investment context, however, did not follow this line of argument, and while there have been certain rhetorical nods, as mentioned above, those tribunals have, for the most part, found human rights norms to lie outside the realm of the law they could interpret and enforce.[85] This disconnect probably concerns the divergent interests, cognitive frames and stereotypes among the different communities,[86] but it also reflects the limited recognition of the authority of human rights bodies in the investment field.

Activating paths in another issue area, then, will often come with particular promise—it might help to break out of established patterns and facilitate broader change. At the same time, it also comes with greater risk: as the authority of activated institutions is likely to be circumscribed in the target regime, the benefits of this strategy will often be more limited as well. Success in another issue area may simply not travel back to the regime initially in focus.

Moving sideways into another context is then a frequent step—and one with considerable promise. In our cases, those involving more than one sphere of

[81] See, e.g., on the biotech dispute, Mark A Pollack and Gregory C Shaffer, *When Cooperation Fails: The International Law and Politics of Genetically Modified Foods* (Oxford University Press, 2009); Nico Krisch, *Beyond Constitutionalism: The Pluralist Structure of Postnational Law* (Oxford University Press, 2010), ch. 6.

[82] ICJ. Application of the International Convention on the Elimination of All Forms of Racial Discrimination (Qatar v United Arab Emirates) (Preliminary Objections) [2021] ICJ Rep 71, para. 100.

[83] See Moshe Hirsch, 'Social Movements, Reframing Investment Relations, and Enhancing the Application of Human Rights Norms in International Investment Law', *Leiden Journal of International Law* 34, (2021): p. 127; Dorothea Endres, 'The Human Side of Protecting Foreign Investment', *Transnational Legal Theory* 12, (2021): p. 249.

[84] UN CESCR, 'General Comment 24 (2017) on State obligations in the context of business activities' (10 August 2017) UN E/C.12/GC/24, para. 13; UN Working Group on the Issue of Human Rights and Transnational Corporations and Other Business Enterprises, 'Report on Human Rights-compatible International Investment Agreements' (27 July 2021) UN Doc A/76/238.

[85] See, e.g., ICSID, *Bear Creek Mining Corporation v Peru* (30 November 2017) ICSID Case No ARB/14/21.

[86] See Hirsch (n 83); Endres (n 83).

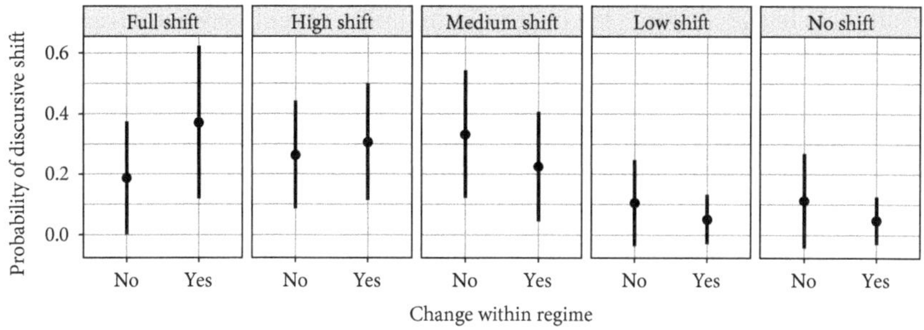

Figure 6.3 Probability of success in change within or beyond a distinct regime

authority were almost equal in number to those operating within a distinct regime. Of these, more than 40 % were largely successful, resulting in a high or full discursive shift. As already shown in Chapter 4, this success rate was lower than that for change processes taking place within a distinct regime, and a predicted probability test using ordinal logistic regression—as shown in Figure 6.3—indicates that the likelihood of a full shift or high shift is on average greater when change attempts are processed within a single regime, although the confidence intervals are wide and overlap substantially. However, we also saw in the regression analysis in Chapter 4 that 'change within a distinct regime' was negatively correlated with successful outcomes, but this relationship was not statistically significant.[87] Given the statistical limitations of our sample, one should not draw far-reaching conclusions from this. But it is noteworthy that 'sideways moves'—although probably less likely to lead to full change than change processes within a distinct regime—still offer meaningful chances of success.

Sideways moves open up the possibility of mounting more fundamental challenges to existing understandings than change attempts within one regime, but they face the risk of being ignored because the authority of norms and statements generated in this way may not reach back into the target regime. This reproduces—and exacerbates—the general dynamics of the paths of least resistance introduced above. When faced with (actual or expected) resistance in central authorities in a given field, actors tend to seek first more receptive paths even if these come with less weight and a less extensive authority. Step by step, as authority accumulates and widens, they seek to increase the likelihood of success in the central paths themselves. The path-dependence built into this sequence can smooth the change process. But if the authority of initially targeted institutions is too limited, this positive sequence is disrupted and the desired effect fails to materialize—with the

[87] See 'Findings II: Regression Analysis' in Chapter 4.

result that change attempts fail or remain in limbo, caught between diverging interpretations in different contexts.[88]

4. Paths around International Law

The paths of least resistance we have explored in this chapter have remained inside the realm of international law, broadly understood. When faced with legal and institutional complexity on the different paths of international law, actors pursue particular sequences, often moving from more proximate but peripheral to more central actors and institutions and accumulating authority step by step. This account was driven by the receptivity/resistance of authorities to a particular change attempt and the possibility, in a context of complexity, to exploit differences in the degree of such resistance across institutional settings. But what if, from the perspective of a given change agent, all paths of change in international law are inaccessible or too resistant—where does their change attempt move then?

Even in the more flexible, gradualist account of legal change we develop in this book, international law is still relatively static. Although widespread state support is not always necessary to bring about change—as we have seen in Chapter 4—the usual disagreement among states in a diverse international society nevertheless renders change difficult; after all, opposition by a significant number of states reduces the likelihood of success and will often (although not always) derail change attempts.[89] Moreover, many institutions are not easily accessible to all actors. Many are limited to states (at least formally), and those that can be accessed by other actors will often be hesitant to engage in open change for fear of backlash by states. Change on a larger scale or in a shorter timeframe is, in any event, difficult to bring about on many of the paths we have encountered. The more interpretive paths—especially those involving judicial or expert authority—can effect incremental change, but broader and quicker ruptures frequently require treaty-making, and the threshold for success at initiating and negotiating a universal treaty with sufficient ambition is often prohibitively high.

When the paths of international law are too resistant, change efforts are then likely to seek other outlets.[90] In the historical-institutionalist picture we have drawn above, we would expect that too many veto points (for displacing an existing norm) and too little room for interpretive change (for a conversion of its meaning) are likely to lead to 'layering'—whereby change agents create other

[88] We will return to this latter effect of such contestation in Chapter 7.
[89] See 'Findings I: Descriptive Analysis' in Chapter 4.
[90] See also Nico Krisch, 'The Decay of Consent: International Law in an Age of Global Public Goods', *American Journal of International Law* 108, (2014): p. 1.

norms and institutions to effectuate change, and potentially later generate feedback effect on the resistant institution.[91] We have already observed some of that with the 'sideways moves' within international law—where change was too cumbersome within one field and its institutions, actors move into adjacent areas to initiate change processes with a view to layering on new norms, interpretive statements, or even institutions.

Towards Informal International Rules

We can see similar forms of layering, on a larger scale, through moves outside of international law—or at least into areas that are not traditionally considered to be part of public international law proper. The most obvious such move is that to 'informal international law' or 'soft law'—to forms of normative regulation that do not come with a claim to be legally binding.[92] The rise of informal rule-making has attracted much attention, and it is often portrayed as a result of the excessive difficulties of effecting change through formal law. The stagnation of treaty-making, already visible since the 1980s but exacerbated since the turn of the millennium, is a frequently cited factor.[93] Likewise, the greater ease of creating informal rules and the flexibility in changing them makes them attractive for change agents wary of facing the domestic ratification hurdles and sovereignty costs of locking themselves into overly static regimes.[94] Some governments operate with a guidance to work, if at all possible, through non-binding rules instead of treaties.[95] Another important factor concerns accessibility: for many actors, including national regulators, formal processes of international law-making are not directly accessible; other forms, such as memoranda of understanding or informal institutions, will often be more easily available to them.[96]

The classic example for this is financial regulation, which—in contrast with other areas of economic law, such as trade or investment—largely comes in informal clothes. Institutions such as the Basel Committee on Banking Regulation,

[91] See 'Paths of Least Resistance'; Mahoney and Thelen (n 20).

[92] See Joost Pauwelyn, Ramses Wessel and Jan Wouters, eds., *Informal International Lawmaking* (Oxford University Press, 2012); also Kenneth W Abbott and Thomas J Biersteker, eds., *Informal Governance in World Politics* (Cambridge University Press, 2024).

[93] See Joost Pauwelyn, Ramses A Wessel and Jan Wouters, 'When Structures Become Shackles: Stagnation and Dynamics in International Lawmaking', *European Journal of International Law* 25, (2014): p. 733.

[94] See Charles B Roger, *The Origins of Informality: Why the Legal Foundations of Global Governance Are Shifting, and Why It Matters* (Oxford University Press, 2020).

[95] See, e.g., for Germany 'Auswärtiges Amt, Richtlinien für die Behandlung völkerrechtlicher Verträge' (2021), para. 5 https://www.auswaertiges-amt.de/resource/blob/2481616/31364feaa9019e4a9281796ceda6362d/rvv-data.pdf.

[96] See, e.g., Anne-Marie Slaughter, *A New World Order* (Princeton University Press, 2004).

the Financial Stability Board, or the Financial Action Task Force populate an area in which formal rules are largely missing. The ease and flexibility mentioned above are widely seen as an important factor behind this architecture, as is the ability of financial regulators to cooperate directly with one another through such institutions, without traditional diplomatic involvement. Informal regulation in this area also appears less 'resistant' from another angle. For governments in powerful economies, the compromise costs of formal, relatively inclusive law-making often seem too high, especially since the structure of financial markets allows regulation and enforcement by a few central players through minilateral tools.[97]

A very direct move away from an overly resistant process of change in international law is on display in the area of corporate accountability since the 1990s.[98] Activists had sought to achieve the recognition of direct obligations of corporations to respect and protect human rights in international law, but their efforts in the UN Commission on Human Rights floundered. The 2003 *Draft Norms on the Responsibilities of Transnational Corporations and Other Business Enterprises with regard to Human Rights*, elaborated in an expert working group of the Sub-Commission on the Promotion and Protection of Human Rights, met with opposition from a range of (especially Northern) states and was never taken further.[99] After this failure, efforts moved into another process, less geared towards formal law and pushed forward from within the UN Secretariat, and with ample participation by civil society organizations and businesses. This eventually resulted in the UN Guiding Principles on Business and Human Rights (UNGPs), adopted by the HRC in 2011, which refrain from invoking binding obligations for corporations and instead merely talk about their 'responsibilities'. The UNGPs became the centre of gravity for a multitude of other informal guidelines and standards in the area.[100] And while a renewed push for a legally binding instrument has been made since 2014 (with limited success so far), the question of direct obligations for corporations has been largely left out of the process.[101] The definition of corporate 'responsibilities' has thus shifted away from international law into the informal realm.

[97] See Chris Brummer, *Soft Law and the Global Financial System: Rule Making in the 21st Century*, 2nd ed. (Cambridge University Press, 2015); David Zaring, *The Globalized Governance of Finance* (Cambridge University Press, 2019).

[98] See Dorothea Endres, 'Direct Human Rights Obligations of Corporations', in *The Paths of International Law: Case Studies*, edited by Pedro Martínez Esponda and others (SSRN, 2023).

[99] Giovanni Mantilla, 'Emerging International Human Rights Norms for Transnational Corporations', *Global Governance* 15, (2009): p. 279.

[100] Elise Groulx Diggs, Mitt Regan and Beatrice Parance, 'Business and Human Rights as a Galaxy of Norms', *Georgetown Journal of International Law* 50, (2018): p. 309; John Gerard Ruggie, 'The Social Construction of the UN Guiding Principles on Business and Human Rights', in *Research Handbook on Human Rights and Business*, edited by Surya Deva and David Birchall (Edward Elgar Publishing, 2020).

[101] See Surya Deva, 'Treaty Tantrums: Past, Present and Future of a Business and Human Rights Treaty', *Netherlands Quarterly of Human Rights* 40, (2022): pp. 211, 218–19.

Other Forms, Other Actors

The turn towards informality is not the only path 'around' international law. In the business and human rights context, informal international processes are increasingly coupled with domestic legislation of a transnational character. Various countries, and also the European Union, have in recent years begun to enact rules on corporate due diligence in supply chain governance in order to protect human rights and foster sustainability.[102] This is a response to civil society pressure, which, in light of the slow progress in international fora, increasingly focuses on national regulation and litigation. From the perspective of governments, this domestic path is also—even more so than informal international rules—particularly receptive to their own agenda. It involves less of a need for compromise with other states and offers the flexibility to change rules relatively easily in the future. If domestic law promises to be reasonably effective—and this is often the case for powerful economies in the context of market regulation[103]—international law can appear as overly resistant and problematic. Competition law is a classic example in which the availability of unilateral tools reduced the interest (especially of the US) in binding regulation at the international level considerably and frustrated attempts at treaty-making in the WTO context.[104]

The dynamics of going around international law, and the multiplicity of tools available for that purpose, are nowhere nearly as visible as in the area of climate change law. With the long stagnation of negotiations to replace the Kyoto Protocol and the (for many) disappointing Paris Agreement, actors have pursued a host of different avenues to effectuate change in the norms, laws, and more broadly, the governance of climate change. The result is a transnational regime complex with myriad institutions and norms at different levels and developed in different contexts, from finance to human rights, which now create intricate overlaps.[105] Many of these have been created in fora that are more accessible to non-state actors than most international legal sites. Private and hybrid institutions—driven partly, sometimes jointly, by civil society groups or businesses—count among these just as sub-state initiatives, such as the C40 network or the Global Covenant of Mayors, which brings together more than 12,000 cities.[106]

[102] See Surya Deva, 'Mandatory Human Rights Due Diligence Laws in Europe: A Mirage for Rightsholders?', *Leiden Journal of International Law* 36, (2023): p. 389.

[103] See Anu Bradford, *The Brussels Effect: How the European Union Rules the World* (Oxford University Press, 2020).

[104] See Krisch (n 90), pp. 12–15.

[105] Kenneth W Abbott, 'The Transnational Regime Complex for Climate Change', *Environment and Planning C: Government and Policy* 30, (2012): p. 571; Harriet Bulkeley and Peter Newell, *Governing Climate Change*, 3rd ed. (Taylor & Francis, 2023).

[106] David J Gordon, *Cities on the World Stage: The Politics of Global Urban Climate Governance* (Cambridge University Press, 2020). For an analysis of the drivers of different forms of transnational governance, see Harriet Bulkeley and others, *Transnational Climate Change Governance* (Cambridge University Press, 2014), ch. 4.

Many of the governance initiatives on climate change (as in other areas) do not come in the guise of norms, but instead through other governance tools, such as funding, infrastructure, or technology. Perhaps most importantly, many are informational in nature and operate through indicators or rankings.[107] The UN Sustainable Development Goals, adopted by the General Assembly in 2015, are the most prominent and ambitious example, with goals for seventeen areas, among them clean energy and climate action.[108] Formulating these as goals, with targets and indicators for progress, made their adoption possible—crafting a treaty, or even a General Assembly resolution with openly normative content on so many issues, would have been close to impossible. Moreover, indicators and rankings do not necessarily involve states—even more so than informal rules, they are open to non-state actors of various kinds with the necessary resources, expertise, and technology to generate and process data.

The limited receptivity and accessibility of international law's paths of change is, as we have seen, one factor behind the use of such other tools—informal, informational, or otherwise. In order to achieve their goals, many actors turn to paths of less resistance. This does not have to be a conscious weighing of alternatives (although it often will be), and international law may not even be among the instruments considered by certain actors, especially non-state actors with little direct access to the paths of international law. In climate change, for example, few activists would think of initiating a new treaty process, given the experiences with the Paris Agreement. Instead, progress can be pursued through alternative paths, with climate litigation being one of them.[109] Recently, international courts may have attracted more attention in this respect, with cases in different human rights courts and expert bodies and advisory opinion requests in the ICJ, the ITLOS, and the Inter-American Court of Human Rights. For most change agents in the field, however, the promise associated with these international legal avenues is limited (and they may not be directly available to them), and they are pursuing action in a variety of other—potentially more receptive—sites, especially in domestic courts where climate change cases are burgeoning.[110]

[107] See Kevin E Davis and others, eds., *Governance by Indicators: Global Power through Classification and Rankings* (Oxford University Press, 2012).

[108] UNGA Res 70/1, 'Transforming Our World: The 2030 Agenda for Sustainable Development' (21 October 2015) UN Doc A/Res/70/1. See also Jaye Ellis, 'The Turn to Metrics in International Environmental Law', in *The Many Paths of Change in International Law*, edited by Nico Krisch and Ezgi Yildiz (Oxford University Press, 2023).

[109] See César Rodríguez-Garavito, ed., *Litigating the Climate Emergency: How Human Rights, Courts, and Legal Mobilization Can Bolster Climate Action* (Cambridge University Press, 2022).

[110] César Rodríguez-Garavito, 'Litigating the Climate Emergency: The Global Rise of Human Rights-Based Litigation for Climate Action', in *Litigating the Climate Emergency: How Human Rights, Courts, and Legal Mobilization Can Bolster Climate Action*, edited by César Rodríguez-Garavito (Cambridge University Press, 2022); Joana Setzer and Catherine Higham, 'Global Trends in Climate Change Litigation: 2024 Snapshot' (Grantham Research Institute on Climate Change and the Environment and Centre for Climate Change Economics and Policy, London School of Economics and Political Science, 2024).

Many other areas are shaped by forms of governance other than formal international law. Think only of internet governance in which private, transnational rules, and standards play a major role, and attempts at creating international legal rules have been hampered by states' disagreement and the slow pace of multilateral fora.[111] A full account of the areas in which such alternative forms prevail is beyond the scope of this chapter, but the brief survey here should suffice to show that the reasons for choosing other sites and forms are manifold—international legal paths may be too slow, too costly, too difficult to access, or too unlikely to lead to success. At the same time, alternative avenues and tools for change are available in many contexts, and sometimes new paths can be created. These alternatives may not promise solutions that are as universal and mandatory as binding international legal rules, but they will often appear as more receptive to change agents and hold out better chances for realizing some of their goals in a more timely and effective fashion.[112] As a result, international law may lose relevance in certain issue areas—or may be altogether sidelined.

5. Conclusion

This chapter has presented a simple but powerful model for understanding the paths on which international legal change travels in a world of fragmented institutions and regime complexity. Using the literature of institutional choice and historical institutionalism, the model is built on the receptiveness or resistance of different paths. Especially in contexts of diffuse authority, actors will often choose paths of least resistance—paths that may be relatively peripheral but are available to change agents and hold the promise of greater receptivity for a particular change attempt. Building on the authority gained in such sites, actors then target more central institutions. In areas with default focal paths, actors may choose these first. However, even in such contexts, they often first engage secondary authorities to lay the groundwork and increase their chances of success on the focal path. And as we have also seen, when the paths of one regime are, or promise to be, resistant to a given change attempt, actors often turn to authorities in other fields with greater receptivity to their cause—thus increasing support for their change attempt before returning to their target field.

The multiplicity of available paths—within and across fields—thus often smooths change efforts. The threshold for initiating them is reduced, and among the many available institutions, some may be receptive to the change attempt,

[111] See Roxana Radu, *Negotiating Internet Governance* (Oxford University Press, 2019).

[112] On the relative effectiveness of soft law, see Gregory Shaffer and Mark A Pollack, 'Hard vs. Soft Law: Alternatives, Complements, and Antagonists in International Governance', *Minnesota Law Review* 94, (2010): p. 706.

support it, and thereby potentially pave the way for further success. The cumulation of authority is key here, and it stands in contrast with typical models based on ideas of forum-shopping and binary choices. But cumulation can also go the other way. When paths diverge, change attempts tend to stagnate, leaving the law in an in-between state: a state of abeyance.

The picture in this chapter—and in the book overall—is one of relative dynamism, but it is dynamism only when compared to standard images of a very static (and statist) international law. Often enough, the paths of international law are not responsive—or not responsive enough in the eyes of change agents. In the last section, we saw how paths of least resistance can, and often do, lead outside of international law. Other forms and sites may promise greater receptivity—greater ease in bringing about change—and more flexibility for further change in the future, including for many non-state actors for whom international legal paths appear distant.

In an accelerating world, with increasing functional pressures to effect change to deal with new challenges, many actors' temptation to turn elsewhere is bound to grow, and this leaves international law in an uneasy situation. As legal institutions, especially courts, become more assertive and expansive in dealing with such challenges, they also invite politicization and ever-increasing contestation as international society becomes more polarized. Contestation is, of course, a necessary element for legal change as it triggers change processes and challenges existing norms and interpretations. At the same time, it can also become potentially threatening to existing institutions and paths. It is this ambivalent, but inherently dynamic, character of contestation that we turn to in the next chapter.

7
Contestation, Consolidation, Change

Change goes through contestation: the change attempts we have analysed in this book are all challenges to the law as it stands. Contestation has been present throughout the previous chapters, but we have so far not paid more focused attention to its structure and consequences. Yet it has been a major theme in international relations scholarship, especially with a view to norm contestation, and in the present chapter, we draw on and take further the insights of this literature. Contestation, we argue, is key to understanding change in international legal rules, as well as change in the paths of change themselves.

Contestation is typically understood to 'involve . . . the range of social practices, which discursively express disapproval of norms',[1] and it is often seen as a core factor in the operation of norms, both sustaining and undermining the robustness of norms in international society. Processes of contestation bring norms to light and mobilize actors around them, and they may lead to adjustments and changes in norms.[2] However, when challenging the validity, rather than merely the content, of certain norms, contestation can have serious corrosive effects, undermining the acceptance of and consequently compliance with a given norm—and potentially leading to its decay.[3]

Even though contestation is widespread in norm practices, it has received less attention in the study of international *legal* norms.[4] For scholars of international law, it has become a central theme primarily in its more extreme form, 'backlash'—usually with a view to a backlash against international institutions, especially courts.[5] In this context, contestation is typically seen as a threat to legal institutions

[1] Antje Wiener, *A Theory of Contestation* (Springer, 2014), p. 1.

[2] See Antje Wiener, *Contestation and Constitution of Norms in Global International Relations* (Cambridge University Press, 2018).

[3] See Nicole Deitelhoff and Lisbeth Zimmermann, 'Things We Lost in the Fire: How Different Types of Contestation Affect the Robustness of International Norms', *International Studies Review* 22, (2020): p. 51.

[4] But see Jakob H Holtermann, Mikael Rask Madsen and Nora Stappert, 'International Lawyers, Legal Norms, and Contestations of Legal Validity', in *Contesting the World: Norm Research in Theory and Practice*, edited by Phil Orchard and Antje Wiener (Cambridge University Press, 2024).

[5] See, e.g., Karen J Alter, James T Gathii and Laurence R Helfer, 'Backlash against International Courts in West, East and Southern Africa: Causes and Consequences', *European Journal of International Law* 27, (2016): p. 293; Mikael Rask Madsen, Pola Cebulak and Micha Wiebusch, 'Backlash against International Courts: Explaining the Forms and Patterns of Resistance to International Courts', *International Journal of Law in Context* 14, (2018): p. 197; Ezgi Yildiz and Umut Yüksel, 'International Courts and Selective Restraint in Times of Backlash', Prepared for the Political Economy of International Organization (PEIO) Conference (22–25 January 2025, Harvard University), https://papers.ssrn.com/sol3/papers.cfm?abstract_id=5102435.

Change in International Law. Nico Krisch, Ezgi Yildiz, and Pedro Martínez Esponda, Oxford University Press.
 DOI: 10.1093/9780198918325.003.0007

that risks undermining their force in favour of (power) politics. This is true also for most analyses of contestation in particular areas of international law, although in recent years interest in more varied forms of contestation has increased, for example, with respect to the laws of war.[6]

For the study of change in international law, contestation is a central element—it is typically through some form of contestation that previous norms or their understandings change. At the same time, law and contestation also stand in tension. On the one hand, law is associated with an imagery of firmness that sets it apart from the shifting sands of politics and society and aims at 'stabilizing normative expectations' of societal actors.[7] Contestation, on the other hand, destabilizes—at least in a first step, it aims at unsettling existing norms and understandings.

In this chapter, we explore this tension between contestation and stability in international law at two levels. In section 1, we focus on the consequences of contestation for the stability and strength of international legal norms and trace how different forms of contestation pursue—and result in—different degrees of consolidation. Whether, and to what extent, normative practices are reconsolidated after a change attempt depends on the type of contestation at issue, but also—and especially—on the authority structure in place in a given area. In contexts of diffuse authority, reconsolidation is less likely than in contexts with a focal authority. As diffuse authority is significantly more common, much international law remains at intermediate levels of consolidation. It remains 'liquid' rather than 'solid'[8]—a fact that sits uneasily with binary conceptualizations of law and legality, but one that legal scholars should do more to understand and integrate into their theories.

Yet contestation does not only affect (primary) norms of behaviour, but often operates also at a second level—that of the secondary norms which regulate how norms are applied, interpreted, and changed. The distinction between these two levels (often ignored in international relations scholarship[9]) is commonplace for legal scholars and practitioners. In section 2, we pursue the consequences of contestation for those secondary norms—or better: for the normative practices that define the paths on which international law travels. The paths of international law are heavily time-bound, and a focus on contestation can help us shed light on changes in those paths of change. We thus look back and contrast today's paths

6 See, e.g., Max Lesch and Christian Marxsen, 'Norm Contestation in the Law Against War: Towards an Interdisciplinary Analytical Framework', *Zeitschrift für ausländisches öffentliches Recht und Völkerrecht* 83, (2023): p. 11.

7 See, e.g., Niklas Luhmann, *Das Recht der Gesellschaft* (Suhrkamp, 1993).

8 See Nico Krisch, 'Liquid Authority in Global Governance', *International Theory* 9, (2017): p. 237.

9 But see Paul F Diehl and Charlotte Ku, *The Dynamics of International Law* (Cambridge University Press, 2010); Theresa Reinold and Michael Zürn, '"Rules about Rules" and the Endogenous Dynamics of International Law: Dissonance Reduction as a Mechanism of Secondary Rule-Making', *Global Constitutionalism* 3, (2014): p. 236; Mark Raymond, *Social Practices of Rule-Making in World Politics* (Oxford University Press, 2019).

with those of previous periods of international law. Looking forward, we analyse the processes through which certain paths are currently challenged or blocked and are likely to be further contested in the fractured world we are entering. Understanding the shape of international law at any point requires understanding its 'path' dependence—the ways in which paths at one moment in time are reaffirmed or contested, strengthened, weakened, or abandoned.

1. Contestation and (Degrees of) Consolidation

Contestation is now a common *topos* in the analysis of international norms, but it was not always regarded as so central—initially, norms researchers focused primarily on the structuring effects of norms and depicted them as stable guides for states' behaviour. It was only in a second wave that scholars shifted attention to the malleable character norms exhibit in practice.[10] This led to a greater interest in norm dynamics and the transitions from one stable state of norms to another, with a frequent focus on the emergence of new norms.

Contestation appears as one element of such norm dynamics, but it gained particular prominence in a third wave, in which scholars began to see norms themselves as a process, as being constituted through practices which are always more or less in flux.[11] Contestation is then a normal element in this process, frequently present and sometimes with major, at other times more marginal relevance for the practices around norms. Some observers go further: for them, contestation goes 'all the way down'[12] and norms are constituted only through processes of contestation that lead to formal, social, or cultural validation as norms become increasingly internalized among actors.[13] Even though we follow the general thrust of this third wave in that we regard norms—including legal norms—as processual,[14] we understand contestation as a contingent, not a necessary element in those processes. While some degree of challenge, divergence, or dissensus around norms will often be present, normative practices may also show no or little sign of contestation—some norms might be taken for granted, providing the undisputed

[10] For an overview, see Phil Orchard and Antje Wiener, 'Introduction: Norm Research in Theory and Practice', in *Contesting the World: Norm Research in Theory and Practice*, edited by Phil Orchard and Antje Wiener (Cambridge University Press, 2024), pp. 4–12.

[11] See, e.g., Mona Lena Krook and Jacqui True, 'Rethinking the Life Cycles of International Norms: The United Nations and the Global Promotion of Gender Equality', *European Journal of International Relations* 18, (2012): p. 103; Holger Niemann and Henrik Schillinger, 'Contestation "All the Way Down"? The Grammar of Contestation in Norm Research', *Review of International Studies* 43, (2017): p. 29; Simon Frankel Pratt, 'From Norms to Normative Configurations: A Pragmatist and Relational Approach to Theorizing Normativity in IR', *International Theory* 12, (2020): p. 59.

[12] See Niemann and Schillinger (n 11).

[13] Wiener (n 2); Orchard and Wiener (n 10).

[14] See the discussion in 'Gradual Change' in Chapter 1 and in 'Actors, Practices, Authority' in Chapter 2.

ground or boundary for actors' behaviour, and they might even be constitutive for actors or a particular kind of international order.[15] Whether and to what extent a given norm is contested or consolidated then becomes an empirical issue.[16]

In assessing the stability of norms in the wake of contestation, our study focuses primarily on the degree of discursive shift: we are mainly interested in the extent to which legal discourses remain or become (re)consolidated after a change attempt has occurred.[17] This discursive approach corresponds closely with conceptualizations in the international relations literature, which understand norm strength as 'the extent of collective expectations related to a principled idea' and the result of both concordance (an acceptance of and reference to a given norm by actors) and institutionalization (a codification of the norm through institutions and international law).[18] Other scholars theorize the 'robustness' of norms as comprising further elements, especially compliance and implementation.[19] For our purposes, the greater emphasis on states' behaviour in the latter approach is analytically problematic as it makes it more difficult to distinguish questions around the status of a norm from those concerning violations and compliance. It might also undervalue norms that are strongly established at a rhetorical and institutional level despite frequent (overt or covert) violations—the prohibition on the use of force, for example.[20] We thus take non-compliance and erosion into view only insofar as they affect the discursive strength and status of a norm.

Attempts at understanding the impact of contestatory practices on the strength of norms have recently focused especially on the type of contestation at issue. The distinction between applicatory and validity contestation has had particular resonance in this respect—with an expectation that the strength or robustness of norms is affected more heavily by challenges to their validity rather than to their application.[21] While this may be plausible in principle, the distinction between both is often difficult, as it depends on a (rather subjective) definition of what constitutes the core and boundaries of a given norm. The contrast between these two types did thus not seem to find much resonance in our cases.

Another attempt at distinguishing different types of contestation finds greater reflection in our material: that between proactive, interpretive, and reactive contestation.[22] Proactive and interpretive forms of contestation are structurally similar: while one seeks to establish a new norm and the other a new understanding

[15] See, e.g., Christian Reus-Smit, 'The Constitutional Structure of International Society and the Nature of Fundamental Institutions', *International Organization* 51, (1997): p. 555.

[16] See also Anette Stimmer, 'Beyond Internalization: Alternate Endings of the Norm Life Cycle', *International Studies Quarterly* 63, (2019): p. 270.

[17] See 'Identifying 'Change' in Chapter 2 and 'Methodology: Cases and Measurement' in Chapter 4.

[18] See Michal Ben-Josef Hirsch and Jennifer M Dixon, 'Conceptualizing and Assessing Norm Strength in International Relations', *European Journal of International Relations* 27, (2021): p. 521.

[19] Deitelhoff and Zimmermann (n 3).

[20] See also the distinctions in Ben-Josef Hirsch and Dixon (n 18), pp. 523–24; Stimmer (n 16).

[21] Deitelhoff and Zimmermann (n 3).

[22] See, e.g., Orchard and Wiener (n 10), pp. 14–18.

of an existing norm, they both aim ultimately at the reconsolidation of normative practices along new lines.[23] The destabilization of the *status quo* is an important stage on this path, as it creates the space necessary for the discursive uptake of the envisaged new norm or interpretation. Reactive contestation, in contrast, seeks to weaken existing norms without necessarily aiming at establishing a new norm.[24] Instances of this type often have as their primary goal to loosen constraints—for example, constraints associated with human rights norms which governments may find too onerous. Autocratic and populist governments, especially, have recently pushed back against regional and universal human rights norms, and while they may have had limited success in changing norm contents, their efforts at destabilization may well be consequential in the long run.[25]

We can expect that such reactive contestation will often leave norms in a less solid state—its proponents are typically not even interested in reconsolidation. The Trump administration in the United States, for example, seems to content itself with an erosion of international legal limits and often does not even attempt at defining new norms.[26] However, for proactive and interpretive contestation, too, reconsolidation may not occur if they are not fully successful—the effort at consolidation may face counter-contestation, or it may simply not muster enough active support. In line with our general approach in this book, we expect that the institutional structure prevailing in the respective context will play an important role here, and in the following, we lay out the findings from our cases on contestation, its consequences, and the factors conditioning those consequences.

International Law in Degrees

Legal rules are typically portrayed in binary terms, as either validly in place or not. Many norms in international law are indeed widely accepted and do not attract much contestation—states' right to police their territory, or their obligation to respect the status of other countries' diplomats, for example. In the cases that provide the basis for this book, we have not taken such instances into view—being interested in legal change, we focus on cases in which certain actors undertake attempts

[23] As the distinction between new norms and new understandings of a given norm is often difficult—and because the dynamics of proactive and interpretive contestation are often described in similar ways—it is better to treat both as part of one category, 'proactive' contestation.

[24] For elaboration and examples, see ibid.

[25] On such effects, see Laurence R Helfer and Erik Voeten, 'Walking Back Human Rights in Europe?', *European Journal of International Law* 31, (2020): p. 797; Wayne Sandholtz, 'Resurgent Authoritarianism, Rights, and Legal Change', in *The Many Paths of Change in International Law*, edited by Nico Krisch and Ezgi Yildiz (Oxford University Press, 2023).

[26] See, e.g., Mark A Pollack, 'Trump as a Change Agent in International Law Ends, Means, and Legacies', in *The Many Paths of Change in International Law*, edited by Nico Krisch and Ezgi Yildiz (Oxford University Press, 2023); Oona A Hathaway and Scott J Shapiro, 'Might Unmakes Right: The Catastrophic Collapse of Norms against the Use of Force', *Foreign Affairs* 104, (2025): p. 80.

at modifying the rules. Yet as we observe these cases over time, the degree of contestation varies, and, although most change agents initially aim for consolidated change—an undisputed new norm or understanding—the result in many of the cases is more ambiguous than that, and contestation is characteristic not just of the initiation of a change attempt or its uptake by (some) institutions, but also of the normal life of many legal norms. Rather than following a binary form, those norms come in degrees.

Among the cases we analyse, the average success rate—in terms of a 'discursive shift' including aspects of both concordance and institutionalization[27]—is 2.6 on a scale from 0 to 4. While successful cases are somewhat more prevalent in our sample, as already discussed in Chapter 4,[28] the data still show a significant spread in the degree of consolidation. In particular, we do not find a binary distribution with results clustered around negative and positive outcomes. Instead, the majority of cases (about two-thirds) lie in the middle, in a zone of more or less limited consolidation with values ranging from 1 to 3. Figure 7.1 shows this distribution.

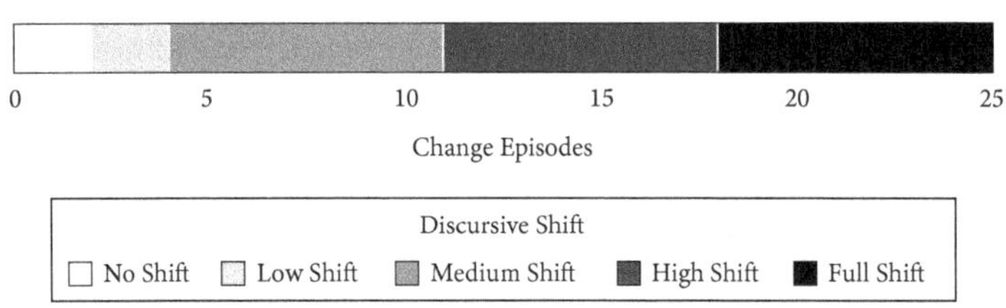

Figure 7.1 Cases with different degrees of discursive shift

Our cases then reveal some clear and consolidated outcomes (with either no or full shift) but also many situations in which the law is 'debatable'—in which it is not immediately clear which norm or understanding applies. Practitioners are familiar with such situations; much of the work of the best practitioners lies in persuading courts and other actors of one or the other arguable position in such instances. Theorists have often addressed the issue as one of a contrast between a (fixed) core of a rule and a (debatable) penumbra,[29] although the boundary between the two categories (if there is any) is itself subject to shifts in legal discourse—there is no fixity in (legal) language.[30] This is perhaps best expressed through reference to the generally 'arguable character' of the law, which renders legal certainty often elusive and recognizes that the scope and limits of plausible legal argument are

[27] See 'Methodology: Cases and Measurement' in Chapter 4 for a further explanation of the measure.
[28] See ibid.
[29] See, e.g., Frederick Schauer, *Thinking Like a Lawyer: A New Introduction to Legal Reasoning* (Harvard University Press, 2009), pp. 18–23.
[30] See, e.g., Ingo Venzke, *How Interpretation Makes International Law: On Semantic Change and Normative Twists* (Oxford University Press, 2012); Charlotte Epstein, 'Constructivism or the Eternal Return of Universals in International Relations. Why Returning to Language Is Vital to Prolonging the Owl's Flight', *European Journal of International Relations* 19, (2013): p. 499.

defined and redefined through legal processes themselves.[31] The relevance of those limits—and shared, consolidated understandings of what cannot be argued—should not be underestimated; they constitute a core pillar of the operation of any legal system. But if legal norms are indeed ultimately processual and constituted through social practices, any such consolidation will be contingent and may be undone at a later point by changing practices.

The effects of unconsolidated, arguable norms may be more limited than those of fully consolidated ones, but they can nevertheless be significant. This is perhaps particularly so in cases of permissive norms or interpretations—cases in which contestation is aimed at limiting existing restrictions or creating exceptions from them. Especially in the absence of formal dispute settlement mechanisms, having an 'arguable case' will often provide significant advantages—especially reputational ones—for countries making use of more permissive understandings. Among our cases, those related to jurisdictional rules stand out most in this respect. In the case of effects jurisdiction, for example, the United States initially faced significant criticism for its claims to be able to regulate transboundary practices on the basis of the 'effects' these produced in the United States, despite lacking more traditional territorial links. US courts and regulators used effects jurisdiction, especially with a view to anti-competitive practices—cartels and the like—that had an impact on the US market. This approach was not widely accepted for more than half a century, but once it had been established as an arguable position, the reputational costs of using it became considerably weaker, and other countries came to adopt similar approaches towards the late twentieth century.[32] Similar dynamics can be observed in our case on illegal, unreported, and unregulated (IUU) fishing as jurisdictional limits for port state measures became destabilized.[33] But these dynamics are also visible well beyond—for example, in the well-known shift from absolute to restrictive state immunity. Here, some Western countries began to restrict immunity for non-sovereign acts (*acta iure gestionis*) from the early twentieth century on—once this position had gained traction among more than a handful of states by the 1950s, the reputational effects for countries adopting it decreased, and more and more countries shifted—including, in 2023, China, the longest-standing major opponent.[34]

[31] See Neil MacCormick, *Rhetoric and The Rule of Law: A Theory of Legal Reasoning* (Oxford University Press, 2005).

[32] See Pedro Martínez Esponda, 'The Effects Doctrine of Jurisdiction', in *The Paths of International Law: Case Studies*, edited by Pedro Martínez Esponda and others (SSRN, 2023).

[33] See Ezgi Yildiz, 'The Emergence of Port State Measures Against IUU Fishing', in *The Paths of International Law: Case Studies*, edited by Pedro Martínez Esponda and others (SSRN, 2023).

[34] See Pierre-Hugues Verdier and Erik Voeten, 'How Does Customary International Law Change? The Case of State Immunity', *International Studies Quarterly* 59, (2015): p. 209; on China, Xinxiang Shi, 'Foreign State Immunity Law of China: A Preliminary Appraisal', *Chinese Journal of International Law* 23, (2024): p. 341.

Yet the effects of unconsolidated norms are not limited to cases of greater permissiveness. Even in contexts in which contestation has sought to broaden obligations or require cooperation among states, we can observe significant implications. This is especially clearly on display in cases of norms characterized as 'emerging' or 'in the making'. For example, the precautionary principle has often been described in this way—while widely invoked in a range of contexts (and formalized in some of them), it continues to have a somewhat undefined status in customary law. After being included in the Rio Declaration in 1992, it was enshrined in a number of treaties and recognized by the Seabed Disputes Chamber of the International Tribunal of the Law of the Sea (ITLOS) in 2011. However, other courts and tribunals—from the International Court of Justice (ICJ) to the European Court of Human Rights (ECtHR) and World Trade Organization (WTO) panels—have avoided explicit pronouncements on its status. The precautionary principle is then the quintessential norm 'in limbo', but the frequent references to it in resolutions and judicial decisions also signal that it is not devoid of effect. Instead, it appears to shape legal discourses in a less direct way than a clearly applicable, precise norm would.[35]

Likewise, the right to a healthy environment was for a long time 'in the making' before it became more strongly consolidated through the UN Human Rights Council (UNHRC) and the General Assembly in the early 2020s. During this time, it was seen to affect the way in which other human rights—with an explicit basis in human rights instruments—were interpreted. Courts, reluctant to recognize the right to a healthy environment as such, for example, have understood other rights in light of environmental considerations. The widely noted judgment of the ECtHR in the *KlimaSeniorinnen* case in 2024 is a good reflection of this approach—in line with previous jurisprudence on environmental issues, it established far-reaching obligations with respect to climate change on the basis of the right to life and the right to a private life, which are explicitly set out in the European Convention on Human Rights (ECHR).[36] The Inter-American Court of Human Rights, too, has read the right to life and the right to personal integrity as having an important environmental dimension, and it has emphasized the close interrelationship with the right to a healthy environment enshrined in the 1988 Protocol of San Salvador.[37]

[35] See Ezgi Yildiz, 'The Precautionary Principle: Ubiquitous Yet Hollow and Marginal', in *The Paths of International Law: Case Studies*, edited by Pedro Martínez Esponda and others (SSRN, 2023).

[36] ECtHR. Verein KlimaSeniorinnen Schweiz and Others v Switzerland [2024] App no 53600/20, paras. 507–20.

[37] IACtHR. The Environment and Human Rights (Advisory Opinion OC-23/17 of November 15, 2017) paras. 176– 78. See also IACtHR. Climate Emergency and Human Rights (Advisory Opinion AO-32/25 of 29 May 2025), paras. 270-278. On the possibility of adjudicating rights under the Protocol in conjunction with rights under the American Convention, see IACtHR, Judgment of August 31, 2017 *Case of Lagos del Campo v Peru,* Preliminary objections, merits, reparations and costs).

Judicial and quasi-judicial proceedings face particular constraints associated with the need to state the law to decide cases—a court cannot normally point to a norm as 'in-between' or undecided.[38] For other participants in the international legal process, these constraints are less severe, and they can capture semi-consolidated states more easily. With a view to the right to a healthy environment, the Independent Expert on Human Rights and the Environment appointed by the UNHRC could thus conclude in 2013:

> Despite the diversity of the sources from which [different interpretive statements on the right to a healthy environment] arise, however, the statements are remarkably coherent. Taken together, they provide strong evidence of converging trends towards greater uniformity and certainty in the human rights obligations relating to the environment. These trends are further supported by State practice reflected in the universal periodic review process and international environmental instruments . . . In this light, the Independent Expert encourages States to accept these statements as evidence of actual or emerging international law.[39]

Many international legal norms remain subject to contestation to a significant extent. But even in an unconsolidated state, they exert significant effects. As the scope of arguable positions widens, actors can more easily justify actions otherwise clearly prohibited, activists can make new claims that are now in the range of the plausible, and courts and tribunals can, and do, take such shifts into account for their interpretation, even if norms remain emerging or in the making. Legal in-between states—law in degrees or even 'liquid' law[40]—are then not just an artefact of processual understandings of (international legal) norms or an exceptional aberration from binary modes of doing law. Instead, they constitute a pervasive feature of the practices and discourses of international law.

Destabilization Strategies

Not all change attempts leave norms unconsolidated, but all of them aim, in a first step, at destabilizing existing norms and understandings. This allows opening up space that can be filled with new meanings. Yet in some cases—for forms of

[38] But see ICJ, *Legality of the Threat or Use of Nuclear Weapons*, Advisory Opinion, [1996] ICJ Rep 226, para. 97; and the discussion in Prosper Weil, 'The Court Cannot Conclude Definitively . . . Non Liquet Revisited', *Columbia Journal of Transnational Law* 36, (1998): p. 109.

[39] John H Knox, 'Report of the Independent Expert on the issue of human rights obligations relating to the enjoyment of a safe, clean, healthy and sustainable environment' (30 December 2013) UN Doc A/HRC/25/53, para. 27.

[40] See Krisch (n 8).

reactive rather than proactive or interpretive contestation—destabilization is the primary goal. It will often be deployed to loosen constraints, and as we have seen above, when change aims at greater permissiveness, undermining the stability of previously existing prohibitions may well serve the purposes of change agents well enough. Especially if the consolidation of a new norm would be prohibitively costly or run the risk of failure, actors are more likely to engage in merely reactive contestation.[41]

A good illustration of this point is the case of the right to self-defence against non-state actors, which came to the fore especially after the terrorist attacks of 11 September 2001.[42] Invocations of self-defence against non-state actors throughout the 2000s provoked a certain amount of criticism, but mostly not in principled legal terms. However, generating sufficient institutional support to shift towards a new, consolidated norm would have faced obstacles. Such support was forthcoming in individual instances with significant salience—especially in the Security Council response to the 9/11 attacks—but a broader affirmation in principle would have been difficult, given the widespread resistance against widened rights to use force, especially among countries from the Global South.[43] The ICJ, too, had signalled its opposition.[44] In this context, proponents of a right to self-defence against non-state actors did not pursue further institutional support. For the US, the UK, and Israel (the most frequent users of the right), the resulting lack of consolidation may not have been too harmful—the destabilization of more rigid limits to the use of force may have been enough for them to create a semblance of legality and thus reduce the reputational costs of engaging in such actions.[45] By emphasizing the state action path for change, they could make the new norm 'arguable', even in the face of opposition on more institutional paths over which they had less influence.[46] These countries were, of course, also materially so powerful that they could bear the remaining reputational costs rather easily—and more broadly, reactive contestation may be particularly attractive for powerful states that have the means to act on their own and the strength to ignore criticism.

[41] See Pedro Martínez Esponda, 'Norm-Instability as a Strategy in International Law-Making: The Case of Self-Defence against Non-State Actors', in *The Many Paths of International Legal Change*, edited by Nico Krisch and Ezgi Yildiz (Oxford University Press, 2023).

[42] See ibid pp. 72–85.

[43] See also Jutta Brunnée and Stephen J Toope, 'Self-Defence against Non-State Actors: Are Powerful States Willing but Unable to Change International Law?', *International & Comparative Law Quarterly* 67, (2018): p. 263.

[44] See ICJ, *Legal Consequences of the Construction of a Wall in the Occupied Palestinian Territory* (Advisory Opinion) [2004] ICJ Rep 136, para. 139. But see also the more ambiguous statement in ICJ, *Armed Activities on the Territory of the Congo (DRC v Uganda)* [2005] ICJ Rep 168, para. 147.

[45] For a similar analysis of different strategies of change in the law on the use of force, see Michael Byers, 'Preemptive Self-Defense: Hegemony, Equality and Strategies of Legal Change', *Journal of Political Philosophy* 11, (2003): p. 171.

[46] See also the contrast in Monica Hakimi and Jacob Katz Cogan, 'The Two Codes on the Use of Force', *European Journal of International Law* 27, (2016): p. 257.

In order to obtain the destabilizing effect sought by contestation, a certain degree of recognition is necessary. Contestation becomes visible and consequential only when it has found some form of validation that destabilizes existing understandings—validation that can come in formal, social, or cultural forms.[47] In international law, it is generated and recognized primarily through the paths of change identified in previous chapters. In order to destabilize existing norms, however, thresholds are lower than for the consolidation of a new norm. As we have seen above, we typically find multiple paths available, and destabilization may already be achieved if action on one of them finds some success. In the example of self-defence against non-state actors, the invocation of such a right on the state action path, coupled with muted reactions by other states, may well have been sufficient to counter, and thus unsettle, the previous understanding built especially around institutional statements.

The validation of destabilization efforts is more challenging if a norm is embedded in a 'norm cluster', with other, interlinked norms and its own institutions to uphold it.[48] The institutional side of this point is exemplified in the difficulties of change agents to curtail the scope of rights under the ECHR. Especially since the 2010s, different governments have initiated serious challenges against the ECtHR, seeking to limit the reach of its jurisprudence and the scrutiny of national practices and policies. These efforts resulted in certain changes—the Court has been found to be more lenient, especially with respect to critics among Western democracies, and it is also seen to have moved towards more restrictive interpretations on a number of issues that had generated particular discontent. Yet these adjustments remained relatively limited and, most importantly, they were enacted (and controlled) by the Court itself.[49] In the presence of a gatekeeping focal institution, the effects of an attempt at norm contestation will typically depend on that institution primarily.

In contrast, destabilization will often be facilitated by institutional multiplicity and complexity. As highlighted in the previous chapter, such multiplicity offers important opportunities—for both change agents as well as their opponents, it allows for broader access to sympathetic authorities to bolster their positions. This eases change processes as it provides actors with an entry point into the process. For example, the contestation of restrictive rules on port state measures against IUU fishing on the high seas was enhanced by the possibility of using institutional

[47] See Wiener (n 2), ch. 2.

[48] Jeffrey S Lantis and Carmen Wunderlich, 'Resiliency Dynamics of Norm Clusters: Norm Contestation and International Cooperation', *Review of International Studies* 44, (2018): p. 570.

[49] On those adjustments, see Helfer and Voeten (n 25); Mikael Rask Madsen, '"Unity in Diversity" Reloaded: The European Court of Human Rights' Turn to Subsidiarity and Its Consequences', *The Law & Ethics of Human Rights* 15, (2021): p. 93; Sandholtz (n 25); Dilek Kurban, 'Authoritarian Resistance and Judicial Complicity: Turkey and the European Court of Human Rights', *European Journal of International Law* 35, (2024): p. 355; Ezgi Yildiz, *Between Forbearance and Audacity: The European Court of Human Rights and the Norm Against Torture* (Cambridge University Press, 2023).

settings open to challengers' claims. The UN Food and Agriculture Organization (FAO) was a more sympathetic forum for attacks against IUU fishing than typical institutions of the law of the sea, and challengers of restrictive jurisdictional rules could exploit this in order to set a change process in motion and achieve destabilization, even if through the FAO alone full change was less likely to occur.[50] As we saw in the previous chapter, multiplicity may make the *consolidation* of new norms and understandings more difficult—where authorities diverge, a change attempt may remain in limbo. But it makes *contestation* and its validation easier: using a 'path of least resistance' by activating peripheral but more sympathetic authorities, change agents will often be successful in destabilizing previous norms.

Contestation, Authority, and (Re)Consolidation

Most contestation—apart from reactive forms geared at mere destabilization—pursues a consolidation of change by establishing a new norm as 'settled law'. Most accounts of norm change reflect this finality of contestation—change, tipping points, and norm cascades are seen to lead eventually to restabilization; in 'cycles of change', action and argument challenges prior understandings and leads to new, settled structures; and in imageries of punctuated equilibria, short phases of movement are followed by longer phases of stability.[51]

In our account of gradual change—just as in some of the 'third wave' theories of norm contestation[52]—the contrast between both phases is not so marked. Movement is a normal state of affairs, and a certain residual contestation will often be present. In a very diverse international society and a relatively decentralized setting of international law, this is unsurprising—in this context, it is the consolidation of norms, more than their instability, that requires explanation.

We then need to understand when and how the unstable situations brought about by the contestation of existing norms give way to more settled understandings. While the conclusion of treaties may fix norms and meanings between the parties (but often enough also leave them purposely vague), the processes of gradual change in the meaning of a treaty after its conclusion, or in rules of customary international law, are less structured, and the frequent divergences of more than 190 states are likely to make convergence and settlement the exception rather than the norm. In fact, as we saw above, almost two-thirds of our cases resulted in a somewhat unsettled outcome.[53]

[50] See Yildiz (n 33).

[51] See, e.g., Martha Finnemore and Kathryn Sikkink, 'International Norm Dynamics and Political Change', *International Organization* 52, (1998): p. 887; Wayne Sandholtz and Kendall W Stiles, *International Norms and Cycles of Change* (Oxford University Press, 2009); Diehl and Ku (n 9).

[52] See the overview in Orchard and Wiener (n 10).

[53] See Figure 7.1 and accompanying text above. The category of settled/unsettled cases is distinct from that of successful/unsuccessful change attempts—we count as settled the cases lying at both

In order to understand this result, it is worth returning to the discussion in the previous section about the factors facilitating destabilization in the first place. If institutional multiplicity and complexity favour attempts at unsettling existing norms, they also render reconsolidation and new settlement more difficult, as we have already seen in Chapter 6. Where a variety of paths and institutions—potentially from different issue areas—are available to process change, reconsolidation typically comes about only as a result of widespread and consistent support from multiple authorities in a complex process over time. This is visible, for example, in the creation of the right to water or the right to a healthy environment.[54] In such cases, actors have managed to 'knit' a tight web of supportive statements, often using normative resources from different contexts and eventually eclipsing remaining challenges.[55] In many other cases, residual contestation—or simply a lack of sufficiently visible acceptance—leads to more limited discursive shifts and less solid recognition.[56] We can observe the same result where there is a widespread convergence of state positions, but not enough acceptance by international authorities to lead to full recognition. For example, the effects doctrine mentioned above has by now been widely embraced in state practice, at least in the area of competition law, but in the absence of support from an international authority—in the form of jurisprudence, a declaration, or a treaty—this has not found full reflection in accounts of the law of jurisdiction.[57]

The challenges of multiplicity and divergence are further exacerbated where change processes take place in contexts in which different communities of practice coexist. As we saw in Chapter 2, such communities (whether understood as interpretive, epistemic communities, or communities of practice in a strict sense) play a major role in the social process of international legal change. It is primarily through them that authority is construed in a given field, that common understandings of norms emerge, and that hierarchies are produced between different actors. For Jutta Brunnée and Stephen Toope, the 'shared understandings' generated in such

ends of the spectrum (both fully unsuccessful and fully successful change attempts) and as unsettled those in the middle in which understandings have shifted (to different degrees) but have not led to full consolidation.

[54] See Nina Reiners, 'Despite or Because of Contestation? How Water Became a Human Right', *Human Rights Quarterly* 43, (2021): p. 329; Dorothea Endres, 'The Human Right to a "Good" Environment', in *The Paths of International Law: Case Studies*, edited by Pedro Martínez Esponda and others (SSRN, 2023).

[55] See also the discussion in Chapter 6; and Dorothea Endres, 'Conceptualizing Legal Change as "Norm-Knitting" through the Example of the Environmental Human Right', *Leiden Journal of International Law* 36(4), (2023): pp. 879.

[56] The trajectories of state-official immunities or port state obligations on IUU fishing are cases in point. See Pedro José Martínez Esponda, 'Change in International Law Through Informal Means: The Rise of Exceptions to State Official Immunity for International Crimes', *Revista Latinoamericana de Derecho Internacional (LADI)* 9, (2019): p. 175; Yildiz (n 32).

[57] Martínez Esponda (n 32).

communities are at the core of international legality.[58] This evokes associations of convergence and commonality, but communities of practice are not necessarily cohesive, and often different communities are at play on a particular issue.[59] This is most obvious when change processes unfold in different subfields—where investment and human rights law meet, it is also the communities associated with these areas that come into play, with their different actors, authorities, and cognitive and ideational starting points.[60] A similar disjuncture can occur inside one area. In international humanitarian law, for example, we can observe two relatively distinct communities—those centred on the humanitarian and human rights-orientation of this body of law, and those highlighting the importance of military necessity in striking the right balance between different considerations in what they more often call 'the law of armed conflict'.[61] The divergence of these groups also leads them to different notions of authority in the field—while the former give much weight to ICRC positions for guidance, the latter place greater weight on military practices, especially of those states frequently engaged in conflict. This often results in incompatible assessments of where the law stands and whether a given change process has been successful or not. On issues of the use of force, we might find a similar cleavage between those looking to institutional pronouncements (especially from UN bodies) and those emphasizing the element of practice, thus often privileging the positions of militarily active states.[62] More broadly, geographical and geopolitical factors have shaped particular national or regional communities, with different understandings of what counts as an authority and what threshold is needed for law to change.[63] The more such cleavages are prominent in a given field, the more likely it becomes that, in cases of disagreement, the law remains in abeyance—that it might be understood in one way in one community and differently in another.

If the institutional and social structure in a given field is heavily fragmented, reconsolidation efforts will thus face greater obstacles. In contrast, in areas in which a focal institution exists, change processes are likely to result in more clear-cut

[58] See Jutta Brunnée and Stephen J Toope, 'Shared Understandings: The Underpinnings of Law', in *Legitimacy and Legality in International Law. An Interactional Account* (Cambridge University Press, 2010).

[59] See Michael Waibel, 'Interpretive Communities in International Law', in *Interpretation in International Law*, edited by Andrea Bianchi, Daniel Peat and Matthew Windsor (Oxford University Press, 2014).

[60] See the discussion in 'Sideways Moves' in Chapter 6 and Moshe Hirsch, 'Social Movements, Reframing Investment Relations, and Enhancing the Application of Human Rights Norms in International Investment Law', *Leiden Journal of International Law* 34, (2021): p. 127; Dorothea Endres, 'The Human Side of Protecting Foreign Investment', *Transnational Legal Theory* 12, (2021): p. 249.

[61] See Dorothea Endres, 'Whose International Law Is Changing? The Practice of Fragmented Communities Constructing Legal Change', in *The Many Paths of International Law*, edited by Nico Krisch and Ezgi Yildiz (Oxford University Press, 2023).

[62] See Hakimi and Cogan (n 46).

[63] See, e.g., Anthea Roberts, *Is International Law International?* (Oxford University Press, 2017); Anthea Roberts and others, eds., *Comparative International Law* (Oxford University Press, 2018).

outcomes. The social recognition of a focal institution already implies that the success of a change attempt will often be measured primarily with a view to the stance of that institution—it becomes a gatekeeper. Where it rejects a change attempt, the attempt counts as failed; where it supports it, it will often be regarded as successful, even if a certain degree of contestation among actors (including states) remains. For example, on the question of subsidies for state-owned entities, the Appellate Body's shift in 2011 towards a new, more flexible line—closer to the Chinese position on 'public bodies'—was heavily criticized on substance by a number of countries, but it was nevertheless widely accepted as reflecting 'the law' in the following years.[64] The remaining contestation and non-compliance by the United States did not prevent such consolidation, even though its persistence provoked a later backpedalling by WTO panels and the Appellate Body (and renewed destabilization after the US had blocked the latter's continued operation).[65]

This suggests that the authority structure in a given area plays a key role in the consolidation of change attempts—a point clearly on display across our cases. As shown in Figure 7.2, of those cases in which we observe a full discursive shift—consolidated change—more than 70% have been processed by a focal authority, and less than 30% are the result of the work of peripheral authorities. For all other categories, peripheral authority is the more frequent (or sole) context. This is in line with the observation in the examples above that, in the context of dispersed authority, residual contestation—especially if it finds some support from a recognized authority—will usually prevent full consolidation even if most of the interpretive community converges. In contrast, where a focal authority sides with a change attempt, residual contestation is often ignored in the reception of change.

The importance of the authority structure is also suggested by Figure 7.3, which presents the results of an ordinal logistic regression model analysing the probability of discursive shift based on different types of authority. The involvement or endorsement of focal authorities leads to a higher probability of full (to some extent also high) shifts, whereas the presence of peripheral authorities is associated here with a greater likelihood of medium, low, or no shifts.

A settled ending to a change process is thus more likely in integrated areas with a focal authority that acts as a gatekeeper. Where that authority embraces change, change often becomes accepted; where it rejects it, the law typically stays the same. Yet authorities do not always position themselves clearly—they may also remain ambiguous towards a particular change attempt. In the case of self-defence

[64] See Nico Krisch, 'The Dynamics of International Law Redux', *Current Legal Problems* 74, (2021): p. 269, 280–82.

[65] See Dukgeun Ahn, 'Why Reform Is Needed: WTO "Public Body" Jurisprudence', *Global Policy* 12, (2021): p. 61; Nina Teresa Kiderlin, 'World Trade Law and the Rise of China: Struggles over Subsidy Rules', in *The Many Paths of Change in International Law*, edited by Nico Krisch and Ezgi Yildiz (Oxford University Press, 2023).

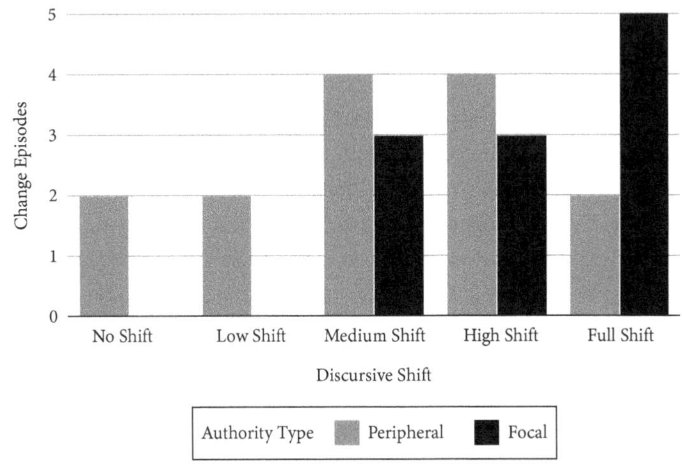

Figure 7.2 Discursive shift by activated authority (peripheral versus focal)

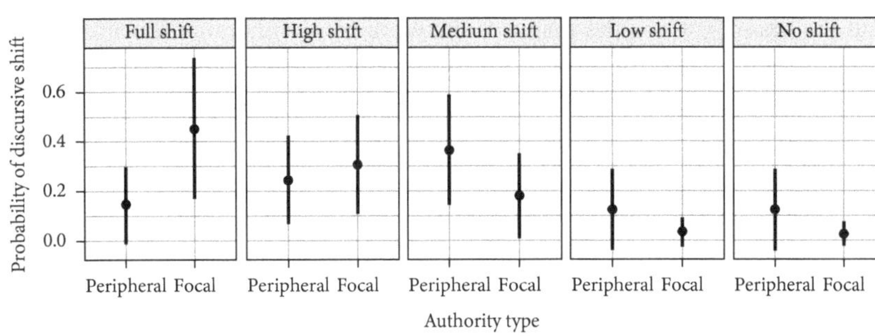

Figure 7.3 Probability of discursive shift depending on authority type

against non-state actors, the ICJ seemed to have rejected the proposition only then to cryptically point out that there was no need to decide 'as to whether and under what conditions contemporary international law provides for a right of self-defence against large-scale attacks by irregular forces'.[66] Yet more visibly, the ICJ evaded a clear positioning on change attempts concerning the delimitation of the continental shelf since the late 1960s. Despite a push on the part of many states towards a recognition of the equidistance principle, the court distanced itself from this trend, left the law relatively open, and provided inconsistent guidance over the next two decades, allowing states to adopt widely diverging positions. Whether the

[66] ICJ, *Armed Activities on the Territory of the Congo* (n 44), para. 147.

ICJ is best described as 'focal' in the field or not, the effect of its ambiguous stance was certainly one of defocalization.[67]

Likewise, even a clear position of a focal authority is not necessarily the end of the matter. Challenges against it may succeed, but they tend to face a higher threshold. Here too, institutional multiplicity will often play a role—as we have seen in Chapter 6, mobilization in one area of international law may help to destabilize a settled understanding promoted by a focal authority in another. The adoption of the Biosafety Protocol to counteract the less precaution-oriented approach of the WTO Appellate Body on trade related to genetically modified organisms in the late 1990s may be a case in point.[68]

Discontent over the position of a focal authority may also spill over into attempts to undermine the authority itself. Widely noted backlash attempts follow this logic—they are typically directed at consolidated institutions which, in the eyes of some governments, have overstepped their boundaries and taken change too far and in the wrong direction.[69] United States contestation of the WTO Appellate Body resulted from discontent with its interpretive moves, just as the backlash of some European countries against the ECtHR was provoked, in part, by judgments on sensitive issues—prisoners' rights, migration, etc.[70] The results of such backlash vary. While some have only led to certain adjustments in the orientation of focal bodies, as for example in the ECtHR, others—such as in the Appellate Body case, or in the Zimbabwean challenge of the South African Development Community (SADC) Tribunal—have successfully disabled the respective institutions.[71] In doing so, they have not only destabilized the law but also modified the paths of change within their respective domains. It is such change in the paths of change that we turn to in the next section.

2. Contestation and the Changing Paths of Change

Contestation operates at two levels: it shapes not only the content of international legal norms but also the very paths through which norms change. These paths are not fixed—more stable than individual norms, they are nevertheless subject to challenge and modification, and it is through such processes that the landscape of

[67] Ezgi Yildiz and Umut Yüksel, 'The Defocalizing Effect of International Courts: Evidence from Maritime Delimitation Practices', *The Review of International Organizations* 20, (2024): p. 825.

[68] See Nico Krisch, 'Pluralism in Postnational Risk Regulation: The Dispute over GMOs and Trade', *Transnational Legal Theory* 1, (2010): p. 237.

[69] See, e.g., Madsen, Cebulak and Wiebusch (n 5).

[70] See Mikael Madsen, 'The Challenging Authority of the European Court of Human Rights: From Cold War Legal Diplomacy to the Brighton Declaration and Backlash', *Law and Contemporary Problems* 79, (2016): p. 141.

[71] See, e.g., Helfer and Voeten (n 25); Alter, Gathii and Helfer (n 5); Daniel Abebe and Tom Ginsburg, 'The Dejudicialization of International Politics?', *International Studies Quarterly* 63, (2019): p. 521.

international law is defined over time. Change here occurs on a different level—if the processes we describe in this book concern primary norms of behaviour, change in the 'paths' is concerned more with the secondary norms that structure the ways in which primary norms emerge and change, are interpreted and enforced.[72]

The paths of change in international law are then time-bound—the modes of change we describe in this book are different from those in the seventeenth, eighteenth, or nineteenth centuries, if only for the density of interactions and of the institutional contexts in which they take place, and they are likely to be different from the paths prevailing in the future. This does not mean that everything about change in international law is different across time—some aspects feature (in varying ways) throughout the history of international law. Yet to understand the place of the particular paths we have taken into focus here requires us to gain greater distance by taking a step back in time.

Paths of the Past

For centuries after the emergence of the modern state system in Europe, the paths of change in international law (European international law, that is) were not clearly defined—change occurred through rather unstructured processes and often over long periods of time. The shift from the notion of closed seas to the freedom of the seas is a good example. Dominant up until then, claims to sovereignty over the high seas were increasingly contested towards the end of the sixteenth century, largely by rising powers who challenged the trade dominance of Spain and Portugal in the Americas and the East Indies.[73] Hugo Grotius, also advising the Dutch East India Company, formulated the new position most cogently in his *Mare Liberum*, part of his broader work on the law of prize.[74] Although countered by Italian, Portuguese, and English writers, most famously John Selden, in the 'battle of the books' that ensued, the state of the law became contested and remained so for some time. Yet with the ascendancy of Britain, its own claims to maritime sovereignty gained new weight, and throughout the seventeenth century, the principle of *mare clausum* was still defended by many.[75] After that, state positions and scholarly treatises shifted in favour of open seas—at least during peacetime—and this position most

[72] See Raymond (n 9); Diehl and Ku (n 9). On the distinction between primary and secondary norms in legal theory, see H L A Hart, 'Law as the Union of Primary and Secondary Rules', in *The Concept of Law*, 2nd ed. (Clarendon Press, 1994).

[73] See R P Anand, 'Mare Liberum vs. Mare Clausum', in *Origin and Development of the Law of the Sea: History of International Law Revised* (Brill Nijhoff, 2022).

[74] Hugo Grotius, *The Freedom of the Seas* (CreateSpace Independent Publishing Platform, 2018).

[75] Mark Somos, 'Open and Closed Seas: The Grotius-Selden Dialogue at the Heart of Liberal Imperialism', in *Empire and Legal Thought* (Brill Nijhoff, 2020), pp. 331–45.

likely became consolidated around 1700,[76] although some observers see a more nuanced and variegated picture unfolding during the eighteenth century.[77]

Regardless of when precisely the consolidation of the principle of *mare liberum* occurred, the change process on this crucial legal question of the times lasted at least a century, was driven by changing positions of states and scholarly accounts grounded in arguments and analogies from Roman law, Christian theology, and natural law, each deployed for one or the other position. While the Pope's authority to settle such issues was no longer accepted, secular authorities that could have authoritatively shaped the change process did not exist. This extended to states—customary international law, with its reliance on the practice of states, was not fully recognized as a source of law in its own right, and more generally, international law was not understood to be simply subject to the will of states.[78] The result in this case was a law in abeyance, with space to adopt flexible positions throughout the seventeenth century,[79] until convergence later settled the issue and made the freedom of the seas appear as the almost natural principle of international law it is today.

The paths of legal change visible here resemble theories of norm emergence and change widespread in international relations. Wayne Sandholtz and Kenneth Stiles' account, mentioned in Chapter 1, reflects this in the emphasis on norm cycles which proceed through concrete arguments that challenge existing rules and can generate new settlements before another cycle of argument is initiated.[80] This recognizes that norm change is not merely a function of state interests but takes place in a social context in which argument and justification are important, but it also does not leave out aspects of power which are present in most norm change episodes—Sandholtz and Stiles note that 'agreement of the leading powers of the time' was key to the conclusion of norm change in practically all of the cases they studied.[81]

Such accounts have many virtues, but in their quest for a general model of international norm change (with most examples concerning *legal* change), they largely ignore structural variation over time. This is common among many approaches to norm change in international relations, although some do mention elements of temporality. Martha Finnemore and Kathryn Sikkink, in their seminal piece on norm emergence and change, point especially to the impact of greater

[76] Tullio Treves, 'Historical Development of the Law of the Sea', in *The Oxford Handbook of the Law of the Sea*, edited by Donald Rothwell and others (Oxford University Press, 2015), pp. 3–5.

[77] See Anand (n 73); Stefano Cattelan, 'In the Shadow of the Great Powers: Freedom of the Sea and Neutrality in the Long Eighteenth Century', *Grotiana* 44, (2023): p. 145, 149–52.

[78] See Yasuaki Onuma, *A Transcivilizational Perspective on International Law* (Brill, 2010), pp. 220–22; B S Chimni, 'Customary International Law: A Third World Perspective', *American Journal of International Law* 112, (2018): pp. 1, 16.

[79] Andrea Weindl, 'Grotius's Mare Liberum in the Political Practice of Early-Modern Europe', *Grotiana* 30, (2009): pp. 131, 140.

[80] Sandholtz and Stiles (n 51).

[81] ibid p. 334.

institutionalization on change processes throughout the twentieth century—institutions, in their account, provide platforms through which actors can interact more effectively, and they allow for faster change processes as a result.[82] This does not capture fully the role authority plays in the cases we study here—nor the lesser role of powerful states—but it suggests a greater sensitivity for change over time: change not only of the norms themselves but also of the paths on which norm change travels.

Some approaches to norm change with a focus on legal issues go further. Paul Diehl and Charlotte Ku, for example, highlight the expansion of the 'operating system' of international law to include a growing number of actors throughout the twentieth century, even if they leave somewhat unclear how these other actors become relevant.[83] This contrasts with the more general, timeless accounts in the international relations literature, but also those in much doctrinal international law scholarship which often limit themselves to the contemporary sources of international law.[84] Yet it would be surprising if change processes in international law did not differ radically between European early modernity—steeped as it was in Christianity, practising mercantilist economic policies and continuously engaged in (colonial) expansionism—and today's world, thought of in universal frames and often with a secular leaning, highly diverse in terms of societies and religions and linked to a late capitalist economic system.[85] In our account, the 'changing paths' of international law are the result of (contingent) practices, varying across contexts and over time in respect of the relevant actors, institutions, the grounds of authority, and the types of legal argument.

The (Contested) Paths of the Present

The particular paths we describe in this book are then a product of their times. They build on the state-based paths of positive international law, such as those associated with customary law and state practice,[86] which became dominant in the nineteenth century as natural law ideas were increasingly contested and marginalized. Yet they moved beyond these in their close linkage with multilateral institutions, a phenomenon of the twentieth century and especially of its second half, when a particular proliferation and complexification occurred.[87] Many of

[82] Finnemore and Sikkink (n 51).

[83] Diehl and Ku (n 9), pp. 37–42.

[84] See also the observation in Onuma (n 78), p. 220.

[85] For historical engagements with international law sources, see, e.g., chapters 1–6 in Samantha Besson and Jean d'Aspremont, eds., *The Oxford Handbook on the Sources of International Law* (Oxford University Press, 2017).

[86] On the emergence of customary international law as a source see Onuma (n 78).

[87] See, e.g., José E Alvarez, 'International Organizations: Then and Now', *American Journal of International Law* 100, (2006): p. 324; Karen J Alter and Kal Raustiala, 'The Rise of International Regime Complexity', *Annual Review of Law and Social Science* 14, (2018): p. 329.

today's paths are also related to a specific form of institutionalization, namely the judicialization of international relations—a development that gained momentum in the 1990s.[88] And they are related to the rise of non-state authority in the international sphere—non-governmental organizations, private institutions, and experts with important roles on many paths—which has likewise gained ground in recent decades.[89]

Not all the paths that have arisen in this phase are equally accepted—some remain subject to contestation themselves. Different states have questioned the authority of non-state paths in principle, emphasizing instead the centrality of traditional, state-based avenues for legal interpretation and change.

The US has been among the most vocal critics of judicial and quasi-judicial institutions as lawmakers. It has pushed back, for example, against attempts by the UN Human Rights Committee to insist on the authoritative nature of its interpretations of the International Covenant on Civil and Political Rights. This became most visible in 2008 in a dispute over a draft general comment in which the Committee had sought to frame itself as quasi-judicial and as an 'authentic interpreter' of the Covenant whose views were to be regarded 'as determinative', with principles of good faith leading to 'an obligation to respect the view of the Committee in a given case'.[90] In its observations on the draft, the US set out a broader, principled view on the primacy of state-based mechanisms:

> It is a fundamental and long-standing principle of customary international law that treaties are authoritatively interpreted by the Parties themselves through mutual agreement, either directly through the ordinary channels of international relations or indirectly as the result of recourse to good offices, mediation, or conciliation. A treaty may be authoritatively interpreted by an international body in the case of a dispute regarding the interpretation of a provision, but only if and only to the extent that the Parties agree, either in the treaty at issue or through a separate agreement, to submit the dispute to such an international organ. With respect to the Covenant, States Parties have given no such authority to the Committee under the Covenant or the Optional Protocol. The Committee is not a body established pursuant to the Covenant that is intended to provide authoritative interpretations of the treaty. Rather, the Committee is intended to assist and facilitate States Parties' implementation of the Covenant. The States Parties

[88] See, e.g., Karen Alter, *The New Terrain of International Law: Courts, Politics, Rights* (Princeton University Press, 2014); Karen J Alter, Emilie M Hafner-Burton and Laurence R Helfer, 'Theorizing the Judicialization of International Relations', *International Studies Quarterly* 63, (2019): p. 449.

[89] See, e.g., Bruce Rodney Hall and Thomas Biersteker, eds., *The Emergence of Private Authority in Global Governance* (Cambridge University Press, 2002).

[90] See UN Human Rights Committee, 'Draft General Comment No 33' (25 August 2008) UN Doc CCPR/C/GC/CRP.3. See also Geir Ulfstein, 'The Legal Status of Views Adopted by the Human Rights Committee: From Genesis to Adoption of General Comment No. 33', in *Making Peoples Heard: Essays on Human Rights in Honour of Gudmundur Alfredsson* (Brill, 2011).

to the Covenant and Optional Protocol remain the authoritative interpreters of the instruments.[91]

Faced with such opposition (and criticism from other governments as well[92]), the Human Rights Committee chose somewhat softer language for the final version of its general comment. Still referring to some quasi-judicial characteristics and to its views as an 'authoritative determination', it dropped mention of its role as an authentic interpreter and of the obligation to respect its views.[93] This was not enough to appease the United States, which largely reiterated its principled criticism in its reaction to the General Comment.[94]

Similar concerns underlay some of the discontent of the United States with the WTO Appellate Body—a discontent that led to the Appellate Body's demise as a result of the US decision to block reappointments.[95] In this context, the US took issue especially with the fact that the Appellate Body had come to assume a law-making role in the WTO system, much in contrast with what the US saw as its more limited original function, namely that of providing case-specific review in the dispute settlement process. In this vein, the US criticized the Appellate Body for 'holding itself out as an ersatz "Supreme Court of International Trade" that creates "WTO law"' and, in particular, for its practice of using earlier cases as precedent and for its readiness to fill gaps left in the WTO agreements.[96] In the view of the US, rather than settling cases applying existing law, the Appellate Body had made 'findings that appear to go beyond the text of the WTO Agreement' and thus violated the Dispute Settlement Understanding which provides that the dispute settlement system 'cannot add to or diminish the rights and obligations provided in the covered agreements'.[97]

Criticism of non-state paths of change is not limited to the United States. Especially, Russia and China have in recent years renewed their emphasis on

[91] 'Comments of the United States of America on the Human Rights Committee's "Draft General Comment 33: The Obligations of States Parties Under the Optional Protocol to the International Covenant Civil and Political Rights"' (17 October 2008), https://www.ohchr.org/Documents/HRBodies/CCPR/GC33/USA.doc.

[92] See Ulfstein (n 90), pp. 163–64.

[93] UN Human Rights Committee, 'General Comment 33: Obligations of States parties under the Optional Protocol to the International Covenant on Civil and Political Rights' (25 June 2009), UN Doc CCPR/C/GC/33.

[94] 'Observations of the United States of America on the Human Rights Committee's General Comment 33: The Obligations of States Parties under the Optional Protocol to the International Covenant on Civil and Political Rights' (22 December 2008), pp. 2–3, https://2009-2017.state.gov/documents/organization/138852.pdf.

[95] See, e.g., Mark A Pollack, 'International Court Curbing in Geneva: Lessons from the Paralysis of the WTO Appellate Body', *Governance* 36, (2023): p. 23.

[96] United States Trade Representative, 'Report on the Appellate Body of the World Trade Organization' (February 2020), p. 120, https://ustr.gov/sites/default/files/Report_on_the_Appellate_Body_of_the_World_Trade_Organization.pdf.

[97] ibid p. 13. Understanding on Rules and Procedures Governing the Settlement of Disputes, Marrakesh Agreement Establishing the World Trade Organization, Annex 2 (entered into force 1 January 1995) 1869 UNTS 40 (DSU), art. 3.2 and art. 19.2.

sovereignty and sovereign equality as pillars of international law.[98] They have typically kept a distance from international courts and have insisted that the work of international courts and tribunals be circumscribed by the consent provided by states.[99] In the aftermath of the arbitration award on the South China Sea, China reemphasized this point: '[n]o matter what mechanism or means is chosen for settling disputes between any countries, the consent of states concerned should be the basis of that choice, and the will of sovereign states should not be violated.'[100] With a view to UN human rights institutions, it has likewise expressed concern about 'human rights treaty bodies acting beyond their treaty mandates, in particular, making general comments/recommendations that have the effect of interpreting the provisions of the treaties', and it has emphasized that treaty bodies 'should operate strictly within the terms of their mandates provided for under the respective treaties'.[101]

Other states, too, have voiced reservations against the law-making roles of particular institutions. As already mentioned, several states challenged the Human Rights Committee's assertive stance on the authoritative nature of its decisions, even as they recognized that they have a duty to take these decisions into account in good faith.[102] Sometimes challenges go further and constitute warning shots, reflecting an unwillingness to comply in a particular case, as recently in the Swiss challenge of the ECtHR's *KlimaSeniorinnen* judgment.[103] At other times, they lead individual states to engage in further backlash and withdraw from the ambit of certain institutions, as in the series of withdrawals from the individual complaints procedure before the African Court on Human and Peoples' Rights.[104] In yet other

[98] On Russia, see, e.g., Lauri Mälksoo, *Russian Approaches to International Law* (Oxford University Press, 2015).

[99] 'The Declaration of the Russian Federation and the People's Republic of China on the Promotion of International Law', The Ministry of Foreign Affairs of the Russian Federation (25 June 2016), https://archive.mid.ru/en/foreign_policy/news/-/asset_publisher/cKNonkJE02Bw/content/id/2331698. See Lauri Mälksoo, 'Russia and China Challenge the Western Hegemony in the Interpretation of International Law', *EJIL: Talk!* (15 July 2016), https://www.ejiltalk.org/russia-and-china-challenge-the-western-hegemony-in-the-interpretation-of-international-law/.

[100] See Congyan Cai, *The Rise of China and International Law: Taking Chinese Exceptionalism Seriously* (Oxford University Press, 2019), pp. 281–82.

[101] Submission by the Government of the People's Republic of China on the Consideration of the State of the UN Human Rights Treaty Body System (2020), https://www.ohchr.org/sites/default/files/Documents/HRBodies/TB/HRTD/CoFacilitationProcess/States/China_.docx. See also Vincent Ploton and Sarah M Brooks, 'China and the UN Treaty Body System' (International Service for Human Rights 2023) Briefing Paper 11–14, https://ishr.ch/defenders-toolbox/resources/china-and-the-un-treaty-body-system/.

[102] Ulfstein (n 90), pp. 163–64.

[103] See the Declaration of the National Council (12 June 2024), ('limits of permissible legal development exceeded'), https://www.parlament.ch/de/ratsbetrieb/amtliches-bulletin/amtliches-bulletin-die-verhandlungen?SubjectId=64937; see also that of the Federal Council (28 August 2024), https://www.admin.ch/gov/de/start/dokumentation/medienmitteilungen.msg-id-102244.html.

[104] Oliver Windridge, 'Under Attack? Under the Radar? Under-Appreciated? All of the Above? A Time of Reckoning for the African Court on Human and Peoples' Rights', *Opinio Juris* (7 May 2020), https://opiniojuris.org/2020/05/07/under-attack-under-the-radar-under-appreciated-all-of-the-above-a-time-of-reckoning-for-the-african-court-on-human-and-peoples-rights/.

cases, as mentioned above, they may even result in the dismantling of certain institutions and their powers, as in the case of the SADC Tribunal.[105]

However, as we have seen throughout the book, principled reservations of some actors against the role of certain paths in international law-making have not necessarily proven to be an obstacle for their factual relevance in processes of legal change. Perhaps the best example here is the UN General Assembly, whose law-making powers—heavily debated especially in the 1960s and 1970s, as we already saw in Chapter 1[106]—have consistently been rejected by a significant number of (especially Northern) states.[107] Despite this challenge in principle, the General Assembly has become a core institution for the validation of change attempts in different areas, from human rights and the law of the sea to general international law.[108] It may not be able to effectuate change in and of itself—change typically comes about through the confluence of statements across multiple paths—but it plays a key role in the consolidation of change efforts that muster broad support.

As a result, change occurs in many instances despite such reservations and challenges in principle. As intimated already in Chapter 1, governments, including those from the Global South, seem to be unwilling to accept the binding force of statements on paths other than the state-action path as such. However, except in cases of stark disagreement, they are often ready to go along with such statements if these find significant support in the relevant communities of practice. De facto, many of these paths—built around international organizations, courts, treaty bodies, or expert groups—have thus become key anchors for change processes. This allows for greater fluidity in international legal change while permitting contestability *ex post*, thus providing states with a certain safety valve against the imposition of new obligations.[109]

Looking Ahead: Contestation and Change in a Fractured World

The paths we trace in this book are, to some extent, those of the post-war world and of what many call the 'liberal international order'.[110] They are linked to the rise of multilateral institutions and the many political and expert bodies within them that are engaged in the development of international norms and rules. They are also linked to post-Cold War processes of intense legalization and judicialization (for

[105] See Abebe and Ginsburg (n 71).

[106] See 'Contested Modes of Change' in Chapter 1.

[107] See, e.g., Jorge G Castañeda, *Legal Effects of United Nations Resolutions* (Columbia University Press, 1969); Antonio Cassese and Joseph H H Weiler, eds., *Change and Stability in International Law-Making* (Walter de Gruyter, 1988).

[108] See, e.g., Reiners (n 53). On variation in the effects of GA resolutions, see Rossana Deplano, *Empirical and Theoretical Perspectives on International Law: How States Use the UN General Assembly to Create International Obligations* (Cambridge University Press, 2022).

[109] See also the discussion in 'The Politics of Change' in Chapter 1.

[110] See, e.g., David A Lake, Lisa L Martin and Thomas Risse, 'Challenges to the Liberal Order: Reflections on International Organization', *International Organization* 75, (2021): p. 225.

example, around the creation of the WTO Appellate Body, the international criminal tribunals, and the explosion of investment arbitration), as well as a greater role of non-state actors in international affairs.[111] In this respect, then, they are also related to a particular geopolitical constellation—the concentration of material and ideational power in North America and Western Europe in the late twentieth and the beginning of the twenty-first centuries. Despite all struggle and contestation, this was a phase of particular convergence in international politics, with images of an 'international community' gaining ground and shared understandings of core political values on the horizon.[112]

Today's world is of a different kind, and it is characterized by growing contestation of fundamentals. Material power has shifted, liberal values are increasingly challenged even in places in which they were long embraced, and Western dominance is progressively tested. Observers diverge in their assessments of the extent of the shift, both in terms of competing values and institutional confrontation. While some see limited adaptations of the liberal frame, others see a transformation towards a multiplex order with different spheres alongside each other.[113] Yet others diagnose rupture, with a turn to increasing discord and conflict over influence, control, and values—a genuinely fractured world.[114]

How will this shift affect the paths of change in international law? Many observers believe that, with the onset of greater conflictuality, we are likely to return to an international law of coexistence in Wolfgang Friedmann's terms—that the law of cooperation and community is giving way to a thinner international legal order that regulates the boundaries of states' different spheres and refrains from stronger demands, especially as concerns liberal norms related to democracy and human rights.[115] Sovereigntist, anti-liberal, and even authoritarian tendencies have been on the rise in Europe and North America for some time and have posed significant challenges for international law, not just since Donald Trump rose to power.[116] Some emerging (or re-emerging) powers may share such orientations—many Asian countries have long been associated with notions of a sovereigntist 'Eastphalia',[117] and the 2015 declaration on international law by Russia and China

[111] See Judith L Goldstein and others, eds., *Legalization and World Politics* (MIT Press, 2001).

[112] See Bruno Simma, 'From Bilateralism to Community Interest in International Law', in *Recueil des Cours*, vol 250 (Martinus Nijhoff, 1994); Eyal Benvenisti, Georg Nolte and Keren Yalin-Mor, eds., *Community Interests Across International Law* (Oxford University Press, 2018).

[113] See, e.g., Daniel Deudney and G John Ikenberry, 'Liberal World: The Resilient Order', *Foreign Affairs* 97, (2018): p. 16; Amitav Acharya, *The End of American World Order* (John Wiley & Sons, 2014).

[114] See Paul Tucker, *Global Discord: Values and Power in a Fractured World Order* (Princeton University Press, 2022).

[115] See Heike Krieger and Andrea Liese, eds., *Tracing Value Change in the International Legal Order: Perspectives from Legal and Political Science* (Oxford University Press, 2023).

[116] See, e.g., Michael Goodhart and Stacy Bondanella Taninchev, 'The New Sovereigntist Challenge for Global Governance: Democracy without Sovereignty', *International Studies Quarterly* 55, (2011): p. 1047; Tom Ginsburg, 'Authoritarian International Law?', *American Journal of International Law* 114, (2020): p. 221.

[117] Sung Won Kim, David P Fidler and Sumit Ganguly, 'Eastphalia Rising? Asian Influence and the Fate of Human Security', *World Policy Journal* 26, (2009): p. 53; David P Fidler, 'Introduction: Eastphalia

is full of references to coexistence, non-interference, and the protection of state sovereignty.[118] This reflects a common thread among states critical of Western dominance across the Global South—captured cogently in the 1955 Bandung Declaration[119]—and it is likely to be an important element in an alternative imagination of order. However, we should not overlook that such a pluralist imagery coexists with solidaristic visions that emphasize commonality and mutual obligations of distributive justice. In contemporary Chinese discourse, this is perhaps best expressed through notions such as a 'community with a shared future for humankind'.[120] Other countries of the Global South have expressed more solidaristic approaches from the struggle for a new international economic order to today's claims for climate justice.[121]

It is thus unlikely that attempts at change in international law will pursue one coherent direction in the coming years or decades—a continuing struggle between different visions and approaches with greater pressure on liberal elements is a more probable scenario.[122] Even if a more sovereigntist order might reflect the vision of some powers (and potentially, in varying shapes, of the US, Russia, and China), it is less clear how it would come about. As we have seen throughout the book, institutional change is not merely a function of the current interests of actors, even of powerful actors—change can typically not be brought about by powerful states alone. It is instead shaped and conditioned by the institutional setting itself. Institutions may be more or less path-dependent, but they typically evince a certain degree of stickiness that prevents actors from shifting immediately to another institutional form when their cost-benefit calculus changes. This is especially so when existing institutions contain veto positions that are not easily overcome.[123] Contestation, even by great powers, then does not necessarily have the desired effect, at least not in the short run—it may be resisted by existing institutions, may lead to some (modest) adaptations, but it may also trigger reactive sequences that

Emerging?: Asia, International Law, and Global Governance', *Indiana Journal of Global Legal Studies* 17, (2010): p. 1.

[118] See Rodney Hall and Biersteker (n 89).

[119] See the Final Communiqué of the Asian-African Conference (24 April 1955), https://bandungspirit.org/IMG/pdf/anri-bandung_conference-final_communique.pdf.

[120] See Björn Ahl, 'Chinese Positions on Global Constitutionalism, Community of Common Destiny for Mankind, and the Future of International Law', *The Chinese Journal of Comparative Law* 9, (2021): p. 304; Ignacio de la Rasilla and H A O Yayezi, 'The Community of Shared Future for Mankind and China's Legalist Turn in International Relations', *Chinese Journal of International Law* 20, (2021): p. 341.

[121] See, e.g., Marco Vieira, 'Rising States and Distributive Justice: Reforming International Order in the Twenty-First Century', *Global Society* 26, (2012): p. 311; Jochen von Bernstorff and Philipp Dann, eds., *The Battle for International Law: South-North Perspectives on the Decolonization Era* (Oxford University Press, 2019).

[122] See also Krieger and Liese (n 115).

[123] See Chapters 1 and 6 in this volume.

can undermine an existing constellation and bring about more radical change.[124] In order to assess the likely trajectory of international law, we thus need more fine-grained expectations about the ways in which the current constellation of paths might undergo change. Here we can only point to some such expectations in a rough form. They relate to four directions—continuity, erosion, fragmentation, and circumvention—but much more work would be necessary to refine them, and much more time to assess the extent to which they hold.

Continuity. If the general account of institutional change is correct, we should see quite some stickiness—a significant amount of continuity in the operation of the different paths of international law. This is certainly what we have been able to observe in our cases so far—even as power began to shift and divergences increased since the turn of the twenty-first century, change processes continued to travel on the paths outlined in this book. As we highlighted in Chapter 4, the success rate of change processes post-2000 was slightly lower than that for earlier cases, and it would be surprising if it were otherwise given the greater discrepancies among countries and the resulting inability to reach agreements.[125] Substantive divergence translates into an inability to reach compromises if the positions are too far apart, if too many disagreements are connected with one another, and if no actor has the tools to bring about solutions through incentives or coercion. This is bound to affect the state-led paths of change—as has in fact been observed for some time for a stagnation in treaty-making, with declining numbers of new multilateral treaties and an emphasis on regional rather than universal treaties.[126]

However, we did observe significant informal change in many of our cases even during this period—on issues as varied as the right to truth, rape as a war crime, deep-seabed mining, or port-state measures against IUU fishing.[127] On some paths—for example, the multilateral path around the UNHRC—norm production has continued but seen certain shifts in content, with less emphasis on liberal elements, especially civil and political rights.[128] Moreover, as we explored in the 'paths of

[124] See Stacie E Goddard and others, 'Contestation in a World of Liberal Orders', *Global Studies Quarterly* 4, (2024): p. 26; Michael Zürn, 'Historical Institutionalism and International Relations - Strange Bedfellows?', in *Historical Institutionalism and International Relations: Explaining Institutional Development in World Politics*, edited by Thomas Rixen, Lora Anne Viola and Michael Zürn (Oxford University Press, 2016); Karen J Alter and Stephen C. Nelson. 'Global Governance in Time: Institutional Sequences, International Regime Complexes, and the Politics of Global Governance', *World Politics* 76, (2024): p. 379.

[125] See already the diagnosis in Thomas Hale, David Held and Kevin Young, *Gridlock: Why Global Cooperation Is Failing When We Need It Most* (Polity, 2013).

[126] See Robert A Denemark and Matthew J Hoffmann, 'Just Scraps of Paper? The Dynamics of Multilateral Treaty-Making', *Cooperation and Conflict* 43, (2008): p. 185; Joost Pauwelyn, Ramses A Wessel and Jan Wouters, 'When Structures Become Shackles: Stagnation and Dynamics in International Lawmaking', *European Journal of International Law* 25, (2014): p. 733.

[127] See Pedro Martínez Esponda and others, *Paths of Change in International Law: Case Studies* (SSRN, 2023).

[128] Gino Pauselli, Francisco Urdínez and Federico Merke, 'Shaping the Liberal International Order from the inside: A Natural Experiment on China's Influence in the UN Human Rights Council', *Research & Politics* 10, (2023): p. 1; Anna M Meyerrose and Irfan Nooruddin, 'Trojan Horses in Liberal

least resistance' in Chapter 6, increased contestation seems to have shifted change processes from (blocked) state paths towards alternative paths with less state involvement. This was most visible in the trade law context, where the stagnation of the Doha Round negotiations shifted the focus of change attempts to the judicial path and especially the WTO Appellate Body.[129] A similar shift may be diagnosed today in the area of climate change where the slow pace of change through intergovernmental processes has led change agents to turn to bureaucratic, judicial, and private authority paths—with expert bodies, international secretariats, regional human rights courts, domestic courts, and now the International Tribunal for the Law of the Sea and the ICJ playing important roles.[130] Here we can potentially observe shifts between (and in the weight of) existing paths, but the constellation of change avenues remains largely the same.

Erosion. Yet continuity is, of course, not the whole story; it is accompanied by other, more frictious processes in which increasing contestation affects the paths of change themselves. Some of them can be understood as erosion—erosion as regards the scope and weight of authority of institutions and actors on different paths of change. Such erosion can be formal, as in the withdrawal from international courts and quasi-judicial bodies. This is not new—the US withdrawal from the optional-clause recognition of ICJ jurisdiction after the *Nicaragua* case is the most prominent, but by far not the only, example from earlier times. Tendencies of 'dejudicialization' today include withdrawals from the Human Rights Committee's individual complaint process, from the International Criminal Court, or from investment arbitration under bilateral or multilateral investment agreements.[131] More frequently, erosion is informal in nature, through processes of contestation that result in certain paths of change seeing their authority weakened. Instances of backlash are the most visible expression of such informal erosion, and they may lead to institutional adaptation, but also, at times, to institutional breakdown, as in the case of the WTO Appellate Body or the South African Development Community (SADC) Tribunal.[132] Erosion can also happen—with or without overt contestation—through reduced levels of compliance, signalling a more

International Organizations? How Democratic Backsliders Undermine the UNHRC', *The Review of International Organizations* 20, (2025): p. 125.

[129] See Jae Sundaram and Ayodele S Owolabi, 'Impasse at the WTO Dispute Settlement Body: The Slow Demise of Multilateralism?', *Trade, Law and Development* 14, (2022): p. 127; Kathleen Claussen, 'The Experimental Evolution of Trade Law', in *Is the International Legal Order Unraveling?*, edited by David L Sloss (Oxford University Press, 2022). See also Nicolas Lamp, 'Arrested Norm Development: The Failure of Legislative-Judicial Dialogue in the WTO', *Leiden Journal of International Law* 38, (2025): p. 570.

[130] See, e.g., César Rodríguez-Garavito, ed., *Litigating the Climate Emergency: How Human Rights, Courts, and Legal Mobilization Can Bolster Climate Action* (Cambridge University Press, 2022).

[131] Joost Pauwelyn and Rebecca J Hamilton, 'Exit from International Tribunals', *Journal of International Dispute Settlement* 9, (2018): p. 679; Abebe and Ginsburg (n 70).

[132] Madsen, Cebulak and Wiebusch (n 5).

limited scope of influence and recognition of a given authority.[133] The Trump administration's policy of ignoring WTO law in its trade wars is certainly a case in point,[134] even though it does not necessarily lead to an unravelling of the world trading regime as between other countries.[135]

Fragmentation. A third direction, sometimes related to erosion, is fragmentation. This relates to earlier processes of fragmentation, much discussed in international law in the 2000s,[136] but now bears a stronger political dimension because of the diverging orientations of different (groups of) states. Institutionally, the greatest attention has been paid to the creation of rival international organizations, as in the establishment of the Asian Infrastructure Investment Bank, often seen as a competitor to the World Bank and with a noticeable impact on the scope and influence of the World Bank and its conditions on project funding.[137] In terms of international law, fragmentation is most visible in trade and economic cooperation where the universal frame of the WTO is increasingly displaced—partly as a result of the contestation and blockade of the WTO's multilateral and judicial pathways—by regional or megaregional agreements with somewhat diverging policies. The Regional Comprehensive Economic Partnership (RCEP), developed in the context of the Association of Southeast Asian Nations (ASEAN) and with significantly weaker social and environmental provisions than other, Western-led regional agreements, is a good example here.[138] In other areas, too, fragmentation may come through institutional developments—as in the attempt to generate an African (interpretation of) international criminal law through the African Court of Justice and Human Rights (so far unsuccessful)[139]—or through increasing divergence in the recognition of certain authorities. As pointed out above, in some contexts, different communities of practice, with different normative orientations and recognized authorities, stand alongside each other, leaving the law fragmented as a result.[140] On human rights, this may be a potential trajectory to come, especially if competing approaches find expression in diverging (regional) contexts and institutions. Divergences around the freedom of expression with a view to political

[133] Sandholtz (n 25).

[134] See Mark A Pollack, 'Trump as a Change Agent in International Law Ends, Means, and Legacies', in *The Many Paths of Change in International Law*, edited by and Ezgi Yildiz (Oxford University Press, 2023).

[135] See Claussen (n 129); Shamel Azmeh, '"Saving the WTO": Middle Power Insiders and Joint Statement Initiatives at the World Trade Organisation', *New Political Economy* 29, (2024): p. 60, https://www.tandfonline.com/doi/abs/10.1080/13563467.2023.2221637 (accessed 22 April 2025).

[136] See, e.g., Martti Koskenniemi and Päivi Leino, 'Fragmentation of International Law? Postmodern Anxieties', *Leiden Journal of International Law* 15, (2002): p. 553.

[137] Jing Qian, James Raymond Vreeland and Jianzhi Zhao, 'The Impact of China's AIIB on the World Bank', *International Organization* 77, (2023): p. 217.

[138] Henry Gao and Gregory Shaffer, 'The RCEP: Great Power Competition and Cooperation over Trade' (UC Irvine School of Law Research Paper No. 2021-09, 2021), https://ssrn.com/abstract=3777604.

[139] See Oumar Ba, 'Exit from Nuremberg to the Hague: The Malabo Protocol and the Pan-African Road to Arusha', *Global Studies Quarterly* 3, (2023): p. 47.

[140] See section 1 above.

opponents— 'terrorists', 'extremists', 'separatists'—may signal future directions just as much as regional contrasts in the recognition of economic and social rights.[141]

Circumvention. The fourth direction of change we can expect is the circumvention of international law in favour of other forms of ordering. We have observed such moves around international law already in Chapter 6 as a result of the obstacles international law puts in the way of change attempts.[142] These obstacles are bound to increase as divergences among states rise, state-led paths are less receptive, and more dynamic paths of change erode. If change attempts cannot be accommodated by international law—or if working through international law appears as too onerous and costly—the use of informal norms and organizations is likely to increase, as is the use of domestic law to regulate transboundary challenges and also the recourse to power politics to reshape the global order. Threats of force belong to the latter category, but there are, of course, more benign forms of circumvention. The turn to goals and indicators, as in the UN's Millennium and Sustainable Development Goals, points in this direction,[143] as does, for example, China's legal construction of its Belt-and-Road initiative out of bilateral, informal, and contractual tools.[144] The turn towards unilateral regulation by states in areas such as environmental protection, digital regulation, or human rights in recent years is likewise an indication of trends to come when global cooperation becomes too cumbersome.[145] However, as the relative economic power of the primary users of those tools—the US and the EU—wanes, unilateral regulation may also become more ineffective over time, leaving important gaps in global governance—but potentially also inducing actors to return to cooperative forms even if they imply painful compromises.

The expectations associated with these four directions follow the recent theorizing among historical institutionalists we have used throughout this book.[146] In this model, change agents pursue their change attempts in receptive institutions, but when existing paths appear too resistant, they will turn elsewhere. In a more fractured world, this resistance is bound to grow in response to attempts from all sides, although with variation across issue areas. Areas embodying stronger liberal orientations—such as human rights—are likely to be more affected than others, such as climate change. More geopolitically salient ones—such as trade—are also

[141] On the former, see Tom Ginsburg, *Democracies and International Law* (Cambridge University Press, 2021), pp. 219–25.

[142] See 'Paths Around International Law' in Chapter 6.

[143] See Kevin E Davis and others, eds., *Governance by Indicators: Global Power through Classification and Rankings* (Oxford University Press, 2012).

[144] See Gregory Shaffer and Henry Gao, 'A New Chinese Economic Order?', *Journal of International Economic Law* 23, (2020): p. 607; Jianfu Chen, 'Tension and Rivalry: The "Belt and Road" Initiative, Global Governance, and International Law', *The Chinese Journal of Comparative Law* 8, (2020): p. 177.

[145] See, e.g., Anu Bradford, *The Brussels Effect: How the European Union Rules the World* (Oxford University Press, 2020); Anu Bradford, *Digital Empires: The Global Battle to Regulate Technology* (Oxford University Press, 2023).

[146] See Chapters 1, 4, and 6.

a likely focus of increasing tensions, as has been visible for some time in the US–China trade wars that have hampered universal cooperation in the area.[147] What the pressures in these areas will lead to is a matter of speculation, but they will not easily be accommodated by international legal practices. To the extent that the paths of change in international law require a certain convergence of states, they will produce increasingly unsatisfactory results for all concerned, with advances for one side seen as losses for the other, potentially provoking further contestation and backlash. As actors turn away from existing paths, these erode and, where possible, more receptive avenues are chosen, within or outside formal international law. New paths are difficult to create in today's contested context, and where they are created, their scope will often be more limited than the often quasi-universal ambit of the paths of international law we have traced in this book. At the same time, power politics and geopolitical rivalry may increasingly impose a logic that is antithetical to that of rules, norms and law in global ordering—potentially leading to a more fractured (and embattled) international law as a result.

3. Conclusion

Change typically proceeds through contestation—contestation keeps international law in motion, generates change attempts and, if sufficiently validated, leads to new settled law. But as we have seen in this chapter, even if contestation is present in all norm-related practices, its strength and relevance vary heavily across areas. Many rules of international law are largely internalized and provide relatively unquestioned ground rules. Change processes also often lead, after a shorter or longer period of contestation, to forms of reconsolidation, especially when focal authorities exist to stabilize common understandings. However, in the majority of our cases, we have found contestation to persist, thus leaving the law to some extent unsettled and opening up space for continued legal argument.

The contestation we have taken into view here is, a priori, neither good nor bad. In the literature on international norms and law, some regard contestation as problematic—as destabilizing, as undermining the rule of law or the stability of common norms. Others see it as a necessary tool to challenge the *status quo*—as the crack through which 'the light gets in'.[148] For the normative assessment, all depends on the direction of contestation. Social change always comes about through challenges to the *status quo*, and those challenges might serve progressive or reactionary causes. Sometimes the destabilization of existing rules will serve to create emancipatory space from excessive constraints; sometimes it will remove much-needed constraints on the powerful. How one understands current processes of

[147] See Goddard and others (n 124); Krieger and Liese (n 115).
[148] Wiener (n 2), ix. For a discussion of both approaches, see Deitelhoff and Zimmermann (n 3).

contestation will then also depend on one's assessment of the existing order: those who see today's international law as furthering the cause of justice will regard contestation with scepticism; those who are critical of international law—from the left or the right, from standpoints of distributive justice or nationalism—will greet (certain forms of) contestation as necessary.[149] After all, contestation is a pervasive but largely ambivalent feature of international legal processes.

The effect of contestation on international law is likely to grow as power shifts and divergences in world society become more accentuated. The impact will be felt on the level of individual norms, quite likely with challenges against liberal and neoliberal norms from sovereigntist and authoritarian directions, but likely also with challenges from more solidarist perspectives reclaiming economic justice and countering structural domination. But contestation will affect not only individual norms but also the way international law changes—the paths of change themselves. These paths have been historically time-bound, and we can already observe increased contestation of certain (especially judicial) authorities central to some of the paths that have defined international legal change over the past decades. As existing paths decline or are more difficult to use—and some powerful states turn away from the idea of rules towards power politics—change is likely to seek other avenues, leading to a more fragmented landscape in which the role of international law itself may well be reduced. In some contexts, it is likely to remain relatively dynamic; in others, it may no longer be able to respond to change attempts which consequently turn to other fora.

What will international law become as a result? Contestation in a fractured world is likely to engender a fractured international law over time—potentially up until the point when the need for common responses drives actors back into stronger cooperation. Countervailing forces of fragmentation and (re)integration are thus likely to be at play, with different strengths and relations, across different states, regions, and areas of international law. Yet as the future international legal order grows out of the existing one—and develops, in the first place, on the existing paths of change—it is likely to reflect not so much a coherent logic but more a highly variegated, rugged landscape, with uneven developments across issues and geographical contexts.

[149] See also the discussion in 'The Politics of Change' in Chapter 1.

8
Paths of Change
A Conclusion

International law is not quite what it seems. When we look at legal doctrine and textbooks, international law does indeed appear as 'more static than any other law', to take up the quote from Hersch Lauterpacht with which we began this book.[1] But the reality we have traced is far more dynamic.

On a formal level, not much may have changed in the past century. The sources of international law—treaties, custom, and general principles—are today still treated in much the same way as when the Statute of the Permanent Court of International Justice was drafted in 1920. The threshold for making new law in this context is high, typically requiring near-unanimity of states for the creation of custom or an accord of the parties to an agreement. Treaties—especially multilateral treaties—have, of course, been concluded far more frequently in past decades, often with broad law-making aspirations. Yet their negotiation remains cumbersome and frequently produces limited results (if any results at all). Likewise, many international courts, tribunals, and quasi-judicial bodies have been established, but they have not been recognized as law-makers as such. Legal change, at least on the formal level, rests in the hands of states and can only come about if a large number of them converge.

A different, more dynamic picture emerges when we consider the actual practice of international law—the way new understandings and norms are brought about de facto by social and political actors. With this book, we have taken this practice into view. In the picture that results from our analysis, states—including powerful ones—play a more limited role, institutions are more prominent, and rules are more fluid. The picture is also not one of international law as such, but rather one of many international laws with rather distinct avenues of change in different issue areas and institutional contexts. However, change in international law is not quite as smooth as many would hope; despite the greater dynamism, it often leaves proponents of change frustrated and in search of alternatives.

[1] Hersch Lauterpacht, *The Function of Law in the International Community*, 2nd ed. (Oxford University Press, 2011), p. 257.

Change in International Law. Nico Krisch, Ezgi Yildiz, and Pedro Martínez Esponda, Oxford University Press.
 DOI: 10.1093/9780198918325.003.0008

In this conclusion, we lay out these and other key findings in a synthetic way (section 1). On this basis, we reflect on some of the implications for broader questions in international law and international politics—particularly the role of sources, the process of norm change, and the path dependence of international rules (section 2). We then return to a central question we posed at the outset: are the modes of change as we have described them adequate to meet the needs of international society today (section 3)? As global challenges increase in scope and urgency, even a more dynamic international law may still fall short.

1. International Legal Change: Eight Lessons

Lesson 1: Change Is (Often) Gradual

With formal thresholds high, change in international law is often imagined as coming in big leaps, often associated with new settlements through major treaties. As we traced in the first chapter, scholarly accounts reflect this image by theorizing change around punctuated equilibria—long periods of stability punctuated by (relatively) short periods of movement.

In contrast, our cases paint a picture of gradual change—one in which change in international rules comes about step by step, often over a longer period of time, with incremental moves towards a consolidation of new meanings. Change, then, is a process, not an event; it is typically constituted by interventions of multiple actors, institutions, and authorities which, taken together, bring about a rearticulation of legal meaning/recognition of a changed understanding of international law.[2]

Gradual change in international law sits alongside more sudden forms, often expressed in treaties. But treaties are (increasingly) difficult to negotiate and, because of disagreements among states, often cannot adequately respond to demands for change. As a result, in many areas of international law, change has come about gradually and in less formalized ways. The creation of new rights (to water, to a healthy environment) in international human rights law is a good example, as is the progressive expansion of core concepts such as indirect expropriation and fair and equitable treatment in international investment law. Likewise, in the absence of new agreements, especially since the blocked Doha Round, world trade law has been largely shaped in gradual processes around the World Trade Organization (WTO) Appellate Body, and the criminalization of acts in non-international armed conflicts has been the result of a series of consequential interventions, in part by the International Criminal Tribunal for the Former Yugoslavia.

[2] See Chapter 1, 'Change in Small Steps'; Chapter 2, 'Actors, Practices, Authority: The Social Frame of Change'; and Chapter 6, 'Paths of Least Resistance'.

In all these (and more) areas, gradual change through incremental steps has been prominent and often more influential than other, more sudden forms of change. This mode of change is best understood as evolutionary: as a process of adaptation whereby new understandings are built upon or layered onto existing norms. Such developments may appear more modest compared to the revolutionary transformations that some hope for—but revolutions (or even major new treaties) are few and far between in the history of international law. In practice, most change in international law is gradual. Yet, as we have seen in the examples above, gradualism does not render change less transformative or relegate its role to the margins. On the contrary, gradual change episodes often reshape the core structures and concepts of international law, driving meaningful and lasting transformations.[3]

Lesson 2: Change Travels on Distinct (and Often Non-state) Paths

Change does not come about by itself but is part of a process in which actors advance new understandings of international legal rules and strategically pursue particular avenues of influence to gain support for their position and eventually see it recognized by the broader community of practice. The core of this process is composed of the different 'paths' on which change travels—distinct sets of institutions, actors, and sources of authority that can provide change attempts with support and validation. Some of these paths—the state-action and multilateral paths—are built around states and can (to varying degrees) effect direct change, while the other paths—the bureaucratic, judicial, and private-authority paths—typically build on expert (non-state) authority and operate through interpretation rather than open change.[4]

All paths other than the state-action path are typically regarded as subsidiary or secondary in formalist understandings of the identification of customary law or the interpretation of treaties. In the change processes we study, they are, however, far more consequential than this image suggests. The multilateral and bureaucratic paths are present in more than half, and the judicial path in more than three-quarters of our successful cases—while the state-action path only figures in around one-third of them. This gap becomes even clearer when we look at the dominant paths in these cases: the state-action path is among the dominant paths only in one-fifth of successful cases, whereas bureaucratic and judicial paths were among the dominant ones in over one-third. In only one of the eight areas we surveyed is the state-action path the primary path of change.[5] Moreover, paths also often appear in combination, with more than two-thirds of our case population

[3] See the overview of our cases in 'Change Across Issue Areas' in Chapter 3.
[4] See 'Paths of Change' in Chapter 2.
[5] See the introduction to Chapter 3.

reflecting the activation of three or more types of paths.[6] These patterns suggest that successful change is more often than not the result of a variety of steps along the multilateral, bureaucratic, and judicial paths.

Lesson 3: International Law Is Not One But Many

The paths of change are socially constructed and emerge from the social practices in a given context. With a growing differentiation of international law over the past decades, its subfields have generated their own paths (and constellations of frequently interacting paths) —and these vary significantly.

While the formal, doctrinal framework around change is typically portrayed as unchanging across the entirety of international law, the actual processes through which change is produced are rather distinct in many issue areas.[7] In some areas, states, their pronouncements, and practice remain at the centre of such processes—general international law is the most prominent example, which in our cases comprised issues of responsibility, jurisdiction, immunities, and the use of force. In other areas, change travels primarily on the judicial path: international investment law, international criminal law, and international trade law (in the days of the World Trade Organization's Appellate Body) are examples here. To an extent, the judicial path acts as a gatekeeper—without judicial or quasi-judicial pronouncements, change is unlikely to be recognized in these areas. In other areas, such as international human rights or humanitarian law, the bureaucratic path is more central, although often alongside judicial and/or multilateral paths.

As a result, today's international law is not a single unified system, but a plurality of legal regimes. The thresholds and criteria for change vary across subfields, leading to differences in the shape and speed of change processes, as well as the actors and institutions involved. Even if the subfields remain connected and processes show considerable similarities, this result nevertheless suggests a significant and continuing fragmentation of international law. The fact that international courts increasingly reach across different fields for their interpretative efforts is then perhaps less a sign of convergence than an indicator of a need to bridge increasingly salient divergences.[8] International law certainly moves increasingly on different tracks.

[6] See 'Paths of Least Resistance' in Chapter 6.
[7] See Chapter 3.
[8] See also the discussion in 'Sideways Moves: Cumulation across Issue Areas' in Chapter 6.

Lesson 4: Authority Matters (More than States)

The traditional picture of international legal change is centred around states: change succeeds if states converge (most states in the case of customary international law, and the state parties when it comes to changes in the case of treaties), and change fails if a significant number of states (or parties to a treaty) oppose it.

Our findings contrast heavily with this picture. Several of our cases resulted in successful change despite limited support from states, and we also have a significant number of cases in which change came about despite discernible—sometimes even broad—opposition from states. Yet, more significantly, our regression analysis showed that state *support* fell below the threshold of statistical significance, while only state *opposition* had a statistically significant (negative) effect on change outcomes. This does not imply that state positions are irrelevant to international legal change, but it does suggest that states matter far less than is commonly assumed, and that their impact is felt primarily in obstructing change rather than in bringing it about.[9]

In contrast, the most decisive factor influencing change outcomes is the authority structure in a given issue area. Descriptive statistics show that where a focal authority was present and actively engaged in a change process, the proportion of successful cases was much higher than in cases involving only peripheral authorities. This pattern is reinforced by our regression analysis, which identifies focal authority intervention as the statistically most significant predictor for positive change outcomes. Remarkably, even state opposition had a diminished effect in undermining change attempts when the change was endorsed by a focal authority.

This result may be surprising when viewed through the lens of the typical statist imagery of international law. However, if international law is understood as a discursive, social practice with particular mechanisms in different subfields, it becomes clearer that who and what matters in shaping legal change is itself socially constructed. In contemporary international law, this is no longer exclusively the state—sometimes it is states acting in conjunction (as in intergovernmental bodies in international organizations), sometimes it is non-state actors, and often expert bodies of a public (and sometimes even private) nature. It is this authority structure that matters more for change outcomes across our cases than states' positions themselves.

[9] See the detailed discussion in 'Findings I: Descriptive Analysis', 'Findings II: Regression Analysis', and 'Assessing Interactions and Predictions' in Chapter 4.

Lesson 5: Power Cannot Effect (or Even Obstruct) Change

It is a truism in international relations—and not just among realists—that powerful states matter more than others, and most observers assume the same holds true in the context of international law. Our cases, however, paint a more nuanced picture—power plays a much smaller role than would be expected.

Across our cases, the position of major powers appeared to be of limited consequence. In the regression analysis, neither support nor opposition by them showed statistically significant effects on outcomes, and the success rate of cases with support by a major power was largely the same as that of cases without such support. Descriptive statistics reveal a complementary picture. The opposition of major powers appeared as somewhat more consequential—cases facing such opposition, on average, were less successful than those that did not. However, even with opposition by a major power, close to half the cases achieved high or full discursive shift—a remarkable finding that suggests that great powers are not even able to block change when they so wish.

This relative inconsequentiality has to do with the fact that, frequently, support and opposition from major powers are both present in the same case; their effects may thus cancel each other out. But we also suggest that the limited impact of powerful states is linked to the particularities of international law as a discursive practice. In Chapter 5, we examine the role of power in detail and contrast material power—usually associated with major-power status—with other forms of power, especially ideational ones. In legal discourses, and especially so in interpretive discourses, ideational power is particularly relevant. It is through discourse mobilization that such power can be exercised—through framing, through the activation of institutions and authorities, and through the use of procedural rules and possibilities. The materially powerful are not necessarily in a position—or not invested enough—to make good use of such discourse mobilization tools.

This does not mean that international law is simply a 'weapon of the weak'. But the paths of informal change—especially those involving multilateral fora and non-state actors and authorities—do not recreate privileges for the powerful in the same way as other forms of change do. It is thus unsurprising that powerful countries are especially critical of non-state law-making, and that they often turn to other forms of international law—(bilateral) treaties in particular—or pursue change outside international law altogether, including through violence or other traditional tools of power politics.

Lesson 6: Change Takes Paths of Least Resistance

Actors interested in change do not necessarily pick the paths of change with full consciousness of all options—they may use opportunities that open up or respond to the need to define a position on questions that arise, as they arise. Change agents act with bounded rationality, but many of them—in governments as well as non-governmental organizations—operate with a core understanding of which fora may be more receptive to their cause and begin by targeting these.

As a result, change processes often follow a recognizable pattern, moving along 'paths of least resistance'. They begin in rather peripheral fora potentially sympathetic to the envisaged change and, if successful there, build on the authority of those fora to target more central ones. Even where a focal path exists in a given area, change agents often lay the groundwork by first generating support in other, more sympathetic contexts whose support may generate greater receptivity in the focal institution itself.[10]

These paths of least resistance, at times, straddle different issue areas. Change agents may activate, for example, human rights bodies to achieve change in contexts of trade or investment which may initially appear (or prove) to be less receptive. The availability of institutions in other issue areas lowers the threshold for the initiation of change processes, but the support gained from success there will also often not command as much authority in the target context. Regime complexity and fragmentation thus make change processes more fluid, but they also often leave them ultimately unresolved.

Lesson 7: International Law Comes in Degrees and Often Remains Contestable

Law is usually portrayed in solid, binary terms: a certain behaviour is either lawful or unlawful; a rule is established or not; an interpretation is either right or wrong. In our cases, however, international law often comes in degrees—it is more 'liquid' than the typical picture of solid law promises.

The contestation typical of change processes serves to destabilize existing norms. Whether this leads to reconsolidation—around a new meaning or, if the change attempt is unsuccessful, the previous understanding—depends on the strategies of change agents, the reception by others, and, crucially, the authority structure in which the change attempt is embedded. Contexts of focal authority favour reconsolidation, while contexts of diffuse authority will often leave the result of a change attempt unsettled, as different actors and institutions may continue to hold competing views. When change attempts use paths across different issue areas, a consolidated result is even less likely. Overall, we observed that in nearly two-thirds of our cases, the outcome was not entirely settled.

Unsettled norms are, however, not irrelevant. To the contrary: even despite a certain degree of contestation around them, they often play a significant role in

[10] See 'Paths of Least Resistance' in Chapter 6.

international legal discourse and practice. The precautionary principle or the right to a healthy environment—to take two prominent examples—have been frequently invoked despite their unsettled status, and they have been found to influence the interpretation of other norms.[11]

International legal norms then lie on a spectrum of consolidation. This also has to do with the fact that, in our observation, the assessment of whether a change attempt is successful or not is largely done ex post by the relevant communities of practice. Most of the paths of international law we have identified in this book are relevant de facto, but they are not widely recognized as being able to generate legislative effects themselves. Formally, UN General Assembly resolutions are regarded as recommendatory; the bindingness of international courts' pronouncements is seen as limited to the parties in a given case; and quasi-judicial bodies only have the power to issue 'views', not binding decisions. Change often comes about on those paths despite these formal limitations, but many governments want to retain the possibility of contesting such change if it turns out to be undesirable. This residual contestability increases the likelihood that change processes lead to unsettled states of the law.

Lesson 8: Paths Are Timebound

The modes of change in international law are not immutable. Much to the contrary—being constructed through practice, they fluctuate over time.

The current paths of international law are the result of the confluence of two developments: first, a formal process of international institutionalization (including judicialization) throughout the twentieth century; secondly, an informal, social process through which many institutions, courts, and expert bodies came to be recognized as authorities in particular areas. This has complemented the more traditional mechanisms of change around state practice and treaty-making and in many contexts opened up a variety of parallel paths—some with greater, some with less weight in generating change.[12]

Just as these paths have arisen over time, they may also transform or disappear over time. In recent decades, various paths have come to be contested, and some of that contestation has resulted in curtailing the role of certain institutions—especially courts—in adjudication as well as law-making. Most prominently, the demise of the WTO Appellate Body has led to a serious transformation of the modes of change in world trade law, and it has, by most accounts, provoked a shift from universal to regional trade regimes.

[11] See the discussion in 'Contestation and (Degrees of) Consolidation' in Chapter 7.

[12] See 'Contestation and the Changing Paths of Change' in Chapter 7.

This may foreshadow a broader trend towards an erosion and increased fragmentation of international law, but for now, it occurs alongside processes that reflect greater continuity and incremental adaptation. In most areas of international law, it is the existing paths of change that condition the transformations of international law towards a future of greater diversity, multipolarity, and—potentially—fracture in international society.

2. Implications: Sources, Norms, and Paths

Throughout this book, we have tried to understand better how dynamic international law is—whether it is as static as often claimed, which actors can propel change and block it, and under which circumstances change is most likely to come about. In the previous section, we have synthetized some of our core findings—and painted a picture of international legal change which, in some key respects, differs from standard accounts among scholars of international law and international relations. In this section, we take a step back and briefly distil some implications for debates in both disciplines in the hope of suggesting further lines of inquiry.

International Law: Process versus Sources

Our findings about the paths of change in international law stand in some tension with the traditional doctrine of sources of international law. They urge us to reconsider what we consider as sources, but they also pose broader questions about whether 'sources' are ultimately the right category to capture law-making and legal change in international law.

In the first place, of course, this book is not about legal sources as such. It analyses how international law actually changes—how change comes about de facto as opposed to what legal rules say about how it ought to change de iure. As we outlined in Chapter 1, much anecdotal evidence indicates a significant difference between these two dimensions—one to which our case studies and analysis lend empirical support. In the lessons compiled above, we have already hinted at different aspects of the difference: the relative unimportance of states (while doctrinal accounts focus almost entirely on states), the possibility of change despite significant opposition (while doctrine requires widespread or full agreement among states or treaty parties), the variation across issue areas (while most scholarly accounts treat the sources of international law as applying throughout), or the fact that legal norms may come in degrees rather than in binary form, as normally assumed.

What relevance does this gap between actual process and legal doctrine have? The typical answer would see both as operating in distinct spheres—it would insist that it is through its sources doctrine that international law determines how facts are processed as a matter of law and that legal authorities identify 'valid' law to support their decisions.[13] Recent accounts of the actual processes of international law-making have then also professed simply not to deal with sources.[14] Yet a proper response would have to go further (and we can only hint here at its contours). It would have to take into account the complication that sources do not simply precede facts, but that they are themselves constituted by facts—the doctrine of sources is also meant to reflect the way international law is practised.[15] When the International Law Commission recently developed its conclusions on the identification of customary international law, for example, it (at least rhetorically) sought to 'reflect the approach adopted by States, as well as by international courts and organizations and most authors'.[16] On this account, the definition of sources is itself a product of international interactions, and it is susceptible to change as those interactions change over time. This corresponds with the fact that, in positivist jurisprudence, law eventually derives from social facts, and the foundations of the law derive from social practices.[17] On this basis, it is also by no means guaranteed that all parts of international law operate according to the same set of sources. Some areas may well develop their own sources or at least a variation on the sources used in other areas, as commentators have increasingly come to recognize.[18]

[13] See, e.g., the description of the role of sources in James Crawford, *Brownlie's Principles of Public International Law*, 9th ed. (Oxford University Press, 2019), p. 18; Hugh Thirlway, *The Sources of International Law* (Oxford University Press, 2019), p. 17.

[14] Alan Boyle and Christine Chinkin, *The Making of International Law* (Oxford University Press, 2007), p. 1; Catherine Brölmann and Yannick Radi, 'Introduction: International Lawmaking in a Global World', in *Research Handbook on the Theory and Practice of International Lawmaking*, edited by Catherine Brölmann and Yannick Radi (Edward Elgar Publishing, 2016), p. 2.

[15] See Jean d'Aspremont, *Formalism and the Sources of International Law: A Theory of the Ascertainment of Legal Rules* (Oxford University Press, 2011), chs. 7–8. But note also attempts at theorizing sources on the basis of normative considerations, as in Samantha Besson, 'Theorizing the Sources of International Law', in *The philosophy of International Law* (Oxford University Press, 2010). The tension between both poles is the subject of Martti Koskenniemi, *From Apology to Utopia: The Structure of International Legal Argument* (Cambridge University Press, 2005), ch. 5. However, most authors do not inquire further into the theoretical origins or 'ontology' of the sources but content themselves with a reference to their historical development in general terms; see, e.g., Thirlway (n 13), ch 1. On the lack of theorization of sources in general, see Jean d'Aspremont, *International Law as a Belief System* (Cambridge University Press, 2017), pp. 55–63.

[16] UN Doc A/73/10 (2018), p. 123. See also the reference to 'evidence . . . in international practice' in the ILC's commentary on interpretation rules in the draft of the Vienna Convention on the Law of Treaties, Yearbook of the International Law Commission 1966, vol II, 218. However, in fact, the ILC often refers to decisions of the International Court of Justice which in turn relies on the work of the ILC, opening it to criticism of a 'Ponzi scheme' and moving it further away from the aspiration to reflect the practice on the ground. See S Villalpando, 'On the International Court of Justice and the Determination of Rules of Law', *Leiden Journal of International Law* 26, (2013): pp. 243, 245–51; B S Chimni, 'Customary International Law: A Third World Perspective', *American Journal of International Law* 112, (2018): pp. 1, 20–36.

[17] See, e.g., Liam Murphy, *What Makes Law: An Introduction to the Philosophy of Law* (Cambridge University Press, 2014). Most prominently, for H L A Hart the foundation of the rule of recognition lies in the recognition by legal officials; see H L A Hart, *The Concept of Law*, 2nd ed. (Clarendon Press, 1994).

[18] See also the chapters in Part IV of Samantha Besson and Jean d'Aspremont, eds., *The Oxford Handbook on the Sources of International Law* (Oxford University Press, 2017).

A reconstruction of the sources in each area would then have to take account of the way in which international law is practised therein—thus potentially reflecting the 'paths of change' laid out in this book.[19]

Yet our account here might suggest an even deeper challenge—a challenge to the notion of 'sources' as such.[20] Unlike traditional sources, the paths of change we have traced here are often not stable and fixed but instead part of a process that stretches over time, moves through different degrees of consolidation, and is often stabilized only through convergence at the reception stage. Moreover, many actors—especially governments—reject the idea that those paths, especially non-state paths, can themselves create rights and obligations under international law. At the same time, they often accept (or at least tolerate) the outcomes of the change processes travelling on those paths if these outcomes find a generally positive reception in the respective field. This seems to stand in contrast with the idea, often associated with the notion of sources, that sources should make it possible to identify the law independently from, and with some distance to, the way it is practised.[21] A similar problem has long been posed by customary international law, and custom has accordingly been portrayed as an 'extended process of challenge and response', often with undefined states during the process of emergence and change: '[w]hile that process is ongoing, it will be difficult to ascertain from an observer's standpoint whether customary norm C exists.'[22] If we follow our analysis in this book, much of international law shares this characteristic—it is often only in retrospect that we can identify what the law is and whether change has taken place.

This state of affairs seems to reflect H.L.A. Hart's depiction of international law as a 'set', rather than a 'system', of legal norms. In a 'system'—replete with a rule of recognition and secondary rules—one can say in advance whether a rule will be valid if it conforms to certain criteria, but '[i]n the simpler form of society [with a set of laws] we must wait and see whether a rule gets accepted as a rule or not'.[23] While some aspects of international law-making correspond to the former type—treaty-making in particular—many of the processes of change we have analysed in this book point us in the latter direction. This means that the vocabulary of

[19] For a similar argument, see Anthea Roberts and Sandesh Sivakumaran, 'The Theory and Reality of the Sources of International Law', in *International Law*, edited by Malcolm D Evans, 6th ed. (Oxford University Press, 2024).

[20] For a brief overview over other such challenges see Jean d'Aspremont, 'Towards a New Theory of Sources in International Law', in *The Oxford Handbook of the Theory of International Law*, edited by Anne Orford and Florian Hoffmann (Oxford University Press, 2016), pp. 550–56.

[21] On the fundamental tension between concreteness and normativity in the sources doctrine, see Koskenniemi (n 15), ch. 5.

[22] David Lefkowitz, 'Sources in Legal-Positivist Theories: Law as Necessarily Posited and the Challenge of Customary Law Creation', in *The Oxford Handbook of the Sources of International Law*, edited by Samantha Besson and Jean d'Aspremont (Oxford University Press, 2017), pp. 334–35.

[23] Hart (n 17), p. 235. For a useful recent discussion, see David Lefkowitz, *Philosophy and International Law: A Critical Introduction* (Cambridge University Press, 2020), ch. 3.

'sources' does not quite fit this normative practice: many paths of international law do not really have a defined origin from which the rest can be deduced; the law's content is not determined through secondary rules but ultimately defined by acceptance in practice.[24]

Such an account of the course of international law is likely to disappoint those who hope that the recourse to sources would help to distinguish law from non-law—and especially law from politics.[25] The enlightenment project of sources as a counterpoint to sheer facticity seems frustrated when law is equated with practice. Yet the legal practice we focus on in this book is not just *any* practice—it is a discursive, normative practice which centres on arguments and justification, not mere action itself.[26] This practice does not lack markers—it often operates around authorities recognized by participants—but these markers are typically not as decisive as we would expect in the context of classical sources doctrine. A widely supported UN General Assembly resolution may not make new law in and of itself, but it typically represents a crucial element in actors' recognition of change.

The legal process is then still more normative and discursive in character than other political processes, although the distinction between both will often be less formalized and obvious. But then, with the turn to positivism, the distinction between law and politics has always been tenuous, and critical voices have long highlighted that both the creation and the interpretation of international law are eminently political acts.[27] Understanding international law as a flow, a process, or practice helps illuminate its entanglement with politics—an entanglement that is easily obscured by a rhetoric dominated by formality, doctrine, and the language of sources.

International Norms, Change, and Authority

The account we have developed throughout this book also adds an important dimension—authority—to our understanding of international norms, their emergence, change, and decay.

Norms have become a key object of study in international relations since the 1990s, and after an initial focus primarily on the effect of (and compliance with)

[24] Related emphases can be found in the work of the New Haven School of International Law; see Myres S McDougal, 'International Law, Power, and Policy: A Contemporary Conception', *Recueil des Cours* vol 82 (1953). Interactional approaches are also built around continued practices (although with a more normative orientation): see Jutta Brunnée and Stephen J Toope, *Legitimacy and Legality in International Law. An Interactional Account* (Cambridge University Press, 2010).

[25] See Samantha Besson and Jean d'Aspremont, 'The Sources of International Law: An Introduction' in *The Oxford Handbook of the Sources of International Law*, edited by Samantha Besson and Jean d'Aspremont (Oxford University Press, 2017), pp. 10–12.

[26] See 'Actors, Practices, Authority: The Social Frame of Change' in Chapter 2 above.

[27] See only Koskenniemi (n 15).

international norms, interest soon grew in how norms change and evolve.[28] This interest has, over the years, led to a rich body of literature, now increasingly interwoven with the study of norm contestation.[29]

The literature on norm change in international politics has generated important insights into the relevant factors behind successful or failed change attempts—we have drawn on them already in our discussion of potential factors in Chapter 4.[30] Many of these factors focus on states—emphasizing the necessary degree of state support required to enable change, or conversely, the level of resistance sufficient to derail it,[31] as well as the important role ascribed to powerful states in the process.[32] The other main group of factors concerns the properties of the norms in question—the adjacency of a new understanding to existing ones, contradictions between existing norms and the availability of precedent, the degree to which a norm belongs to a supportive cluster, the strength of and support for a norm, or whether a challenge concerns the validity or merely the application of a given norm.[33]

In most of these accounts, institutions and authorities appear frequently throughout the empirical observations, but analytically they are treated as secondary—typically as fora in and through which actors (states and other norm entrepreneurs) pursue change proposals and gather support for them, or as sites to voice contestation. For example, Finnemore and Sikkink's foundational account portrays institutions as 'platforms' for change agents, as sites to pursue greater norm precision and enforcement, or as fora for negotiations. A stronger role for institutions comes into view only as part of the socialization processes that make new norms stick.[34] Many later contributions have, implicitly or explicitly, used a similar

[28] See Ann Florini, 'The Evolution of International Norms', *International Studies Quarterly* 40, (1996): p. 363; Martha Finnemore and Kathryn Sikkink, 'International Norm Dynamics and Political Change', *International Organization* 52, (1998): p. 887.

[29] See Wayne Sandholtz, 'International Norm Change', Oxford Research Encyclopedia of Politics, 2017, https://oxfordre.com/view/10.1093/acrefore/9780190228637.001.0001/acrefore-9780190228637-e-588; Antje Wiener, *Contestation and Constitution of Norms in Global International Relations* (Cambridge University Press, 2018).

[30] See 'Towards an Institutionalist Account' in Chapter 4.

[31] Finnemore and Sikkink (n 28); Alan Bloomfield, 'Norm Antipreneurs and Theorising Resistance to Normative Change', *Review of International Studies* 42, (2016): p. 310.

[32] Wayne Sandholtz and Kendall W Stiles, *International Norms and Cycles of Change* (Oxford University Press, 2008); Roland Paris, 'The Right to Dominate: How Old Ideas About Sovereignty Pose New Challenges for World Order', *International Organization* 74, (2020): p. 453.

[33] See Finnemore and Sikkink (n 28); Sandholtz and Stiles (n 32); Mona Lena Krook and Jacqui True, 'Rethinking the Life Cycles of International Norms: The United Nations and the Global Promotion of Gender Equality', *European Journal of International Relations* 18, (2012): p. 103; Jeffrey S Lantis and Carmen Wunderlich, 'Resiliency Dynamics of Norm Clusters: Norm Contestation and International Cooperation', *Review of International Studies* 44, (2018): p. 570; Michal Ben-Josef Hirsch and Jennifer M Dixon, 'Conceptualizing and Assessing Norm Strength in International Relations', *European Journal of International Relations* 27, (2021): p. 521; Beth A Simmons and Hyeran Jo, 'Measuring Norms and Normative Contestation: The Case of International Criminal Law', *Journal of Global Security Studies* 4, (2019): p. 18; Nicole Deitelhoff and Lisbeth Zimmermann, 'Things We Lost in the Fire: How Different Types of Contestation Affect the Robustness of International Norms', *International Studies Review* 22, (2018): p. 51.

[34] Finnemore and Sikkink (n 28) 899–909.

frame.[35] Institutions and authorities are de facto key to the processes in question, but their role is not central to theorizing those processes.[36]

In this book, we focus on international *legal* norms—a subcategory of norms which features heavily in the study of norms in international relations. Insights about legal norms cannot necessarily be generalized to norms more broadly, but given the importance of legal norms for the study of the latter, they should carry significant weight in the broader debate and spur further research with a view to other categories of international norms as well.

As we have laid out especially in Chapter 4 (and summarized above), in our account, 'authority' emerges as perhaps *the* key factor behind the success or failure of change attempts.[37] In our descriptive statistics, the regression analysis, as well as many of our detailed case studies, successful change depends on the ability to mobilize institutions in authority—be they inter-governmental organs, expert groups, international courts, or quasi-judicial bodies. In the discursive process of international law, authoritative statements provide reference points and induce deference among actors, thus facilitating convergence around a new norm.[38] In their absence, a change attempt is far more likely to remain unrecognized and unconsolidated—even if it is supported by a significant number of states. Authority also helps to overcome state opposition; where focal institutions are at play, change attempts have significantly greater success chances even in the face of opposition from states.

This suggests that scholarship on international norm change and the contestation of norms should pay far more structured attention to authority and institutions. This would also help to account for variation over time. The relative unimportance of institutions and authorities in many accounts of norm change may in part be due to the objective of creating timeless models. This is perhaps most obvious in the work of Wayne Sandholtz and Kendall Stiles, who construe their cycles-of-change model across a long time period with relatively fixed and recurring elements. The appearance of authorities in some of their cases, for

[35] See, e.g., Mona Lena Krook and Jacqui True, 'Rethinking the Life Cycles of International Norms: The United Nations and the Global Promotion of Gender Equality', *European Journal of International Relations* 18, (2012): p. 103; Ingvild Bode and John Karlsrud, 'Implementation in Practice: The Use of Force to Protect Civilians in United Nations Peacekeeping', *European Journal of International Relations* 25, (2019): p. 458; Elvira Rosert, 'Norm Emergence as Agenda Diffusion: Failure and Success in the Regulation of Cluster Munitions', *European Journal of International Relations* 25, (2019): p. 1103. But see also the emphasis on institutional norm entrepreneurs in Daisuke Madokoro, 'International Commissions as Norm Entrepreneurs: Creating the Normative Idea of the Responsibility to Protect', *Review of International Studies* 45, (2019): p. 100; Druscilla Scribner and Tracy Slagter, 'Recursive Norm Development: The Role of Supranational Courts', *Global Policy* 8, (2017): p. 322.

[36] See, e.g., Amitav Acharya, *Constructing Global Order: Agency and Change in World Politics* (Cambridge University Press, 2018); Deitelhoff and Zimmermann (n 33). See also the discussion in 'Towards an Institutionalist Account' in Chapter 4.

[37] See 'Findings I: Descriptive Analysis', 'Findings II: Regression Analysis', and 'Assessing Interactions and Predictions' in Chapter 4.

[38] See 'Actors, Practices, Authority: The Social Frame of Change' in Chapter 2.

example, the emergence of a right to democracy, simply does not fit the broader pattern. Their generalization over time favours the agency of states: 'Norm change in the international system . . . generally occurs in the absence of an authoritative third-party dispute resolver, or judge. Actions trigger a dispute, which generates normative arguments, which states (not judges) decide.'[39] But the fact that there is, in most cases, not a single authoritative dispute settler or law-maker does not mean that norm development occurs outside of authority structures altogether. In many cases, as we have seen, not accounting for the importance of authorities misses an important element of the norm change process—and a key reason why processes of norm change today have a different shape and pace than those in previous times.[40]

Rational Designs and Paths Dependencies

Our focus on paths and authorities also highlights the limitations of rationalist accounts of international law. International legal rules have often been understood through a rationalist lens as the result of coordination or cooperation between states to further their national interests.[41] Treaties, in particular, have been analysed in this way, and elements of rational design have been traced in provisions on issues ranging from withdrawal clauses to reservations and dispute resolution.[42] Broader accounts of the legalization of international politics have also employed a rationalist frame, portraying the growing relevance of law and legal institutions largely as the result of state choices and design.[43]

Such rationalist accounts provide important insights, but their limits have long been emphasized by other scholarly traditions in international relations. Constructivist scholars especially have insisted that legal rules cannot be reduced to interest-based exchange alone but also reflect ideas and norms embedded in international society.[44] Legalization, in this view, results from 'many moves' by different actors, producing a complex set of transformations.[45] Moreover, the effects

[39] Sandholtz and Stiles (n 32), p. 325.

[40] This point has already been alluded to in Finnemore and Sikkink (n 28), p. 909.

[41] See, e.g., Andrew T Guzman, *How International Law Works: A Rational Choice Theory* (Oxford University Press, 2008).

[42] Barbara Koremenos, *The Continent of International Law: Explaining Agreement Design* (Cambridge University Press, 2016).

[43] Judith L Goldstein and others, eds., *Legalization and World Politics* (MIT Press, 2001). For a critique of the underlying rationalist frame, see Martha Finnemore and Stephen J Toope, 'Alternatives to "Legalization": Richer Views of Law and Politics', *International Organization* 55, (2001): p. 743.

[44] See Jutta Brunnée and Stephen Toope, 'Constructivism and International Law', in *Interdisciplinary Perspectives on International Law and International Relations: The State of the Art*, edited by Jeffrey L Dunoff and Mark A Pollack (Cambridge University Press, 2012).

[45] Christian Brütsch and Dirk Lehmkuhl, 'Complex Legalization and the Many Moves to Law', in *Law and Legalization in Transnational Relations*, edited by Christian Bruetsch and Dirk Lehmkuhl (Routledge, 2007).

of international law are seen as extending beyond the resolution of collective-action problems to shaping the very constitution of relationships, identities, and preferences.[46]

Building on these broader engagements, our account in this book highlights the limitations of rationalist approaches for understanding change in international law. The authorities that matter in international legal change processes—beyond the negotiation of treaties—are not necessarily designed by states, and where they are (as for international courts or institutions), they have typically not been formally tasked to develop the law. The norms and understandings produced on the many paths of international law are not easily captured by an interest-based framework—and this holds as much for the International Committee of the Red Cross's role in shaping customary humanitarian law as it does for the international criminal tribunals' recognition of rape as a war crime. Likewise, the evolution of international investment law, with enhanced protections against indirect expropriation established by arbitral tribunals to scrutinize all kinds of regulatory measures, is not something one could imagine lying in the interest of all state parties to these agreements. Nor are these outcomes simply the result of power relations, as realists would expect[47]—after all, we have found power to have a limited bearing on change processes.

The relative 'inefficiency' of these results of legal change thus challenges both rationalist and realist approaches, yet this cannot be explained solely by reference to ideas, shared understandings, frames, or cognitive biases, as many constructivist or behaviouralist accounts suggest.[48] Instead, the embedding of certain ideas and interests into new rules and understandings was enabled by authority constellations, typically formed around special institutions. The recognition of these authorities, institutions, and paths of legal change shaped the conditions under which particular ideas and interests gained prominence in the discursive process.

These findings largely correspond with historical institutionalist approaches which see unintended consequences and 'irrational' outcomes as the typical consequence of institutional arrangements and their path dependencies.[49] In this sense, the 'paths' of international law, once accepted in a given issue area, condition interactions in ways that may run counter to previously existing interests and power

[46] See, e.g., Christian Reus-Smit, ed., *The Politics of International Law* (Cambridge University Press, 2004).

[47] See Richard H Steinberg, 'Wanted—Dead or Alive: Realism in International Law', in *Interdisciplinary Perspectives on International Law and International Relations: The State of the Art*, edited by J L Dunoff and M A Pollack (Cambridge University Press, 2012).

[48] See Brunnée and Toope (n 24); Andrea Bianchi and Moshe Hirsch, eds., *International Law's Invisible Frames: Social Cognition and Knowledge Production in International Legal Processes* (Oxford University Press, 2021); Anne van Aaken and Moshe Hirsch, eds., *International Legal Theory and the Cognitive Turn* (Oxford University Press, 2025).

[49] Paul Pierson, *Politics in Time: History, Institutions, and Social Analysis* (Princeton University Press, 2004); Orfeo Fioretos, 'Historical Institutionalism in International Relations', *International Organization* 65, (2011): p. 367.

relations. The paths and authority constellations in a particular field are not only the result of state interactions but also of social processes of recognition, and they are often difficult to unsettle even if they produce undesired results from the perspective of states or groups of states. Except in a few prominent cases of backlash, challenges of institutions engaged in legal change have often only marginally affected their course.[50]

Historical institutionalism has not found much attention so far in scholarship around international law, but it holds significant promise. Insights on the mechanisms of path dependence, on modes of gradual change, or on reactive sequences can all illuminate important international legal processes,[51] and there is ample space for further work than we can accomplish here.

One of the appeals of historical institutionalism is that it does not portray institutions as simply determining outcomes—actors make active choices, but these choices are in many ways conditioned (rationally or socially) by the authority constellation actors find themselves in. The paths of least resistance we have explored reflect both agency and structure in the ways in which change processes in international law unfold. This becomes particularly clear in the context of regime complexity: actors do not simply seek (or resist) change by reference to particular ideas, norms, or interests, but instead seek to mobilize authorities closer to their understandings to generate institutional support. Actors pursue rational strategies here, but these strategies operate in an existing structure, and the results are conditioned by that structure. International law is, in this sense, heavily 'paths-dependent'.

3. Assessment: Paths and their Adequacy

International law is thus more dynamic than is often thought, but—to return to our initial question from the beginning of the book—is that dynamism sufficient? Is it enough to cope with the challenges of an accelerating world, one increasingly described as facing a 'polycrisis'?[52]

Whether (and how much) change is desirable on any particular issue is, in the first place, a function of values and priorities. Our cases date from the past few decades, and many of them reflect the liberal or neo-liberal attitudes of this period—with the creation of new rights, advances in the fight against impunity, and the expansion of property protections (followed later by some increased emphasis on

[50] See the discussion in Chapter 7.

[51] On such insights and their application to international politics and institutions, see Thomas Rixen, Lora Anne Viola and Michael Zürn, eds., *Historical Institutionalism and International Relations: Explaining Institutional Development in World Politics* (Oxford University Press, 2016); Orfeo Fioretos, ed., *International Politics and Institutions in Time* (Oxford University Press, 2017).

[52] On the term polycrisis and its uses, see Eric Helleiner, 'Economic Globalization's Polycrisis', *International Studies Quarterly* 68, (2024): p. 1.

the police powers of governments).[53] Environmental concerns, too, played a major role (although often not as much as observers hoped). However, change in international law can also take other directions. In recent years, shifts towards an authoritarian international law have been diagnosed, and in the current ideological climate, anti-liberal tendencies may well gain greater traction still.[54] The more dynamic international law is, the more it tracks the broader political and ideational trends of the time—and depending on these trends, change can be progressive or regressive.

Yet we also need to ask whether, on a structural level, international law is sufficiently dynamic to address new demands and to cope with new and growing challenges. Our findings throughout this book suggest that its dynamism remains too limited to tackle global problems effectively. The change processes we have described here reflect important adaptations on a variety of pressing issues, but we have also seen that actors often turned to other forms than international law to make better progress.[55] The Sustainable Development Goals are perhaps the most striking example—they seek to bring about change through goals and indicators rather than through rules and their enforcement. On issues such as poverty, inequalities, climate, or clean water, the SDGs have sidelined international law as a vehicle of change.[56]

This result is not surprising if we consider the limitations built into the processes of change in international law. The gradual processes we have traced here typically cannot effect big leaps in short timespans, and they remain contestable as long as they do not rest on formally recognized powers to enact law. Formal law-making powers are usually not associated with the paths we explored. Apart from the UN Security Council, international institutions tend to hold such powers, if at all, only in narrowly defined areas, often limited to technical issues, and usually include mechanisms that allow states to opt out if they do not want to be bound.[57] International courts are not formally recognized as law-makers; their jurisdiction is limited, and the binding effects of their decisions typically apply only to the parties to a given case. Treaties can generate formal change, but they require the consent of the parties and are thus often not able to transcend disagreement but instead reflect limited compromises and lowest common denominators (or even leave out the dissenting states). The agreements reached on two of the greatest

[53] See the overview in 'Change Across Issue Areas' in Chapter 3.

[54] See Tom Ginsburg, 'Authoritarian International Law?', *American Journal of International Law* 114, (2020), p. 221; Heike Krieger and Andrea Liese, eds., *Tracing Value Change in the International Legal Order: Perspectives from Legal and Political Science* (Oxford University Press, 2023).

[55] See 'Sideways Moves: Cumulation across Issue Areas' in Chapter 6.

[56] On the gaps and interactions between the SDGs and international law, see Jonas Ebbesson and Ellen Hey, 'Introduction: The Sustainable Development Goals, Agenda 2030, and International Law', in *The Cambridge Handbook of the Sustainable Development Goals and International Law*, edited by Jonas Ebbesson and Ellen Hey (Cambridge University Press, 2022).

[57] See Liesbet Hooghe, Tobias Lenz and Gary Marks, *A Theory of International Organization* (Oxford University Press, 2019), ch. 3.

global challenges of the past decade—the Paris Agreement on Climate Change and the WHO Pandemic Agreement, both of which contain few hard and fast obligations and come with limited adherence—reflect these limitations rather vividly. The gradual change processes we have taken into view in this book may have made some progress, but they remain far from providing an adequate response to challenges of this urgency and magnitude.

A potentially more effective alternative would be a turn to majoritarian processes—processes by which a majority of states (or potentially other actors) would create obligations for all (and establish mechanisms to enforce and implement them). Eliminating the requirement of state consent and moving towards non-consensual law-making is for many an obvious response to political deadlock and intractable problems of global public goods.[58] As we have seen earlier in the book, similar proposals were mooted by scholars in the 1930s interested in more flexible forms of peaceful change, and they returned later in discussions over the powers of the General Assembly.[59] Majority decision-making has, of course, been institutionalized in certain regional contexts, most prominently in the European Union. Here, decisions on most issues—from the internal market to police and security cooperation, and environmental policies—are today taken by a qualified majority in the EU's Council and Parliament.[60] But it has not found widespread recognition in other regional systems, let alone at the universal level.

Would such legislative mechanisms for international law be desirable more generally? In terms of output, they would certainly generate greater flexibility and render more effective responses to global challenges possible. But they would, today just as a century ago, provoke doubts as to their societal foundations. Writing about legislation as a mechanism of change in the international order, E.H. Carr noted in 1939 that 'the difficulty lies not in the lack of machinery of international legislation, but in the absence of an international political order sufficiently well integrated to make possible the establishment of a legislative authority whose decrees will be recognized as binding on states without their specific assent'.[61] Such doubts may have seemed less relevant after the end of the Cold War, when the notion of an international community took centre stage and the possibility of a constitutionalization of international law appeared on the horizon.[62] A cosmopolitan democracy, based no longer solely on states but rather on a worldwide citizenry, was seen to require (and render possible) new institutions to tackle global

[58] See, e.g., Andrew Guzman, 'Against Consent', *Virginia Journal of International Law* 52, (2012): p. 747.
[59] See 'Contested Modes of Change' in Chapter 1.
[60] See Robert Schütze, *European Constitutional Law*, 3rd ed. (Oxford University Press, 2021), ch. 7.
[61] E H Carr, *The Twenty Years' Crisis, 1919-1939* (Springer, 2016), pp. 193–94.
[62] Bardo Fassbender, 'The United Nations Charter as Constitution of the International Community', *Columbia Journal of Transnational Law* 36, (1998): p. 529; Jürgen Habermas, *Der Gespaltene Westen* (Suhrkamp, 2004); Jan Klabbers, Anne Peters and Geir Ulfstein, *The Constitutionalization of International Law* (Oxford University Press, 2009).

challenges in the interest of all. Such institutions would, in the influential formulation of David Held, include 'the creation of an effective transnational legislative and executive' around an 'international democratic assembly' to tackle pressing global problems, such as health, global warming, and the risks of nuclear and chemical warfare.[63]

There are strong normative reasons to back such a vision, not least the democratic imperative of self-government by which people ought to be able to take political decisions on issues affecting them—including in a transnational, global context if the relevant issues are of a transboundary nature.[64] A merely inter-state, consent-based order is insufficient in this respect. However, global law-making by majority risks creating tensions with other democratic imperatives, such as freedom from domination and the possibility of self-government by the different communities people identify with.[65] In international law, the principle of self-determination points to the salience of this latter point. As a result, even proponents of a constitutionalization of international law have moved away from ideas of binding global decisions towards more open and heterarchical structures.[66] In a pluralist order, global rules would stand alongside rules and decisions adopted at other legitimate levels, without a claim to supremacy and thus always subject to mutual challenges.[67]

If the problems associated with the idea of global legislation were visible in the 1990s and 2000s, they are yet clearer today in a more diverse and politically fragmented, potentially even 'fractured' international society.[68] As values and interests diverge more sharply, finding common ground becomes increasingly difficult. In this context, collective decision-making—especially when driven by majority rule or asymmetrical influence—carries a heightened risk of domination by stronger or more organized actors. Fear of such domination has provoked a growing insistence on safeguards to protect self-government and prevent overreach by institutions and mechanisms perceived as being controlled by others.[69] Growing

[63] David Held, *Democracy and the Global Order* (Cambridge University Press, 1995), pp. 272–74.

[64] On output and governance capability as key elements of global political legitimacy, see Jens Steffek, 'The Output Legitimacy of International Organizations and the Global Public Interest', *International Theory* 7, (2015): p. 263; Terry Macdonald, 'Sovereignty, Democracy, and Global Political Legitimacy', in *The Oxford Handbook of International Political Theory*, edited by Chris Brown and Robyn Eckersley (Oxford University Press, 2018). On principles of inclusion in global decision-making, see Robert E Goodin, 'Enfranchising All Subjected, Worldwide', *International Theory* 8, (2016): p. 365.

[65] For an emphasis on non-domination, see Philip Pettit, 'A Republican Law of Peoples', *European Journal of Political Theory* 9, (2010): p. 70.

[66] See, e.g., Anne Peters, 'Dual Democracy', in *The Constitutionalization of International* Law, edited by J Klabbers, A Peters and G Ulfstein (Oxford University Press, 2009), pp. 333–38.

[67] See Nico Krisch, *Beyond Constitutionalism: The Pluralist Structure of Postnational Law* (Oxford University Press, 2010); Terry Macdonald and Kate Macdonald, 'Towards a "Pluralist" World Order: Creative Agency and Legitimacy in Global Institutions', *European Journal of International Relations* 26, (2020): p. 518.

[68] See the discussion in 'Contestation and the Changing Paths of Change' in Chapter 7.

[69] Michael Zürn, Martin Binder and Matthias Ecker-Ehrhardt, 'International Authority and Its Politicization', *International Theory* 4, (2012): p. 69; Stefanie Walter, 'The Backlash Against Globalization' *Annual Review of Political Science* 24, (2021): p. 421.

anti-internationalist backlash, processes of dejudicialization, and the stagnation of treaty-making can all be seen in this light.[70] As divergence deepens, so too does the need for protective mechanisms to ensure that international law does not merely reflect the preferences of some.

The processes we have traced throughout this book can be seen as a sort of compromise between the need for more flexible change mechanisms and the importance of preserving the possibility of national control and contestation. In the context of customary law, Georges Abi-Saab captured this compromise character perhaps best when he wrote that 'the international community . . . has forged a legislative procedure or process, but . . . without managing to add to it a legislative effect, in the absence of a centralized legislative power'.[71] The paths of change in international law evince this duality more generally. They allow for a relatively smooth de facto transformation of rules even in the face of discontent from some states and great powers, but they usually lack formally binding force and thus remain contestable.

As with any compromise, this state of affairs is unlikely to satisfy either side. For those who prioritize (national) self-determination over competing considerations, it will not allow for enough national control. But it will also frustrate those who seek effective, common responses to global challenges in an international society in which commonality is in short supply—after all, international law's processes are still too slow and cumbersome to save the planet. How a compromise between both positions should best be struck is not something we can conclusively answer here; it would require a much deeper engagement with questions of political philosophy, moral theory, and institutional design. But in the face of important countervailing values, some sort of compromise is likely to be the only option.[72]

4. Paths Ahead

'Law must be stable and yet it cannot stand still. Hence all thinking about law has struggled to reconcile the conflicting demands of the need of stability and of the need of change', wrote US legal scholar, Roscoe Pound, a century ago.[73]

[70] See, e.g., Heike Krieger, 'Populist Governments and International Law' *European Journal of International Law* 30, (2019): p. 971; Daniel Abebe and Tom Ginsburg, 'The Dejudicialization of International Politics?' *International Studies Quarterly* 63, (2019): p. 521; Joost Pauwelyn, Ramses A Wessel and Jan Wouters, 'When Structures Become Shackles: Stagnation and Dynamics in International Lawmaking' *European Journal of International Law* 25, (2014): p. 733.

[71] Georges Abi-Saab, *Cours général de droit internationale public*, vol 207 (Martinus Nijhoff Publishers, 1996), p. 179 (translation by authors).

[72] On the virtues and limits of compromise, see Avishai Margalit, *On Compromise and Rotten Compromises* (Princeton University Press, 2010).

[73] Roscoe Pound, *Interpretations of Legal History* (Cambridge University Press, 1967), p. 1.

This tension continues to run through international law; it has not been resolved, and perhaps it cannot be fully resolved. It is being navigated, however, and in this book, we have analysed how this navigation occurs. The resulting image has been one of greater dynamism than is often thought. On the different paths of international law, change attempts often succeed even if states (including powerful states) show limited support or even engage in opposition. Authority and institutions, we find, are key to such processes, and they help to render change processes more fluid. Many areas of international law have thus seen significant evolution through incremental steps, sometimes resulting in major transformations. Even so, the dynamism of international law remains limited, states seek to retain the possibility to contest change ex post, and change attempts often shift towards other, more accommodating forms than international law.

This book is the first attempt to capture the tension between stability and change in international law, not only theoretically but also on the basis of empirical evidence from cases across the different fields of international law. Other, more detailed studies will need to dig deeper into particular areas, take into account a greater number of cases, and extend the scope over time. But we hope that our findings about authority, states, and power in international legal change provide a solid starting point for such further inquiries.

Are the paths of international law here to stay? As time progresses, we will be able to draw clearer conclusions about the time-bound nature of the paths as we have described them. The current modes of change in international law are of relatively recent origin and are subject to contestation and change. In today's more fractured international society, it might well be that, as a result of geopolitical shifts, growing anti-internationalism, and a narrower definition of national interests among governments, international law will recede. Processes of erosion and fragmentation, coupled with increasing circumvention, may further reduce the relevance of international legal rules.[74] As we finish writing this book, the wars in Ukraine, Sudan, Gaza and Iran have made a mockery of the laws of war, and the US government is taking a sledgehammer not only to the rules of international trade law but also to foundational principles of sovereignty and territorial integrity.

Gloomy predictions see us return to a world of power politics, and if this comes to pass, the thick international law built after the Second World War may at some point appear as an historical exception. This is not a foregone conclusion, however—in today's interdependent world, many value international law highly. This includes the many people around the world who have come to look to the International Court of Justice to speak truth (and law) to power. But it also includes many governments that seek international rules for their own protection and to achieve common goals—they may yet rise to uphold and construe international

[74] See 'Contestation and the Changing Paths of Change' in Chapter 7.

law independently of the destructive policies of one or the other great power. What international law will look like in decades to come is anyone's guess. But for now, it continues to travel on the paths that lie at the centre of this book, and much of the change ahead will have to pass through them as well. After all, these paths remain international law's most viable routes for adaptation in a fractured world in which agreement among states is ever more elusive.

APPENDIX

Part A. Main Regression Analyses

OLS Regression Models

We compare in Table A1 Model 1 (existing accounts) and Model 2 (expanded accounts including permissive norms, focal authority, location of change attempt [within or outside a regime], and breadth of discursive opening). Model 2 shows improved fit and identifies additional significant predictors of discursive shift.

Table A1 OLS regression results

	Dependent variable:	
	Discursive Shift	
	Model 1	**Model 2**
Broad state support	0.916 (0.555)	0.283 (0.518)
Full state support	−0.263 (1.243)	0.143 (1.082)
Limited state opposition	−0.755 (0.693)	−1.476** (0.633)
Broad state opposition	−1.565* (0.866)	−2.055** (0.749)
Major power support	0.008 (0.655)	0.714 (0.582)
Major power opposition	0.028 (0.625)	0.689 (0.578)
Loose norm adjacency (ref: no adjacency)	−0.257 (0.801)	0.363 (0.833)
Clear norm adjacency (ref: no adjacency)	−0.624 (0.755)	−0.339 (0.793)
Rival norm	−0.314 (0.621)	−1.019* (0.548)
Permissive norm		0.962* (0.444)
Focal authority		1.564** (0.600)

(*continued*)

Table A1 Continued

	Dependent variable:	
	Discursive Shift	
	Model 1	Model 2
Change within a regime		−0.858 (0.554)
Narrow discursive opening		0.130 (0.500)
Timing (post-2000s) (ref: pre-1990s)	−1.295 (0.968)	−2.262** (0.832)
Timing (1900s) (ref: pre-1990s)	0.248 (1.075)	−0.753 (0.979)
Constant	5.272*** (1.228)	5.116*** (1.069)
Observations	25	25
R^2	0.646	0.847
Adjusted R^2	0.346	0.593
Residual Std. Error	0.990 (df = 13)	0.781 (df = 9)
F Statistic	2.154* (df = 11; 13)	3.331** (df = 15; 9)

Note: *p < 0.1; **p < 0.05; ***p < 0.01

Interaction Effects

We present in Table A2 below the regression output of a model including an interaction between authority type and breadth of state opposition. Results indicate that focal authority combined with limited state opposition is associated with higher rates of discursive shift.

Table A2 The interaction between authority type and breadth of state opposition

	Dependent variable:
	Discursive shift
Focal authority	−0.250 (0.902)
Limited state opposition	−1.500** (0.638)
Broad state opposition	−1.750* (0.902)
Focal authority * Limited state opposition	1.875* (1.042)

Table A2 Continued

	Dependent variable:
	Discursive shift
Focal authority * Broad state opposition	0.750 (1.563)
Constant	3.250*** (0.521)
Observations	25
R^2	0.427
Adjusted R^2	0.276
Residual Std. Error	1.042 (df = 19)
F Statistic	2.833** (df = 5; 19)

Note: *p < 0.1; **p < 0.05; ***p < 0.01

Part B. Regression Diagnostics

All regression diagnostics and robustness checks are conducted on the same analytic sample of N = 25 cases with complete data on all variables.

Table A3 describes the results from regression diagnostics assessing key model assumptions. Tests for normality (Jarque–Bera, $p = 0.29$), homoskedasticity (studentized Breusch–Pagan, $p = 0.35$), and functional form (Ramsey RESET, $p = 0.85$) indicate no violations. Adjusted GVIF values are all below 2, suggesting no multicollinearity concerns (see Table A4). Influential observations were identified through Cook's Distance, leverage, and

Table A3 Summary of tests assessing model assumptions

Diagnostic	**Test**	**Statistic**	**P-value/Result**
Normality	Jarque–Bera	$X^2 = 2.51$	p = 0.29 (no violation)
Homoskedasticity	Studentized Breusch–Pagan	BP = 16.44, df = 15	p = 0.35 (no violation)
Functional Form	Ramsey RESET	F = 0.164, df = 2,7	p = 0.85 (no misspecification)
Multicollinearity	Adjusted GVIF	All < 2	Within acceptable range (see Table A4)
Influential Observations	Cook's Distance, leverage, studentized residuals	Flagged Cases: 19, 4, 11 (see Figure A2)	See Table A5 for a regression analysis without outliers

studentized residuals (Cases 19, 4, and 11), and models excluding these cases are presented in Table A5.

Figure A1 below presents a Q–Q plot of the model residuals, showing that the points closely follow the 45-degree reference line. This visual inspection supports the Jarque–Bera test result (p = 0.29), which together indicate that the residuals are approximately normally distributed.

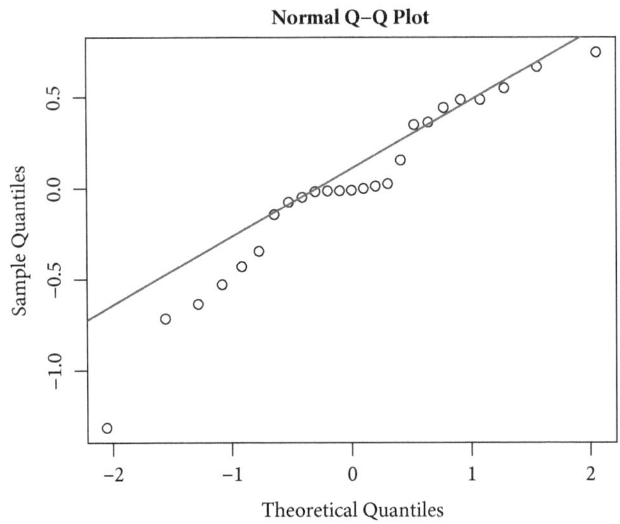

Figure A1 Q–Q plot of regression residuals

Table A4 Variance inflation factors (VIF) for model 2

Variable	GVIF	Df	Adjusted GVIF
State opposition breadth	4.444	2	1.452
State support breadth	4.036	2	1.417
Major power opposition	3.763	1	1.940
Major power support	2.814	1	1.677
Norm adjacency	8.394	2	1.702
Rival norm	3.480	1	1.866
Norm type	2.088	1	1.445
Change type	1.802	1	1.343
Authority type	3.711	1	1.927
Change within regime	3.200	1	1.789
Discursive opening	2.796	1	1.672
Timing	4.735	2	1.475

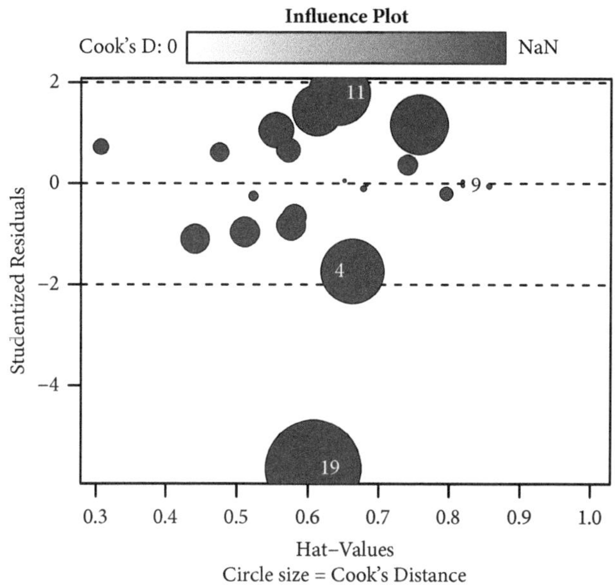

Figure A2 Influence plot showing studentized residuals versus hat values, with circle size proportional to Cook's Distance (Model 2)

Table A4 above reports generalized variance inflation factors (GVIFs) for all predictors in the regression model, adjusted for degrees of freedom (df). All adjusted GVIF values are below 2, well under the common rule-of-thumb thresholds (e.g., 5 or 10), indicating no evidence of problematic multicollinearity.

Figure A2 above presents an influence plot showing studentized residuals (y-axis), hat values (x-axis), and Cook's Distance (circle size). Three observations (Cases 19, 4, and 11) stand out with large residuals. Case 19, in particular, has the largest Cook's Distance value. The highly influential cases in our sample are as follows: Case 19 ('Right to Truth'), Case 11 ('General Exceptions under GATT XX'), and Case 4 ('Cyber Warfare').

Table A5 below presents robustness checks for Model 2 by sequentially excluding observations identified as highly influential based on Cook's Distance studentized residuals. In other words, it re-estimates Model 2 after excluding these influential observations. The first trimmed model excludes only Case 19 (column 2), while the second trimmed model excludes Cases 19, 11, and 4 (column 3). Across both trimmed models, the signs and magnitudes of the key predictors remain substantively consistent with the full sample results (column 1). Removing influential observations changes the pattern of statistical significance for a small set of predictors. In particular, major power support, which is positive but not significant in the full model, becomes positive and significant ($p < 0.05$) once Case 19 is excluded. Case 19 ('Right to Truth') does not itself involve major power support, but its combination of attributes may exert disproportionate leverage on the model. The exclusion of Case 19 also renders loose norm adjacency and change within a regime statistically significant, although these effects are less stable and lose significance when additional outliers are removed.

Table A5 Robustness checks for Model 2 after removing influential observations

	Dependent variable:		
	Discursive shift	Discursive shift	
	(Model 2)	(W/o obs 19)	(W/o obs 19, 11, 4)
Limited state opposition	−1.476** (0.633)	−2.573*** (0.358)	−2.228*** (0.423)
Broad state opposition	−2.055** (0.749)	−2.947*** (0.389)	−2.630*** (0.475)
Broad state support	0.283 (0.518)	−0.417 (0.275)	−0.135 (0.344)
Full state support	0.143 (1.082)	0.099 (0.514)	0.103 (0.526)
Major power opposition	0.689 (0.578)	0.436 (0.278)	0.500 (0.282)
Major power support	0.714 (0.582)	0.879** (0.278)	0.699 (0.377)
Loose norm adjacency (ref: no adjacency)	0.363 (0.833)	1.036** (0.413)	0.730 (0.461)
Clear norm adjacency (ref: no adjacency)	−0.339 (0.793)	0.917* (0.437)	0.655 (0.460)
Rival norm	−1.019* (0.548)	−1.002*** (0.260)	−0.969** (0.340)
Permissive norm	0.962* (0.444)	1.411*** (0.225)	1.171*** (0.270)
Focal authority	1.564** (0.600)	2.427*** (0.323)	1.932*** (0.452)
Change within a regime	−0.858 (0.554)	−1.064*** (0.266)	−0.774* (0.355)
Discursive opening	0.130 (0.500)	−0.313 (0.250)	−0.219 (0.287)
Timing (1990s) (ref: pre-1990s)	−0.753 (0.979)	−1.859*** (0.504)	−1.356* (0.598)
Timing (Post-2000s) (ref: pre-1990s)	−2.262** (0.832)	−3.066*** (0.420)	−2.652*** (0.489)
Constant	4.116*** (1.069)	5.037*** (0.533)	4.741*** (0.629)
Observations	25	24	22
R^2	0.847	0.969	0.971
Adjusted R^2	0.593	0.911	0.898

Note: *p < 0.1; **p < 0.05; ***p < 0.01

Part C. Robustness Checks

OLS Regression on the 10-point Scale DV

The degree of discursive shift was initially measured on a 10-point scale, capturing finer distinctions between cases. This variable was then condensed into a 5-point scale to facilitate interpretation, ensure comparability across cases, and reduce sparsity in underrepresented categories. Figure A3 displays the distribution of the original 10-point measure, illustrating the greater granularity available in the initial coding.

To verify that our findings are not an artefact of this recoding, we re-estimate both main models using the original 10-point scale as the dependent variable. As shown in Table A6, the results are substantively consistent with those reported for the 5-point scale: the same predictors remain statistically significant, and coefficients retain similar signs and relative magnitudes. These include focal authority, state opposition (both limited and broad), the existence of rival norms, and permissive norms, and—only in Model 1—broad state support. Minor differences in p-values reflect the greater variation in the 10-point scale, but these do not alter the substantive interpretation. No unexpected sign changes emerge, and this consistency across codings further strengthens confidence in the robustness of the main findings.

Taken together, these checks show that the main results hold whether influential cases are excluded or the original, more detailed 10-point version of the dependent variable is used.

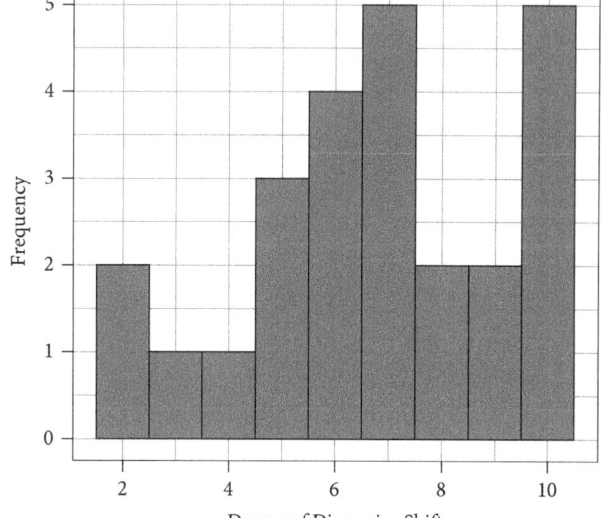

Figure A3 Distribution of the degree of discursive shift (10-point scale)

Table A6 OLS regression results for the degree of discursive shift using the original 10-point scale dependent variable

	Dependent variable:	
	Discursive Shift (10 points scale)	
	(Model 1)	**(Model 2)**
Broad state support	2.013* (1.088)	0.595 (0.937)
Full state support	0.607 (2.436)	1.517 (1.959)
Limited state opposition	−0.981 (1.359)	−2.545* (1.146)
Broad state opposition	−2.431 (1.697)	−3.520** (1.356)
Major power support	−0.305 (1.226)	1.121 (1.047)
Major power opposition	−0.154 (1.283)	1.299 (1.054)
Loose norm adjacency	−1.295 (1.570)	0.229 (1.508)
Clear norm adjacency	−1.474 (1.481)	−0.710 (1.436)
Rival norm	−0.537 (1.217)	−1.914* (0.991)
Permissive norm (ref: collaborative)		1.828** (0.804)
Focal authority (ref: peripheral)		3.424** (1.086)
Change within a regime		−1.736 (1.003)
Narrow discursive opening		−0.252 (0.905)
Timing: post-2000s (ref: pre-1990s)	−2.607 (1.897)	−4.648** (1.505)
Timing: 1990s (ref: pre-1990s)	0.255 (2.108)	−1.996 (1.773)
Constant	10.432*** (2.407)	10.251*** (2.042)
Observations	25	25
R^2	0.661	0.875
Adjusted R^2	0.374	0.668

Note: *$p < 0.1$; **$p < 0.05$; ***$p < 0.01$

Bibliography

Books and Chapters in Books

Aaken, Anne van and Moshe Hirsch, eds. *International Legal Theory and the Cognitive Turn* (Oxford University Press, 2025).

Aalberts, Tanja and Ingo Venzke. 'Moving beyond Interdisciplinary Turf Wars: Towards an Understanding of International Law as Practice'. In *International Law as a Profession*, edited by Jean D'Aspremont, Jean and others (Cambridge University Press, 2017).

Aalberts, Tanja and Thomas Gammeltoft-Hansen. *The Changing Practices of International Law* (Cambridge University Press, 2018).

Abbott, Kenneth W and Thomas J Biersteker, eds. *Informal Governance in World Politics* (Cambridge University Press, 2024).

Abi-Saab, Georges. 'Interprétation et Auto-Interprétation. Quelques Réflexions sur Leur Rôle dans la Formation et la Résolution du Différend International'. In *Recht zwischen Umbruch und Bewahrung Völkerrecht, Europarrecht, Staatsrecht: Festschrift für Rudolf Bernhardt*, edited by Ulrich Beyerlin and others (Springer Verlag, 1995).

Abi-Saab, Georges. *International Change and the International Legal Order* (The Ecumenical Institute Bossey World Council of Churches, 1970).

Acharya, Amitav. *Constructing Global Order: Agency and Change in World Politics* (Cambridge University Press, 2018).

Acharya, Amitav. *The End of American World Order* (John Wiley & Sons, 2014).

Alschner, Wolfgang. *Investment Arbitration and State-Driven Reform: New Treaties, Old Outcomes* (Oxford University Press, 2022).

Alter, Karen J, Laurence R Helfer and Mikael Rask Madsen, eds. *International Court Authority* (Oxford University Press, 2018).

Alter, Karen J. 'The Evolution of International Law and Courts'. In *International Politics and Institutions in Time*, edited by Orfeo Fioretos (Oxford University Press, 2017).

Alter, Karen. *The New Terrain of International Law: Courts, Politics, Rights* (Princeton University Press, 2014).

Alvarez, José E. *International Organizations as Law-Makers* (Oxford University Press, 2005).

Anand, Ram Prakash. 'Mare Liberum vs. Mare Clausum'. In *Origin and Development of the Law of the Sea: History of International Law Revised* (Brill Nijhoff, 2022).

Andenas, Mads and Eirik Bjorge, eds. *A Farewell to Fragmentation: Reassertion and Convergence in International Law* (Cambridge University Press, 2015).

Andreopoulos, George. 'Better Late than Never? The Evolving Responsibility of International Organizations'. In *Contesting Human Rights: Norms, Institutions and Practice*, edited by Alison Brysk and Michael Stohl (Edward Elgar Publishing, 2019).

Arnauld, Andreas von, Kerstin von der Decken and Mart Susi. *The Cambridge Handbook of New Human Rights: Recognition, Novelty, Rhetoric* (Cambridge University Press, 2020).

Arts, Bas. 'Non-State Actors in Global Environmental Governance: New Arrangements Beyond the State'. In *New Modes of Governance in the Global System: Exploring Publicness, Delegation and Inclusiveness*, edited by Mathias Koenig-Archibugi and Michael Zürn (Palgrave Macmillan UK, 2006).

Atapattu, Sumudu. *Emerging Principles of International Environmental Law* (Brill/Nijhoff, 2007).

Avant, Deborah D, Martha Finnemore and Susan K Sell. 'Who Governs the Globe?'. In *Who Governs the Globe?*, edited by Deborah Avant, Martha Finnemore and Susan K Sell (Cambridge University Press, 2010).

Baer, Madeline. *Stemming the Tide: Human Rights and Water Policy in a Neoliberal World* (Oxford University Press, 2017).
Balcerzak. Filip. 'Investor–State Arbitration and Human Rights'. In *Investor–State Arbitration and Human Rights* (Brill Nijhoff, 2017).
Barnett, Michael and Martha Finnemore. *Rules for the World: International Organizations in Global Politics* (Cornell University Press, 2004).
Barton, John H, Judith L Goldstein, Timothy E Josling and Richard H Steinberg. *The Evolution of the Trade Regime: Politics, Law, and Economics of the GATT and the WTO* (Princeton University Press, 2006).
Bassiouni, Cherif M. 'The History of Universal Jurisdiction and Its Place in International Law'. In *Universal Jurisdiction: National Courts and the Prosecution of Serious Crimes under International Law*, edited by Stephen Macedo (University of Pennsylvania Press, 2004).
Basyūnī, M Sharīf. *Introduction to International Criminal Law*, 2nd rev. ed. (Martinus Nijhoff, 2013).
Bates, Edward. 'History'. In *International Human Rights Law*, edited by Daniel Moeckli, Sangeeta Shah and Sandesh Sivakumaran, 3rd ed. (Oxford University Press, 2018).
Behn, Daniel, Ole Kristian Fauchald and Malcolm Langford. *The Legitimacy of Investment Arbitration: Empirical Perspectives* (Cambridge University Press, 2022).
Bellamy, Richard. *A Republican Europe of States: Cosmopolitanism, Intergovernmentalism and Democracy in the EU* (Cambridge University Press, 2019).
Benvenisti, Eyal, Georg Nolte and Keren Yalin-Mor, eds. *Community Interests Across International Law* (Oxford University Press, 2018).
Bernstein, Steven and Marion Laurence, 'Practices and Norms: Relationships, Disjunctures and Change'. In *Conceptualizing International Practices: Directions for the Practice Turn in International Relations*, edited by Alena Drieschova, Christian Bueger and Ted Hopf (Cambridge University Press, 2022).
Bernstorff, Jochen von and Philipp Dann, eds. *The Battle for International Law: South-North Perspectives on the Decolonization Era* (Oxford University Press, 2019).
Besson, Samantha and Jean d'Aspremont, eds. *The Oxford Handbook on the Sources of International Law* (Oxford University Press, 2017).
Besson, Samantha and John Tasioulas, eds. *The Philosophy of International Law* (Oxford University Press, 2010).
Besson, Samantha. 'Sources of International Human Rights Law: How General Is General International Law?'. In *The Oxford Handbook of the Sources of International Law*, edited by Samantha Besson and Jean d'Aspremont (Oxford University Press, 2017).
Beyerlin, Ulrich and Thilo Marauhn. *International Environmental Law* (Hart Publishing, 2011).
Bianchi, Andrea and Moshe Hirsch. *International Law's Invisible Frames: Social Cognition and Knowledge Production in International Legal Processes* (Oxford University Press, 2021).
Bianchi, Andrea. 'Epistemic Communities'. In *Concepts for International Law*, edited by Jean d'Aspremont and Sahib Singh (Edward Elgar Publishing, 2019).
Bianchi, Andrea. *International Law Theories: An Inquiry into Different Ways of Thinking* (Oxford University Press, 2016).
Birnie, Patricia, Alan Boyle and Catherine Redgwell. *International Law and the Environment* (Oxford University Press, 2009).
Bloomfield, Alan and Shirley V Scott, eds. *Norm Antipreneurs and the Politics of Resistance to Global Normative Change* (Taylor & Francis, 2016).
Bodansky, Daniel, Jutta Brunnée and Lavanya Rajamani. *International Climate Change Law* (Oxford University Press, 2017).
Bodansky, Daniel. 'The Precautionary Principle in US Environmental Law'. In *Interpreting the Precautionary Principle*, edited by Timothy O'Riordan and James Cameron (Routledge, 2013).
Bourdieu, Pierre and Loïc J D Wacquant. *An Invitation to Reflexive Sociology*, 1st ed. (University of Chicago Press, 1992).
Bourdieu, Pierre. *Distinction: A Social Critique of the Judgement of Taste* (Harvard University Press, 1984).

Boyle, Alan and Christine Chinkin. *The Making of International Law* (Oxford University Press, 2007).
Bradford, Anu. *Digital Empires: The Global Battle to Regulate Technology* (Oxford University Press, 2023).
Bradford, Anu. *The Brussels Effect: How the European Union Rules the World* (Oxford University Press, 2020).
Bradley, Curtis A. 'Customary International Law Adjudication as Common Law Adjudication'. In *Custom's Future: International Law in a Changing World*, edited by Curtis A Bradley (Cambridge University Press, 2016).
Brölmann, Catherine and Yannick Radi. 'Introduction: International Lawmaking in a Global World'. In *Research Handbook on the Theory and Practice of International Lawmaking*, edited by Catherine Brölmann and Yannick Radi (Edward Elgar Publishing, 2016).
Brown, Chris and Robyn Eckersley, eds. *The Oxford Handbook of International Political Theory* (Oxford University Press, 2018).
Brummer, Chris. *Soft Law and the Global Financial System: Rule Making in the 21st Century*, 2nd ed. (Cambridge University Press, 2015).
Brunnée, Jutta and Stephen J Toope. 'Shared Understandings: The Underpinnings of Law'. In *Legitimacy and Legality in International Law. An Interactional Account* (Cambridge University Press, 2010).
Brunnée, Jutta and Stephen J Toope. *Legitimacy and Legality in International Law. An Interactional Account* (Cambridge University Press, 2010).
Brütsch, Christian and Dirk Lehmkuhl, eds. *Law and Legalization in Transnational Relations* (Routledge, 2007).
Bueger, Christian and Frank Gadinger. *International Practice Theory*, 2nd ed. (Springer, 2018).
Bulkeley, Harriet and others. *Transnational Climate Change Governance* (Cambridge University Press, 2014).
Bulkeley, Harriet and Peter Newell. *Governing Climate Change*, 3rd ed. (Taylor & Francis, 2023).
Bull, Hedley and Adam Watson, eds. *The Expansion of International Society* (Oxford University Press, 1984).
Byers, Michael. *Custom, Power and the Power of Rules: International Relations and Customary International Law* (Cambridge University Press, 1999).
Cai, Congyan. *The Rise of China and International Law: Taking Chinese Exceptionalism Seriously* (Oxford University Press, 2019).
Capoccia, Giovanni. 'Critical Junctures'. In *The Oxford Handbook of Historical Institutionalism*, edited by Orfeo Fioretos and others (Oxford University Press, 2016).
Carr, Edward Hallett. *The Twenty Years' Crisis, 1919-1939* (Springer, 2016).
Cassese, Antonio and Joseph H H Weiler, eds. *Change and Stability in International Law-Making* (Walter de Gruyter, 1988).
Cassese, Antonio and Mireille Delmas-Marty. *Juridictions Nationales et Crimes Internationaux* (Presses Universitaires de France, 2002).
Castañeda, Jorge G. *Legal Effects of United Nations Resolutions* (Columbia University Press, 1969).
Chayes, Abram, Thomas Ehrlich and Andreas F Lowenfeld. *International Legal Process: Materials for an Introductory Course in Two Volumes* (Little, Brown, 1968).
Chimni, Bhupinder Singh. 'Epilogue: Fragmentary Thoughts on Informal Change'. In *The Many Paths of Change in International Law*, edited by Nico Krisch and Ezgi Yildiz (Oxford University Press, 2023).
Clapham, Andrew and Paola Gaeta. *The Oxford Handbook of International Law in Armed Conflict* (Oxford University Press, 2014).
Clapham, Andrew. 'Préface', In *Immunités et violations graves des droits humains: vers une évolution structurelle de l'ordre juridique international?*, edited by Annyssa Bellal (Bruylant, 2011).
Claussen, Kathleen. 'The Experimental Evolution of Trade Law'. In *Is the International Legal Order Unraveling?*, edited by David L Sloss (Oxford University Press, 2022).
Cohen, Harlan Grant. 'Fragmentation'. In *Concepts for International Law*, edited by Jean d'Aspremont and Sahib Singh (Edward Elgar Publishing, 2018).

Condorelli, Luigi and Gaetano Arangio-Ruiz. In *Change and Stability in International Law-Making*, edited by Antonio Cassese and Joseph H H Weiler (Walter de Gruyter, 1988).
Connors, Jane. 'United Nations'. In *International Human Rights Law*, edited by Daniel Moeckli, Sangeeta Shah and Sandesh Sivakumaran, 3rd ed. (Oxford University Press, 2018).
Corell, Elisabeth Corell and Michele M Betsill. 'NGO Influence in International Environmental Negotiations: A Framework for Analysis'. In *International Environmental Governance* (Routledge, 2008).
Cosnard, Michel. 'Les immunités du chef d'état'. In *Le chef d'Etat et le droit international: colloque de Clermont-Ferrand* (A Pedone, 2002).
Crawford and Pert. *International Humanitarian Law* (Brill Nijhoff, 2018).
Crawford, Emily. *Identifying the Enemy* (Oxford University Press, 2015).
Crawford, James. *Brownlie's Principles of Public International Law*, 9th ed. (Oxford University Press, 2019).
Crawford, James. *Chance, Order, Change: The Course of International Law: General Course on Public International Law* (Hague Academy of International Law, 2014).
Crawford, James. *The International Law Commission's Articles on State Responsibility: Introduction, Text and Commentaries* (Cambridge University Press, 2002).
Cryer, Robert. *An Introduction to International Criminal Law and Procedure*, 3rd ed. (Cambridge University Press, 2014).
d'Aspremont, Jean, ed. *Participants in the International Legal System: Multiple Perspectives on Non-State Actors in International Law* (Taylor & Francis, 2011).
d'Aspremont, Jean. *Formalism and the Sources of International Law: A Theory of the Ascertainment of Legal Rules* (Oxford University Press, 2011).
d'Aspremont, Jean. *International Law as a Belief System* (Cambridge University Press, 2017).
d'Aspremont, Jean. 'Towards a New Theory of Sources in International Law'. In *The Oxford Handbook of the Theory of International Law*, edited by Anne Orford and Florian Hoffman (Oxford University Press, 2016).
Davis, Kevin E and others, eds. *Governance by Indicators: Global Power through Classification and Rankings* (Oxford University Press, 2012).
Deplano, Rossana. *Empirical and Theoretical Perspectives on International Law: How States Use the UN General Assembly to Create International Obligations* (Cambridge University Press, 2022).
Derrig, Rián. *The New Haven School: American International Law* (Oxford University Press, 2025).
Diehl, Paul F and Charlotte Ku. *The Dynamics of International Law* (Cambridge University Press, 2010).
Donnelly, Jack. *Universal Human Rights in Theory and Practice*, 3rd ed. (Cornell University Press, 2013).
Duffy, Helen. *Strategic Human Rights Litigation: Understanding and Maximising Impact* (Bloomsbury Publishing, 2018).
Dumouchel, Joelle. 'For a Practice Approach to Authority: The Emergence of Central Bankers' International Authority'. In *Conceptualizing International Practices: Directions for the Practice Turn in International Relations*, edited by Alena Drieschova, Christian Bueger and Ted Hopf (Cambridge University Press, 2022).
Dupuy, Pierre-Marie. *L'unité de l'ordre juridique international: cours général de droit international public* (M Nijhoff, 2003).
Dzehtsiarou, Kanstantsin. *European Consensus and the Legitimacy of the European Court of Human Rights* (Cambridge University Press, 2015).
Ebbesson, Jonas and Ellen Hey. 'Introduction: The Sustainable Development Goals, Agenda 2030, and International Law'. In *The Cambridge Handbook of the Sustainable Development Goals and International Law*, edited by Jonas Ebbesson and Ellen Hey (Cambridge University Press, 2022).

Ellis, Jaye. 'The Turn to Metrics in International Environmental Law'. In *The Many Paths of Change in International Law*, edited by Nico Krisch and Ezgi Yildiz (Oxford University Press, 2023).
Endres, Dorothea. 'The Definition of Investment'. In *The Paths of International Law: Case Studies*, edited by Pedro Martínez Esponda and others (SSRN, 2023).
Endres, Dorothea. 'Direct Participation in Hostilities'. In *The Paths of International Law: Case Studies*, edited by Pedro Martínez Esponda and others (SSRN, 2023).
Endres, Dorothea. 'The Relationship between IHRL and IHL'. In *The Paths of International Law: Case Studies*, edited by Pedro Martínez Esponda and others (SSRN, 2023).
Endres, Dorothea. 'Direct Human Rights Obligations of Corporations'. In *The Paths of International Law: Case Studies*, edited by Pedro Martínez Esponda and others (SSRN, 2023).
Endres, Dorothea. 'Rape as a War Crime'. In *The Paths of International Law: Case Studies*, edited by Pedro Martínez Esponda and others (SSRN, 2023).
Endres, Dorothea. 'The Human Right to a "Good" Environment'. In *The Paths of International Law: Case Studies*, edited by Pedro Martínez Esponda and others (SSRN, 2023).
Endres, Dorothea. 'Whose International Law Is Changing? The Practice of Fragmented Communities Constructing Legal Change'. In *The Many Paths of International Law*, edited by Nico Krisch and Ezgi Yildiz (Oxford University Press, 2023).
Evans, Malcolm D, ed. *International Law*, 3rd ed. (Oxford University Press, 2010).
Fasciglione, Marco. 'A Binding Instrument on Business and Human Rights as a Source of International Obligations for Private Companies: Utopia or Reality?'. In *Legal Sources in Business and Human Rights* (Brill Nijhoff, 2020).
Fioretos, Orfeo and Stephanie Hofmann. 'Global Complexity in Time: Structures, Agency, and Experiences'. In *Experiencing Worlds of Complexity: Creative Agency and Global Governance in Time* (manuscript), edited by Orfeo Fioretos and Stephanie Hofmann.
Fioretos, Orfeo, Tulia G Falleti and Adam Sheingate, eds. *The Oxford Handbook of Historical Institutionalism* (Oxford University Press, 2016).
Fligstein, Neil and Doug McAdam. *A Theory of Fields* (Oxford University Press, 2012).
Forere, Malebakeng Agnes. *The Relationship of WTO Law and Regional Trade Agreements in Dispute Settlement: From Fragmentation to Coherence*, vol 50 (Kluwer Academic, 2015).
Forsythe, David P. *The Humanitarians: The International Committee of the Red Cross* (Cambridge University Press, 2005).
Friedman, Richard. 'On the Concept of Authority in Political Philosophy'. In *Authority*, edited by Joseph Raz (New York University Press, 1990).
Friedmann, Wolfgang. *The Changing Structure of International Law* (Columbia University Press, 1964).
Fukuyama, Francis. *The End of History and the Last Man* (Penguin UK, 1993).
Future Topic and Problems of the International Legislative Process Part V [1998] International Law Commission Fifty Years After: An Evaluation. Proceedings of the Seminar Held to Commemorate the Fiftieth Anniversary of the International Law Commission (UN Publications, 2000).
Gaeta, Paola and Abhimanyu George Jain. 'Individualisation of IHL Through Criminal Responsibility for War Crimes and Some (Un)Intended Consequences'. In *The Individualisation of War*, edited by Dapo Akande and Jennifer Welsh (Oxford University Press, 2021).
Gaeta, Paola. 'The Interplay Between the Geneva Conventions and International Criminal Law'. In *The 1949 Geneva Conventions: A Commentary* (Oxford University Press, 2015).
Garcia, S M. 'Ocean Fisheries Management: The FAO Programme'. In *Ocean Management in Global Change*, edited by Paolo Fabbri (Elsevier Applied Science, 1992).
Gavouneli, Maria. *Functional Jurisdiction in the Law of the Sea* (Brill Nijhoff, 2007).
George, Alexander and Andrew Bennett, *Case Studies and Theory Development in the Social Sciences*, 4th printing ed. (The MIT Press, 2005).
Ginsburg, Tom. 'Political Constraints on International Courts'. In *The Oxford Handbook of International Adjudication*, edited by Cesare P R Romano, Karen J Alter and Yuval Shany (Oxford University Press, 2014).

Ginsburg, Tom. *Democracies and International Law* (Cambridge University Press, 2021).
Goertz, Gary. *International Norms and Decision Making: A Punctuated Equilibrium Model* (Rowman & Littlefield, 2003).
Goffman, Erving. *Frame Analysis: An Essay on the Organization of Experience* (Northeastern University Press, 1986).
Goldsmith, Jack L and Eric A Posner. *The Limits of International Law* (Oxford University Press, 2006).
Goldstein, Judith L and others, eds. *Legalization and World Politics* (MIT Press, 2001).
Gong, Gerrit W. *The Standard of 'Civilization' in International Society* (Clarendon Press Oxford, 1984).
Gordon, David J. *Cities on the World Stage: The Politics of Global Urban Climate Governance* (Cambridge University Press, 2020).
Grewe, Wilhelm G. *The Epochs of International Law* (Walter de Gruyter, 2000).
Grotius, Hugo. *The Freedom of the Seas* (CreateSpace Independent Publishing Platform, 2018).
Habermas, Jürgen. *Der Gespaltene Westen* (Suhrkamp Franfurt, 2004).
Haddad, Heidi Nichols. *The Hidden Hands of Justice: NGOs, Human Rights, and International Courts* (Cambridge University Press, 2018).
Hale, Thomas. David Held and Kevin Young, *Gridlock: Why Global Cooperation Is Failing When We Need It Most* (Polity, 2013).
Hall, Bruce Rodney and Thomas Biersteker, eds. *The Emergence of Private Authority in Global Governance* (Cambridge University Press, 2002).
Halvorssen, Anita M. 'The Origin and Development of International Environmental Law'. In *The Origin and Development of International Environmental Law*, edited by Alam Shawkat and others (Routledge, 2013).
Hart, H L A. *The Concept of Law*, 2nd ed. (Clarendon Press, 1994).
Held, David. *Democracy and the Global Order* (Cambridge University Press, 1995).
Helfer, Laurence. 'Pharmaceutical Patents and the Human Right to Health: The Contested Evolution of the Transnational Legal Order'. In *Transnational Legal Orders*, edited by Terence C Halliday and Gregory Shaffer (Cambridge University Press, 2015).
Heller, Kevin John. *The Nuremberg Military Tribunals and the Origins of International Criminal Law* (Oxford University Press, 2011).
Henderson, Christian. 'The United Nations and the Regulation of Cyber-Security'. In *Research Handbook on International Law and Cyberspace*, edited by Nicholas Tsagourias and Russell Buchan (Edward Elgar Publishing, 2021).
Higgins, Rosalyn. 'The Identity of International Law'. In *Themes and Theories*, edited by Rosalyn Higgins (Oxford University Press, 2009).
Higgins, Rosalyn. *Problems and Process: International Law and How We Use It* (Clarendon Press, 1995).
Hoagland, P, J Jacoby and M E Schumacher. 'Law of the Sea'. In *Encyclopedia of Ocean Sciences*, edited by John H Steele (Academic Press, 2001).
Holst, Rozemarijn Roland. *Change in the Law of the Sea: Context, Mechanisms and Practice* (Brill Nijhoff, 2022).
Holtermann, Jakob v H, Mikael Rask Madsen and Nora Stappert. 'International Lawyers, Legal Norms, and Contestations of Legal Validity'. In *Contesting the World: Norm Research in Theory and Practice*, edited by Phil Orchard and Antje Wiener (Cambridge University Press, 2024).
Hooghe, Liesbet, Tobias Lenz and Gary Marks. *A Theory of International Organization* (Oxford University Press, 2019).
Johnstone, Ian. 'The Power of Interpretive Communities'. In *Power in Global Governance*, edited by M Barnett and R Duvall (Cambridge University Press, 2005).
Johnstone, Ian. 'The Secretary-General as Norm Entrepreneur'. In Simon Chesterman, ed. *Secretary or General? The UN Secretary-General in World Politics* (Cambridge University Press, 2007).
Johnstone, Ian. *The Power of Deliberation: International Law, Politics and Organizations* (Oxford University Press, 2011).

Jupille, Joseph and James A Caporaso. *Theories of Institutions* (Cambridge University Press, 2022).

Jupille, Joseph, Walter Mattli and Duncan Snidal. 'Dynamics of Institutional Choice'. In *International politics and institutions in time*, edited by Orfeo Fioretos (Oxford University Press, 2017).

Jupille, Joseph, Walter Mattli and Duncan Snidal. *Institutional Choice and Global Commerce* (Cambridge University Press, 2013).

Kammerhofer, Jörg. 'Obligations Erga Omnes'. In *Max Planck Encyclopedias of International Law* (Oxford University Press, 2024).

McLachlan, Campbell. *The Principle of Systemic Integration in International Law* (Oxford University Press, 2024).

Keck, Margaret E and Kathryn Sikkink. *Activists Beyond Borders: Advocacy Networks in International Politics* (Cornell University Press, 2014).

Kennedy, David. *International Legal Structures* (Nomos, 1987).

Kiderlin, Nina and Pedro Martínez Esponda. 'Universal Jurisdiction'. In *The Paths of International Law: Case Studies*, edited by Pedro Martínez Esponda and others (SSRN, 2023).

Kiderlin, Nina. 'The Rules of Cyber Warfare'. In *The Paths of International Law: Case Studies*, edited by Pedro Martínez Esponda and others (SSRN, 2023).

Kiderlin, Nina. 'War Crimes in Non-International Armed Conflict'. In *The Paths of International Law: Case Studies*, edited by Pedro Martínez Esponda and others (SSRN, 2023).

Kiderlin, Nina. 'General Exceptions under GATT Article XX'. In *The Paths of International Law: Case Studies*, edited by Pedro Martínez Esponda and others (SSRN, 2023).

Kiderlin, Nina. 'Subsidies and the Definition of "Public Bodies"'. In *The Paths of International Law: Case Studies*, edited by Pedro Martínez Esponda and others (SSRN, 2023).

Kiderlin, Nina. 'World Trade Law and the Rise of China: Struggles over Subsidy Rules'. In *The Many Paths of Change in International Law*, edited by Nico Krisch and Ezgi Yildiz (Oxford University Press, 2023).

Kiderlin, Nina. 'Subsidies: A Changing Approach to "Public Bodies"'. In *The Paths of International Law: Case Studies*, edited by Pedro Martínez Esponda and others (SSRN, 2023).

Klabbers, Jan, Anne Peters and Geir Ulfstein. *The Constitutionalization of International Law*, 1st ed. (Oxford University Press, 2009).

Klabbers, Jan. '(I Can't Get No) Recognition: Subjects Doctrine and the Emergence of Non-State Actors'. In *Nordic Cosmopolitanism: Essays in International Law for Martti Koskenniemi* (Martinus Nijhoff, 2003).

Klinkner, Melanie and Howard Davis. *The Right to the Truth in International Law: Victims' Rights in Human Rights and International Criminal Law*, 1st ed. (Routledge, Taylor & Francis Group, Oxford University Press, 2020).

Knox, John H and Ramin Pejan. 'Introduction'. In *The Human Right to a Healthy Environment*, edited by John H Knox and Ramin Pejan (Cambridge University Press, 2018).

Knox, John H and Ramin Pejan. *The Human Right to a Healthy Environment* (Cambridge University Press, 2018).

Knutsen, Torbjørn L. 'Peaceful Change: The Interwar Era and the Disciplinary Context'. In *The Oxford Handbook of Peaceful Change in International Relations*, edited by T V Paul and others (Oxford University Press, 2022).

Koremenos, Barbara. *The Continent of International Law: Explaining Agreement Design* (Cambridge University Press, 2016).

Koskenniemi, Martti. *From Apology to Utopia: The Structure of International Legal Argument* (Cambridge University Press, 2005).

Koskenniemi Martti. 'Methodology of International Law', *Max Planck Encyclopedias of International Law*, 2007, https://opil.ouplaw.com/display/10.1093/law:epil/9780199231690/law-9780199231690-e1440.

Kothari, Miloon. 'From Commission to the Council: Evolution of UN Charter Bodies'. In *The Oxford Handbook of International Human Rights Law*, edited by Dinah Shelton (Oxford University Press, 2013).

Kratochwil, Friedrich. 'Practices and a "Theory" of Action? Some Conceptual Issues Concerning Ends, Reasons and Happiness'. In *Conceptualizing International Practices: Directions for the Practice Turn in International Relations*, edited by Alena Drieschova, Christian Bueger and Ted Hopf (Cambridge University Press, 2022).

Krieger, Heike and Andrea Liese, eds. *Tracing Value Change in the International Legal Order: Perspectives from Legal and Political Science* (Oxford University Press, 2023).

Krisch, Nico, ed. *Entangled Legalities beyond the State* (Cambridge University Press, 2021).

Krisch, Nico. 'Chapter VII Powers: The General Framework and Articles 39 to 43'. In *The United Nations Charter: A Commentary*, 3rd ed., edited by Bruno Simma and others (Oxford University Press, 2012).

Krisch, Nico. 'More Equal than the Rest? Hierarchy, Equality and US Predominance in International Law'. In *United States Hegemony and the Foundations of International Law*, edited by M Byers and G Nolte (Cambridge University Press, 2003).

Krisch, Nico. 'The Many Fields of (German) International Law'. In *Comparative International Law*, edited by Anthea Roberts and others (Oxford University Press, 2018).

Krisch, Nico. *Beyond Constitutionalism: The Pluralist Structure of Postnational Law* (Oxford University Press, 2010).

Krisch, Nico and Ezgi Yildiz, eds. *The Many Paths of Change in International Law* (Oxford University Press, 2023).

Kucik Jeffrey and Sergio Puig. 'The Appellate Body's Judicial Pathway: Precedent, Resistance and Adaptation'. In *The Many Paths of Change in International Law*, edited by Nico Krisch and Ezgi Yildiz (Oxford University Press, 2023).

Kurosaki, Masahiro. 'The Fight against Impunity for Core International Crimes: Reflections on the Contribution of Networked Experts to a Regime of Aggravated State Responsibility'. *Experts, Networks and Institutional Change*, online ed. (Cambridge University Press, 2017).

Lafontaine, Fannie and William Schabas A. 'National Jurisdictions'. In *International Criminal Law* (Cambridge University Press, 2016).

Lauterpacht, Hersch. 'The Legal Aspect'. In *Peaceful Change: An International Problem*, edited by C A W Manning (Macmillan, 1937).

Lauterpacht, Hersch. *The Function of Law in the International Community*, 2nd ed. (Oxford University Press, 2011).

Lefkowitz, David. *Philosophy and International Law: A Critical Introduction* (Cambridge University Press, 2020).

Lefkowitz, David. 'Sources in Legal-Positivist Theories: Law as Necessarily Posited and the Challenge of Customary Law Creation'. In *The Oxford Handbook of the Sources of International Law*, edited by Samantha Besson and Jean d'Aspremont (Oxford University Press, 2017).

Lewis, Corinne. *UNHCR and International Refugee Law: From Treaties to Innovation* (Routledge, 2012).

Luhmann, Niklas. *Das Recht der Gesellschaft* (Suhrkamp, 1993).

Lukes, Steven. *Power: A Radical View*, 2nd ed. (Palgrave Macmillan, 2004).

MacCormick, Neil. *Rhetoric and The Rule of Law: A Theory of Legal Reasoning* (Oxford University Press, 2005).

Macdonald, Terry. 'Sovereignty, Democracy, and Global Political Legitimacy'. In *The Oxford Handbook of International Political Theory*, edited by Chris Brown and Robyn Eckersley (Oxford University Press, 2018).

Mackenzie, Ruth and others. *Manual on International Courts and Tribunals* (Oxford University Press, 2010).

Mackinnon, Emma Stone. 'Contingencies of Context Legacies of the Algerian Revolution in the 1977 Additional Protocols to the Geneva Conventions'. In *Contingency in international law: on the possibility of different legal histories*, edited by Ingo Venzke and Kevin Jon Heller (Oxford University Press, 2021).

Mahoney, James and Kathleen Thelen. 'A Theory of Gradual Institutional Change'. In *Explaining Institutional Change: Ambiguity, Agency, and Power*, edited by James Mahoney and Kathleen Thelen (Cambridge University Press, 2010).

Mälksoo, Lauri. *Russian Approaches to International Law* (Oxford University Press, 2015).
Malone, Linda and Scott Pasternack. *Defending the Environment: Civil Society Strategies to Enforce International Environmental Law* (Island Press, 2006).
Manning, CAW, ed. *Peaceful Change: An International Problem* (Macmillan, 1937).
Mantilla, Giovanni. *Lawmaking under Pressure: International Humanitarian Law and Internal Armed Conflict* (Cornell University Press, 2020).
Margalit, Avishai. *On Compromise and Rotten Compromises* (Princeton University Press, 2010).
Mark, Stephan, Graham Marshall and Michael McGinnis. 'An Introduction to Polycentricity and Governance'. In *Governing Complexity: Analyzing and Applying Polycentricity*, edited by Andreas Thiel, William A Blomquist and Dustin E Garrick (Cambridge University Press, 2019).
Marks, Susan. *The Riddle of All Constitutions: International Law, Democracy, and the Critique of Ideology* (Oxford University Press, 2003).
Martínez Esponda, Pedro and others. *Paths of Change in International Law: Case Studies* (SSRN, 2023).
Martínez Esponda, Pedro. 'State Official Immunity'. In *The Paths of International Law: Case Studies*, edited by Pedro Martínez Esponda and others (SSRN, 2023).
Martínez Esponda, Pedro. 'The Concept of Internationally Wrongful Act'. In *The Paths of International Law: Case Studies*, edited by Pedro Martínez Esponda and others (SSRN, 2023).
Martínez Esponda, Pedro. 'Differentiated Treatment in the GATT System'. In *The Paths of International Law: Case Studies*, edited by Pedro Martínez Esponda and others (SSRN, 2023).
Martínez Esponda, Pedro. 'The Doctrine of Police Powers in Indirect Expropriation'. In *The Paths of International Law: Case Studies*, edited by Pedro Martínez Esponda and others (SSRN, 2023).
Martínez Esponda, Pedro. 'The Development of Fair and Equitable Treatment'. In *The Paths of International Law: Case Studies*, edited by Pedro Martínez Esponda and others (SSRN, 2023).
Martínez Esponda, Pedro. 'Self-Defense against Non-State Actors'. In *The Paths of International Law: Case Studies*, edited by Pedro Martínez Esponda and others (SSRN, 2023).
Martínez Esponda, Pedro. 'Norm-Instability as a Strategy in International Law-Making: The Case of Self-Defence against Non-State Actors'. In *The Many Paths of International Legal Change*, edited by Nico Krisch and Ezgi Yildiz (Oxford University Press, 2023).
Martínez Esponda, Pedro. 'The Effects Doctrine of Jurisdiction'. In *The Paths of International Law: Case Studies*, edited by Pedro Martínez Esponda and others (SSRN, 2023).
Matsushita, Mitsuo and others. *The World Trade Organization: Law, Practice, and Policy*, 3rd ed. (Oxford University Press, 2015).
Messenger, Gregory. *The Development of World Trade Organization Law: Examining Change in International Law* (Oxford University Press, 2016).
Miéville, China. *Between Equal Rights: A Marxist Theory of International Law* (Brill, 2005).
Milanovic, Marko. 'The Lost Origins of Lex Specialis: Rethinking the Relationship between Human Rights and International Humanitarian Law'. In *Theoretical Boundaries of Armed Conflict and Human Rights*, edited by Jens David Ohlin (Cambridge University Press, 2016).
Miles, Kate, *The Origins of International Investment Law: Empire, Environment and the Safeguarding of Capital* (Cambridge University Press, 2013).
Miller, David. *National Responsibility and Global Justice* (Oxford University Press, 2007).
Molenaar, Erik J. 'Port State Jurisdiction to Combat IUU Fishing: The Port State Measures Agreement'. In *Recasting Transboundary Fisheries Management Arrangements in Light of Sustainability Principles*, edited by Dawn A. Russell and David L. VanderZwaag (Brill|Nijhoff, 2011).
Molenaar, Erik J. 'Port State Jurisdiction'. *Max Planck Encyclopedias of International Law* (Oxford University Press, 2014).
Moore, Sally Falk. *Law as Process: An Anthropological Approach* (Routledge & Kegan Paul, 1978).
Moyn, Samuel and Umut Özsu. 'The Historical Origins and Setting of the Friendly Relations Declaration'. In *The UN Friendly Relations Declaration at 50*, edited by Jorge E Viñuales, 1st ed. (Cambridge University Press, 2020).

Muchlinski, Peter, Federico Ortino and Christoph Schreuer. *The Oxford Handbook of International Investment Law* (Oxford University Press, 2008).

Mührel, Linus. *The Authority of the International Committee of the Red Cross* (DeGruyter Brill, 2024).

Murphy, Liam. *What Makes Law: An Introduction to the Philosophy of Law* (Cambridge University Press, 2014).

Narlikar, Amrita, *International Trade and Developing Countries: Bargaining Coalitions in GATT and WTO* (Routledge, 2004).

Nguyen, Lan Ngoc. *The Development of the Law of the Sea by UNCLOS Dispute Settlement Bodies* (Cambridge University Press, 2023).

Nolte, Georg, ed. *Treaties and Subsequent Practice* (Oxford University Press, 2013).

Noortmann, Math, August Reinisch and Cedric Ryngaert, eds. *Non-State Actors in International Law* (Bloomsbury Publishing, 2015).

Nordhaus, William D. 'Paul Samuelson and Global Public Goods'. In *Samuelsonian Economics and the Twenty-First Century*, edited by Michael Szenberg and others (Oxford University Press, 2006).

Oanta, Gabriela A. 'Illegal Fishing as a Criminal Act at Sea'. In *Crimes at Sea*, edited by K N Trapp and E Papastavridis (Brill, 2014).

Onuma, Yasuaki. *A Transcivilizational Perspective on International Law* (Brill, 2010).

Orchard, Phil and Antje Wiener. 'Introduction: Norm Research in Theory and Practice'. In *Contesting the World: Norm Research in Theory and Practice*, edited by Phil Orchard and Antje Wiener (Cambridge University Press, 2024).

Ortino, Federico. *The Origin and Evolution of Investment Treaty Standards: Stability, Value, and Reasonableness* (Oxford University Press, 2019).

Özsu, Umut. 'An Anti-Imperialist Universalism? *Jus Cogens* and the Politics of International Law'. In *International Law and Empire: Historical Explorations*, edited by Martti Koskenniemi and others (Oxford University Press, 2017).

Özsu, Umut. *Completing Humanity: The International Law of Decolonization, 1960–82* (Cambridge University Press, 2023).

Pahuja, Sundhya. *Decolonising International Law: Development, Economic Growth, and the Politics of Universality* (Cambridge University Press, 2011).

Pappa, Marianthi. *Non-State Actors' Rights in Maritime Delimitation: Lessons from Land* (Cambridge University Press, 2021).

Pauwelyn, Joost, Ramses Wessel and Jan Wouters, eds. *Informal International Lawmaking* (Oxford University Press, 2012).

Pauwelyn, Joost. *Conflict of Norms in Public International Law* (Cambridge University Press, 2003).

Pereira, Eduardo Guedes and Marianthi Pappa. 'The Relationship between Host Government Contracts for Oil and Gas Activities and Public Participation'. In *Regulation of Extractive Industries: Community Engagement in the Arctic*, edited by Rachael Lorna Johnstone and Anne Merrild Hansen (Routledge, 2020).

Perelman, Chaïm. *The Idea of Justice and the Problem of Argument* (Routledge & Kegan Paul, 1963).

Petrov, Anton O. *Expert Laws of War: Restating and Making Law in Expert Processes* (Edward Elgar Publishing, 2020).

Pierson, Paul. *Politics in Time: History, Institutions, and Social Analysis* (Princeton University Press, 2004).

Pilar, Elizalde. 'A Horizontal Pathway to Impact? An Assessment of the Universal Periodic Review at 10'. In *Contesting Human Rights: Norms, Institutions and Practice*, edited by Alison Brysk and Michael Stohl (Edward Elgar Publishing, 2019).

Pollack, Mark A and Gregory C Shaffer. *When Cooperation Fails: The International Law and Politics of Genetically Modified Foods* (Oxford University Press, 2009).

Pollack, Mark A. 'Trump as a Change Agent in International Law Ends, Means, and Legacies'. In *The Many Paths of Change in International Law*, edited by Nico Krisch and Ezgi Yildiz (Oxford University Press, 2023).

Porter, Theodore M. *Trust in Numbers*, reprint ed. (Princeton University Press, 1996).

Posner, Eric A and A O Sykes. *Economic Foundations of International Law* (Harvard University Press, 2013).

Pound, Roscoe. *Interpretations of Legal History* (Cambridge University Press, 1967).

Purcell, Kate, *Geographical Change and the Law of the Sea* (Oxford University Press, 2019).

Radu, Roxana. *Negotiating Internet Governance* (Oxford University Press, 2019).

Rajamani, Lavanya and Jacqueline Peel, eds. *The Oxford Handbook of International Environmental Law*, 2nd edition (Oxford University Press, 2021).

Rajkovic, Nikolas M, Tanja E Aalberts and Thomas Gammeltoft-Hansen. 'Introduction: Legality, Interdisciplinarity and the Study of Practices'. In *The Power of Legality: Practices of International Law and their Politics*, edited by Nikolas M Rajkovic, Tanja E Aalberts and Thomas Gammeltoft-Hansen (Cambridge University Press, 2016).

Ranganathan, Surabhi. *Strategically Created Treaty Conflicts and the Politics of International Law* (Cambridge University Press, 2014).

Rao, Pemmaraju Sreenivasa. 'International Law Commission (ILC)'. In *Max Planck Encyclopedia of Public International Law* (Oxford University Press, 2017).

Raymond, Mark. *Social Practices of Rule-Making in World Politics* (Oxford University Press, 2019).

Reiners, Nina. 'World Trade Law and the Rise of China: Struggles over Subsidy Rules'. In *The Many Paths of Change in International Law*, edited by Nico Krisch and Ezgi Yildiz (Oxford University Press, 2023).

Reiners, Nina. 'Transnational Lawmaking Coalitions as Change Agents in International Law'. In *The Many Paths of Change in International Law*, edited by Nico Krisch and Ezgi Yildiz (Oxford University Press, 2023).

Reiners, Nina. *Transnational Lawmaking Coalitions for Human Rights* (Cambridge University Press, 2021).

Reydams, Luc. *Universal Jurisdiction: International and Municipal Legal Perspectives* (Oxford University Press, 2004).

Roberts, Anthea and others, eds. *Comparative International Law* (Oxford University Press, 2018).

Roberts, Anthea and Sandesh Sivakumaran. 'The Theory and Reality of the Sources of International Law'. In *International Law*, edited by Malcolm D Evans, 5th ed. (Oxford University Press, 2018).

Roger, Charles B. *The Origins of Informality: Why the Legal Foundations of Global Governance Are Shifting, and Why It Matters* (Oxford University Press, 2020).

Rosa, Hartmut. *Beschleunigung: Die Veränderung der Zeitstrukturen in der Moderne* (Suhrkamp Verlag, 2005).

Rosendorff, Peter. 'Domestic Politics and International Disputes (Chapter 8)'. In *The Oxford Handbook of the Political Economy of International Trade*, edited by Lisa L Martin, 1st ed. (Oxford University Press, 2015).

Rothwell, Donald R and others, eds. *The Oxford Handbook of the Law of the Sea*, 1st edition (Oxford University Press, 2017).

Ruggie, John G. 'The Social Construction of the UN Guiding Principles on Business and Human Rights'. In *Research Handbook on Human Rights and Business*, edited by Surya Deva and David Birchall (Edward Elgar Publishing, 2020).

Ruggie, John G. *Just Business* (Norton & Company, 2013).

Sadat, Leila Nadya. *Forging a Convention for Crimes against Humanity* (Cambridge University Press, 2011).

Sand, Peter H. 'Origin and History'. In *The Oxford Handbook of International Environmental Law*, edited by Lavanya Rajamani and Jacqueline Peel, 2nd ed. (Oxford University Press, 2021).

Sandholtz, Wayne and Adam Feldman. 'The Trans-Regional Construction of Human Rights'. In *Contesting Human Rights: Norms, Institutions and Practice*, edited by Alison Brysk and Michael Stohl (Edward Elgar Publishing, 2019).
Sandholtz, Wayne and Kendall W Stiles. *International Norms and Cycles of Change* (Oxford University Press, 2009).
Sandholtz, Wayne. *Prohibiting Plunder: How Norms Change* (Oxford University Press, 2007).
Sandholtz, Wayne. 'International Norm Change'. *Oxford Research Encyclopedia of Politics*, 2017. https://oxfordre.com/view/10.1093/acrefore/9780190228637.001.0001/acrefore-9780190228637-e-588.
Sandholtz, Wayne. 'Resurgent Authoritarianism, Rights, and Legal Change'. In *The Many Paths of Change in International Law*, edited by Nico Krisch and Ezgi Yildiz (Oxford University Press, 2023).
Sands, Philippe, ed. *Greening International Law* (Routledge, 1993).
Sarfaty, Galit. *Values in Translation: Human Rights and the Culture of the World Bank* (Stanford University Press, 2012).
Sassan, Gholiagha and others, eds. *The Oxford Handbook of Norms Research in International Relations* (Oxford University Press, 2025).
Sassòli, Marco. *International Humanitarian Law: Rules, Controversies, and Solution as to Problems Arising in Warfare* (Edward Elgar Publishing, 2019).
Sassòli, Marco, Antoine A Bouvier and Anne Quintin avec la collab de Juliane Garcia. *Un Droit dans la Guerre?* (Comité International de la Croix-Rouge, 2012).
Schabas, William A. 'Time, Justice, and Human Rights: Statutory Limitation on the Right to Truth?'. In Understanding the Age of Transitional Justice (Rutgers University Press, 2018).
Scharf, Michael P. *Customary International Law in Times of Fundamental Change: Recognizing Grotian Moments* (Cambridge University Press, 2013).
Schauer, Frederick. *Thinking like a Lawyer: A New Introduction to Legal Reasoning* (Harvard University Press, 2009).
Schill, Stephan W. *The Multilateralization of International Investment Law* (Cambridge University Press, 2009).
Schmidt, Vivien A. 'The State and Political Economic Change: Beyond Rational Choice and Historical Institutionalism to Discursive Institutionalism'. In *State, Globalization and Multilateralism: The Challenges of Institutionalizing Regionalism*, edited by Mario Telò (Springer Netherlands, 2012).
Schröder, Meinhard. 'Precautionary Approach/Principle'. In *Max Planck Encyclopedias of International Law* (Oxford University Press, 2014).
Schwebel, Stephen M. 'The Inter-Active Influence of the International Court of Justice and the International Law Commission'. In *Liber Amicorum `In Memoriam' of Judge José María Ruda*, edited by Calixto A Armas Barea and others (Brill, 2000).
Schwöbel-Patel, Christine. *Marketing Global Justice: The Political Economy of International Criminal Law*, vol Series Number 151 (Cambridge University Press, 2021).
Scott, Joanne. 'Unilateralism, Extraterritoriality and Climate Change'. In *Climate Change Law*, edited by Daniel A Farber and Marjan Peeters (Edward Elgar Publishing, 2016).
Sending, Ole Jacob. *The Politics of Expertise: Competing for Authority in Global Governance* (Michigan University Press, 2015).
Setzer, Joana and Catherine Higham. 'Global Trends in Climate Change Litigation: 2024 Snapshot' (Grantham Research Institute on Climate Change and the Environment and Centre for Climate Change Economics and Policy, London School of Economics and Political Science, 2024).
Shaffer, Gregory C. *Emerging Powers and the World Trading System: The Past and Future of International Economic Law* (Cambridge University Press, 2021).
Shaw, Malcolm N. *International Law* (Cambridge University Press, 2017).
Shelton, Dinah, ed. *The Oxford Handbook of International Human Rights Law*, Reprint edition (Oxford University Press, 2015).
Schütze, Robert. *European Constitutional Law* (Oxford University Press, 2021).

Simma, Bruno. 'From Bilateralism to Community Interest in International Law'. In *Recueil des Cours*, vol 250 (Martinus Nijhoff, 1994).

Sinclair, Guy Fiti. 'A Battlefield Transformed: The United Nations and the Struggle over Postcolonial Statehood'. In *The Battle for International Law: South-North Perspectives on the Decolonization Era*, edited by Jochen von Bernstorff and Philipp Dann (Oxford University Press, 2019).

Sinclair, Guy Fiti. *To Reform the World: International Organizations and the Making of Modern States* (Oxford University Press, 2017).

Sivakumaran, Sandesh. *The Law of Non-International Armed Conflict*, 1st ed. (Oxford University Press, 2012).

Slaughter, Anne-Marie. *A New World Order* (Princeton University Press, 2004).

Slobodian, Quinn. *Globalists: The End of Empire and the Birth of Neoliberalism* (Harvard University Press, 2018).

Soave, Tommaso. *The Everyday Makers of International Law: From Great Halls to Back Rooms* (Cambridge University Press, 2022).

Somos, Mark. 'Open and Closed Seas: The Grotius-Selden Dialogue at the Heart of Liberal Imperialism'. *Empire and Legal Thought* (Brill Nijhoff, 2020).

Sornarajah, M. *Resistance and Change in the International Law on Foreign Investment* (Cambridge University Press, 2015).

St. John, Taylor. *The Rise of Investor-State Arbitration: Politics, Law, and Unintended Consequences* (Oxford University Press, 2018).

Steinberg, Richard H. 'Wanted—Dead or Alive: Realism in International Law'. In *Interdisciplinary Perspectives on International Law and International Relations: The State of the Art*, edited by Jeffrey L Dunoff and Mark A Pollack (Cambridge University Press, 2012).

Stephen, Matthew. 'Contestation Overshoot: Rising Powers, NGOs, and the Failure of the WTO Doha Round'. In *Contested World Orders*, edited by Matthew Stephen and Michael Zürn (Oxford University Press, 2019).

Stimmer, Anette. *The Politics of International Norms: A Rhetorical Approach* (Cambridge University Press, 2025).

Streeck, Wolfgang and Kathleen Thelen, eds. *Beyond Continuity: Institutional Change in Advanced Political Economies* (Oxford University Press, 2005).

Streeck, Wolfgang and Kathleen Thelen. 'Introduction: Institutional Change in Advanced Political Economies'. In *Beyond continuity: institutional change in advanced political economies*, edited by Wolfgang Streeck and Kathleen Thelen (Oxford University Press, 2005).

Strupp, Karl. *Legal Machinery for Peaceful Change* (Constable & Company Limited, 1937).

Sweet, Alec Stone. 'Path Dependence, Precedent, and Judicial Power'. In *On Law, Politics, and Judicialization*, edited by M Shapiro and A Stone Sweet (Oxford University Press, 2002).

Tallberg, Jonas and others. *The Opening up of International Organizations: Transnational Access in Global Governance* (Cambridge University Press, 2013).

Tanaka, Yoshifumi. *The International Law of the Sea* (Cambridge University Press, 2012).

Theilen, Jens T. *European Consensus between Strategy and Principle* (Nomos Publishers, 2021).

Thirlway, Hugh. *The Sources of International Law* (Oxford University Press, 2019).

Thomas Rixen and Lora Anne Viola, 'Historical Institutionalism and International Relations: Towards Explaining Change and Stability in International Institutions'. In *Historical Institutionalism & International Relations*, edited by Thomas Rixen, Lora Anne Viola and Michael Zuern (Oxford University Press, 2016).

Toope, Stephen. 'Powerful but Unpersuasive? The Role of the United States in the Evolution of Customary International Law'. In *United States Hegemony and the Foundations of International Law*, edited by M Byers and G Nolte (Cambridge University Press, 2003).

Trebilcock, Michael John and Robert Howse. *The Regulation of International Trade*, 3rd ed. (Routledge, 2005).

Treves, Tullio. 'Historical Development of the Law of the Sea'. In *The Oxford Handbook of the Law of the Sea*, edited by Donald Rothwell and others (Oxford University Press, 2015).

Trevisanut, Seline. 'The Future of the Oceans: The Role of Human Rights and International Environmental Law in Shaping the Law of the Sea'. In *The Many Paths of International Law*, edited by Nico Krisch and Ezgi Yildiz (Oxford University Press, 2023).
Tucker, Paul, *Global Discord: Values and Power in a Fractured World Order* (Princeton University Press, 2022).
Tzouvala, Ntina. *Capitalism as Civilisation: A History of International Law* (Cambridge University Press, 2020).
Ulfstein, Geir. 'The Legal Status of Views Adopted by the Human Rights Committee–From Genesis to Adoption of General Comment No. 33'. In *Making Peoples Heard: Essays on Human Rights in Honour of Gudmundur Alfredsson* (Brill, 2011).
Venzke, Ingo 'The Path Not Taken: On Legal Change and Its Context'. In *The Many Paths of International Law*, edited by Nico Krisch and Ezgi Yildiz (Oxford University Press, forthcoming).
Venzke, Ingo and Kevin Jon Heller, eds. *Contingency in International Law: On the Possibility of Different Legal Histories* (Oxford University Press, 2021).
Venzke, Ingo. *How Interpretation Makes International Law: On Semantic Change and Normative Twists* (Oxford University Press, 2012).
Vincent Pouliot, *International Pecking Orders: The Politics and Practice of Multilateral Diplomacy* (Cambridge University Press, 2016).
Vinjamuri, Leslie. 'Human Rights Backlash'. In *Human Rights Futures*, edited by Stephen Hopgood, Jack Snyder and Leslie Vinjamuri (Cambridge University Press, 2017).
Viñuales, Jorge E, ed. *The UN Friendly Relations Declaration at 50: An Assessment of the Fundamental Principles of International Law* (Cambridge University Press, 2020).
Waibel, Michael and others. 'The Backlash Against Investment Arbitration: Perceptions and Reality'. In *The Backlash Against Investment Arbitration*, edited by Michael Waibel and others (Kluwer Law International, 2010).
Waibel, Michael. 'Interpretive Communities in International Law'. In *Interpretation in International Law*, edited by Andrea Bianchi, Daniel Peat and Matthew Windsor (Oxford University Press, 2014).
Watson Institute. *Strengthening Targeted Sanctions Through Fair and Clear Procedures* (Brown University, 2006).
Webb, Philippa. *International Judicial Integration and Fragmentation* (Oxford University Press, 2013).
Weber, Max. *Wirtschaft Und Gesellschaft* (*Mohr Siebeck* [1922], 1980).
Weber, Max. *Politik als Beruf*, 2nd ed. (Duncker & Humblot, 1926).
Wegner, Etienne. *Communities of Practice: Learning, Meaning, and Identity* (Cambridge University Press, 1999).
Weiler, Joseph and Joseph H H Weiler. *The EU, the WTO, and the NAFTA: Towards a Common Law of International Trade?* (Oxford University Press, 2001).
Werner, Wouter. 'The Making of Lawmaking: The ILC Draft Conclusions on the Identification of Customary Law'. In *The Many Paths of Change in International Law*, edited by Nico Krisch and Ezgi Yildiz (Oxford University Press, 2023).
Werner, Wouter. *Repetition and International Law* (Cambridge University Press, 2022).
Wiener, Antje. *A Theory of Contestation* (Springer, 2014).
Wiener, Antje. *Contestation and Constitution of Norms in Global International Relations* (Cambridge University Press, 2018).
Williams, Sir John Fischer. *International Change and International Peace* (Oxford University Press, H Milford, 1932).
Yildiz, Ezgi and Isabel Silagy. 'Norms, Legitimacy, and Compliance: Between International Law and Politics.' In *The Oxford Handbook of Norms Research in International Relations*, edited by Sassan Gholiagha and others (Oxford University Press, 2025).
Yildiz, Ezgi and Pedro Martínez Esponda. 'The Right to Truth'. In *The Paths of International Law: Case Studies*, edited by Pedro Martínez Esponda and others (SSRN, 2023).

Yildiz, Ezgi. 'The Equidistance Principle'. In *The Paths of International Law: Case Studies*, edited by Pedro Martínez Esponda and others (SSRN, 2023).
Yildiz, Ezgi. 'Revising the "Parallel System of Access" Rule for Seabed Mining'. In *The Paths of International Law: Case Studies*, edited by Pedro Martínez Esponda and others (SSRN, 2023).
Yildiz, Ezgi. 'The Emergence of Port State Measures Against IUU Fishing'. In *The Paths of International Law: Case Studies*, edited by Pedro Martínez Esponda and others (SSRN, 2023).
Yildiz, Ezgi. 'The Precautionary Principle: Ubiquitous Yet Hollow and Marginal'. In *The Paths of International Law: Case Studies*, edited by Pedro Martínez Esponda and others (SSRN, 2023).
Yildiz, Ezgi. 'The Protection of Women from Domestic Violence'. In *The Paths of International Law: Case Studies*, edited by Pedro Martínez Esponda and others (SSRN, 2023).
Yildiz, Ezgi. 'CITES and the Changing Definition of Conservation'. In *The Paths of International Law: Case Studies*, edited by Pedro Martínez Esponda and others (SSRN, 2023).
Yildiz, Ezgi. 'Evolving Rules of Continental Shelf Delimitation: The Fate of the Equidistance Principle'. In *The Paths of International Law: Case Studies*, edited by Pedro Martínez Esponda and others (SSRN, 2023).
Yildiz, Ezgi. 'Port State Measures Against IUU Fishing'. In *The Paths of International Law: Case Studies*, edited by Pedro Martínez Esponda and others (SSRN, 2023).
Yildiz, Ezgi. 'The Right to Truth'. In *The Paths of International Law: Case Studies*, edited by Pedro Martínez Esponda and others (SSRN, 2023).
Yildiz, Ezgi. *Between Forbearance and Audacity: The European Court of Human Rights and the Norm Against Torture* (Cambridge University Press, 2023).Young, Margaret A. *Trading Fish, Saving Fish: The Interaction between Regimes in International Law* (Cambridge University Press, 2011).
Zarbiyev, Fuad. 'A Quiet Revolution in the Making? The Changing State Authority in Treaty Interpretation'. In *The Many Paths of Change in International Law*, edited by Nico Krisch and Ezgi Yildiz (Oxford University Press, 2023).
Zaring, David. *The Globalized Governance of Finance* (Cambridge University Press, 2019).
Zumbansen, Peer, ed. *The Oxford Handbook of Transnational Law* (Oxford University Press, 2021).
Zürn, Michael. 'Historical Institutionalism and International Relations: Strange Bedfellows?'. In *Historical Institutionalism and International Relations: Explaining Institutional Development in World Politics*, edited by Thomas Rixen, Lora Anne Viola and Michael Zürn (Oxford University Press, 2016).
Zürn, Michael. *A Theory of Global Governance: Authority, Legitimacy, and Contestation* (Oxford University Press, 2018).

Journal Articles and Working Papers

Abbott, Kenneth W and others, 'The Concept of Legalization', *International Organization* 54, (2000): 401.
Abbott, Kenneth W. 'The Transnational Regime Complex for Climate Change', *Environment and Planning C: Government and Policy* 30, (2012): 571.
Abebe, Daniel and Tom Ginsburg. 'The Dejudicialization of International Politics?'. *International Studies Quarterly* 63, (2019): 521.
Abi-Saab, Georges. 'The Newly Independent States and the Rules of International Law: An Outline Symposium: International Law Standards in an Era of Rapid Historical Change: Leading Article'. *Howard Law Journal* 8, (1962): 97.
Acharya, Amitav, Antoni Estevadeordal and Louis W Goodman. 'Multipolar or Multiplex? Interaction Capacity, Global Cooperation and World Order'. *International Affairs* 99, (2023): 2339.
Adler, Emanuel and Vincent Pouliot. 'International Practices'. *International Theory* 3, (2011): 1.

Adler-Nissen Rebecca and Vincent Pouliot. 'Power in Practice: Negotiating the International Intervention in Libya'. *European Journal of International Relations* 20, (2014): 889.

Ahl, Björn. 'Chinese Positions on Global Constitutionalism, Community of Common Destiny for Mankind, and the Future of International Law'. *The Chinese Journal of Comparative Law* 9, (2021): 304.

Ahn, Dukgeun. 'Why Reform Is Needed: WTO "Public Body" Jurisprudence'. *Global Policy* 12, (2021): 61.

Akande, Dapo. 'Clearing the Fog of War?'. *International & Comparative Law Quarterly* 59, (2010): 180.

Alexander, Amanda. 'International Humanitarian Law, Postcolonialism and the 1977 "Geneva Protocol I"'. *Melbourne Journal of International Law* 17, (2016): 15.

Alter, Karen and Kal Raustiala. 'The Rise of International Regime Complexity'. *Annual Review of Law and Social Science* 14, (2018): 329.

Alter, Karen J and Sophie Meunier. 'The Politics of International Regime Complexity'. *Perspectives on Politics* 7(1) (2009): 13.

Alter, Karen J, Emilie M Hafner-Burton and Laurence R Helfer. 'Theorizing the Judicialization of International Relations'. *International Studies Quarterly* 63, (2019): 449.

Alter, Karen J, James T Gathii and Laurence R Helfer. 'Backlash against International Courts in West, East and Southern Africa: Causes and Consequences'. *European Journal of International Law* 27, (2016): 293.

Alter, Karen J. 'From Colonial to Multilateral International Law: A Global Capitalism and Law Investigation'. *International Journal of Constitutional Law* 19, (2021): 798.

Alter, Karen J. 'The Promise and Perils of Theorizing International Regime Complexity in an Evolving World'. *The Review of International Organizations* 17, (2022): 375.

Alter, Karen, Laurence Helfer and Mikael Madsen. 'How Context Shapes the Authority of International Court'. *Law and Contemporary Problems* 79, (2016): 1.

Alter, Karen J and Stephen C. Nelson. 'Global Governance in Time: Institutional Sequences, International Regime Complexes, and the Politics of Global Governance'. *World Politics* 76 (2) (2024): 379.

Alvarez, José E. 'International Organizations: Then and Now'. *American Journal of International Law* 100, (2006): 324.

Anderson, David. 'Resolution and Agreement Relating to the Implementation of Part XI of the UN Convention on the Law of the Sea: A General Assessment'. *ZaöRV* 55, (1995): 275.

Azaria, Danae. '"Codification by Interpretation": The International Law Commission as an Interpreter of International Law'. *European Journal of International Law* 31, (2020): 171.

Azmeh, Shamel. '"Saving the WTO": Middle Power Insiders and Joint Statement Initiatives at the World Trade Organisation'. *New Political Economy* 29, (2024): 60.

Ba, Oumar. 'Exit from Nuremberg to the Hague: The Malabo Protocol and the Pan-African Road to Arusha'. *Global Studies Quarterly* 3, (2023): 47.

Bacchus, James and Simon Lester. 'The Rule of Precedent and the Role of the Appellate Body'. *Journal of World Trade* 54, (2020): 183.

Baisley, Elizabeth. 'Reaching the Tipping Point?: Emerging International Human Rights Norms Pertaining to Sexual Orientation and Gender Identity'. *Human Rights Quarterly* 38, (2016): 134.

Barnett, Michael and Raymond Duvall. 'Power in International Politics'. *International Organization* 59, (2005): 39.

Beesley, Alan. 'The Negotiating Strategy of UNCLOS III: Developing and Developed Countries as Partners: A Pattern for Future Multilateral International Conferences'. *Law and Contemporary Problems* 46, (1983): 183.

Benvenisti, Eyal. 'The Birth and Life of the Definition of Military Objectives'. *International and Comparative Law Quarterly* 71, (2022): 269.

Biersteker, Thomas J. 'Targeted Sanctions and Individual Human Rights'. *International Journal* 65, (2010): 99.

Bloomfield, Alan. 'Norm Antipreneurs and Theorising Resistance to Normative Change'. *Review of International Studies* 42, (2016): 310.
Bodansky, Daniel. 'The United Nations Framework Convention on Climate Change: A Commentary'. *Yale Journal of International Law* 18, (1993): 451.
Bodansky, Daniel. 'What's in a Concept? Global Public Goods, International Law, and Legitimacy'. *European Journal of International Law* 23, (2012): 651.
Bode, Ingvild and John Karlsrud. 'Implementation in Practice: The Use of Force to Protect Civilians in United Nations Peacekeeping'. *European Journal of International Relations* 25, (2019): 458.
Bordin, Fernando Lusa. 'Reflections of Customary International Law: The Authority of Codification Conventions and ILC Draft Articles in International Law'. *International & Comparative Law Quarterly* 63, (2014): 535.
Borgese, Elizabeth. 'The New International Economic Order and the Law of the Sea'. *San Diego Law Review* 14, (1977): 584.
Bourdieu, Pierre. 'La force du droit: Eléments pour une sociologie du champ juridique'. *Actes de la recherche en sciences sociales* 64, (1986): 3.
Bradley, Miriam. 'Unintended Consequences of Adjacency Claims: The Function and Dysfunction of Analogies between Refugee Protection and IDP Protection in the Work of UNHCR'. *Global Governance: A Review of Multilateralism and International Organizations* 25, (2019): 620.
Brunnée, Jutta and Stephen J Toope. 'Self-Defence against Non-State Actors: Are Powerful States Willing but Unable to Change International Law?'. *International & Comparative Law Quarterly* 67, (2018): 263.
Brunnée, Jutta. 'COPing with Consent: Law-Making Under Multilateral Environmental Agreements'. *Leiden Journal of International Law* 15, (2002): 1.
Bugnion, François. 'Law of Geneva and Law of The Hague'. *International Review of the Red Cross* 83, (2005): 901.
Burke-White, William W. 'Power Shifts in International Law: Structural Realignment and Substantive Pluralism'. *Harvard International Law Journal* 56, (2015): 1.
Byers, Michael. 'Preemptive Self-Defense: Hegemony, Equality and Strategies of Legal Change'. *Journal of Political Philosophy* 11, (2003): 171.
Camins, Emily. 'The Past as Prologue: The Development of the "Direct Participation" Exception to Civilian Immunity'. *International Review of the Red Cross* 90, (2008): 853.
Capoccia, Giovanni and R Daniel Kelemen. 'The Study of Critical Junctures: Theory, Narrative, and Counterfactuals in Historical Institutionalism'. *World Politics* 59, (2007): 341.
Carstensen, Martin B and Vivien A Schmidt. 'Power through, over and in Ideas: Conceptualizing Ideational Power in Discursive Institutionalism'. *Journal of European Public Policy* 23, (2016): 318.
Carty, Anthony. 'Critical International Law: Recent Trends in the Theory of International Law'. *European Journal of International Law* 2, (1991): 66.
Castañeda, Jorge. 'The Underdeveloped Nations and the Development of International Law'. *International Organization* 15, (1961): 38.
Cater, Charles and David M Malone. 'The Origins and Evolution of Responsibility to Protect at the UN'. *International Relations* 30, (2016): 278.
Cattelan, Stefano. 'In the Shadow of the Great Powers: Freedom of the Sea and Neutrality in the Long Eighteenth Century'. *Grotiana* 44, (2023): 145.
Cerna, Christina M. 'The Inter-American System for the Protection of Human Rights'. *Florida Journal of International Law* 16, (2004): 195.
Charlesworth, Hilary. 'International Law: A Discipline of Crisis'. *Modern Law Review* 65, (2002): 377.
Checkel, Jeffrey T. 'International Institutions and Socialization in Europe: Introduction and Framework'. *International Organization* 59, (2005): 801.
Chen, Jianfu. 'Tension and Rivalry: The "Belt and Road" Initiative, Global Governance, and International Law'. *The Chinese Journal of Comparative Law* 8, (2020): 177.

Cheng, Bin. 'United Nations Resolutions on Outer Space: "Instant" International Customary Law?'. *Indian Journal of International Law* 5, (1965): 23.
Chimni, B S. 'Customary International Law: A Third World Perspective'. *American Journal of International Law* 112, (2018): 1.
Cho, Sungjoon. 'The Demise of Development in the Doha Round Negotiations'. *Texas International Law Journal* 45, (2010): 573.
Cima, Elena. 'The Right to a Healthy Environment: Reconceptualizing Human Rights in the Face of Climate Change'. *Review of European, Comparative & International Environment Law* 31, (2022): 38.
Cogan, Jacob Katz. 'Competition and Control in International Adjudication'. *Virginia Journal of International Law* 48, (2007): 411.
Corten, Olivier. 'A Plea Against the Abusive Invocation of Self-Defence as a Response to Terrorism'. *EJIL: Talk!*, 14 July 2016. https://www.ejiltalk.org/a-plea-against-the-abusive-invocation-of-self-defence-as-a-response-to-terrorism/.
Cosbey, Aaron and Petros C Mavroidis. 'Heavy Fuel: Trade and Environment in the GATT/WTO Case Law'. *Review of European, Comparative & International Environmental Law* 23, (2014): 288.
Cottier, Thomas. 'The Common Law of International Trade and the Future of the World Trade Organization'. *Journal of International Economic Law* 18, (2015): 3.
Davidson, Natalie R. 'Everyday Lawmaking in International Human Rights Law: Insights from the Inclusion of Domestic Violence in the Prohibition of Torture'. *Law & Social Inquiry* 47, (2022): 205.
de Nevers, Renee. 'Imposing International Norms: Great Powers and Norm Enforcement'. *International Studies Review* 9, (2007): 53.
De Schutter, Olivier and others. 'Commentary to the Maastricht Principles on Extraterritorial Obligations of States in the Area of Economic, Social and Cultural Rights'. *Human Rights Quarterly* 34, (2012): 1084.
Deitelhoff, Nicole and Harald Müller. 'Theoretical Paradise: Empirically Lost? Arguing with Habermas'. *Review of International Studies* 31, (2005): 167.
Deitelhoff, Nicole and Lisbeth Zimmermann. 'Things We Lost in the Fire: How Different Types of Contestation Affect the Robustness of International Norms'. *International Studies Review* 22, (2020): 51.
Deitelhoff, Nicole. 'The Discursive Process of Legalization: Charting Islands of Persuasion in the ICC Case'. *International Organization* 63, (2009): 33.
Denemark, Robert A and Matthew J Hoffmann. 'Just Scraps of Paper? The Dynamics of Multilateral Treaty-Making'. *Cooperation and Conflict* 43, (2008): 185.
Deudney, Daniel and G John Ikenberry. 'Liberal World: The Resilient Order'. *Foreign Affairs* 97, (2018): 16.
Deva, Surya. 'Mandatory Human Rights Due Diligence Laws in Europe: A Mirage for Rightsholders?'. *Leiden Journal of International Law* 36, (2023): 389.
Deva, Surya. 'Treaty Tantrums: Past, Present and Future of a Business and Human Rights Treaty'. *Netherlands Quarterly of Human Rights* 40, (2022): 211.
Diggs, Elise Groulx, Mitt Regan and Beatrice Parance. 'Business and Human Rights as a Galaxy of Norms'. *Georgetown Journal of International Law* 50, (2018): 309.
Doswald-Beck, Louise. 'San Remo Manual on International Law Applicable to Armed Conflict at Sea'. *International Review of the Red Cross* 35, (1995): 583.
Drezner, Daniel W. 'The Power and Peril of International Regime Complexity'. *Perspectives on Politics* 7, (2009): 65.
Dupuy, Pierre-Marie. 'The Danger of Fragmentation or Unification of the International Legal System and the International Court of Justice'. *NYU Journal of International Law and Politics* 31, (1998): 791.
Durkee, Melissa J. 'The Business of Treaties'. *UCLA Law Review* 63, (2016): 264.
Elkins, Zachary, Andrew T Guzman and Beth A Simmons. 'Competing for Capital: The Diffusion of Bilateral Investment Treaties, 1960-2000'. *International Organization* 60, (2006): 811.

Ellis, Mark E. 'The New International Economic Order and General Assembly Resolutions: The Debate over the Legal Effects of General Assembly Resolutions Revisited'. *California Western International Law Journal* 15, (1985): 647.
Emmenegger, Patrick. 'Agency in Historical Institutionalism: Coalitional Work in the Creation, Maintenance, and Change of Institutions'. *Theory and Society* 50, (2020): 607.
Endres, Dorothea. 'Conceptualizing Legal Change as "Norm-Knitting" through the Example of the Environmental Human Right'. *Leiden Journal of International Law* 36(4) (2023): 879.
Endres, Dorothea. 'The Human Side of Protecting Foreign Investment'. *Transnational Legal Theory* 12, (2021): 249.
Englehart, Neil A and Melissa K Miller. 'The CEDAW Effect: International Law's Impact on Women's Rights'. *Journal of Human Rights* 13, (2014): 22.
Englehart, Neil. 'CEDAW and Gender Violence: An Empirical Assessment'. *Michigan State Law Review* (2014): 265.
Epstein, Charlotte. 'Constructivism or the Eternal Return of Universals in International Relations. Why Returning to Language Is Vital to Prolonging the Owl's Flight'. *European Journal of International Relations* 19, (2013): 499.
Ertürk, Yakın and Bandana Purkayastha. 'Linking Research, Policy and Action: A Look at the Work of the Special Rapporteur on Violence against Women'. *Current Sociology* 60(2) (2012): 144.
Eslava, Luis and Sundhya Pahuja. 'Beyond the (Post)Colonial: TWAIL and the Everyday Life of International Law'. *Verfassung und Recht in Über/Law and Politics in Africa, Asia and Latin America* 45, (2012) 195.
Fassbender, Bardo. 'The United Nations Charter as Constitution of the International Community'. *Columbia Journal of Transnational Law* 36, (1998): 529.
Feichtner, Isabel. 'Sharing the Riches of the Sea: The Redistributive and Fiscal Dimension of Deep Seabed Exploitation'. *European Journal of International Law* 30, (2019): 601.
Fidler, David P. 'Introduction: Eastphalia Emerging?: Asia, International Law, and Global Governance'. *Indiana Journal of Global Legal Studies* 17, (2010): 1.
Finnemore, Martha and Kathryn Sikkink. 'International Norm Dynamics and Political Change', *International Organization* 52(4) (1998): 887.
Finnemore, Martha and Stephen J Toope. 'Alternatives to "Legalization": Richer Views of Law and Politics'. *International Organization* 55, (2001): 743.
Finnemore, Martha. 'Dynamics of Global Governance: Building on What We Know'. *International Studies Quarterly* 58, (2014): 221.
Fioretos, Orfeo. 'Historical Institutionalism in International Relations'. *International Organization* 65, (2011): 367.
Fischer-Lescano, Andreas and Gunther Teubner. 'Regime-Collisions: The Vain Search for Legal Unity in the Fragmentation of Global Law'. *Michigan Journal of International Law* 25, (2004): 999.
Florini, Ann. 'The Evolution of International Norms'. *International Studies Quarterly* 40, (1996): 363.
Franck, Thomas M. 'The Power of Legitimacy and the Legitimacy of Power: International Law in an Age of Power Disequilibrium'. *American Journal of International Law* 100, (2006): 88.
Frost, Neli. 'Transnational Corporations as Agents of Legal Change: The Role of Corporate Social Responsibility'. *Cambridge International Law Journal* 5, (2016): 502.
Gao, Henry and Gregory Shaffer. 'The RCEP: Great Power Competition and Cooperation over Trade'. UC Irvine School of Law Research Paper No. 2021-09. 2021. https://ssrn.com/abstract=3777604.
Garraway, Charles. 'The Use and Abuse of Military Manuals'. *Yearbook of International Humanitarian Law* 7, (2004): 425.
Gathorne-Hardy, G M. 'Territorial Revision and Article 19 of the League Covenant'. *International Affairs* 14, (1935): 818.
Gerring, John and Lee Cojocaru. 'Selecting Cases for Intensive Analysis: A Diversity of Goals and Methods'. *Sociological Methods & Research* 45, (2016): 392.

Gerschewski, Johannes. 'Explanations of Institutional Change: Reflecting on a "Missing Diagonal"'. *American Political Science Review* 115, (2021): 218.
Gilman, Nils. 'The New International Economic Order: A Reintroduction'. *Humanity* 6, (2015): 1.
Ginsburg, Tom. 'Authoritarian International Law?'. *American Journal of International Law* 114, (2020): 221.
Goddard, Stacie E and others. 'Contestation in a World of Liberal Orders'. *Global Studies Quarterly* 4, (2024): 26.
Goodhart, Michael and Stacy Bondanella Taninchev. 'The New Sovereigntist Challenge for Global Governance: Democracy without Sovereignty'. *International Studies Quarterly* 55, (2011): 1047.
Goodin, Robert E. 'Enfranchising All Subjected, Worldwide'. *International Theory* 8, (2016): 365.
Goodman, Ryan and Derek Jinks. 'Incomplete Internalization and Compliance with Human Rights Law'. *European Journal of International Law* 19, (2008): 725.
Gowa, Joanne and Soo Yeon Kim. 'An Exclusive Country Club: The Effects of the GATT on Trade, 1950-94'. *World Politics* 57, (2005): 453.
Greenhill, Brian. 'The Company You Keep: International Socialization and the Diffusion of Human Rights Norms'. *International Studies Quarterly* 54, (2010): 127.
Greenwood, Christopher. 'The Development of International Humanitarian Law by the International Criminal Tribunal for the Former Yugoslavia'. *Max Planck Yearbook of United Nations Law Online* 2, (1998): 97.
Grgić, Iva. 'The Future of Investor–State Dispute Settlement: Reforming Law, Practice and Perspectives for a Fast-Changing World'. *ICSID Review - Foreign Investment Law Journal*, forthcoming.
Guellali, Amna. 'Lex Specialis, Droit International Humanitaire et Droits de l'homme: Leur Interaction Dans Les Nouveaux Conflits Armés'. *Revue Générale de Droit International Public* 111, (2007): 539.
Guzman, Andrew T. 'Against Consent'. *Virginia Journal of International Law* 52, (2012): 747.
Guzman, Andrew T. 'Why LDCs Sign Treaties That Hurt Them: Explaining the Popularity of Bilateral Investment Treaties'. *Virginia Journal of International Law* 38, (1997): 639.
Guzzini, Stefano. 'On the Measure of Power and the Power of Measure in International Relations'. *2009 DIIS Working Paper*, no 28. (2009): 9, https://www.econstor.eu/handle/10419/44660.
Guzzini, Stefano. 'Structural Power: The Limits of Neorealist Power Analysis'. *International Organization* 47, (1993): 443.
Guzzini, Stefano. 'The Concept of Power: A Constructivist Analysis'. *Millennium* 33, (2005): 495.
Hajjar, Lisa. 'International Humanitarian Law and "Wars on Terror": A Comparative Analysis of Israeli and American Doctrines and Policies', *Journal of Palestine Studies* 36, (2006): 21.
Hakimi, Monica. 'Making Sense of Customary International Law'. *Michigan Law Review* 118, (2020): 1487.
Hakimi, Monica and Jacob Katz Cogan. 'The Two Codes on the Use of Force'. *European Journal of International Law* 27, (2016): 257.
Halley, Janet. 'Rape at Rome: Feminist Interventions in the Criminalization of Sex-Related Violence in Positive International Criminal Law'. *Michigan Journal of International Law* 30, (2008): 1.
Hathaway, Oona A. 'Between Power and Principle: An Integrated Theory of International Law'. *The University of Chicago Law Review* 72, (2005): 469.
Hathaway, Oona A and Scott J Shapiro, 'Might Unmakes Right: The Catastrophic Collapse of Norms against the Use of Force'. *Foreign Affairs* 104 (4) (2025): 80
Heikkila, Tanya Sergio Villamayor-Tomas and Dustin Garrick. 'Bringing Polycentric Systems into Focus for Environmental Governance'. *Environmental Policy and Governance* 28, (2018): 207.
Helal, Mohamed. 'Common African position on the application of international law to the use of information and communication technologies in cyberspace, and all associated communiques adopted by the peace and security council of the African Union'. Ohio State Legal

Studies Research Paper No. 823, (2024) https://papers.ssrn.com/sol3/papers.cfm?abstract_id=4714756.
Helfer, Laurence R and Erik Voeten. 'International Courts as Agents of Legal Change: Evidence from LGBT Rights in Europe'. *International Organization* 68, (2014): 77.
Helfer, Laurence R and Erik Voeten. 'Walking Back Human Rights in Europe?'. *European Journal of International Law* 31, (2020): 797.
Helfer, Laurence R. 'Forum Shopping for Human Rights'. *University of Pennsylvania Law Review* 148, (1999): 285.
Helfer, Laurence R. 'Regime Shifting: The TRIPS Agreement and New Dynamics of International Intellectual Property Lawmaking'. *Yale Journal of International Law* 29, (2004): 1.
Helleiner, Eric. 'Economic Globalization's Polycrisis'. *International Studies Quarterly* 68, (2024): 1.
Hemmings, Jess. 'Does CITES Conserve Biodiversity'. *Asia Pacific Journal of Environmental Law* 7, (2002): 95.
Hensel, Paul R and Sara M Mitchell. 'The Issue Correlates of War (ICOW) Project Issue Data Set: Territorial Claims Data'. *Harvard Dataverse*, 2007. https://dataverse.harvard.edu/dataset.xhtml?persistentId=doi:10.7910/DVN/E6PSGZ.
Hickey, Michael J. 'Acceptance of Sustainable Use within the Cites Community'. *Vermont Law Review* 23, (1998): 861.
Higgins, Rosalyn. 'Policy Considerations and the International Judicial Process'. *International & Comparative Law Quarterly* 17, (1968): 58.
Hirsch, Michal Ben-Josef and Jennifer M Dixon. 'Conceptualizing and Assessing Norm Strength in International Relations'. *European Journal of International Relations* 27, (2021): 521.
Hirsch, Moshe. 'Social Movements, Reframing Investment Relations, and Enhancing the Application of Human Rights Norms in International Investment Law'. *Leiden Journal of International Law* 34, (2021): 127.
Hodson, Loveday. 'Women's Rights and the Periphery: CEDAW's Optional Protocol'. *European Journal of International Law* 25, (2014): 561.
Hofmann, Stephanie C. 'Overlapping Institutions in the Realm of International Security: The Case of NATO and ESDP'. *Perspectives on Politics* 7, (2009): 45.
Holsti K J. 'The Concept of Power in the Study of International Relations'. *Background* 7, (1964): 179.
Hopf, Ted. 'Change in International Practices'. *European Journal of International Relations* 24, (2018): 687.
Howse, Robert. 'The World Trade Organization 20 Years On: Global Governance by Judiciary'. *European Journal of International Law* 27, (2016): 9.
Huijbers, Leonie M and Claire M S Loven. 'Pushing for Political and Legal Change: Protecting the Cultural Identity of Travellers in the Netherlands', *Journal of Human Rights Practice* 11, (2019): 508.
Huneeus, Alexandra. 'International Criminal Law by Other Means: The Quasi-Criminal Jurisdiction of the Human Rights Courts'. *American Journal of International Law* 107, (2013): 1.
Hurd, Ian. 'Legitimacy and Authority in International Politics'. *International Organization* 53, (1999): 379.
Hurd, Ian. 'The Permissive Power of the Ban on War'. *European Journal of International Security* 2, (2017): 1.
Ikenberry, G John. 'Three Worlds: The West, East and South and the Competition to Shape Global Order'. *International Affairs* 100, (2024): 121.
Jaeckel, Aline, Jeff A Ardron and Kristina M Gjerde. 'Sharing Benefits of the Common Heritage of Mankind: Is the Deep Seabed Mining Regime Ready?'. *Marine Policy* 70, (2016): 198.
Jahan, Mitali. 'How Legal Change Happened through Effective Policy Advocacy in Bangladesh: Adoption of the Domestic Violence Law'. *Asian Journal of Women's Studies* 23, (2017): 401.

Jennings, Robert. 'The Role of the International Court of Justice'. *British Yearbook of International Law* 68, (1998): 1.
Kim, Sung Won, David P Fidler and Sumit Ganguly, 'Eastphalia Rising? Asian Influence and the Fate of Human Security'. *World Policy Journal* 26, (2009): 53.
Kingsbury, Benedict. 'Sovereignty and Inequality'. *European Journal of International Law* 9, (1998): 599.
Kirgis, Frederic L. 'Custom on a Sliding Scale'. *American Journal of International Law* 81, (1987): 146.
Kirton, Allan G and Stephen C Vasciannie. 'Deep Seabed Mining Under the Law of the Sea Convention and the Implementation Agreement: Developing Country Perspectives'. *Social and Economic Studies* 51(2) (2002): 63.
Kiyani, Asad G. 'The Three Dimensions of Selectivity in International Criminal Law'. *Journal of International Criminal Justice* 15, (2017): 624.
Krieger, Heike. 'Populist Governments and International Law'. *European Journal of International Law* 30, (2019): 971.
Knox, John H. 'Obligations of States in Respect of Climate Change (Advisory Opinion)'. *American Journal of International Law* 120 (2026): forthcoming.
Koh, Harold Hongju. 'Transnational Legal Process'. *Nebraska Law Review* 75, (1996): 181.
Koh, Harold Hongju. 'Why Do Nations Obey International Law?'. *The Yale Law Journal* 106, (1997): 2599.
Koskenniemi, Martti and Päivi Leino. 'Fragmentation of International Law? Postmodern Anxieties'. *Leiden Journal of International Law* 15, (2002): 553.
Kovras, Iosif. 'Explaining Prolonged Silences in Transitional Justice: The Disappeared in Cyprus and Spain'. *Comparative Political Studies* 46, (2013): 730.
Krasner, Stephen D. 'Sovereignty: An Institutional Perspective'. *Comparative Political Studies* 21, (1988): 66.
Kravik, Andreas Motzfeldt. 'An Analysis of Stagnation in Multilateral Law-Making—and Why the Law of the Sea Has Transcended the Stagnation Trend'. *Leiden Journal of International Law* 34, (2021): 935.
Kreß, Claus. 'On Recent Events Concerning the Crime of Aggression', *Journal of International Criminal Justice* 23 (3-4) (2025): 405.
Kreuder-Sonnen, Christian and Michael Zürn. 'After Fragmentation: Norm Collisions, Interface Conflicts, and Conflict Management'. *Global Constitutionalism* 9(2) (2020): 241.
Krieps, Catharine L. 'Sustainable Use of Endangered Species under Cites: Is It a Sustainable Alternative'. *University of Pennsylvania Journal of International Economic Law* 17, (1996): 461.
Krisch, Nico, Francesco Corradini and Lucy Lu Reimers. 'Order at the Margins: The Legal Construction of Interface Conflicts over Time'. *Global Constitutionalism* 9, (2020): 343.
Krisch, Nico. 'Entangled Legalities in the Postnational Space'. *International Journal of Constitutional Law* 20, (2020): 476.
Krisch, Nico. 'International Law in Times of Hegemony: Unequal Power and the Shaping of the International Legal Order'. *European Journal of International Law* 16, (2005): 369.
Krisch, Nico. 'Liquid Authority in Global Governance'. *International Theory* 9, (2017): 237.
Krisch, Nico. 'Pluralism in Postnational Risk Regulation: The Dispute over GMOs and Trade'. *Transnational Legal Theory* 1, (2010): 237.
Krisch, Nico. 'The Decay of Consent: International Law in an Age of Global Public Goods'. *American Journal of International Law* 108, (2014): 1.
Krisch, Nico. 'The Dynamics of International Law Redux'. *Current Legal Problems* 74, (2021): 269.
Kristensen, Peter Marcus. '"Peaceful Change" in International Relations: A Conceptual Archaeology'. *International Theory* 13, (2021): 36.
Krook, Mona Lena and Jacqui True. 'Rethinking the Life Cycles of International Norms: The United Nations and the Global Promotion of Gender Equality'. *European Journal of International Relations* 18, (2012): 103.
Kunz, Josef L. 'The Problem of Revision in International Law'. *American Journal of International Law* 33, (1939): 33.

Kurban, Dilek. 'Authoritarian Resistance and Judicial Complicity: Turkey and the European Court of Human Rights'. *European Journal of International Law* 35, (2024): 355.

Kustermans, Jorg and Rikkert Horemans. 'Four Conceptions of Authority in International Relations'. *International Organization* 76, (2022): 204.

Lake, David A, Lisa L Martin and Thomas Risse. 'Challenges to the Liberal Order: Reflections on International Organization'. *International Organization* 75, (2021): 225.

Lake, David A. 'Relational Authority and Legitimacy in International Relations'. *American Behavioral Scientist* 53, (2009): 331.

Lake, David A. 'Rightful Rules: Authority, Order, and the Foundations of Global Governance'. *International Studies Quarterly* 54, (2010): 587.

Lamp, Nicolas. 'Arrested Norm Development: The Failure of Legislative-Judicial Dialogue in the WTO'. *Leiden Journal of International Law* 38, (2025): 570.

Langford, Malcolm and Daniel Behn. 'Managing Backlash: The Evolving Investment Treaty Arbitrator?'. *European Journal of International Law* 29, (2018): 551.

Lantis, Jeffrey S and Carmen Wunderlich. 'Resiliency Dynamics of Norm Clusters: Norm Contestation and International Cooperation'. *Review of International Studies* 44, (2018): 570.

Larson, David L. 'Deep Seabed Mining: A Definition of the Problem'. *Ocean Development & International Law* 17(4) (1986): 271.

Latorre, Andrés Felipe Lopez. 'In Defence of Direct Obligations for Businesses Under International Human Rights Law'. *Business and Human Rights Journal* 5, (2020): 56.

laViolette, Nicole. '"UNHCR Guidance Note on Refugee Claims Relating to Sexual Orientation and Gender Identity": A Critical Commentary'. *International Journal of Refugee Law* 22, (2010): 173.

Lennan, Mitchell and Stephanie Switzer. 'Agreement on Fisheries Subsidies'. *International Journal of Marine and Coastal Law* 38, (2023): 161.

Lesch, Max and Christian Marxsen. 'Norm Contestation in the Law Against War: Towards an Interdisciplinary Analytical Framework'. *Zeitschrift für ausländisches öffentliches Recht und Völkerrecht* 83, (2023): 11.

Levy, Jack S. 'Case Studies: Types, Designs, and Logics of Inference'. *Conflict Management and Peace Science* 25, (2008): 1.

Lovat, Henry and Shaina Western. 'Behind Backlash: The ICC and "African Backlash" in Context'. *GCILS Working Paper Series*, no. 11 (2021).

Macdonald, Terry and Kate Macdonald, 'Towards a "Pluralist" World Order: Creative Agency and Legitimacy in Global Institutions', *European Journal of International Relations* 26, (2020): 518.

Madokoro, Daisuke. 'International Commissions as Norm Entrepreneurs: Creating the Normative Idea of the Responsibility to Protect'. *Review of International Studies* 45, (2019): 100.

Madsen, Mikael Rask, Pola Cebulak and Micha Wiebusch, 'Backlash against International Courts: Explaining the Forms and Patterns of Resistance to International Courts'. *International Journal of Law in Context* 14, (2018): 197.

Madsen, Mikael Rask. '"Unity in Diversity" Reloaded: The European Court of Human Rights, Turn to Subsidiarity and Its Consequences'. *The Law & Ethics of Human Rights* 15, (2021): 93.

Madsen, Mikael. 'From Boom to Backlash? The European Court of Human Rights and the Transformation of Europe'. *iCourts Working Paper Series*, no. 211 (2020): 15, https://papers.ssrn.com/sol3/papers.cfm?abstract_id=3681925.

Madsen, Mikael. 'The Challenging Authority of the European Court of Human Rights: From Cold War Legal Diplomacy to the Brighton Declaration and Backlash'. *Law and Contemporary Problems* 79, (2016): 141.

Mahoney, James. 'Path Dependence in Historical Sociology'. *Theory and Society* 29, (2000): 507.

Mallin, Felix and Mads Barbesgaard. 'Awash with Contradiction: Capital, Ocean Space and the Logics of the Blue Economy Paradigm'. *Geoforum* 113, (2020): 121.

Mallin, Marc-Andrej Felix. 'From Sea-Level Rise to Seabed Grabbing: The Political Economy of Climate Change in Kiribati', *Marine Policy* 97, (2018): 244.

Mantilla, Giovanni. 'Emerging International Human Rights Norms for Transnational Corporations'. *Global Governance* 15, (2009): 279.

Mantilla, Giovanni. 'From Treaty to Custom: Shifting Paths in the Recent Development of International Humanitarian Law'. *Leiden Journal of International Law* 37, (2024): 359.

Martínez Esponda, Pedro . 'Change in International Law Through Informal Means: The Rise of Exceptions to State Official Immunity for International Crimes'. *Revista Latinoamericana de Der echo Internacional (LADI)* 9, (2019): 175.

Matz-Lück, Nele. 'Framework Conventions as a Regulatory Tool'. *Goettingen Journal of International Law* 1, (2009): 439.

Mazower, Mark. 'The Strange Triumph of Human Rights, 1933-1950'. *The Historical Journal* 47, (2004): 379.

McDougal, Myres S, Harold D Lasswell and W Michael Reisman. 'The World Constitutive Process of Authoritative Decision'. *Journal of Legal Education* 19, (1966): 253.

McDougal, Myres S. 'International Law, Power, and Policy: A Contemporary Conception'. *Recueil des Cours* 82, (1953).

McQuigg, Ronagh J A. 'The Responses of States to the Comments of the CEDAW Committee on Domestic Violence'. *The International Journal of Human Rights* 11, (2007): 461.

Meierhenrich, Jens. 'The Practice of International Law: A Theoretical Analysis'. *Law and Contemporary Problems* 76, (2013): 1.

Meyerrose, Anna M and Irfan Nooruddin. 'Trojan Horses in Liberal International Organizations? How Democratic Backsliders Undermine the UNHRC'. *The Review of International Organizations* 20, (2025): 125.

Milanovic, Marko and Sandesh Sivakumaran. 'Assessing the Authority of the ICRC Customary IHL Study: How Does IHL Develop?'. *International Review of the Red Cross* 104, (2022): 1856.

Mitrany, David. 'Territorial Revision and Article 19 of the League Covenant'. *International Affairs* 14, (1935): 818.

Modirazeh, Naz K. 'Folk International Law: 9/11 Lawyering and the Transformation of the Law of Armed Conflict to Human Rights Policy and Human Rights Law to War Governance'. *Harvard National Security Journal* 5, (2014): 225.

Morgenthau, Hans J. 'Positivism, Functionalism, and International Law'. *American Journal of International Law* 34, (1940): 260.

Mutua, Makau. 'What Is TWAIL?'. *Proceedings of the ASIL Annual Meeting* 94, (2000): 31.

NAFTA Free Trade Commission. 'Notes of Interpretation of Certain Chapter 11 Provisions'. http://www.sice.oas.org/tpd/nafta/commission/ch11understanding_e.asp.

Naftali, Patricia. 'Crafting a "Right to Truth" in International Law: Converging Mobilizations, Diverging Agendas?'. *Justice penale internationale* XIII, (2016), https://doi.org/10.4000/cha mppenal.9245.

Naqvi, Yasmin. 'The Right to the Truth in International Law: Fact or Fiction?'. *International Review of the Red Cross* 88, (2006): 245.

Nardin, Terry. 'Theorising the International Rule of Law'. *Review of International Studies* 34, (2008): 385.

Nayyeri, Mohammad. 'Populism, Backlash Morality and Immigrants'. *International Journal of Law in Context* 21(2025): pp. 58.

Neuwirth, Rostam J. 'The "Culture and Trade Debate" Continues: The UNESCO Convention in Light of the WTO Reports in China - Publications and Audiovisual Products: Between Amnesia or Déjá Vu?'. *Journal of World Trade* 44, (2010): 1333.

Niemann, Holger and Henrik Schillinger. 'Contestation "All the Way Down"? The Grammar of Contestation in Norm Research'. *Review of International Studies* 43, (2017): 29.

O'Connor, Cliodhna and Helene Joffe. 'Intercoder Reliability in Qualitative Research: Debates and Practical Guidelines'. *International Journal of Qualitative Methods* 19, (2020): 1.

Paris, Roland. 'The Right to Dominate: How Old Ideas About Sovereignty Pose New Challenges for World Order'. *International Organization* 74, (2020): 453.

Pauselli, Gino, Francisco Urdínez and Federico Merke. 'Shaping the Liberal International Order from the inside: A Natural Experiment on China's Influence in the UN Human Rights Council'. *Research & Politics* 10, (2023): 1.

Pauwelyn, Joost and Rebecca J Hamilton. 'Exit from International Tribunals'. *Journal of International Dispute Settlement* 9, (2018): 679.

Pauwelyn, Joost, Ramses A Wessel and Jan Wouters. 'When Structures Become Shackles: Stagnation and Dynamics in International Lawmaking'. *European Journal of International Law* 25, (2014): 733.

Pauwelyn, Joost. 'The Rule of Law without the Rule of Lawyers? Why Investment Arbitrators Are from Mars, Trade Adjudicators from Venus'. *American Journal of International Law* 109, (2015): 761.

Peters, Anne. 'The Refinement of International Law: From Fragmentation to Regime Interaction and Politicization'. *International Journal of Constitutional Law* 15, (2017): 671.

Peters, B Guy, Jon Pierre and Desmond S King. 'The Politics of Path Dependency: Political Conflict in Historical Institutionalism'. *The Journal of Politics* 67, (2005): 1275.

Pettit, Philip. 'A Republican Law of Peoples'. *European Journal of Political Theory* 9, (2010): 70.

Petrova, Margarita H. 'Naming and Praising in Humanitarian Norm Development'. *World Politics* 71, (2019): 586.

Pollack, Mark A. 'International Court Curbing in Geneva: Lessons from the Paralysis of the WTO Appellate Body'. *Governance* 36, (2023): 23.

Porterfield, M C. 'An International Common Law of Investor Rights'. *University of Pennsylvania Journal of International Economic Law* 27, (2006): 79.

Posse, Hortensia D T Gutierrez. 'The Relationship between International Humanitarian Law and the International Criminal Tribunals'. *International Review of the Red Cross* 88, (2006): 65.

Pratt, Simon Frankel. 'From Norms to Normative Configurations: A Pragmatist and Relational Approach to Theorizing Normativity in IR'. *International Theory* 12, (2020): 59.

Puchala, Donald J and Raymond F Hopkins. 'International Regimes: Lessons from Inductive Analysis'. *International Organization* 36, (1982): 245.

Puig, Sergio. 'Social Capital in the Arbitration Market'. *European Journal of International Law* 25, (2014): 387.

Purvis, Nigel. 'Critical Legal Studies in Public International Law'. *Harvard International Law Journal* 32, (1991): 81.

Qian, Jiangtao, Kangjie Sun and Yen-Chiang Chang. 'The Impact of the ITLOS Climate Change Advisory Opinion on the Development of International Law'. *Marine Policy* 170, (2024): 106406.

Qian, Jing, James Raymond Vreeland and Jianzhi Zhao, 'The Impact of China's AIIB on the World Bank'. *International Organization* 77, (2023): 217.

Rasilla, Ignacio de la and HAO Yayezi. 'The Community of Shared Future for Mankind and China's Legalist Turn in International Relations'. *Chinese Journal of International Law* 20, (2021): 341.

Raustiala, Kal and David G Victor. 'The Regime Complex for Plant Genetic Resources'. *International Organization* 58, (2004): 277.

Raustiala, Kal. 'The "Participatory Revolution" in International Environmental Law'. *Harvard Environmental Law Review* 21, (1997): 537.

Reckwitz, Andreas. 'Toward a Theory of Social Practices: A Development in Culturalist Theorizing'. *European Journal of Social Theory* 5, (2002): 243.

Reiners, Nina. 'Despite or Because of Contestation? How Water Became a Human Right'. *Human Rights Quarterly* 43, (2021): 329.

Reiners, Nina. 'States as Bystanders of Legal Change: Alternative Paths for the Human Rights to Water and Sanitation in International Law'. *Leiden Journal of International Law* 37, (2024): 22.

Reinold, Theresa and Michael Zürn. '"Rules about Rules" and the Endogenous Dynamics of International Law: Dissonance Reduction as a Mechanism of Secondary Rule-Making'. *Global Constitutionalism* 3, (2014): 236.

Reus-Smit, Christian. 'The Constitutional Structure of International Society and the Nature of Fundamental Institutions'. *International Organization* 51, (1997): 555.
Rickard, Stephanie J. 'International Negotiations over the Global Commons'. *The Review of International Organizations* 20, (2024): 999.
Ridi, Niccolò. 'The Shape and Structure of the "Usable Past": An Empirical Analysis of the Use of Precedent in International Adjudication'. *Journal of International Dispute Settlement* 10, (2019): 200.
Risse, Thomas. '"Let's Argue!": Communicative Action in World Politics'. *International Organization* 54, (2000): 1.
Roberts, Anthea and Taylor St John. 'The Originality of Outsiders: Innovation in the Investment Treaty System'. *European Journal of International Law* 33, (2023): 1153.
Roberts, Anthea Elizabeth. 'Traditional and Modern Approaches to Customary International Law: A Reconciliation'. *American Journal of International Law* 95, (2001): 757.
Roberts, Anthea. 'Clash of Paradigms: Actors and Analogies Shaping the Investment Treaty System'. *American Journal of International Law* 107, (2013): 45.
Roberts, Anthea. 'Incremental, Systemic, and Paradigmatic Reform of Investor-State Arbitration'. *American Journal of International Law* 112, (2018): 410.
Roberts, Anthea. 'Power and Persuasion in Investment Treaty Interpretation: The Dual Role of States'. *American Journal of International Law* 104, (2010): 179.
Rosert, Elvira. 'Norm Emergence as Agenda Diffusion: Failure and Success in the Regulation of Cluster Munitions'. *European Journal of International Relations* 25, (2019): 1103.
Ruggie, John G. 'The Social Construction of the UN Guiding Principles on Business & Human Rights'. *Harvard Kennedy School Faculty Research Working Paper Series 8*, no. RWP17-030 (2017), https://www.hks.harvard.edu/publications/social-construction-un-guiding-principles-business-human-rights.
Sand, Peter H. 'Whither CITES? The Evolution of a Treaty Regime in the Borderland of Trade and Environment'. *European Journal of International Law* 8, (1997): 29.
Sands, Philippe. 'Of Courts and Competition: Dispute Settlement under Part XV of Unclos'. *Contemporary Developments in International Law*, (2016): 789.
Schittecatte, Catherine. 'The Politics of the MAI: On the Social Opposition of the MAI and Its Role in the Demise of the Negotiations'. *Journal of World Investment & Trade* 1, (2000): 329.
Schultz, Thomas. 'International Law in the Minds: On the Ideational Basis of the Making, the Changing, and the Unmaking of International Law'. *Leiden Journal of International Law* 37, (2024): 649.
Scott, Joanne. 'International Trade and Environmental Governance: Relating Rules (and Standards) in the EU and the WTO'. *European Journal of International Law* 15, (2004): 307.
Scott, Shirley. 'International Law as Ideology: Theorizing the Relationship between International Law and International Politics'. *European Journal of International Law* 5, (1994): 313.
Scribner, Druscilla and Tracy Slagter. 'Recursive Norm Development: The Role of Supranational Courts'. *Global Policy* 8, (2017): 322.
Seawright, Jason and John Gerring. 'Case Selection Techniques in Case Study Research: A Menu of Qualitative and Quantitative Options'. *Political Research Quarterly* 61, (2008): 294.
Sending, Ole Jacob. 'Recognition and Liquid Authority'. *International Theory* 9, (2017): 311.
Shaffer, Gregory C and Henry Gao. 'A New Chinese Economic Order?'. *Journal of International Economic Law* 23, (2020): 607.
Shaffer, Gregory C, Manfred Elsig and Sergio Puig. 'The Extensive (But Fragile) Authority of the WTO Appellate Body'. *Law and Contemporary Problems* 79, (2016): 237.
Shaffer, Gregory C and Mark A Pollack, 'Hard vs. Soft Law: Alternatives, Complements and Antagonists in International Governance'. *Minnesota Law Review* 94, (2010): 706.
Shi, Xinxiang. 'Foreign State Immunity Law of China: A Preliminary Appraisal'. *Chinese Journal of International Law* 23, (2024): 341.
Simmons, Beth A and Hyeran Jo. 'Measuring Norms and Normative Contestation: The Case of International Criminal Law'. *Journal of Global Security Studies* 4, (2019): 18.

Simmons, Beth A. 'Bargaining over BITs, Arbitrating Awards: The Regime for Protection and Promotion of International Investment'. *World Politics* 66, (2014): 12.
Sivakumaran, Sandesh and Marko Milanovic. 'Assessing the Authority of the ICRC Customary IHL Study'. *International Review of the Red Cross* 104, (2022): 1856.
Sivakumaran, Sandesh. 'Beyond States and Non-State Actors: The Role of State-Empowered Entities in the Making and Shaping of International Law'. *Columbia Journal of Transnational Law* 55, (2017): 343.
Sivakumaran, Sandesh. 'Making and Shaping the Law of Armed Conflict'. *Current Legal Problems* 71, (2018): 119.
Slaughter, Anne-Marie. 'A Global Community of Courts Focus: Emerging Fora for International Litigation (Part 2)'. *Harvard International Law Journal* 44, (2003): 191.
Soifer, Hillel David. 'The Causal Logic of Critical Junctures'. *Comparative Political Studies* 45, (2012): 1572.
Sovacool, Benjamin K and Kelly E Siman-Sovacool. 'Creating Legal Teeth for Toothfish: Using the Market to Protect Fish Stocks in Antarctica'. *Journal of Environmental Law* 20, (2008): 15.
Spees, Pam. 'Women's Advocacy in the Creation of the International Criminal Court: Changing the Landscapes of Justice and Power'. *Journal of Women in Culture and Society* 28, (2003): 1233.
Stahn, Carsten. 'Evolution, Revolution or New Culture? The Changing Anatomy of International Criminal Justice (and Some of Its Curiosities)'. *International Criminal Law Review*, 15 (2015): 1122.
Stappert, Nora. 'Practice Theory and Change in International Law: Theorizing the Development of Legal Meaning through the Interpretive Practices of International Criminal Courts'. *International Theory* 12, (2020): 33.
Steffeck, Jens. 'The Output Legitimacy of International Organizations and the Global Public Interest'. *International Theory* 7, (2015): 263.
Steinberg, Richard H and Jonathan M Zasloff. 'Power and International Law'. *American Journal of International Law* 100, (2006): 64.
Steinberg, Richard H. 'Judicial Lawmaking at the WTO: Discursive, Constitutional, and Political Constraints'. *American Journal of International Law* 98, (2004): 247.
Stewart, James and Asad Kiyani. 'The Ahistoricism of Legal Pluralism in International Criminal Law'. *American Journal of Comparative Law* 65, (2017): 393.
Stimmer, Anette and Lea Wisken. 'The Dynamics of Dissent: When Actions Are Louder than Words'. *International Affairs* 95, (2019): 515.
Stimmer, Anette. 'Beyond Internalization: Alternate Endings of the Norm Life Cycle'. *International Studies Quarterly* 63, (2019): 270.
Stinnett, Douglas M and others. 'The Correlates of War (Cow) Project Direct Contiguity Data, Version 3.0'. *Conflict Management and Peace Science* 19, (2002): 59.
Sundaram, Jae and Ayodele S Owolabi. 'Impasse at the WTO Dispute Settlement Body: The Slow Demise of Multilateralism?'. *Trade, Law and Development* 14, (2022): 127.
Talmon, Stefan. 'Determining Customary International Law: The ICJ's Methodology between Induction, Deduction and Assertion'. *European Journal of International Law* 26, (2015): 417.
Talmon, Stefan. 'The Responsibility of Outside Powers for Acts of Secessionist Entities'. *The International and Comparative Law Quarterly* 58, (2009): 493.
Taylor, Marshall A. 'Visualization Strategies for Regression Estimates with Randomization Inference', *The Stata Journal* 20, (2020): 309.
Thomas, Dorothy Q and Michele E Beasley. 'Domestic Violence as a Human Rights Issue'. *Human Rights Quarterly* 15, (1993): 36.
Tzanakopoulos, Antonios. 'Domestic Courts in International Law: The International Judicial Function of National Courts'. *Loyola of Los Angeles International & Comparative Law Review* 34, (2011): 133.
Vagts, Detlev F. 'Hegemonic International Law'. *American Journal of International Law* 95, (2001): 843.
Vander Zwaag, David L. 'The ICJ, ITLOS and the Precautionary Approach. Paltry Progressions, Jurisprudential Jousting'. *University of Hawai'i Law Review* 35, (2013): 617.

Venzke, Ingo. 'Understanding the Authority of International Courts and Tribunals: On Delegation and Discursive Construction'. *Theoretical Inquiries in Law* 14, (2013): 381.
Venzke, Ingo. 'What Makes for a Valid Legal Argument?'. *Leiden Journal of International Law* 27, (2014): 811.
Verdier, Pierre-Hugues and Erik Voeten. 'How Does Customary International Law Change? The Case of State Immunity'. *International Studies Quarterly* 59, (2015): 209.
Verdier, Pierre-Hugues and Erik Voeten. 'Precedent, Compliance and Change in Customary International Law: An Explanatory Theory'. *American Journal of International Law* 108, (2014): 389.
Vieira, Marco. 'Rising States and Distributive Justice: Reforming International Order in the Twenty-First Century'. *Global Society* 26, (2012): 311.
Villalpando S. 'On the International Court of Justice and the Determination of Rules of Law'. *Leiden Journal of International Law* 26, (2013): 243.
Vincent Ploton and Sarah M Brooks, 'China and the UN Treaty Body System' (International Service for Human Rights 2023) Briefing Paper 11–14, https://ishr.ch/defenders-toolbox/resources/china-and-the-un-treaty-body-system/.
Vivien A Schmidt, 'Discursive Institutionalism: The Explanatory Power of Ideas and Discourse', *Annual Review of Political Science* 11, (2008): 303.
Vivien A Schmidt, 'Taking Ideas and Discourse Seriously: Explaining Change through Discursive Institutionalism as the Fourth "New Institutionalism"', *European Political Science Review* 2, (2010): 1.
Voeten, Erik. 'The Politics of International Judicial Appointments: Evidence from the European Court of Human Rights'. *International Organization* 61, (2007): 669.
Voeten, Erik, 'Is the Public Backlash against Globalization a Backlash against Legalization and Judicialization?'. *International Studies Review* 24 (2) (2022).
Walter, Stefanie. 'The Backlash Against Globalization'. *Annual Review of Political Science* 24, (2021): 421.
Washburn, John. 'The Negotiation of the Rome Statute for the International Criminal Court and International Lawmaking in the 21st Century'. *Pace International Law Review* 11, (1999): 361.
Weil, Prosper. 'The Court Cannot Conclude Definitively . . . Non Liquet Revisited'. *Columbia Journal of Transnational Law* 36, (1998): 109.
Weiler, Joseph H H. 'The Geology of International Law: Governance, Democracy and Legitimacy'. *Zeitschrift für ausländisches öffentliches Recht und Völkerrecht* 64, (2004): 547.
Weindl, Andrea. 'Grotius's Mare Liberum in the Political Practice of Early-Modern Europe'. *Grotiana* 30, (2009): 131.
Weiner, Phillip. 'The Evolving Jurisprudence of the Crime of Rape in International Criminal Law'. *Boston College Law Review* 54, (2013): 1207.
Weiss, Edith Brown. 'The Contribution of International Environmental Law to International Law: Past Achievements and Future Expectation - The Evolution of International Environmental Law'. *Japanese Yearbook of International Law* 54 (2011): 1.
Wiener, Antje. 'Enacting Meaning-in-Use: Qualitative Research on Norms and International Relations'. *Review of International Studies* 35, (2009): 175.
Yildiz, Ezgi and others. 'New Norms in Old Regimes: Judicial Strategies for Importing Environmental Norms'. Unpublished manuscript. 2022.
Yildiz, Ezgi and Umut Yüksel. 'International Courts and Selective Restraint in Times of Backlash' (Prepared for the Political Economy of International Organization (PEIO) Conference, January 22-25, 2025, Harvard University), https://papers.ssrn.com/sol3/papers.cfm?abstract_id=5102435.
Yildiz, Ezgi and Umut Yüksel. 'The Defocalizing Effect of International Courts: Evidence from Maritime Delimitation Practices'. *The Review of International Organizations* 20, (2024): 825.
Yildiz, Ezgi and Umut Yüksel. 'Understanding the Limitations of Behavioralism: Lessons from the Field of Maritime Delimitation'. *German Law Journal* 23 (2022): 413.
Yildiz, Ezgi. 'A Court with Many Faces: Judicial Characters and Modes of Norm Development in the European Court of Human Rights'. *European Journal of International Law* 31, (2020): 73.

Yildiz, Ezgi. 'Enduring Practices in Changing Circumstances: A Comparison of the European Court of Human Rights and the Inter-American Court of Human Rights'. *Temple International & Comparative Law Journal* 34, (2020): 309.
Yip, Ka Lok. 'The ICRC's Interpretive Guidance on the Notion of Direct Participation in Hostilities: Sociological and Democratic Legitimacy in Domestic Legal Orders'. *Transnational Legal Theory* 8, (2017): 224.
Young, Saskia. 'Contemporary Issues of the Convention on International Trade in Endangered Species of Wild Fauna and Flora (CITES) and the Debate over Sustainable Use'. *Colorado Journal of International Environmental Law and Policy* 14, (2003): 167.
Zarbiyev, Fuad. 'Saying Credibly What the Law Is: On Marks of Authority in International Law'. *Journal of International Dispute Settlement* 9, (2018): 291.
Zimmermann Wim. 'Self-Presentation in International Law: On Reputation and Interpretation'. *German Law Journal, forthcoming.*
Zürn, Michael, Martin Binder and Matthias Ecker-Ehrhardt. 'International Authority and Its Politicization'. *International Theory* 4, (2012): 69.
Zürn, Michael. 'On the Role of Contestations, the Power of Reflexive Authority, and Legitimation Problems in the Global Political System'. *International Theory* 13, (2021): 192.
Zwingel, Susanne. 'From Intergovernmental Negotiations to (Sub)National Change'. *International Feminist Journal of Politics* 7, (2005): 400.

Online Sources and Blog Posts

Centre de Droit International. 'Plea Against the Abusive Invocation of Self-Defence as a Response to Terrorism'. June 2016. https://cdi.ulb.ac.be/wp-content/uploads/2016/06/A-plea-against-the-abusive-invocation-of-self-defence.pdf.
House of Lords, International Relations and Defence Committee. 'UNCLOS: Fit for Purpose for the 21st Century, Witness Statement from Sir Malcolm Evans'. 20 October 2021. https://committees.parliament.uk/oralevidence/2853/pdf.
Koh, Tommy T B. 'A Constitution for the Oceans'. *Remarks by the President of the Third United Nations Conference on the Law of the Sea.* 11 December 1982. Montego Bay. https://www.un.org/depts/los/convention_agreements/texts/koh_english.pdf.
Lester, Simon. 'Ending the WTO Dispute Settlement Crisis: Where to from Here?'. *International Institute for Sustainable Development.* 2 March 2022. https://www.iisd.org/articles/united-states-must-propose-solutions-end-wto-dispute-settlement-crisis.
Mälksoo, Lauri. 'Russia and China Challenge the Western Hegemony in the Interpretation of International Law'. *EJIL: Talk!*. 15 July 2016. https://www.ejiltalk.org/russia-and-china-challenge-the-western-hegemony-in-the-interpretation-of-international-law.
Riemer, Lena. 'From "Original Intentions" to "Unforeseeable Change of Circumstances": The 2025 Escalation of Pressure Towards the ECtHR'. *EJIL: Talk!* 5 January 2026). https://www.ejiltalk.org/fromoriginalintentionstounforeseeablechangeofcircumstances.
Ugale, Anastasiya and Vanina Sucharitkul. 'Backlash in Investment Arbitration (Wiki Note)'. *Jus Mundi.* 23 December 2024. https://jusmundi.com/en/document/wiki/en-backlash-in-investment-arbitration.
Windridge, Oliver. 'Under Attack? Under the Radar? Under-Appreciated? All of the Above? A Time of Reckoning for the African Court on Human and Peoples' Rights'. *Opinio Juris.* 7 May 2020. https://opiniojuris.org/2020/05/07/under-attack-under-the-radar-under-appreciated-all-of-the-above-a-time-of-reckoning-for-the-african-court-on-human-and-peoples-rights/.
Zarbiyev, Fuad. 'Of Bullshit, Lies and "Demonstrably Rubbish" Justifications in International Law'. *Völkerrechtsblog.* 18 March 2022. https://voelkerrechtsblog.org/of-bullshit-lies-and-demonstrably-rubbish-justifications-in-international-law/.

Cases

ECtHR. *Verein KlimaSeniorinnen Schweiz and Others v Switzerland* [2024] App no 53600/20.
GATT Panel Report. *United States—Restrictions on Imports of Tuna* (3 September 1991) WT/DS21/R, unadopted, GATT BISD 39S/155.
GATT Panel Report. *United States—Restrictions on Imports of Tuna* (16 June 1994) WT/DS29/R, unadopted.
Hague District Court (Rechtbank Den Haag). *Milieudefensie and Others v Royal Dutch Shell plc* [2021] ECLI:NL:RBDHA:2021:5339.
IACtHR. The Environment and Human Rights (Advisory Opinion OC-23/17 of November 15, 2017). https://www.corteidh.or.cr/docs/opiniones/seriea_23_ing.pdf
IACtHR. *Climate Emergency and Human Rights* (Advisory Opinion AO-32/25 of 29 May 2025). https://www.corteidh.or.cr/docs/opiniones/seriea_32_en.pdf.
IACtHR. *Judgement of August 31, 2017 Case of Lagos del Campo v Peru* (Preliminary objections, merits, reparations and costs) https://www.corteidh.or.cr/docs/casos/articulos/seriec_340_ing.pdf.
ICJ. *Application of the International Convention on the Elimination of All Forms of Racial Discrimination (Qatar v United Arab Emirates) (Preliminary Objections)* [2021] ICJ Rep 71.
ICJ. *Case Concerning Ahmadou Sallio Diallo (Republic of Guinea v Democratic Republic of the Congo)* [2010] ICJ Rep 639.
ICJ. *Armed Activities on the Territory of the Congo (DRC v Uganda)* [2005] ICJ Rep 168.
ICJ. *Barcelona Traction, Light and Power Company Limited (Belgium v Spain)* [1970] ICJ Rep 3.
ICJ. *Legal Consequences of the Construction of a Wall in the Occupied Palestinian Territory* (Advisory Opinion) [2004] ICJ Rep 136.
ICJ. *Legality of the Threat or Use of Nuclear Weapons* (Advisory Opinion) [1996] ICJ Rep 226.
ICJ. *Maritime Delimitation in the Area between Greenland and Jan Mayen (Denmark v Norway)* (Judgment) [1993] ICJ Rep 38.
ICJ. *Maritime Delimitation in the Black Sea (Romania v Ukraine)* (Judgment) [2009] ICJ Rep 61.
ICJ. *Military and Paramilitary Activities in and against Nicaragua (Nicaragua v United States of America)* [1986] ICJ Rep 392.
ICJ. *North Sea Continental Shelf Cases (Federal Republic of Germany v Denmark Federal Republic of Germany v Netherlands)* [1969] ICJ Rep 3.
ICJ. *Obligations of States in respect of Climate Change* (Advisory Opinion) [2025] ICJ Rep 2025.
ICSID. *Bear Creek Mining Corporation v Peru* (30 November 2017) ICSID Case No ARB/14/21.
ICSID. *Urbaser SA and Consorcio de Aguas v Argentina* (Award of 8 December 2016) ICSID Case No ARB/07/26.
ITLOS. *Request for an Advisory Opinion submitted by the Commission of Small Island States on Climate Change and International Law* (Advisory Opinion of 21 May 2024).
Supreme Court of the Netherlands (Hoge Raad). *Urgenda Foundation v State of Netherlands* [2019] ECLI:NL:HR:2019:2007 C/09/571932.
UKHL. *R v Bartle and the Commissioner of Police for the Metropolis and Others, ex parte Pinochet*, 38 ILM 581 (HL 1999).
UKHL. *R v Evans and Another and the Commissioner of Police for the Metropolis and Others, ex parte Pinochet* [1999] UKHL 17.
UKHL. *Secretary of State for the Home Department v Fornah* [2006] UKHL 46.
UN Human Rights Committee. *Daniel Billy and others v Australia* (2023), No 3624/2019.
UN Human Rights Committee. *Teitiota v New Zealand* (2019), No 2728/2016.
US Circuit Court of Appeals. *United States v Aluminum Co of America* 148 F.2d 416 (US Circuit Court of Appeals, Second Circuit 1945).
WTO Appellate Body. *European Communities—EC Measures Concerning Meat and Meat Products (Hormones)* (1998) WT/DS26/AB/R.
WTO Appellate Body. *United States—Import Prohibition of Certain Shrimp and Shrimp Products* (12 October 1998) WT/DS58/AB/R.

WTO Appellate Body. *United States—Standards for Reformulated and Conventional Gasoline (US—Gasoline)* WT/DS2/AB/R, adopted 20 May 1996.

Official Documents

Auswärtiges Amt, Germany. 'Richtlinien für die Behandlung völkerrechtlicher Verträge'. 2021. https://www.auswaertiges-amt.de/resource/blob/2481616/31364feaa9019e4a9281796ceda6362d/rvv-data.pdf.

Bray, Kevin. 'A Global Review of Illegal, Unreported and Unregulated (IUU) Fishing'. 2000 AUS:IUU/2000/6 AUS:IUU/2000/6. http://www.fao.org/3/y3274c/y3274e08.htm#fn67.

CCAMLR. 'Report of the Twenty-first Meeting of the Commission' (21 October–1 November 2002). https://www.ccamlr.org/en/ccamlr-xxi.

'Comments of the United States of America on the Human Rights Committee's Draft General Comment 33: The Obligations of States Parties Under the Optional Protocol to the International Covenant Civil and Political Rights'. 7 October 2008. https://www.ohchr.org/Documents/HRBodies/CCPR/GC33/USA.doc.

'Declaration of the National Council'. 12 June 2024. https://www.parlament.ch/de/ratsbetrieb/amtliches-bulletin/amtliches-bulletin-die-verhandlungen?SubjectId=64937.

'Declaration on the Establishment of a New International Economic Order'. UNGA Res 3201 (1974) UN Doc A/RES/3201(S-VI)).

'Informe Del Estado Mexicano (En relación con la Comunicación Conjunta OL MEX 3/19)'. 24 January 2020. https://spcommreports.ohchr.org/TMResultsBase/DownLoadFile?gId=35129.

'Observations of the United States of America on the Human Rights Committee's General Comment 33: The Obligations of States Parties under the Optional Protocol to the International Covenant on Civil and Political Rights'. 22 December 2008. https://2009-2017.state.gov/documents/organization/138852.pdf.

'The Declaration of the Russian Federation and the People's Republic of China on the Promotion of International Law'. The Ministry of Foreign Affairs of the Russian Federation. 25 June 2016. https://archive.mid.ru/en/foreign_policy/news/-/asset_publisher/cKNonkJE02Bw/content/id/2331698.

Documents of the United Nations Conference on International Organization (United Nations, 1945), vol IX, 70.

FAO. 'International Plan of Action to Prevent, Deter and Eliminate Illegal, Unreported and Unregulated Fishing'. (IPOA-IUU) (2001). https://www.fao.org/3/y1224e/Y1224E.pdf.

Federal Council, Switzerland. 28 August 2024. https://www.admin.ch/gov/de/start/dokumentation/medienmitteilungen.msg-id-102244.html.

Final Communiqué of the Asian-African Conference. 24 April 1955. https://bandungspirit.org/IMG/pdf/anri-bandung_conference-final_communique.pdf.

GATT document (25 November 1988) L/ 6437.

Human Rights Treaty Body System. 2020. https://www.ohchr.org/sites/default/files/Documents/HRBodies/TB/HRTD/CoFacilitationProcess/States/China_.docx.

ICC-OTP. 'Strategic Plan 2019-2021, by M. Fatou Bensouda, Prosecutor'. (2019). https://www.icc-cpi.int/news/office-prosecutor-issues-its-strategic-plan-2019-2021.

ILC. 'Articles on Responsibility of States for Internationally Wrongful Acts' (2001).

ILC. 'Conclusions of the work of the Study Group on the Fragmentation of International Law: Difficulties arising from the Diversification and Expansion of International Law' (2006) UN Doc A/61/10.

ILC. 'Draft Conclusions on Identification of Customary International Law with Commentaries' (2018) UN Doc A/73/10.

ILC. 'Draft Conclusions on Subsequent Agreements and Subsequent Practice in Relation to the Interpretation of Treaties, with Commentaries' (2018) UN Doc A/73/10.

ILC. 'Fourth Report on State Responsibility, by Mr. James Crawford, Special Rapporteur' (A/CN.4/517 and Add.1).

ILC. 'Report of the Study Group of the International Law Commission', finalized by Martti Koskenniemi (13 April 2006) UN Doc A/CN.4/L.682.

ILC. 'Second Report on Identification of Customary International Law, by Sir Michael Wood, Special Rapporteur' (22 May 2014) UN Doc A/CN.4/672.

ILC. 'Draft Articles on Prevention and Punishment of Crimes Against Humanity' (2019) UN Doc A/74/10.

International Committee on Legal Aspects of a New International Economic Order. 'Third Report of the International Committee on Legal Aspects of a New International Economic Order' in International Law Association Report of the Sixty-first Conference (International Law Association, 1965).

ISA Secretariat. (6 February 2018) ISBA/24/LTC/4.

ISBA. 'Considerations relating to the regulations for prospecting and exploration for hydrothermal polymetallic sulphides and cobalt-rich crusts in the Area' (29 May 2001) ISBA/7C/2.

ISBA. 'Issues related to the possible alignment of the Authority's regulations on prospecting and exploration concerning the offer of an equity interest in a joint venture arrangement' (6 February 2018) ISBA/24/LTC/4.

Knox, John H. 'Report of the Independent Expert on the issue of human rights obligations relating to the enjoyment of a safe, clean, healthy and sustainable environment' (30 December 2013) UN Doc A/HRC/25/53.

Office of the United States Trade Representative. 'Report on the Appellate Body of the World Trade Organization'. 202 https://ustr.gov/sites/default/files/enforcement/DS/USTR.Appellate.Body.Rpt.Feb2020.pdf.

OHCHR. Comments of the United States of America on the Human Rights Committee's "Draft General Comment 33". 17 October 2008. https://www.ohchr.org/Documents/HRBodies/CCPR/GC33/USA.doc.

'Request for an advisory opinion on the Climate Emergency and Human Rights submitted to the Inter-American Court of Human Rights by the Republic of Colombia and the Republic of Chile'. 9 January 2023. https://www.corteidh.or.cr/docs/opiniones/soc_1_2023_en.pdf.

The White House, 'Presidential Memoranda: Withdrawing the United States from International Organizations, Conventions, and Treaties that Are Contrary to the Interests of the United States' (7 January 2026), https://www.whitehouse.gov/presidential-actions/2026/01/withdrawing-the-unitedstates-from-international-organizations-conventions-and-treaties-that-are-contrary-to-the-interestsof-the-united-states/.

UN Committee on Economic, Social and Cultural Rights. 'General Comment 24 (2017) on State obligations under the International Covenant on Economic, Social and Cultural Rights in the context of business activities' (10 August 2017) UN E/C.12/GC/24.

UN Committee on the Elimination of Discrimination against Women. 'General Recommendation No 12: Violence against Women' (1989) UN Doc A/44/38.

UN Committee on the Elimination of Discrimination against Women. 'General Recommendation 35: Gender-based Violence against Women' (26 July 2017) CEDAW/C/GC/35.

UN Committee on the Elimination of Discrimination against Women. 'General Recommendation 19: Violence against Women' (1992) UN Doc/A/47/38.

UN Working Group on the Issue of Human Rights and Transnational Corporations and Other Business Enterprises. 'Report on Human Rights-compatible International Investment Agreements' (IIAs) (27 July 2021) UN Doc A/76/238.

UNCHR Res 11 (2004) UN Doc E/CN.4/2004/L.73/Rev1.

UNCTAD. 'Draft Convention on Investments Abroad (Abs–Shawcross Convention), International Investment Instruments: A Compendium—Volume V, p. 395, https://www.international-arbitration-attorney.com/wp-content/uploads/137-volume-5.pdf.

UNGA Res 217 A (III), 'Universal Declaration of Human Rights' (10 December 1948) UN Doc Resolution 217 A (III).
UNGA Res 3281 (XXIX) (12 December 1974).
UNGA Res 48/104 (20 December 1993).
UNGA Res 70/1 'Transforming Our World: The 2030 Agenda for Sustainable Development' (21 October 2015) UN Doc A/Res/70/1.
UNGA Res 76/300 (28 July 2022) UN Doc A/Res/76/300.
UNGA Res 76/L.75 (28 July 2022) UN Doc A/76/L.75.
UNGA Res 77/276 (19 April 2023) UN Doc A/RES/77/276.
UNGA. 'Report of the World Commission on Environment and Development: Our Common Future' (1987) UN Doc A/42/427.
UNGA. 'Rio Declaration on Environment and Development', (3–4 June 1992) UN Doc A/CONF.151/26 (Vol. I).
UNGA. 'Report of the United Nations Conference on Environment and Development' (12 August 1992) UN Doc A/CONF.151/26.
UNHRC Res 32/19 (1 July 2016) UN/A/HRC/Res/32/19, adopted without a vote.
UNHRC Res 48/13 (8 October 2021) UN Doc A/HRC/RES/48/13.
UNHRC. 'Draft General Comment No 33' (25 August 2008) UN Doc CCPR/C/GC/CRP.3.
UNHRC. 'General Comment 33: Obligations of States parties under the Optional Protocol to the International Covenant on Civil and Political Rights' (25 June 2009) UN Doc CCPR/C/GC/33.
United Nations Commission on International Trade Law. 'Possible Reform of Investor-State Dispute Settlement (ISDS). Note by the Secretariat' (2019) UN Doc A/CN.9/WG.III/WP.166.
United States Trade Representative, 'Report on the Appellate Body of the World Trade Organization'. February 2020. https://ustr.gov/sites/default/files/Report_on_the_Appellate_Body_of_the_World_Trade_Organization.pdf.
UNSC Meetings 8262 (17 May 2018) S/PV.8262 at https://documents.un.org/doc/undoc/pro/n18/151/80/pdf/n1815180.pdf,
UNSC Meetings 8395 (9 November 2018) S/PV.8395 at https://documents.un.org/doc/undoc/pro/n18/368/63/pdf/n1836863.pdf.
WTO. Ministerial Decision on Trade and Environment. 15 April 1994. https://www.wto.org/english/tratop_e/envir_e/issu5_e.htm.

Index

For the benefit of digital users, indexed terms that span two pages (e.g., 52–53) may, on occasion, appear on only one of those pages.